A STREET-SMART GUIDE BOOK. EVERY CITY SHOULD HAVE ONE.—RONALD LIEM, D[...]AZINE A MUST-HA[...]AS: VERA GOODWIN [...] EVERYTHING YOU NEED TO KNOW ABOUT FASHION IN HONG KONG, FROM HARD TO FIND TAILORS TO LUXE BOUTIQUES.—DIVIA HARILELA, SOUTH CHINA MORNING POST EVERYTHING PARENTS NEW TO HONG KONG WILL NEED TO KNOW IS IN THIS BOOK: BIRTHDAY PARTY IDEAS, CHILD-FRIENDLY RESTAURANTS, WHERE TO BUY SHOES. I RECOMMEND IT TO ALL NEW FAMILIES WHO JOIN OUR COMMUNITY.—ROCHELLE SNEDDON, HONG KONG INTERNATIONAL SCHOOL, NEW PARENT MENTOR PROGRAM THIS BOOK IS A VALUABLE RESOURCE FOR ALL NEWCOMERS TO HONG KONG, AS WELL AS FOR ANYONE WHO HAS LIVED HERE AND STRUGGLED TO FIND THOSE 'HARD-TO-LOCATE' ITEMS OR SERVICES.—LANCE ALLEN, MANAGING DIRECTOR, SANTA FE EVEN AFTER LIVING HERE FOR SEVEN YEARS, THIS IS STILL

MY PRIMARY REFERENCE BOOK FOR FINDING EVERY POSSIBLE RESOURCE IN THIS CITY. IT'S A FAVOURITE GIFT FOR ANYONE MOVING TO HONG KONG.—FIONA KOTUR, HANDBAG DESIGNER, KOTUR FROM WHERE TO FIND HONG KONG'S BEST BOWL OF NOODLES TO THE CITY'S BEST TAILOR, VERA GOODWIN HAS COVERED IT ALL. NO REQUEST, WHETHER IT'S ESSENTIAL OR INDULGENT, GOES UNANSWERED HERE.—DEBORAH KAN, REPORTER, REUTERS WHETHER YOU'VE BEEN HERE 15 MINUTES OR 15 YEARS, THIS BOOK IS A GREAT RESOURCE FOR ALL THAT YOU COULD POSSIBLY NEED (AND THINGS YOU DIDN'T KNOW YOU NEEDED!) TO GET THE MOST OUT OF HONG KONG.—KAREN KOH, FREELANCE TV JOURNALIST A HOUSEHOLD STAPLE! EVERYTHING HONG KONG IS A ONE-STOP LIFE-SIMPLIFIER WITH HIGH IMPACT ON THE VALUE OF MY TIME. I'M GETTING THE BEST ADVICE IN TOWN SO I DON'T NEED TO LOOK ANYWHERE ELSE.—SONYA MADDEN, FASHION DESIGNER

EVERY THING
HONG KONG

THE ESSENTIAL LIVING GUIDE.
VERA GOODWIN

HAVEN BOOKS

To my own everything,
Tyler, Connor and Talia

EVERYTHING HONG KONG

Published in Hong Kong by Haven Books

www.havenbooksonline.com

Copyright © 2010 by Haven Books

'E Guides' and 'Everything' are imprints of Haven Books.

All rights reserved. No part of this book may be reproduced, extracted for electronic media, copied or translated in any form without the express permission of the publisher.

Although the author and publisher have tried to make the information herein as accurate as possible, they accept no responsibility for any loss, injury or inconvenience sustained by any person using this book.

ISBN 978-988-18094-7-6

EVERYTHING HONG KONG

A WORD FROM THE AUTHOR

I've often felt like a professional expat. Since first moving to Hong Kong in 1994, I went on to live in Jakarta, Los Angeles and New York, which led to my return to Hong Kong once again in 2001. Having had to settle in new cities several times, I leaned on savvy friends, acquaintances and sometimes total strangers for advice. They provided me with first-hand information on the best dry-cleaner to use, where to go for old-fashioned comfort food, or where to get high-quality biking gear. Why waste time trying mediocre services when you can just ask?

EVERYTHING HONG KONG started six years ago because of a decision to gather this invaluable information into one useful reference tool that everyone can use. When someone gives you a flyer as you walk down the street, you naturally feel wary. On the other hand, when friends and people you trust make a recommendation, you try it!

The resulting book is just that: a compilation of useful, practical, essential information gathered from the direct recommendations of people-in-the-know. No one has paid to be mentioned in this book—they are in it because they've been recommended personally.

I am very grateful to the following people (and quite a few others), without whose support, recommendations and friendship this project would never have been possible.

Victoria A.	Melody F.	Lucy M.
Pam A.	Kelly G.	Alli M.
Amber B.	Jessica G.	Judith M.
Miki B.	Annie H.	Karmei M.
Sandrine C.	Gisele H.	Jennifer M.
Alison C.	Deborah K.	Joanne O.
Mandy D.	Karen K.	Michelle P.
Judy D.	Jeannie L.	Ruby P.
Rhea D.	Sarah L.	Lily R.
Allison F.	Marcy L.	Heather S.
Rochelle F.	Sonya M.	Toland S.
Lynly F.	Angelique M.	Lorie T.
Carolyn F.	Fiona M.	Teresa W.

I'd also like to thank the fantastic team at Haven Books whose hard work, dedication and countless hours have resulted in a product we are all very proud of: Annie Das, Liz Lee, Cecilia Chan, Michelle Low, Wayne Mok, and Jeff Tang. Thanks too to our design partners at Whitespace, and to Candace Campos for all their creative input. Finally, I'd like to thank Dania Shawwa Abuali, whose vision, support and friendship has been paramount to this project.

With sincere thanks,

Vera Goodwin

Email: veragoodwin@everythingguides.com

TABLE OF CONTENTS

HONG KONG MAP   10

EVERYTHING FOOD & ENTERTAINMENT

entertain and **IMPRESS**   14
dining **AL FRESCO**   18
EXPLORE eateries off the beaten track   21
book a **PRIVATE KITCHEN**   26
BRUNCH around town   29
let's do **LUNCH**   31
light & **HEALTHY**   35
comfy **WESTERN** favourites   40
DRINK till the last drop   49
DIM SUM & dumplings   56
oodles of **NOODLES**   60
more **ASIAN** dining   61
satisfy your **SWEET** tooth   74
GROCERIES and gourmet   81
BETTY CROCKER does Hong Kong   92
a taste of fine **WINE**   95
DIAL it in   101

EVERYTHING FASHION & SHOPPING

the trendiest shopping **SPOTS**   104
finding your **SIZE**   105
the **LOOK** for **LESS**   107
find the **LABEL** without the price   110
FANCY party dresses   114
DENIM you can't live without   117
if the **SHOE** fits   120
the **BARE** necessities   122
MEN need to look stylish too   126
custom **MAKE** it   129
world famous **TAILORS**   133
ALTER it to perfection   136
bags to **CARRY** around   137

clothes to **SWEAT** in 144

for the great **OUTDOORS** 147

blinded by **BLING** 149

BABIES a to z 160

TOYS for tots and big boys 165

KIDS' clothing that rocks 168

relax with a good **BOOK** 176

the lost art of **PRINT** 185

STANLEY for dummies 187

find your way in **SHAM SHUI PO** 189

EVERYTHING LIFESTYLE & WELL BEING

no pain, no gain, it's time to hit the **GYM** 194

SPORTS for all seasons 196

EQUIP yourself with the best 212

TRAVEL the world and the seven seas 219

EVENTS—is your name on the list? 223

ahoy matey, let's hit the open **WATER** 225

a **PARTY** to remember 227

there's more to **KIDS'** parties than clowns 231

a **PHOTO** is worth a thousand words 236

don't mess with the **BRIDE** 238

MUSIC lessons for our inner Beethoven 252

ACTIVITIES to get the kids out of the house 257

only the best **SCHOOLS** for your children 266

what's up, **DOC?** 272

9 months and **BABY** makes 3 282

an **ALTERNATIVE** to western medicine 284

BEAUTY or the beast? it's all about maintenance 286

guys need to **PRIMP** too 296

restore, reverse, **REJUVENATE** 297

EVERYTHING HOUSE & HOME

there's a **PICASSO** for all of us 304

timeless **TREASURES** 310

FURNITURE a to z 312

make it **NEW** again 318

dim the **LIGHTS** 320

kingdom for **KIDS** 322

SLEEPING in style 324

ACCESSORIES to add that final touch 328

everyone ends up in the **KITCHEN** 335

satisfy your home **APPLIANCE** needs 337

CLEANLINESS is godliness 340

DOMESTIC divas and caregivers 346

the grass is always **GREENER** 348

man's **BEST FRIEND** 353

i need some help: **DESIGN** for dummies 359

who's **HANDY** with a hammer? 362

FLAT hunting 101 366

book a **ROOM** for out-of-towners 370

there's a **TECH** geek in all of us 373

what has four wheels and goes **VROOM** 379

don't worry, it's a **RENTAL** 380

DELIVER it fast 381

consult the **EXPERTS** 382

EVERYTHING BY PHONE 386

EVERYTHING ONLINE 387

EVERYTHING CANTONESE 392

EVERYTHING INDEX 397

SYMBOL LEGEND

Chinese Speaking

Green / Healthy

Open Late

Good Value

For Men

Great for Kids

HONG KONG MAP

Tai Po

Yuen Long

NEW TERRITORIES

Sha Tin

Tsuen Wan

Tuen Mun

KOWLOON

Kowloon Tong

Sai Kung

Clear Water Bay

Hang Hau Village

Po Toi Island

Tsing Yi

Sham Shui Po

Mong Kok

Yau Ma Tei

Kowloon Bay

Tsim Sha Tsui

Tin Hau

Causeway Bay

North Point

Quarry Bay

Tai Koo

Chai Wan

Shek O

Wan Chai

Happy Valley

Tai Tam

Admiralty

Sheung Wan

Central

Mid-Levels

The Peak

HONG KONG ISLAND

Repulse Bay

Stanley

Aberdeen

Pok Fu Lam

Ap Lei Chau

Lamma Island

Discovery Bay

Cheung Chau

EVERYTHING
FOOD &
ENTERTAINMENT

entertain and **IMPRESS**	14
dining **AL FRESCO**	18
EXPLORE eateries off the beaten track	21
book a **PRIVATE KITCHEN**	26
BRUNCH around town	29
let's do **LUNCH**	31
light & **HEALTHY**	35
comfy **WESTERN** favourites	40
DRINK till the last drop	49
DIM SUM & dumplings	56
oodles of **NOODLES**	60
more **ASIAN** dining	61
satisfy your **SWEET** tooth	74
GROCERIES and gourmet	81
BETTY CROCKER does Hong Kong	92
a taste of fine **WINE**	95
DIAL it in	101

WHERE CAN I TAKE VISITORS FOR A MEMORABLE WESTERN MEAL WITH **GREAT VIEWS**?

Aqua Tokyo, Aqua Roma, Aqua Spirit
29/F & 30/F, 1 Peking Rd, Tsim Sha Tsui
3427-2288
www.aqua.com.hk
Ultra-stylish restaurant offering both Italian and Japanese cuisines. Great spot for a drink or stay for dinner. Incredible views of Hong Kong Island.

Watermark
Level P, Central Pier 7, Central
2167-7251
www.igors.com
Spectacular 270-degree view of Victoria Harbour towards Kowloon. An elegant dining room with 30-ft.-plus ceilings by the waterfront.

Pearl on the Peak
1/F, The Peak Tower, 128 Peak Rd, The Peak
2849-5123
www.maxconcepts.com.hk
Geoff Lindsay, Australia's 2005 Chef of the Year, oversees Pearl's modern Australian cuisine. The view is unbelievable, with floor-to-ceiling windows overlooking Hong Kong.

Felix
28/F, The Peninsula Hotel, Salisbury Rd, Tsim Sha Tsui
2315-3188
www.hongkong.peninsula.com
A minimalist avant-garde restaurant designed by Philippe Starck. Stunning views and enticing "east meets west" fare. Gentlemen, make sure you check out the memorable bathroom experience.

Caprice
6/F, Four Seasons Hotel Hong Kong
8 Finance St, Central
3196-8860
www.fourseasons.com/hongkong
2-star Michelin-rated restaurant featuring contemporary French cuisine, Hong Kong's widest selection of artisanal French cheeses and an extensive wine list.

Pierre
25/F, Mandarin Oriental Hotel
5 Connaught Rd Central
2825-4001
www.mandarinoriental.com/hongkong
3-star Michelin chef, Pierre Gagnaire, creates French-influenced cuisine set against spectacular views of Victoria Harbour.

Azure ....*)
29/F, Hotel LKF, 33 Wyndham St, Central
3518-9330
www.azure.hk
Stylish, trendy restaurant with a small outdoor deck, great city views and slick bar in the heart of Lan Kwai Fong.

Grissini
2/F, Grand Hyatt Hotel, 1 Harbour Rd, Wan Chai
2584-7722
www.hongkong.grand.hyatt.com
Northern Italian homestyle cuisine, enormous Italian wine list, with panoramic view.

Petrus
56/F, Island Shangri-La Hotel, Pacific Place
Supreme Court Rd, Admiralty
2820-8590
www.shangri-la.com
Traditional French cuisine with unparalleled views from the 56th floor and refined ambience.

SPOON by Alain Ducasse
Lobby, InterContinental Hotel
18 Salisbury Rd, Tsim Sha Tsui
2313-2256 / 2313-2323
hongkong-ic.dining.intercontinental.com
Modern French fusion cuisine by Michelin-starred chef Alain Ducasse with panoramic views of Hong Kong Island.

Angelini
Mezzanine, Kowloon Shangri-La Hotel
64 Mody Rd, East Tsim Sha Tsui
2733-8750
www.shangri-la.com
Contemporary Italian with great views and good service.

Harlan's
L2, IFC Mall, 8 Finance St, Central
2805-0566
www.jcgroup.hk
Popular for business lunches and fine dining, the restaurant offers good food with views of the harbour.

H One
L4, IFC Mall, 8 Finance St, Central
2805-0638
www.h-one.com.hk
Sleek interior with some tables offering great harbour views. Good value set lunch with buffet appetisers and choices of main course.

Café Gray Deluxe
49/F, The Upper House Hotel
Pacific Place, 88 Queensway, Admiralty
3968-1106
www.cafegrayhk.com
Highly acclaimed chef Gray Kunz returns from New York to open this spectacular 21st-century grand café with breathtaking views, offering interpretations of classic European cuisine with an accent on local organic produce and relaxed service.

ANY SUGGESTIONS FOR A MORE **RELAXED RESTAURANT WITH VIEWS**?

Café Deco
1/F & 2/F, Peak Galleria, 118 Peak Rd, The Peak
2849-5111
www.cafedecogroup.com
Large restaurant at the top of the Peak, offering spectacular views of Hong Kong, Kowloon and Victoria Harbour. There is something on offer for everyone, with cuisine including Western, Indian, Japanese seafood and fresh oysters, and even selections for kids.

Bubba Gump Shrimp Co.
3/F, The Peak Tower, 128 Peak Rd, The Peak
2849-2867
www.bubbagump.com
Shrimp and Southern fare in a casual "down home" setting.

BLT Steak
G/F, Ocean Terminal, Harbour City
Canton Rd, Tsim Sha Tsui
2730-3508
www.diningconcepts.com.hk
Great views of Hong Kong from the outdoor deck
overlooking the harbour. Try the brunch on Sundays.

Isola
L3, IFC Mall, 8 Finance St, Central
2383-8765
www.isolabarandgrill.com
Open, bright, airy restaurant with a great outdoor deck
and good value set lunch with antipasto buffet and
choices of main course. Book several days ahead for lunch.

The Box
L4, IFC Mall, 8 Finance St, Central
2234-7738
www.jcgroup.hk
Part of the JC Group that also runs Harlan's and H One.
The Box offers more casual buffet lunches and à la carte
dining for dinner. Call before going to make sure it
hasn't been booked out for a private function.

HABITU Ristorante ....
G/F, Ocean Terminal, Harbour City
Canton Rd, Tsim Sha Tsui
3101-0901
www.habitu.com.hk
Large outdoor deck with city views, international cuisine.

HOW ABOUT AN **ASIAN RESTAURANT** OFFERING
GREAT VIEWS?

Hutong
28/F, 1 Peking Rd, Tsim Sha Tsui
3428-8342
www.hutong.com.hk
Northern Chinese cuisine and old world minimalist
décor, with spectacular views of Hong Kong Island.

Nobu
2/F, InterContinental Hotel
18 Salisbury Rd, Tsim Sha Tsui
2313-2345 / 2313-2323
hongkong-ic.dining.intercontinental.com
Innovative contemporary Japanese cuisine.

Tien Yi
2/F & 3/F, The Peak Tower, 128 Peak Rd, The Peak
2907-3888
www.rcgastronomic.com/tienyi/tienyi.html
Contemporary Chinese cuisine with spectacular harbour
views and a large wine list.

Kyo Hachi
2/F, The Peak Tower, 128 Peak Rd, The Peak
2907-2888
www.rcgastronomic.com/kyo/kyo.html
Modern Japanese with panoramic harbour views.

Cuisine Cuisine
L3, IFC Mall, 8 Finance St, Central
2393-3933
www.cuisinecuisine.hk
Contemporary Cantonese in an elegant setting with
harbour views.

Lung King Heen
4/F, Four Seasons Hotel Hong Kong
8 Finance St, Central
3196-8880
www.fourseasons.com/hongkong
*Michelin-rated fine Cantonese cuisine in an elegant
setting. Also try their innovative dim sum menu.*

WHAT ABOUT COFFEE SHOPS/CAFÉS WITH GREAT VIEWS?

Pacific Coffee ....
G/F, The Peak Tower, 128 Peak Rd, The Peak
2849-6608
www.pacificcoffee.com
Arguably the best views from any café in Hong Kong.
Caffè HABITU ....
G/F, Ocean Terminal, Harbour City
Canton Rd, Tsim Sha Tsui
2115-9170
www.caffehabitu.com
*Spectacular views of Hong Kong side while sitting in an
al fresco setting. See also HABITU Ristorante (page 16).*

HOW ABOUT A BAR WITH GREAT VIEWS?

Red ....
L4, IFC Mall, 8 Finance St, Central
8129-8882
www.pure-red.com
Huge outdoor seating area, very popular after work or gym.
Pier 7 Café & Bar
Level R, Central Pier 7, Central
2167-8377
www.igors.com
SPOON by Alain Ducasse
Lobby, InterContinental Hotel
18 Salisbury Rd, Tsim Sha Tsui
2313-2256 / 2313-2323
www.hongkong-ic.dining.intercontinental.com
Isola Bar
L3, IFC Mall, 8 Finance St, Central
2383-8765
www.isolabarandgrill.com
G Bar
L4, IFC Mall, 8 Finance St, Central
2234-7739
www.jcgroup.hk
Sheraton Oyster & Wine Bar
18/F, Sheraton Hong Kong Hotel and Towers
20 Nathan Rd, Tsim Sha Tsui
2324-7739
www.starwoodhotels/sheraton
M Bar
25/F, Mandarin Oriental Hotel, 5 Connaught Rd Central
2825-4002
www.mandarinoriental.com/hongkong
ToTT's
34/F, Excelsior Hotel, 281 Gloucester Rd, Causeway Bay
2837-6786
www.excelsiorhongkong.com

Sevva .... *☽

25/F, Prince's Bldg, 10 Chater Rd, Central

2537-1388

www.sevvahk.com

Chic setting, the place to be seen.

Café Gray Deluxe

49/F, The Upper House Hotel

Pacific Place, 88 Queensway, Admiralty

3968-1106

www.cafegrayhk.com

Seductive and sophisticated bar and lounge with spectacular views highlighted by a 14-m-long bar.

Wooloomooloo Steakhouse

31/F, The Hennessy, 256 Hennessy Rd, Wan Chai

2893-6960

www.wooloo-mooloo.com

Although a bit of a destination in terms of the bar scene, this is a fantastic spot for drinks in this completely open rooftop bar with amazing views all around. Great spot for a party too!

THE WEATHER IS FANTASTIC, CAN YOU SUGGEST A RESTAURANT WITH A PATIO OR **AL FRESCO DINING**?

The Peak Lookout .... ◉

121 Peak Rd, The Peak

2849-1000

www.peaklookout.com.hk

Extensive menu, with something for everyone.

Spices .... ◉

The Repulse Bay, 109 Repulse Bay Rd, Repulse Bay

2292-2821

www.therepulsebay.com/restaurants.html

Great courtyard setting where kids can run around.

Cococabana .... ◉

UG/F, Beach Bldg, Island Rd, Deep Water Bay

2812-2226 / 2328-2138

www.toptables.com.hk

Mediterranean-style, casual al fresco dining overlooking Deep Water Bay beach.

Top Deck .... ◉

Top Floor, Jumbo Kingdom, Shum Wan Pier Drive

Wong Chuk Hang, Aberdeen

2552-3331

www.cafedecogroup.com

Chilled-out, al fresco, lounge-like atmosphere.

Gaia

G/F, Grand Millennium Plaza

181 Queen's Rd Central, Sheung Wan

2167-8200

www.gaiaristorante.com

City al fresco dining that feels remarkably outside of the city.

The Boathouse .... ◉

88 Stanley St, Stanley

2813-4467

www.igors.com

Casual dining overlooking the water. Get a table on the patio.

Simpatico
1/F, Peak Galleria, 118 Peak Rd, The Peak
2849-0001
www.epicurean.com.hk
Rustic Italian cuisine and pizzas; make a booking on the very popular outdoor terrace.

Red
L4, IFC Mall, 8 Finance St, Central
8129-8882
www.pure-red.com
Popular bar/lounge that offers self-serve dining; first-come, first-served for outdoor seating.

Mijas
1/F, Murray House, Stanley Plaza, Stanley
2899-0858
www.kingparrot.com
Wraparound deck in the historical Murray House, offers views over the water.

L16 Café and Bar
Hong Kong Park, 19 Cotton Tree Drive, Admiralty
2522-6333
www.l16cafenbar.com
Casual Thai and Western food, outdoor dining in the park.

Cinecittà
G/F, 9 Star St, Wan Chai
2529-0199
www.elite-concepts.com
Modern Italian cuisine with an extensive wine list and outdoor terrace.

HABITU Ristorante
• 3/F, Lee Gardens Two, 28 Yun Ping Rd, Causeway Bay
  2898-3919
• G/F, Ocean Terminal, Harbour City
  Canton Rd, Tsim Sha Tsui
  3101-0901
www.habitu.com.hk
Large outdoor deck with city views, international cuisine.

The Pawn
1/F–3/F, 62 Johnston Rd, Wan Chai
2866-3444
www.thepawn.com.hk
Outdoor dining and drinks on the rooftop.

Duetto Italian & Indian Dining
2/F, Sun Hung Kai Centre, 30 Harbour Rd, Wan Chai
2598-1222 / 2827-7777
www.chiram.com.hk

The Quarterdeck Club
Fleet Arcade, Fenwick Pier, 1 Lung King St, Wan Chai
2827-8882
www.bulldogsbarandgrill.com/QDHK

Scirocco
1/F, 10–12 Staunton St, SoHo
2973-6605
www.stauntonsgroup.com
Just above Staunton's Wine Bar & Café, this little eatery offers tapas, antipasti and meze with a great terrace in the heart of SoHo.

Elements Mall
R/F, 1 Austin Rd West, Kowloon
Several al fresco dining options with a variety of cuisines, including:
Olive
2810-8585
www.diningconcepts.com.hk
Greek and Middle Eastern.
D Diamond
2196-8126
www.ddiamond.com.hk
El Pomposo
2196-8123
www.epicurean.com.hk
Joia
2382-2323
www.joia.com.hk
Megu
3743-1421
www.megurestaurants.com
Stormies
2196-8098
www.igors.com

I'M LOOKING FOR AN INTIMATE RESTAURANT OR A **ROMANTIC SETTING**.

one-thirtyone
131 Tseng Tau Village Rd, Shap Sze Heung
Sai Kung, New Territories
2791-2684
www.one-thirtyone.com
Located on the bay of Three Fathoms Cove, this converted village house offers an elegant and charming escape for a truly unique dining experience.
The Boathouse ....
88 Stanley St, Stanley
2813-4467
www.igors.com
Gaia
G/F, Grand Millennium Plaza
181 Queen's Rd Central, Sheung Wan
2167-8200
www.gaiaristorante.com
Intimate setting with great food. In good weather try to make a booking outside on the patio.
SPOON by Alain Ducasse
Lobby, InterContinental Hotel, 18 Salisbury Rd, Tsim Sha Tsui
2313-2256 / 2313-2323
www.hongkong-ic.dining.intercontinental.com
Cococabana ....
UG/F, Beach Bldg, Island Rd, Deep Water Bay
2812-2226 / 2328-2138
www.toptables.com.hk
La Fleur
G/F, 16 St. Francis Yard, Wan Chai
2866-7337
Spuntini
G/F, 4–6 St. Francis St, Wan Chai
2528-1060
www.elgrande.com.hk

EVERYTHING FOOD & ENTERTAINMENT

HOW ABOUT A **COSY DATE SPOT** WITHOUT BREAKING THE BANK?

The Peak Lookout
121 Peak Rd, The Peak
2849-1000
www.peaklookout.com.hk
Paul's Kitchen
G/F, 24 Gough St, Sheung Wan
2815-8003
www.pauls-kitchen.com
Scirocco
1/F, 10–12 Staunton St, SoHo
2973-6605
www.stauntonsgroup.com
Classified The Cheese Room ....*)
G/F, 108 Hollywood Rd, Central
2525-3454
www.classifiedfoodshops.com.hk
Excellent selection of cheeses/wines and a great café.
Qing
G/F, 3 Mee Lun St, Central
2815-6739
Babylon
49–51 Gough St, Central
2815-5411
Spoil Café
G/F, 1 Sun St, Wan Chai
3589-5678
Popular little corner café that serves up fresh and light offerings. Save room for some delicious desserts.

I'M IN THE MOOD TO EXPLORE, IS THERE A WESTERN RESTAURANT THAT'S **OFF THE BEATEN TRACK**?

one-thirtyone
131 Tseng Tau Village Rd, Shap Sze Heung
Sai Kung, New Territories
2791-2684
www.one-thirtyone.com
The chef tailors food for you in this French-inspired restaurant that seats up to 20 people.
Black Sheep
350 Shek O Village, Shek O
2809-2021
Excellent pizzas and salads on a casual terrace.
Cococabana ....
UG/F, Beach Bldg, Island Rd, Deep Water Bay
2812-2226 / 2328-2138
www.toptables.com.hk
Always a good choice for Mediterranean food. Right on the water.
Lucy's
G/F, 64 Stanley Main St, Stanley
2813-9055
Fantastic food and warm, intimate ambience. Lucy's Cookbook is also highly recommended.
Concerto Inn ....
28 Hung Shing Yeh Beach, Yung Shue Wan, Lamma Island
2982-1668
www.concertoinn.com.hk

VIEW IT · BRUNCH IT · PATIO IT · VEGGIE IT · **EXPLORE IT** · VALUE IT · BUFFET IT · DRINK IT · SPICE IT · BURGER IT · GOURMET IT · LUNCH IT

Ooh La La ....
Pui O Beach, Lantau Island
2546-3543 ext 4
www.oohlala-hk.com
This beachfront restaurant offers BBQ seafood, meats and fresh salads. A great place to come with kids and other families.

The Stoep ....
32 Lower Cheung Sha Beach, Lantau Island
2980-2699
Mediterranean and South African cuisine right on the beach. Take the ferry to Mui Wo, then taxi or bus to The Stoep, or go by boat.

Anthony's Catch
1826B Po Tung Rd, Sai Kung, New Territories
2792-8474
www.anthonyscatch.com
Western seafood restaurant with a cosy atmosphere, popular amongst expats.

Anthony's Kitchen
45 Market St, Sai Kung, New Territories
2791-2998
Ex-Ritz Carlton chef in a no-frills venue, serves up seafood and Western home-style dishes.

Coco Thai ....
G/F, West Block, Deep Water Bay Beach
Island Rd, Deep Water Bay
2812-1826
www.toptables.com.hk

Paradiso
Shek O Main Beach, Shek O
2809-2080
www.paradiso.com.hk

Stanley Beach Club ....
Stanley Main Beach, Stanley
2813-5005
Surprisingly good food. Try the pizza and chocolate mousse before the kids finish it. The escargot is good too.

Jaspas
13 Sha Tsui Path, Sai Kung, New Territories
2792-6388

Portofino
G/F, 27A Lung Mei Village, Ting Kok Rd
Tai Po, New Territories
2791-4466

Enigma
72–74 Po Tung Rd, Sai Kung, New Territories
2791-7222
www.enigmasaikung.com

Hebe 101
112 Pak Sha Wan, Hebe Haven
Sai Kung, New Territories
2335-5515
www.hebe101.com
Mediterranean-style décor bar and restaurant with international cuisine.

China Bear
G/F, Mui Wo Centre, 3 Ngan Wan Rd
Mui Wo, Lantau Island
2984-9720

La Pizzeria .... 🍭
G/F, Grandview Mansion
11C Mui Wo Ferry Pier Rd, Mui Wo, Lantau Island
2984-8933

Manta Ray
G/F, D Deck, Block A, Discovery Bay Plaza
Discovery Bay, Lantau Island
2987-2298
www.mantaray-hk.com
*One of DB's best, romantic settings, specialising in
seafood, with a great view.*

Koh Tomyums
G/F, D Deck, Block A, Discovery Bay Plaza
Discovery Bay, Lantau Island
2987-0767
www.ddeck.com.hk
*Order the pomelo salad. It's not on the menu, but it's
delicious!*

Hemingway's By The Bay .... 🍭
G/F, D Deck, Block A, Discovery Bay Plaza
Discovery Bay, Lantau Island
2987-8855
www.hemingwaysdb.com
Casual setting with good views.

ZAKS .... 🍭
G/F, D Deck, Block A, Discovery Bay Plaza
Discovery Bay, Lantau Island
2987-6232
*Popular breakfast spot with a great view and good food for
a variety of tastes. Kid friendly with designated play area.*

CAN YOU SUGGEST ANY OTHER UNIQUE
RESTAURANTS WITH **DISTINCTIVE / HISTORIC DÉCOR**?

Luk Yu Tea House
24–26 Stanley St, Central
2523-1970
*Traditional Cantonese fare in a fantastic setting the way
it used to be.*

Dim Sum .... 🉐
G/F, 63 Sing Woo Rd, Happy Valley
2834-8893
*This popular and busy establishment dishes out a wide
assortment of dim sum and traditional fare.*

Island Tang
2/F, The Galleria, 9 Queen's Rd Central
2526-8798
www.islandtang.com
*David Tang's latest creation offers his signature
Shanghai décor at its best.*

OVOlogue
66 Johnston Rd, Wan Chai
2527-6088
www.ovologue.com.hk
*Stylish, minimalist Chinese décor offering a unique
setting for inventive Chinese cuisine.*

The Pawn
1/F–3/F, 62 Johnston Rd, Wan Chai
2866-3444
www.thepawn.com.hk
Colonial, eclectic décor offering modern British cuisine.

Yin Yang
G/F, 18 Ship St, Wan Chai
2866-0868
Set in a 1930's heritage building. Margaret Xu offers a fusion of traditional Chinese cuisine with many ingredients coming from her farm in Yuen Long.

Shu Zhai
G/F, 80 Stanley Main St, Stanley
2813-0123
Dim sum and traditional Chinese cuisine, conveniently located near Stanley Market.

China Tee Club
1/F, Pedder Bldg, 12 Pedder St, Central
2521-0233
www.chinateeclub.com.hk
Traditional tea house, $1,000/year to be a member, however walk-in is OK.

HOW ABOUT **MODERN JAPANESE MEALS** IN HIP SETTINGS?

Nobu
2/F, InterContinental Hotel, 18 Salisbury Rd, Tsim Sha Tsui
2313-2345 / 2313-2323
www.hongkong-ic.dining.intercontinental.com

Zuma
5/F & 6/F, The Landmark, 15 Queen's Rd Central
3657-6388
www.zumarestaurant.com

Roka Robata Grill
LG, Pacific Place, 88 Queensway, Admiralty
3960-5988
www.rokarestaurant.com

Nadaman
7/F, Island Shangri-La Hotel, Pacific Place
Supreme Court Rd, Admiralty
2877-3838
www.shangri-la.com
Upscale restaurant offering everything from sushi to teppanyaki.

Sushi Kuu
1/F, Wellington Place, 2–8 Wellington St, Central
2971-0180

Wasabisabi
13/F, Food Forum, Times Square
1 Matheson St, Causeway Bay
2506-0009
www.aqua.com.hk
Westernised, trendy Japanese food, frequented by foreigners.

Megu
R/F, Elements Mall, 1 Austin Rd West, Kowloon
3743-1421
www.megurestaurants.com

Tokio Joe
16 Lan Kwai Fong, Central
2525-1889
www.lkfe.com
An expat favourite.

Kyoto Joe
G/F, The Plaza, 21 D'Aguilar St, Central
2804-6800
www.lkfe.com

EVERYTHING FOOD & ENTERTAINMENT

WHAT **NOBU** IS TO JAPANESE, IS THERE A **CHINESE EQUIVALENT**?

Green T. House
2/F, The Arcade, Cyberport Rd, Cyberport
2989-6036
www.green-t-house.com
Pairing ultra-modern décor with creative Chinese cuisine and artistic presentation, not for the price-conscious.

Shui Hu Ju
G/F, 68 Peel St, Central
2869-6927

Hutong
28/F, 1 Peking Rd, Tsim Sha Tsui
3428-8342
www.hutong.com.hk

Yun Fu ....*)
Basement, 43 –55 Wyndham St, Central
2116-8855
www.aqua.com.hk

WHERE SHOULD WE GO IF SOMEONE ELSE IS PAYING/**SPECIAL OCCASION**?

L'Atelier de Joël Robuchon
4/F, The Landmark, 15 Queen's Rd Central
2166-9000
www.robuchon.hk

Caprice
6/F, Four Seasons Hotel Hong Kong
8 Finance St, Central
3196-8860
www.fourseasons.com/hongkong

Gaddi's
1/F, The Peninsula Hotel, Salisbury Rd, Tsim Sha Tsui
2315-3171
www.hongkong.peninsula.com
French cuisine at its best. Try the chef's table in the kitchen, where you are at the mercy of the head chef for one extremely memorable night, including the private tour of the kitchen. Advance booking is a must.

Cépage
23 Wing Fung St, Wan Chai
2861-3130
www.lesamis.com.sg

Petrus
56/F, Island Shangri-La Hotel, Pacific Place
Supreme Court Rd, Admiralty
2820-8590
www.shangri-la.com

Amber
7/F, Landmark Mandarin Oriental Hotel
15 Queen's Rd Central
2132-0066
www.mandarinoriental.com/landmark

Pearl on the Peak
1/F, The Peak Tower, 128 Peak Rd, The Peak
2849-5123
www.maxconcepts.com.hk

EVERYTHING FOOD & ENTERTAINMENT

Gaia
G/F, Grand Millennium Plaza
181 Queen's Rd Central, Sheung Wan
2167-8200
www.gaiaristorante.com
Spacious and quiet, including al fresco dining on the outdoor terrace.

Bo Innovation
2/F, J Residence, 60 Johnston Rd, Wan Chai
(Entrance on Ship St)
2850-8371
www.boinnovation.com

Zuma
5/F & 6/F, The Landmark, 15 Queen's Rd Central
3657-6388
www.zumarestaurant.com

SPOON by Alain Ducasse
Lobby, InterContinental Hotel
18 Salisbury Rd, Tsim Sha Tsui
2313-2256 / 2313-2323
www.hongkong-ic.dining.intercontinental.com

Nobu
2/F, InterContinental Hotel
18 Salisbury Rd, Tsim Sha Tsui
2313-2345 / 2313-2323
www.hongkong-ic.dining.intercontinental.com

The Verandah
• 1/F, The Repulse Bay
  109 Repulse Bay Rd, Repulse Bay
  2292-2822
  www.therepulsebay.com
• The Peninsula Hotel, Salisbury Rd, Tsim Sha Tsui
  2315-3166
  www.hongkong.peninsula.com

Brasserie on the 8th
8/F, Conrad Hotel Hong Kong
Pacific Place, 88 Queensway, Admiralty
2521-3838
www.conrad.com.hk

Grissini
2/F, Grand Hyatt Hotel, 1 Harbour Rd, Wan Chai
2584-7722
www.hongkong.grand.hyatt.com

EVERYONE TALKS ABOUT THESE NEW **"PRIVATE KITCHENS"**. ARE THERE ANY **ASIAN** ONES?

Si Jie Sichuan
2/F, Kowa Bldg
285–291 Lockhart Rd, Wan Chai
2802-2250

Mum Chau's Sichuan Kitchen
5/F, Winner Bldg, 37 D'Aguilar St, Central
2522-0338
Back to basics décor but fantastic Sichuan cuisine. Call for reservation.

Kin's Terrace
1/F, 9 Tsing Fung St, Tin Hau
2571-0913
Private kitchen above sister restaurant, Kin's Kitchen.

26

Xi Yan Private Kitchen
3/F, 83 Wan Chai Rd, Wan Chai
2575-6966
www.xiyan.com.hk
Jacky Yu's eclectic mix of East and West will not disappoint you. Book well in advance.

Club Qing
10/F, Cosmos Bldg, 8–11 Lan Kwai Fong, Central
2536-9773
www.clubqing.com
Home-style Cantonese food, set menu.

Da Ping Huo
LG/F, Hilltop Plaza, 49 Hollywood Rd, Central
2559-1317
Seriously spicy Sichuan and northern specialities. The owner's wife will sing opera for you and your guests after the meal.

Yellow Door
6/F, Cheung Hing Comm. Bldg, 37 Cochrane St, Central
2858-6555
www.yellowdoorkitchen.com.hk
Spicy home-cooked Sichuan and Shanghainese food in a simple, cosy setting.

Chow Chung Restaurant
5/F, Kin Tye Lung Bldg
28–29 Bonham Strand West, Sheung Wan
2805-1116
Traditional Chinese cuisine in this ex-Hyatt Regency chef's home. Book well ahead, as there's only space for a table for 10.

Yin Yang
G/F, 18 Ship St, Wan Chai
2866-0868
Margaret Xu Yuan returns to traditional cooking methods to create innovative, modern Chinese cuisine. Passionate about food, she makes everything that is served from scratch. Popular with the serious foodies.

Tim's Kitchen
G/F, 93 Jervois St, Sheung Wan
2543-5919

WHERE ARE THE BEST **WESTERN PRIVATE KITCHENS** OFFERING A **FIXED-PRICE** SET MENU?

Le Blanc
6/F, 83 Wan Chai Rd, Wan Chai
3428-5824
www.blanc.com.hk
Bohemian French cuisine and eclectic décor.

Magnolia
G/F, 17 Po Yan St, Sheung Wan
2530-9880
www.magnolia.hk
Delicious New Orleans Cajun and Creole cuisine. The menu changes regularly and is a surprise.

Chez Patrick
• G/F, 26 Peel St, Central
  2541-1401
• G/F, 8–9 Sun St, Wan Chai
  2527-1408
www.chezpatrick.hk
Traditional home-made French cuisine.

Bonheur
6/F, The Pemberton
22 –26 Bonham Strand, Sheung Wan
2544-6333
www.bonheur-restaurant.com
Fantastic French cuisine.

Bo Innovation
2/F, J Residence, 60 Johnston Rd, Wan Chai
(Entrance on Ship St)
2850-8371
www.boinnovation.com
Chef Alvin Leung prides himself on being self-taught at combining unique ingredients to create a gastronomic experience. Great value in their set lunch, whilst dinner offers a pricier tasting menu, chef's menu or à la carte selections.

La Bouteille
10/F, Pinocine Bldg
80 –82 Queen's Rd Central
2869-1499
Reasonably priced French food prepared by Mr Ha, the chef /owner. Go for the food, if not the venue.

La Fête
1/F, Block 3, Hoover Towers
15 St. Francis St, Wan Chai
2893-5891
French 5-course set menu including fresh seafood. Book in advance.

Le Mieux Bistro ....
4/F, Block B, Ming Pao Ind. Centre
18 Ka Yip St, Chai Wan
2558-2877
Out-of-the-way location offering a creative set menu which is good value given the quality. An added plus: no corkage!

Chez Les Copains
G/F, 117 Pak Sha Wan
Sai Kung, New Territories
2243-1918
www.chezlescopains.com
French food, 4 to 5 tables, wonderful chef, and a great wine list.

Gough 40
G/F, 40 Gough St, Sheung Wan
2851-8498
Former Mandarin Oriental sommelier, Jimmy Yip, has opened this popular, chic neighbourhood bistro.

D17 Seafood Bar & Grill
17/F, Continental Diamond Plaza
525 Hennessy Rd, Causeway Bay
3907-0090
givemefive.hk/d17.php
Intriguing and meticulously prepared French fusion cuisine. This tiny restaurant resembles a quaint French living room on one side and a modern sushi bar on the other. BYOB with $160 corkage fee or a good selection of reasonably-priced wines.

EVERYTHING FOOD & ENTERTAINMENT

HOW ABOUT A GREAT PLACE FOR **BREAKFAST/BRUNCH**?

The Brunch Club ....
G/F, 70 Peel St, SoHo
2526-8861
www.brunch-club.org
*Cosy, refined little eatery, with gourmet breakfast
options. Check out the great selection of magazines that
you can read while there, or buy.*

The Press Room ....
108 Hollywood Rd, Central
2525-3444
www.thepressroom.com.hk
*Sophisticated brasserie-style breakfast. Try their
enormous cappuccinos served in a bowl.*

Wagyu
G/F, The Centrium, 60 Wyndham St, Central
2525-8805

The Flying Pan ....
• G/F, 9 Old Bailey St, SoHo
   2140-6333
• 3/F, 81–85 Lockhart Rd, Wan Chai
   2528-9997
www.the-flying-pan.com
*All-day diner-style breakfast. Open 24 hours. Great for
late-night munchies.*

Brown ....
18A Sing Woo Rd, Happy Valley
2891-8558
This is a real neighbourhood hangout.

Red ....
L4, IFC Mall, 8 Finance St, Central
8129-8882
www.pure-red.com

Al's Diner ....
G/F, Winner Bldg, 27–39 D'Aguilar St, Central
2869-1869

Dublin Jack's ....
1/F, 17 Lan Kwai Fong, Central
2543-0081
www.dublinjack.com.hk

WHERE CAN I FIND THE MOST **IMPRESSIVE BRUNCH/
LUNCH BUFFETS**?

Nicholini's
8/F, Conrad Hotel Hong Kong
Pacific Place, 88 Queensway, Admiralty
2521-3838 ext 8210
www.conrad.com.hk

Café Too ....
7/F, Island Shangri-La, Pacific Place
Supreme Court Rd, Admiralty
2820-8571
www.shangri-la.com
*They offer a huge lunch buffet; you can also go for their
Saturday and Sunday afternoon tea buffet.*

The Lounge
Lobby, JW Marriott Hotel Hong Kong
Pacific Place, 88 Queensway, Admiralty
2841-3846 / 2841-3836
www.jwmarriotthk.com

The Verandah
See page 26

Grissini
2/F, Grand Hyatt Hotel, 1 Harbour Rd, Wan Chai
2584-7722
www.hongkong.grand.hyatt.com

Sabatini Ristorante Italiano
3/F, Royal Garden Hotel, 69 Mody Rd, East Tsim Sha Tsui
2733-2000
www.rghk.com.hk/dining_sabatini.html
*Very notable newcomer and worth the journey! Lunch
buffet only on Sunday.*

Brasserie on the 8th
8/F, Conrad Hotel Hong Kong
Pacific Place, 88 Queensway, Admiralty
2521-3838
www.conrad.com.hk
Sunday brunch buffet, semi-buffet on Mon–Fri.

HOW ABOUT A MORE **CASUAL BRUNCH/LUNCH BUFFET**?

Duetto Italian & Indian Dining
2/F, Sun Hung Kai Centre, 30 Harbour Rd, Wan Chai
2598-1222 / 2827-7777
www.chiram.com.hk
Indian lunch buffet, Mon–Fri.

Tandoor
1/F, Lyndhurst Terrace, 1 Lyndhurst St, Central
2845-2262
Lunch buffet, Mon–Fri.

Red..
L4, IFC Mall, 8 Finance St, Central
8129-8882
www.pure-red.com
Sat and Sun brunch.

The Fringe Club...
2/F & Roof Top, 2 Lower Albert Rd, Central
2521 7251
www.hkfringe.com.hk
Mon–Fri vegetarian lunch buffet, Sat brunch.

H One
L4, IFC Mall, 8 Finance St, Central
2805-0638
www.h-one.com.hk
Sunday brunch and dinner buffet.

ARE THERE ANY GOOD **BUFFETS** SPECIALISING IN
ASIAN CUISINE?

Zuma ....
5/F & 6/F, The Landmark, 15 Queen's Rd Central
3657-6388
www.zumarestaurant.com
*Offers a fantastic Japanese/fusion buffet lunch on
Sundays. One child under 10 per adult eats for free.*

Kaetsu
Mezzanine, Grand Hyatt Hotel
1 Harbour Rd, Wan Chai
2584-7087
www.hongkong.grand.hyatt.com
Sat–Mon lunch and Japanese buffet.

The Spice Market
3/F, The Marco Polo Prince Hotel Hong Kong
23 Canton Rd, Tsim Sha Tsui
2113-6046
www.marcopolohotels.com
Southeast Asian cuisine, Mon–Sun lunch buffet.

Duetto Italian & Indian Dining
2/F, Sun Hung Kai Centre, 30 Harbour Rd, Wan Chai
2598-1222 / 2827-7777
www.chiram.com.hk

Tandoor ....
1/F, Lyndhurst Tower, 1 Lyndhurst Terrace, Central
2845-2262

Nomads ....
G/F, 55 Kimberley Rd, Tsim Sha Tsui
2722-0733
www.igors.com
Mon–Sun lunch buffet.

Jashan ....
1/F, Amber Lodge, 23 Hollywood Rd, Central
3105-5300 / 3105-5311
www.jashan.com.hk

Bombay Dreams
1/F, Carfield Comm. Bldg
75–77 Wyndham St, Central
2971-0001
www.diningconcepts.com.hk
*They offer a buffet lunch for $98 plus 10% service
charge, Monday to Friday.*

HOW ABOUT THE PERFECT PLACE FOR A LITTLE
LADIES' LUNCH AND SOME RETAIL THERAPY?

Harvey Nichols Fourth Floor Restaurant & Bar
4/F, The Landmark, 15 Queen's Rd Central
3695-3389
www.harveynichols.com

Mezz
Mezzanine, Prince's Bldg, 10 Chater Rd, Central
2523-8989
*The food is always reliable and the atmosphere is
calming.*

Sevva ....
25/F, Prince's Bldg, 10 Chater Rd, Central
2537-1388
www.sevvahk.com
*A 360-degree terrace offering spectacular views all
around, ultra-stylish décor and the "it" factor for the
place to be.*

Café Costa
Lane Crawford, L3, IFC Mall, 8 Finance St, Central
2118-7600
www.lanecrawford.com
Outdoor terrace.

agnès b. Café
- L3, IFC Mall, 8 Finance St, Central
  2805-0723
- 3/F, Times Square, 1 Matheson St, Causeway Bay
  2506-3822
- P1, wtc more, 280 Gloucester Rd, Causeway Bay
  2890-2989

www.agnesb-lepaingrille.com

Caffè HABITU ....
- G/F, Hutchison House, 10 Harcourt Rd, Central
  2147-2323
- G/F, Pacific Place Three
  8–10 Queen's Rd East, Wan Chai
  2527-8999
- G/F, Fortis Bank Tower
  77–79 Gloucester Rd, Wan Chai
  2111-2977
- G/F, 33 Leighton Rd, Causeway Bay
  2574-3111
- G.O.D., 2/F, Leighton Centre
  77 Leighton Rd, Causeway Bay
  3579-4050
- 2/F, Cityplaza, 18 Taikoo Shing Rd, Tai Koo
  2904-8676
- G/F, Ocean Terminal, Harbour City
  Canton Rd, Tsim Sha Tsui
  2115-9170
- 1/F, Elements Mall, 1 Austin Rd West, Kowloon
  2196-8466

www.caffehabitu.com

Nadaman
7/F, Island Shangri-La Hotel, Pacific Place
Supreme Court Rd, Admiralty
2877-3838
www.shangri-la.com

Isola
L3, IFC Mall, 8 Finance St, Central
2383-8765
www.isolabarandgrill.com

Domani ....
L4, Pacific Place, 88 Queensway, Admiralty
2111-1197
www.domani.hk

EVERYONE SAYS WHEN IN HONG KONG, YOU
MUST GO FOR **AFTERNOON TEA**. WHAT PLACES ARE
KNOWN FOR THIS?

The Peninsula Hotel
Lobby, Salisbury Rd, Tsim Sha Tsui
2920-2888
www.hongkong.peninsula.com
Afternoon tea served in a grand setting.

The Verandah
1/F, The Repulse Bay, 109 Repulse Bay Rd, Repulse Bay
2292-2822
www.therepulsebay.com
*The 1920s colonial setting offers an authentic
experience for afternoon tea.*

The Lounge
Lobby, Four Seasons Hotel Hong Kong
8 Finance St, Central
3196-8888
www.fourseasons.com/hongkong

Clipper Lounge
Mezzanine, Mandarin Oriental Hotel
5 Connaught Rd Central
2825-4007
www.mandarinoriental.com/hongkong

Antique Patisserie & Fine Chocolates
• G/F, Oriental Crystal Comm. Bldg
  46 Lyndhurst Terrace, Central
  2542-2816
• G/F, Kornhill Plaza (South), 2 Kornhill Rd, Quarry Bay
  2907-2908
www.antiquepatisserie.com
This new little patisserie and fine chocolate store has a cosy, relaxing tea room in the back.

Le Goûter Bernardaud
L2, IFC Mall, 8 Finance St, Central
2295-3955
www.legouter.com
Specialising in macaroons in a myriad of flavours. Try the Valrhona hot cocoa for serious chocoholics.

Portobello ....*)
G/F, 9 Staunton St, SoHo
2523-8999
Unpretentious little patisserie featuring slices of sweet offerings with coffees, teas and cocktails. Open late for that late-night sweet tooth.

COVA Caffè-Ristorante
• 2/F, Alexandra House, 18 Chater Rd, Central
  2522-1833
• 3/F, Pacific Place, 88 Queensway, Admiralty
  2918-9660
• G/F, wtc more, 280 Gloucester Rd, Causeway Bay
  2895-1998
• G/F, Lee Gardens, 33 Hysan Ave, Causeway Bay
  2907-3399
• G/F, Gateway Arcade, Harbour City
  Canton Rd, Tsim Sha Tsui
  2907-3882
• LG1, Festival Walk, 80 Tat Chee Ave, Kowloon Tong
  2265-8688
www.cova.com.hk

WHERE CAN I FIND AN UPSCALE RESTAURANT
WITH A **GREAT VALUE SET LUNCH**?

Bo Innovation ....
2/F, J Residence, 60 Johnston Rd, Wan Chai
2850-837
www.boinnovation.com
A great introduction to the chef's famous creations, without paying dinner prices.

Zuma ....
5/F & 6/F, The Landmark, 15 Queen's Rd Central
3657-6388
www.zumarestaurant.com

Nadaman ....
7/F, Island Shangri-La Hotel, Pacific Place
Supreme Court Rd, Admiralty
2877-3838
www.shangri-la.com

Isola ....
L3, IFC Mall, 8 Finance St, Central
2383-8765
www.isolabarandgrill.com

H One ....
L4, IFC Mall, 8 Finance St, Central
2805-0638
www.h-one.com.hk

Cucina ....
6/F, Marco Polo Hongkong Hotel, Harbour City
Canton Rd, Tsim Sha Tsui
2113-0808
www.cucinahk.com

Lux ....*)
UG/F, California Tower
30–32 D'Aguilar St, Central
2868-9538
www.lkfe.com

L'Atelier de Joël Robuchon ....
4/F, The Landmark, 15 Queen's Rd Central
2166-9000
www.robuchon.hk
*Lunch menu L'Unique available in two sessions for
one hour each, starting from 11:30am–12:15pm and
2–2:30pm. Call for reservation.*

Caviar Kaspia ....
2/F, The Landmark, 15 Queen's Rd Central
2905-1960
www.caviarkaspia.asia

Dakota Prime ....
7/F, LKF Tower, 33 Wyndham St, Central
2526-2366
www.dakotaprime.hk

Gough 40 ....
G/F, 40 Gough St, Sheung Wan
2851-8498

HOW ABOUT JUST A **NO-FRILLS GOOD FOOD**/GOOD
VALUE EATERY?

Wong Chun Chun Thai Restaurant ....
Basement, G/F & 1/F, Belshine Centre
23 Tai Ku Ling Rd, Kowloon City
2716-6269
www.wongchunchun.com.hk

Akune Ra-Men ....
2/F, Hennessy Apartments
48–52 Percival St, Causeway Bay
2890-8234

Katong Laksa ....
G/F, 8 Mercer St, Sheung Wan
2543-4008

EVERYTHING FOOD & ENTERTAINMENT

WHERE CAN I GO FOR A LIGHT HEALTHY MEAL?

Eden Organic Bistro and Bar ....
16 Arbuthnot Rd, Central
2868-0625
www.arcanatables.com

Eat Right ....
23 Staunton St, SoHo
2868-4832
www.eatright.com.hk
*Healthy, high quality food with calories already
calculated for you and many vegetarian options. They
also offer a food/daily meal programme.*

Graze ....
G/F, Chao's Bldg
143–145 Bonham Strand, Sheung Wan
2850-7766
www.graze.hk
Set lunch and dinner, $100 corkage fee.

Duo ....
G/F, 118 Hollywood Rd, Central
2547-0000
www.duo.com.hk

Life Café ....
G/F, 10 Shelley St, SoHo
2810-9043
www.lifecafe.com.hk

WHERE CAN I FIND THE BEST SALAD BARS ?

Dressed ....
• L2, IFC Mall, 8 Finance St, Central
  2295-4848
• G/F, QRE Plaza, 202 Queen's Rd East, Wan Chai
  2893-4848
www.dressedsalads.com.hk

Just Salad ....
• G/F, 30–34 Cochrane St, Central
  2850-6818
• G/F, World-Wide House, 199 Des Voeux Rd Central
  2537-0316
www.justsalad.com.hk
*New York style salad bar; $45 up, they also make
wraps.*

ThreeSixty ....
• 3/F & 4/F, The Landmark, 15 Queen's Rd Central
  2111-4480
• 1/F, Elements Mall, 1 Austin Rd West, Kowloon
  2196-8066
www.threesixtyhk.com

Great Food Hall ....
LG, Pacific Place, 88 Queensway, Admiralty
2918-9986
www.greatfoodhall.com

Duo ....
G/F, 118 Hollywood Rd, Central
2547-0000
www.duo.com.hk

MIX ....
- L1, IFC Mall, 8 Finance St, Central
  2971-0688
- 3/F, Two Exchange Square
  8 Connaught Place, Central
  2843-2128
- ThreeSixty, 4/F, The Landmark, 15 Queen's Rd Central
  2111-4592
- G/F, Amber Lodge, 23 Hollywood Rd, Central
  2851-6038
- G/F, Empire Court, 2–4 Hysan Rd, Causeway Bay
  2869-5234
- Cooked Deli, 3/F, Gateway Arcade, Harbour City
  Canton Rd, Tsim Sha Tsui
  2270-9846
www.mix-world.com

I'M LOOKING FOR SOMETHING ON THE GO.
WHERE I CAN FIND A **HEALTHY TAKE-OUT OPTION**?

See also Salad Bars above
Graze ....
G/F, Chao's Bldg
143–145 Bonham Strand, Sheung Wan
2850-7766
www.graze.hk

Café O ....
- G/F, 2 Arbuthnot Rd, Central
  2868-0450
- G/F & 1/F, 61 Caine Rd, Central
  2111-3131
- G/F, 284 QRC, Sheung Wan
  2851-0890
- G/F, One Capital Place
  18 Luard Rd, Wan Chai
  3543-0224
www.cafeo.hk

Life Café ....
G/F, 10 Shelley St, SoHo
2810-9043
www.lifecafe.com.hk

city'super Deli Counters ....
See page 81
Sandwiches, salads, sushi and lunch sets to go.

Oliver's ....
2/F, Prince's Bldg, 10 Chater Rd, Central
2810-7710

Pure Fitness ....
- L5, IFC Mall, 8 Finance St, Central
  8129-8000
- 2/F, Kinwick Centre, 32 Hollywood Rd, Central
  2970-3366
www.pure-fit.com

Saveur de France ....
G/F, 24 Hollywood Rd, Central
2525-2028

Naturo Plus ....
G/F, 6 Sun St, Wan Chai
2865-0388
www.naturoplus.com.hk

Pumpernickel ....
- G/F, Golden Centre
  188 Des Voeux Rd Central
  2815-3711
- 4/F, Hong Kong Arts Centre
  2 Harbour Rd, Wan Chai
  2588-1001
- G/F, Miami Mansion
  13B Cleveland St, Causeway Bay
  2576-1302
- G/F, 1A Lau Li St, Tin Hau
  2578-0854
- G/F, Riviera Mansion, 20 Hoi Tai St, Quarry Bay
  2811-1361

WHERE CAN I GET A GOOD SANDWICH/WRAP TO GO?

MIX ....
See page 36
Pret A Manger ....
L1, IFC Mall, 8 Finance St, Central
2295-0405
www.pret.com.hk
Many locations. Delivery also available.
La Baguette Ltd ....
18 Lan Kwai Fong, Central
2868-3716
Menu available at www.dialadinner.com.hk.
simplylife Bakery Café ....
- 1/F, Cityplaza, 18 Taikoo Shing Rd, Tai Koo
  2967-8163
- L2, Festival Walk, 80 Tat Chee Ave, Kowloon Tong
  2265-7418
simplylife Bread and Wine ....
L1, IFC Mall, 8 Finance St, Central
2234-7356
Harvest Bagel & Café ....
G/F, 36 Lyndhurst Terrace, Central
3107-1623
www.harvest.com.hk

CAN YOU RECOMMEND A RESTAURANT WITH A RANGE OF ORGANIC FOODS SUITABLE FOR VEGETARIANS/ VEGANS?

Life Café ....
G/F, 10 Shelley St, SoHo
2810-9043
www.lifecafe.com.hk
Vegetarian and organic café offering take-out, delivery service, and eat-in in a simple rustic setting with a fabulous rooftop patio.
Fantasy Vegetarian Restaurant ....
66 Electric Rd, North Point
2887-3886
Chinese vegetarian restaurant and vegetarian dim sum.
Eat Right ....
23 Staunton St, SoHo
2868-4832
www.eatright.com.hk

Bookworm Café .... ♥
G/F, 79 Yung Shue Wan Main St
Yung Shue Wan, Lamma Island
2982-4838
www.bookwormcafe.com.hk
A cosy little café with great Western vegetarian food.

World Peace Café .... ♥
21–23 Tai Wong St East, Wan Chai
2527-5870
www.worldpeacecafe.hk
*Organic and vegetarian food served up completely by
volunteers, with all profits used for building Kadampa
temples around the world.*

Eden Organic Bistro and Bar .... ♥
16 Arbuthnot Rd, Central
2868-0625
www.arcanatables.com

Gingko House .... ♥
G/F, 44 Gough St, Central
2545-1200
www.gingkohouse.org

WHERE CAN I GO FOR AN **ASIAN VEGETARIAN SELECTION**?

Fantasy Vegetarian Restaurant .... ♥ ⊕
66 Electric Rd, North Point
2887-3886

Khana Khazana .... ♥
1/F, Dannies House, 20 Luard Rd, Wan Chai
2520-5308
www.khanakhazana.hk
*Full vegetarian menu, no non-veg options, great for a taste
of South Indian, North Indian and fusion veggie meals.*

Woodlands International Restaurant .... ♥
UG/F, Wing On Plaza
62 Mody Rd, East Tsim Sha Tsui
2369-3718
Great South Indian vegetarian food. Try the Masala Dosa.

Gaia Veggie Shop .... ♥
• 8/F, The Goldmark
  502 Hennessy Rd, Causeway Bay
  2808-1386
• 3/F, Pioneer Centre, 750 Nathan Rd, Prince Edward
  2148-1163
*A wide selection of vegetarian dishes that are cleverly-
masked to appeal to even non-vegetarians. Dishes
range from vegetarian eel sushi to faux Peking duck.*

Po Lin Yuen Vegetarian Food .... ♥
G/F, 69 Jervois St, Sheung Wan
2543-8981

World Peace Café .... ♥
See above

Pure Veggie House .... ♥ ⊕
3/F, Coda Plaza, 51 Garden Rd, Central
2525-0552
www.pureveggie-house.com

Chi Lin Vegetarian .... ♥
Nan Lian Garden, Diamond Hill
3658-9388
www.nanliangarden.org

Po Lin Monastery .... 🌱
Ngong Ping, Lantau Island
2985-5248
Vegan menu.
Tung Fong Siu Kee Yuen .... 🌱
111 Wan Chai Rd, Wan Chai
2575-2542

WHERE CAN I FIND **HALAL FOOD**?

Habibi
11/F, Grand Progress Bldg, 15–16 Lan Kwai Fong, Central
2544-6198
www.habibi.com.hk
Wonderful Egyptian food. Belly dancer performs weekends.
Habibi Café
G/F, 112–114 Wellington St, Central
2544-3886
www.habibi.com.hk
*Great for breakfast or a quick bite. Try the koshary, a
typical street-stall dish in Egypt.*
Islam Food ....
• G/F, 1 Lung Kong Rd, Kowloon City
  2382-2822
• 33–35 Tak Ku Ling Rd, Kowloon City
  2382-1882
www.islamfood.biz.com.hk
Jo Jo Indian Restaurant
2/F, David House, 37–39 Lockhart Rd, Wan Chai
2522-6209
www.jojofood.com
Jo Jo Mess
U/F, 21 Man Nin St, Sai Kung, New Territories
2574-7477
www.jojofood.com
See www.islam.org.hk for more halal restaurants.

WHAT ABOUT **KOSHER FOOD**?

Jewish Community Centre
70 Robinson Rd, Mid-Levels
2801-5440
www.jcc.org.hk
Shalom Grill
2/F, Fortune House, 61 Connaught Rd Central
2851-6300

MY FRIENDS DON'T EAT MEAT. WHERE CAN I TAKE
THEM FOR A GOOD **SEAFOOD MEAL**?

Ocean Grill
G/F, 49 Elgin St, SoHo
2147-0100
www.diningconcepts.com.hk
Sheraton Oyster & Wine Bar
18/F, Sheraton Hong Kong Hotel and Towers
20 Nathan Rd, Tsim Sha Tsui
2324-7739
www.starwoodhotels/sheraton
More than 20 different types of oysters flown in daily.

Dot Cod Seafood Restaurant & Oyster Bar
Basement, Prince's Bldg, 10 Chater Rd, Central
2810-6988
www.dotcod.com

The Mandarin Grill & Bar
1/F, Mandarin Oriental Hotel, 5 Connaught Rd Central
2522-0111 / 2825-4004
www.mandarinoriental.com/hongkong
*Fantastic crustacean selection and excellent fresh
oysters, in addition to a variety of meat selections.*

I WANT TO TAKE MY DATE FOR FRESH **OYSTERS OR
CAVIAR**. WHERE DO YOU SUGGEST WE GO?

Sheraton Oyster & Wine Bar
18/F, Sheraton Hong Kong Hotel and Towers
20 Nathan Rd, Tsim Sha Tsui
2324-7739
www.starwoodhotels/sheraton

Dot Cod Seafood Restaurant & Oyster Bar
See above

The Mandarin Grill & Bar
See above

Café Deco ....
1/F & 2/F, Peak Galleria, 118 Peak Rd, The Peak
2849-5111
www.cafedecogroup.com

The Press Room ....
108 Hollywood Rd, Central
2525-3444
www.thepressroom.com.hk

Oyster Express
• G/F, Redana Centre
  25 Yiu Wa St, Causeway Bay
  2575-0227
• G/F, 6 Hillwood Rd, Tsim Sha Tsui
  2375-6778

Oyster C
G/F, Belle House, 98–104 Hing Fat St, Tin Hau
2834-7748

Caviar Kaspia
2/F, The Landmark, 15 Queen's Rd Central
2905-1960
www.caviarkaspia.asia
*Striking, cosy Parisian chic restaurant offering Hong
Kong's most impressive selection of caviar.*

WHERE CAN I FIND A GOOD **TRADITIONAL
STEAKHOUSE** IN HONG KONG?

Morton's of Chicago
4/F, Sheraton Hong Kong Hotel
20 Nathan Rd, Tsim Sha Tsui
2732-2343
www.mortons.com

Ruth's Chris Steak House
G/F, Lippo Centre, 89 Queensway, Admiralty
2522-9090
www.ruthschris.com

The Steak House Wine Bar and Grill
G/F, InterContinental Hotel
18 Salisbury Rd, Tsim Sha Tsui
2313-2707 / 2313-2323
www.hongkong-ic.dining.intercontinental.com
Prime cuts seared on a charcoal grill and an elaborate salad bar.

Lawry's the Prime Rib
4/F, Lee Gardens, 33 Hysan Rd, Causeway Bay
2907-2218
www.maxconcepts.com.hk

BESIDES THE TRADITIONAL STEAKHOUSES,
WHERE CAN I GO TO GET A REALLY **GOOD STEAK**?

The Press Room ....
108 Hollywood Rd, Central
2525-3444
www.thepressroom.com.hk

Lardos Steak House..
G/F, 4B Hang Hau Village
Tseung Kwan O, New Territories
2719-8168
www.tcdeli.com
Great value for top quality steak in this deceivingly no frills restaurant that is owned by the same owner as T. C. Foods. No wonder the steak is so good.

BLT Steak
G/F, Ocean Terminal, Harbour City
Canton Rd, Tsim Sha Tsui
2730-3508
www.diningconcepts.com.hk

Dakota Prime
7/F, LKF Tower, 33 Wyndham St, Central
2526-2366
www.dakotaprime.hk

Wagyu
G/F, The Centrium, 60 Wyndham St, Central
2525-8805

Wooloomooloo Steakhouse
• G/F & 1/F, Onfem Tower
  29 Wyndham St, Central
  2894-8010
• 31/F, The Hennessy
  256 Hennessy Rd, Wan Chai
  2893-6960
• G/F, Tsim Sha Tsui Centre
  66 Mody Rd, East Tsim Sha Tsui
  2722-7050
• 2/F, Elements Mall
  1 Austin Rd West, Kowloon
  2736-9771
www.wooloo-mooloo.com
Aussie-themed restaurant.

Bistecca
2/F, Grand Progress Bldg
15–16 Lan Kwai Fong, Central
2525-1308
www.diningconcepts.com.hk

EVERYTHING FOOD & ENTERTAINMENT

I'M ON A **BUDGET**, BUT I NEED MY **STEAK FIX**. ANY SUGGESTIONS?

Steak Expert ....
- G/F, 483–499 Jaffe Rd, Wan Chai
  2573-2711
- 1/F, Westview Height, 163 Belcher's St, Kennedy Town
  2816-9111
- 4/F, Carnarvon Plaza, 20 Carnarvon Rd, Tsim Sha Tsui
  2312-6022
- L11, Langham Place, 8 Argyle St, Mong Kok
  3514-9041

Various locations throughout Hong Kong.

WHERE CAN I FIND SOME **TRADITIONAL EUROPEAN FARE**?

Gaia
G/F, Grand Millennium Plaza
181 Queen's Rd Central, Sheung Wan
2167-8200
www.gaiaristorante.com

Da Domenico
G/F, 8 Hoi Ping Rd, Causeway Bay
2882-8013

Grissini
2/F, Grand Hyatt Hotel, 1 Harbour Rd, Wan Chai
2584-7722
www.hongkong.grand.hyatt.com

Cecconi's
G/F, 43 Elgin St, SoHo
2147-5500
www.diningconcepts.com.hk

Chez Patrick
- G/F, 26 Peel St, Central
  2541-1401
- G/F, 8–9 Sun St, Wan Chai
  2527-1408
www.chezpatrick.hk

Gaddi's
1/F, The Peninsula Hotel, Salisbury Rd, Tsim Sha Tsui
2315-3171
www.hongkong.peninsula.com

Rive Droite Rive Gauche
2/F, Onfem Tower, 29 Wyndham St, Central
2525-1681
www.rivedroite-rivegauche.hk
*This modern restaurant/bar offers a classic French menu.
Good value for lunch and happy hour from 6–9pm.*

Chesa
1/F, The Peninsula Hotel, Salisbury Rd, Tsim Sha Tsui
2315-3169
www.hongkong.peninsula.com
Authentic Swiss cuisine including raclette and fondue.

Petrus
56/F, Island Shangri-La Hotel, Pacific Place
Supreme Court Rd, Admiralty
2820-8590
www.shangri-la.com
*Known as Hong Kong's best French restaurant with
spectacular views, an opulent interior, discreet service
and a superb wine list.*

HOW ABOUT **CASUAL EUROPEAN CUISINE**?

Mrs Jones
Upper Basement, Harilela House
79 Wyndham St, Central
2522-8118
www.mrsjones.com.hk

HABITU Ristorante .... ♂
See page 19

Spasso
4/F, Ocean Centre, Harbour City
Canton Rd, Tsim Sha Tsui
2730-8027
www.spassoristorante-bar.com.hk

Simpatico .... ♂
1/F, Peak Galleria, 118 Peak Rd, The Peak
2849-0001
www.epicurean.com.hk

CAN YOU SUGGEST SOME GOOD
MEDITERRANEAN/MIDDLE EASTERN RESTAURANTS?

El Greco
G/F, 5 Wai Fung St, Ap Lei Chau
2328-2138
www.toptables.com.hk/elgreco

Bahce Turkish Restaurant
G/F, Mui Wo Centre, 3 Ngan Wan Rd
Mui Wo, Lantau Island
2984-0222
Casual Turkish food.

Habibi
11/F, Grand Progress Bldg
15–16 Lan Kwai Fong, Central
2544-6198
www.habibi.com.hk

Habibi Café
G/F, 112–114 Wellington St, Central
2544-3886
www.habibi.com.hk

Olive
• G/F, 32 Elgin St, SoHo
  2521-1608
• 3/F, Elements Mall, 1 Austin Rd West, Kowloon
  2810-8585
www.diningconcepts.com.hk
Stylish fusion Greek/Lebanese food.

Marouche Grill
48 Cochrane St, Central
2541-8282

La Kasbah
G/F, 4–8 Arbuthnot Rd, Central
2525-9493
www.kasbah.com.hk
Unique, intimate setting offering North African cuisine.

Assaf Lebanese Cuisine
G/F, Lyndhurst Bldg
37 Lyndhurst Terrace, Central
2851-6550
Reasonably priced, home-style Lebanese cooking in a basic but relaxed setting.

I'M CRAVING **LATIN-STYLE FOOD**, WHERE DO YOU SUGGEST?

Uno Mas
1/F, The Broadway, 54–62 Lockhart Rd, Wan Chai
2527-9111
www.arcanatables.com
Catalan cuisine, paella, tapas and cava sangria.

Ole
1/F, Shun Ho Tower, 24–30 Ice House St, Central
2523-8624

Bacar .... ☽
G/F Wing Lee Bldg, 2 Shelley St, SoHo
2521-8322
Tapas and wine. Sister restaurant to Enoteca.

Fire
1/F, W Hotel, 1 Austin Rd West, Kowloon
3717-2848
www.starwoodhotels.com/whotels/index.html
All-you-can-eat churrascaria barbecue with live Brazilian dancing on Fridays and Saturdays.

Tapeo .... ☽ 🎏
G/F, 19 Hollywood Rd, Central
3171-1989 / 9123-6049
www.tapeo.hk

Scirocco
1/F, 10–12 Staunton St, SoHo
2973-6605
www.stauntonsgroup.com

Mijas
1/F, Murray House, Stanley Plaza, Stanley
2899-0858
www.kingparrot.com

La Bodega
G/F, 42 D'Aguilar St, Central
2524-7790
www.igors.com

Boca
G/F, 65 Peel St, SoHo
2548-1717
www.boca.com.hk

La Comida .... ☽
G/F, 22 Staunton St, SoHo
2530-3118
www.lacomida.com.hk

Rico's
UG/F, 51 Elgin St, SoHo
2840-0937
www.foodxpress.hk

Que Pasa Tequila Bar & Cantina
G/F, 15 Knutsford Terrace, Tsim Sha Tsui
2316-2525
www.mhihk.com

El Taco Loco ....
G/F, 9 Staunton St, SoHo
2522-0214
www.diningconcepts.com.hk

El Pomposo
R/F, Elements Mall, 1 Austin Rd West, Kowloon
2196-8123
www.epicurean.com.hk

Caramba
- 26–30 Elgin St, SoHo
  2530-9963
- G/F, D Deck, Block A, Discovery Bay Plaza
  Discovery Bay, Lantau Island
  2987-2848

www.caramba.com.hk

Agave
- 33 D'Aguilar St, Central
  2521-2010
- 93 Lockhart Rd, Wan Chai
  2866-3228

www.epicurean.com.hk

WHERE CAN I FIND A **THIN CRUST PIZZA**?

Wildfire .... 🍭
- G/F, 13 Bonham Rd, Mid-Levels
  2810-0670
- 2/F, Murray House, Stanley
  2813-6161
- 7/F, East Hall, Terminal 1
  Hong Kong International Airport
  2261-2999

www.igors.com
See website for more locations.

California Pizza Kitchen .... 🍭
- 13/F, Food Forum, Times Square
  1 Matheson St, Causeway Bay
  3102-9132
- LCX, 3/F, Ocean Terminal, Harbour City
  Canton Rd, Tsim Sha Tsui
  3102-0375
- 1/F, Gala Place, 56 Dundas St, Mong Kok
  2374-0032
- L11, MegaBox, 38 Wang Chiu Rd, Kowloon Bay
  3421-2351

www.cpk.com

Pizzeria Italia .... 🍭
G/F, 1–7 Mosque St, Mid-Levels
2525-2519
Great for take-out/delivery.

Pizza Express .... 🍭
- G/F, 21 Lyndhurst Terrace, Central
  2850-7898
- G/F, 10 Wing Fung St, Wan Chai
  3528-0541
- J Residence, 60 Johnston Rd, Wan Chai
  2861-0600
- G/F, Ko On Mansion, 9 Tai Yue Ave, Tai Koo
  3150-8800
- 90 Stanley Main St, Stanley
  2813-7363
- G/F, 35 Ashley Rd, Tsim Sha Tsui
  2317-7432
- L2, Festival Walk, 80 Tat Chee Ave, Kowloon Tong
  3691-8691

www.pizzaexpress.com.hk

Café O .... 🍭 *)
See page 36

EVERYTHING FOOD & ENTERTAINMENT

WHERE CAN I GET A GOOD OLD **DEEP-DISH CHICAGO STYLE PIZZA**?

Capone's Pizza
G/F, 9 Possession St, Sheung Wan
2869-5050 / 2596-0000
www.cuisinecourier.com
Delivery only.

PIZZA BY THE SLICE?

Duke's Deli
G/F, Two Chinachem Plaza, 135 Des Voeux Rd Central
2544-7587
www.dukesdeli.com

Cul-de-Sac ....
• G/F, Block A, Winner Bldg
  17 Wing Wah Lane, Central
  2525-8116
• G/F, 89 Lockhart Rd, Wan Chai
  2529-4116

Café O ....
See page 36

OTHER THAN PIZZA, WHERE DO YOU SUGGEST I TAKE **A BIG GROUP OF KIDS TO EAT**?

Bubba Gump Shrimp Co. ....
3/F, The Peak Tower, 128 Peak Rd, The Peak
2849-2867
www.bubbagump.com
Great views, great food, large portions and very kid friendly! They even do kids' birthday parties.

Ruby Tuesday ....
• 10/F, wtc more, 280 Gloucester Rd, Causeway Bay
  2895-1628
• 5/F, Cityplaza, 18 Taikoo Shing Rd, Tai Koo
  2907-1133
• Podium, Telford Plaza, 33 Wai Yip St, Kowloon Bay
  2376-3122
• 5/F, New Town Plaza, Phase 1
  Sha Tin Centre St, Sha Tin, New Territories
  2699-2838
www.rubytuesday.com.hk

Dan Ryan's Chicago Grill ....
• L1, Pacific Place, 88 Queensway, Admiralty
  2845-4600
• 3/F, Ocean Terminal, Harbour City
  Canton Rd, Tsim Sha Tsui
  2735-6111
• LG, Festival Walk, 80 Tat Chee Ave, Kowloon Tong
  2265-8811
www.danryans.com.hk

Pepperoni's ....
• 8 Staunton St, SoHo
  2525-1439
• 2 Shing Ping St, Happy Valley
  2895-8566
• 1592 Po Tung Rd, Sai Kung, New Territories
  2791-0394

Fat Angelo's ....
- G/F, 49A Elgin St, SoHo
  2973-6808
- 1/F, Elizabeth House
  250 Gloucester Rd, Causeway Bay
  2574-6263
- Basement, 8 Minden Ave, Tsim Sha Tsui
  2730-4788
www.fatangelos.com

WHERE CAN I FIND A GOOD NEW YORK STYLE DELI?

Duke's Deli
G/F, Two Chinachem Plaza, 135 Des Voeux Rd Central
2544-7587
www.dukesdeli.com
Main Street Deli
Langham Hotel, 8 Peking Rd, Tsim Sha Tsui
2375-1133
www.hongkong.langhamhotels.com

WHERE CAN I FIND A GOOD BURGER JOINT?

Triple O's ....
- 1/F, The Forum, Exchange Square
  1 Connaught Rd Central
  3401-4000
- Great Food Hall, LG, Pacific Place
  88 Queensway, Admiralty
  2873-4000
- 1/F, Harbour Centre, 25 Harbour Rd, Wan Chai
  2519-3000
- city'super, B1, Times Square
  1 Matheson St, Causeway Bay
  2506-2600
- city'super, 3/F, Gateway Arcade, Harbour City
  Canton Rd, Tsim Sha Tsui
  2387-7000
- L1, New Town Plaza, Phase 1
  Sha Tin Centre St, Sha Tin, New Territories
  2697-4500
www.tripleo.com.hk
Shake 'em Buns ....
- Mezzanine, 76 Wellington St, Central
  2810-5533
- 60 Johnston Rd, Wan Chai (Entrance at Ship St)
  2866-2060
- G/F, 5 Hoi Ping Rd, Causeway Bay
  2572-6220
www.shakembuns.com
Fatburger ....
G/F, QRE Plaza, Queen's Rd East, Wan Chai
2891-8855
www.fatburger.com
Must try their amazing milkshakes.
Al's Diner ....
G/F, Winner Bldg, 27–39 D'Aguilar St, Central
2869-1869
Atomic Patty ....
G/F, 7 Lan Kwai Fong, Central
2868-3666

Cul-de-Sac
See page 46
If the burgers don't hack it for you, get the poutine!

Gourmet Burger Union ....
1/F, Cheung Fai Bldg
45–47 Cochrane St, Central
2581-0521
www.gourmetburgerunion.com
Unique toppings, design your own, not for the budget conscious.

Burger Republic
39 Gough St, Sheung Wan
2581-1887

HOW ABOUT A GREAT **BURGER IN A RESTAURANT**?

The Press Room ....
108 Hollywood Rd, Central
2525-3444
www.thepressroom.com.hk

Harlan's
L2, IFC Mall, 8 Finance St, Central
2805-0566
www.jcgroup.hk

Duke's Burger
5 Staunton St, SoHo
2526-7062
www.dukesburger.com

Wagyu
G/F, The Centrium, 60 Wyndham St, Central
2525-8805

Kitchen
6/F, W Hotel, 1 Austin Rd West, Kowloon
3717-2222
www.starwoodhotels.com/whotels/index.html

Dan Ryan's Chicago Grill ....
See page 46

WHILE I'M ON BURGERS, WHAT ABOUT OTHER
COMFORT FOOD?

The Chippy ....
Basement, 51 Wellington St, Central
2523-1618
www.thechippy.com.hk

El Taco Loco ....
G/F, 9 Staunton St, SoHo
2522-0214
www.diningconcepts.com.hk

Archie B's ....
LG/F, 7–9 Staunton St, SoHo
2522-1262
www.diningconcepts.com.hk
Burgers, hot dogs, American comfort food.

Yorkshire Pudding ....
G/F, 6 Staunton St, SoHo
2536-9968
www.stauntonsgroup.com

Hot Dog Shop
L/G, Hollywood House
27–29 Hollywood Rd, Central

Hot Dog Link .... 🍭 🎧
67D Waterloo Rd, Kowloon Tong
2624-4002
*Cheap hot dog shop, serving chicken, pork and beef
sausages, also in different flavours like curry, peppered,
chilli, smoked, etc.*

Jed's Just Ribs
2869-5050
*Delivery only, can be ordered through Gourmet Express
(See page 101).*

I'M LOOKING FOR A GOOD CASUAL **NEIGHBOURHOOD
HAUNT**. WHERE SHOULD I GO?

Smugglers Inn ....*·)
90A Stanley Main St, Stanley
2813-8852
A real neighbourhood bar.

The Chapel ....🏷
G/F, 27 Yik Yam St, Happy Valley
2834-6565
*Great neighbourhood restaurant/bar offering tasty
Indian food. Get a group together and check out quiz
night every Thursday at 9pm.*

The Globe
G/F, 39 Hollywood Rd, Central
2543-1941
www.theglobe.com.hk

Café Eos
G/F, 42 Electric Rd, Tin Hau
2571-7968

Pumpernickel ....🍭🍷🏷
See page 37
Great for breakfast.

Classified The Cheese Room ....*·)
G/F, 108 Hollywood Rd, Central
2525-3454
www.classifiedfoodshops.com.hk

Classified Mozzarella Bar ....*·)
31 Wing Fung St, Wan Chai
2528-3454
www.classifiedfoodshops.com.hk

Café Einstein ....*·)
33 Tong Chong St, Quarry Bay
2960-0994
www.ninetysevengroup.com

China Bear
G/F, Mui Wo Centre, 3 Ngan Wan Rd
Mui Wo, Lantau Island
2984-9720

Tivo ....*·)
43 Wyndham St, Central
2116-8055
www.aqua.com.hk

Ali Oli Bakery ....🍭🏷
11 Sha Tsui Path, Sai Kung, New Territories
2792-2655
www.alioli.com.hk

Pane Vino
G/F, 11 Mosque Junction, Central
2521-7366

Brown
18A Sing Woo Rd, Happy Valley
2891-8558

Café O
See page 36

Delaney's
• G/F & 1/F, One Capital Place
 18 Luard Rd, Wan Chai
 2804-2880
• Basement, Mary Bldg
 71 –77 Peking Rd, Tsim Sha Tsui
 2301-3980
www.delaneys.com.hk

The Keg
52 D'Aguilar St, Central
2810-0369
www.igors.com

Dublin Jack's
1/F, 17 Lan Kwai Fong, Central
2543-0081
www.dublinjack.com.hk

The Peak Lookout
121 Peak Rd, The Peak
2849-1000
www.peaklookout.com.hk

Spices
The Repulse Bay
109 Repulse Bay Rd, Repulse Bay
2292-2821
www.therepulsebay.com/restaurants.html

The Boathouse
88 Stanley St, Stanley
2813-4467
www.igors.com

Tapeo
G/F, 19 Hollywood Rd, Central
3171-1989 / 9123-6049
www.tapeo.hk

Yixin Restaurant
G/F, Shanghai Ind. Investment Bldg
50 Hennessy Rd, Wan Chai
2834-9963

The Barn
G/F, 44 –48 Leighton Rd, Causeway Bay
2504-3987

East End Brewery
23 –27 Tong Chong St, Quarry Bay
2811-1907
www.elgrande.com.hk
Also a great place to people watch.

Spoil Café
G/F, 1 Sun St, Wan Chai
3589-5678

WHERE CAN I FIND A **GOOD SPORTS BAR**?

Champs Bar
The Charterhouse
208 –218 Wan Chai Rd, Wan Chai
2833-9086
www.champsbar.com.hk

The Spot Sports Bar .... *)
G/F, 11 Staunton St, SoHo
2973-6886

Amici .... *)
1/F, 83 Lockhart Rd, Wan Chai
2866-1918
www.amicihk.com
Liverpool fans come here! The official Liverpool supporters' bar. A good place to watch sports with food, wine and beer. They also show rugby matches.

Bulldog's Bar & Grill .... *)
• 2/F, Phoenix Bldg
  21–25 Luard Rd, Wan Chai
  2529-2661
• G/F & UG/F, Tsim Sha Tsui Centre
  66 Mody Rd, East Tsim Sha Tsui
  2311-6993
www.bulldogsbarandgrill.com

Skitz Sports Bar .... *)
5/F, Phoenix Bldg
21–25 Luard Rd, Wan Chai
2866-3277
www.skitzbar.com

Slim's .... *)
G/F, 1 Wing Fung St, Wan Chai
2528-1661
www.elgrande.com.hk

ANY SUGGESTIONS FOR SOME GOOD **AFTER-WORK WATERING HOLES**?

Le Jardin .... *)
1/F, 10 Wing Wah Lane, Central
2877-1100

Baby Buddha .... *)
G/F, 18 Wo On Lane, Central
2167-7244

Staunton's Winebar and Café .... *)
G/F, 10–12 Staunton St, SoHo
2973-6611
www.stauntonsgroup.com

Sahara Mezz Bar .... *)
G/F, 11 Elgin St, SoHo
2291-6060
www.aldentegroup.com

Di Vino .... *)
G/F, 73 Wyndham St, Central
2167-8883

Zentro Bar & Eatery .... *)
L2, IFC Mall, 8 Finance St, Central
2899-2221

Café Gray Deluxe
49/F, The Upper House Hotel
Pacific Place, 88 Queensway, Admiralty
3968-1106
www.cafegrayhk.com

Café Einstein .... *)
33 Tong Chong St, Quarry Bay
2960-0994
www.ninetysevengroup.com

The Captain's Bar .... *)
G/F, Mandarin Oriental Hotel
5 Connaught Rd Central
2825-4006
www.mandarinoriental.com/hongkong

Exit Wine & Cigar Bar .... *)
1 St. Francis Yard, Wan Chai
2861-3318
Funky little bar/lounge to hang out and enjoy chilled music, cigars and drinks.

Domani .... *)
L4, Pacific Place, 88 Queensway, Admiralty
2111-1197
www.domani.hk

Lei Dou .... *)
G/F, 20–22 D'Aguilar St, Central
2525-6628

Azure .... *)
29/F, Hotel LKF, 33 Wyndham St, Central
3518-9330
www.azure.hk

Red .... *)
L4, IFC Mall, 8 Finance St, Central
8129-8882
www.pure-red.com

WHERE IS A **GOOD RESTAURANT** THAT ALSO OFFERS A GOOD **BAR SCENE**?

Wagyu
G/F, The Centrium
60 Wyndham St, Central
2525-8805

Wagyu Lounge .... *)
LG/F, Hollywood Comm. House
3–5 Old Bailey St, SoHo
2522-1438

Lotus
37–43 Pottinger St, Central
2543-6290
www.lotus.hk

Sevva .... *)
25/F, Prince's Bldg, 10 Chater Rd, Central
2537-1388
www.sevvahk.com

Zuma
5/F & 6/F, The Landmark, 15 Queen's Rd Central
3657-6388
www.zumarestaurant.com

La Terrasse Wine Bar & Restaurant .... *)
G/F, 19 Old Bailey St, SoHo
2147-2225
www.laterrasse-soho.com

Cinecittà
G/F, 9 Star St, Wan Chai
2529-0199
www.elite-concepts.com

Boca .... *)
G/F, 65 Peel St, SoHo
2548-1717
www.boca.com.hk

EVERYTHING FOOD & ENTERTAINMENT

FINDS .... *)
2/F, LKF Tower, 55 D'Aguilar St, Central
2522-9318

Goccia .... *)
73 Wyndham St, Central
2167-8181
www.goccia.com.hk

Di Vino .... *)
G/F, 73 Wyndham St, Central
2167-8883

Yun Fu .... *)
Basement, 43–55 Wyndham St, Central
2116-8855
www.aqua.com.hk

Aspasia
1/F, The Luxe Manor, 39 Kimberley Rd, Tsim Sha Tsui
3763-8800
www.aspasia.com.hk

WHERE CAN I FIND A **COMEDY CLUB** IN HONG KONG?

The Punchline Comedy Club
Duetto Italian & Indian Dining
2/F, Sun Hung Kai Centre, 30 Harbour Rd, Wan Chai
2598-1222 / 2827-7777
www.punchlinecomedy.com/hongkong
*This restaurant hosts the monthly Punchline Comedy
Club, featuring top acts from the London and
international comedy circuit.*

Takeout Comedy
Basement, 34 Elgin St, SoHo
6220-4436
www.takeoutcomedy.com

WHERE IS A GOOD **BAR/PLACE FOR LIVE MUSIC**?

Makumba .... *)
G/F, Garley Bldg, 48 Peel St, SoHo
2522-0544
www.makumba.com.hk
*African food, live music and drums, in a relaxed, very
un-Hong Kong atmosphere.*

Peel Fresco Music Lounge .... *)
G/F, 49 Peel St, SoHo
2540-2046
www.peelfresco.com

The Cavern .... *)
LG/F, LKF Tower, 55 D'Aguilar St, Central
2121-8969
www.igors.com

Sense 99
2/F–3/F, 99F Wellington St, Central
9466-4695
www.sense99.com
Only opens at weekends or on special occasions.

Backstage .... *)
11/F, Somptuex Central
52–54 Wellington St, Central
2167-8985
www.backstagelive.hk

joyce is not here .... *)
G/F, 44 Peel St, SoHo
2851-2999
www.joycebakerdesign.com

WHERE ARE SOME OF THE **'SCENE AND BE SEEN'**
PLACES TO GO AT NIGHT?

Kee Club .... *)
6/F, 32 Wellington St, Central
2810-9000
www.keeclub.com

Volar .... *)
Basement, 38–44 D'Aguilar St, Central
2810-1272
www.volar.com.hk

M1nt .... *)
108 Hollywood Rd, Central
2261-1111
www.m1nt.com.cn/hongkong.html

Azure .... *)
29/F, Hotel LKF, 33 Wyndham St, Central
3518-9330
www.azure.hk

Dragon-i .... *)
UG/F, The Centrium, 60 Wyndham St, Central
3110-1222
www.dragon-i.com.hk

Privé .... *)
The Centrium, 60 Wyndham St, Central
2810-8199
www.prive.hk

Halo .... *)
LG/F, 10–12 Stanley St, Central
2810-1460 / 2810-1272
www.halo.hk

WHERE CAN I FIND A **BAR/LOUNGE** TO SIT AND TALK?

Domani .... *)
L4, Pacific Place, 88 Queensway, Admiralty
2111-1197
www.domani.hk

Yun Fu .... *)
Basement, 43–55 Wyndham St, Central
2116-8855
www.aqua.com.hk

MO Bar .... *)
G/F, Landmark Mandarin Oriental Hotel
15 Queen's Rd Central, Central
2132-0077 / 2132-0188
www.mandarinoriental.com/landmark

Blue Bar .... *)
Lobby, Four Seasons Hotel Hong Kong
8 Finance St, Central
3196-8830
www.fourseasons.com/hongkong

FINDS .... *)
2/F, LKF Tower, 55 D'Aguilar St, Central
2522-9318
www.finds.com.hk

Vivo .... *)
G/F, Elgin Bldg, 41–43 Elgin St, SoHo
3106-2526
www.ankh-concepts.com
*Good place for a drink, while not feeling like you're
packed in a sardine can.*

Red .... 🍭 *)
L4, IFC Mall, 8 Finance St, Central
8129-8882
www.pure-red.com

Wagyu Lounge .... *)
LG/F, Hollywood Comm. House
3–5 Old Bailey St, SoHo
2522-1438

Solas .... *)
G/F, The Centrium, 60 Wyndham St, Central
3162-3710
www.solas.com.hk

Classified The Cheese Room .... *)
G/F, 108 Hollywood Rd, Central
2525-3454

Classified Mozzarella Bar .... *)
31 Wing Fung St, Wan Chai
2528-3454
www.classifiedfoodshops.com.hk

Lei Dou .... *)
G/F, 20–22 D'Aguilar St, Central
2525-6628

Living Room .... *)
6/F, W Hotel, 1 Austin Rd West, Kowloon
3717-2222
www.starwoodhotels.com/whotels/index.html

Exit Wine & Cigar Bar .... *)
1 St. Francis Yard, Wan Chai
2861-3318

Wooloomooloo Steakhouse
31/F, The Hennessy, 256 Hennessy Rd, Wan Chai
2893-6960
www.wooloo-mooloo.com

WHERE CAN I FIND A GOOD SELECTION OF **BEERS**?

Frites .... *)
1/F, Queen's Palace, 74 Queen's Rd Central
2179-5179
www.fritesbeer.com
Also a great place to go after work for drinks.

King Ludwig .... *)
• G/F, Hopewell Centre
  183 Queen's Rd East, Wan Chai
  2861-0737
• 2/F, Murray House, Stanley Plaza, Stanley
  2899-0122
• G/F, East Tsim Sha Tsui MTR Station, East Tsim Sha Tsui
  2369-8328
web.kingparrot.com

Slim's .... *)
G/F, 1 Wing Fung St, Wan Chai
2528-1661
www.elgrande.com.hk

McSorley's .... *)
- 55 Elgin St, SoHo
  2522-2646
- G/F, D Deck, Block A, Discovery Bay Plaza
  Discovery Bay, Lantau Island
  2987-8280
www.mcsorleys.com.hk

OTHER THAN BIG HOTEL BARS, WHERE CAN I GET
A REALLY GOOD **MARTINI** IN HONG KONG?

Feather Boa .... *)
38 Staunton St, SoHo
2857-2586
Chocolux .... *)
G/F, 57 Peel St, SoHo
2858-8760
www.chocoluxcafe.com
Lei Dou .... *)
G/F, 20–22 D'Aguilar St, Central
2525-6628
Beso .... *)
39A Gough St, Central
2581-3669
www.beso.com.hk

I'M CRAVING A GOOD OL' **CAESAR** (THE DRINK, NOT
THE SALAD). WHERE CAN I GET A GOOD ONE?

The Keg .... *)
52 D'Aguilar St, Central
2810-0369
www.igors.com
Stormies .... *)
G/F & 1/F, 46 D'Aguilar St, Central
2845-5533
The Captain's Bar .... *)
G/F, Mandarin Oriental Hotel
5 Connaught Rd Central
2825-4006
www.mandarinoriental.com/hongkong

WHERE IS A GOOD PLACE FOR **À LA CARTE DIM SUM**?

Dim Sum .... *)
G/F, 63 Sing Woo Rd, Happy Valley
2834-8893
Great old-style décor.
Victoria City Seafood Restaurant
5/F, Citic Tower, 1 Tim Mei Ave, Admiralty
2877-2211
www.eastocean.com.hk
Serenade Chinese Restaurant
1/F, Hong Kong Cultural Centre, Tsim Sha Tsui
2722-0932
Dynasty
1/F, Renaissance Harbour View Hotel
1 Harbour Rd, Wan Chai
2584-6971 / 2802-8888
www.marriott.com

EVERYTHING FOOD & ENTERTAINMENT

Summer Palace
5/F, Island Shangri-La Hotel, Pacific Place
Supreme Court Rd, Admiralty
2820-8552
www.shangri-la.com
Inspired by the décor of Beijing's Summer Palace.
The food is fabulous.

The Square
4/F, Two Exchange Square, 8 Connaught Rd Central
2525-1163
www.thesquare.com.hk

Tsui Hang Village Restaurant
• 2/F, New World Tower
16–18 Queen's Rd Central
2524-2012
• G/F, Miramar Shopping Centre
132 Nathan Rd, Tsim Sha Tsui
2368-1111
• Club Marina Cove
380 Hiram's Highway, Sai Kung, New Territories
2719-4768 / 2376-2882
www.thvr.hk

Lei Garden
• L3, IFC Mall, 8 Finance St, Central
2295-0238
• 1/F, CNT Tower
338 Hennessy Rd, Wan Chai
2892-0333
• 1/F, Block 9–10, City Garden, North Point
2806-0008
• 2/F, Elements Mall, 1 Austin Rd West, Kowloon
2196-8133
• B2, Houston Centre
63 Mody Rd, East Tsim Sha Tsui
2722-1636
• 121 Sai Yee St, Mong Kok
2392-5184
• 2/F, Telford Plaza
33 Wai Yip St, Kowloon Bay
2331-3306
• 5/F, APM, 418 Kwun Tong Rd, Kwun Tong
2365-3238
• 6/F, New Town Plaza, Phase 1
Sha Tin Centre St, Sha Tin, New Territories
2698-9111
www.leigarden.com.hk

Jade Garden
• G/F–2/F, 1 Hysan Ave, Causeway Bay
2577-9332
• 3/F, Causeway Bay Plaza 2
463–483 Lockhart Rd, Causeway Bay
2573-9339
• 4/F, Star House, 3 Salisbury Rd, Tsim Sha Tsui
2730-6888
• 1/F, Telford Plaza 1
33 Wai Yip St, Kowloon Bay
2758-2883
• 1/F, City Walk
1 Yeung Uk Rd, Tsuen Wan, New Territories
2941-0092
www.maxims.com.hk

I'D LIKE A MORE AUTHENTIC HONG KONG EXPERIENCE. WHERE DO THEY STILL DO **TROLLEY SERVICE DIM SUM**?

Metropol Restaurant
4/F, United Centre, 95 Queensway, Admiralty
2865-1988

Lin Heung Tea House ....
G/F–1/F, 160–164 Wellington St, Central
2544-4556
www.linheung.com

Maxim's Palace
- Low Block, City Hall, Connaught Rd Central
  2526-9931 / 2521-1303
- 2/F, Cityplaza, 18 Taikoo Shing Rd, Tai Koo
  2513-1996
- 8/F, Grand Century Place
  193 Prince Edward Rd West, Mong Kok
  2628-9668
- G/F, Telford Plaza, 33 Wai Yip St, Kowloon Bay
  2750-8028
- 8/F, New Town Plaza, Phase I
  Sha Tin Centre St, Sha Tin, New Territories
  2693-6918
- 3/F, Ma On Shan Plaza
  608 Sai Sha Rd, Ma On Shan, New Territories
  2633-5083
- 2/F, Tai Wo Shopping Mall, Tai Wo, New Territories
  2651-0551
- G/F, Luk Yeung Galleria
  22–26 Wai Tsuen Rd, Tsuen Wan, New Territories
  2498-8983
- 5/F, Metroplaza
  223 Hing Fong Rd, Kwai Fong, New Territories
  2420-6933
- Tuen Mun Town Hall
  3 Tuen Hi Rd, Tuen Mun, New Territories
  2430-0688
www.maxims.com.hk

WHAT ABOUT RESTAURANTS THAT SPECIALISE IN **DUMPLINGS AND NORTHERN CHINESE CUISINE**?

Crystal Jade
- L2, IFC Mall, 8 Finance St, Central
  2295-3811
- 310 Tai Yau Plaza, 181 Johnston Rd, Wan Chai
  2573-8844
- 2/F, wtc more, 280 Gloucester Rd, Causeway Bay
  2915-6988
- B2, Times Square, 1 Matheson St, Causeway Bay
  2506-0080
- 3/F, Gateway Arcade, Harbour City
  Canton Rd, Tsim Sha Tsui
  2622-2699
- 5/F, Telford Plaza 2, 33 Wai Yip St, Kowloon Bay
  2305-9990
- 1/F, New Town Plaza, Phase 1
  Sha Tin Centre St, Sha Tin, New Territories
  2699-9811

- 2/F, Tuen Mun Town Plaza, Phase I
  1 Tuen Shun St, Tuen Mun, New Territories
  2430-1909

www.crystaljade.com

A Singapore institution serving up the best xiao long bao and other dumplings, in addition to a huge range of Northern Chinese specialties. Expect to wait for a table during peak hours.

Shanghai Xiao Nan Guo

- 3/F, Man Yee Bldg, 68 Des Voeux Rd Central
  2259-9393
- 12/F, Food Forum, Times Square
  1 Matheson St, Causeway Bay
  2874-8899
- UG/F, Tsim Sha Tsui Centre
  66 Mody Rd, East Tsim Sha Tsui
  2369-8899
- L6, MegaBox, 38 Wang Chui Rd, Kowloon Bay
  2545-0880
- 7/F, New Town Plaza, Phase 1
  Sha Tin Centre St, Sha Tin, New Territories
  2894-8899

www.xnggroup.com

Shanghai Lu Yang Cun Restaurant

11/F, wtc more, 280 Gloucester Rd, Causeway Bay
2881-6669

Shanghai Garden

1/F, Hutchison House, 10 Harcourt Rd, Admiralty
2524-8181

Yè Shanghai

- L3, Pacific Place, 88 Queensway, Admiralty
  2918-9833
- 6/F, The Marco Polo Hongkong Hotel
  3 Canton Rd, Tsim Sha Tsui
  2376-3322

www.elite-concepts.com

Liu Yuan Pavilion

3/F, The Broadway, 54–62 Lockhart Rd, Wan Chai
2804-2000

Bistro Manchu

G/F, 33 Elgin St, SoHo
2536-9218 / 2356-9996

Xia Mian Guan

1/F, Elements Mall, 1 Austin Rd West, Kowloon
2196-8121

Beijing Dumpling Restaurant

G/F, 118 Jaffe Rd, Wan Chai
2527-0289

From the street window, while you are waiting for a table, watch the cooks fill and fold the dumplings as fast as they can boil them.

Dumpling Yuan

- G/F, 69 Wellington St, Central
  2525-9018
- G/F, 10 Morrison St, Sheung Wan
  2541-9737
- 96 Electric Rd, Tin Hau
  2887-9885

Wang Fu

G/F, 98A Wellington St, Central
2121-8006

Home Town Dumpling
G/F, 102 Caine Rd, Mid-Levels
2517-0969

WHERE CAN I FIND THE **BEST CASUAL NOODLE SHOPS**
FOR A REAL HONG KONG EXPERIENCE?

Mak's Noodles .... 🏮 🏷️
- G/F, 77 Wellington St, Central
  2854-3810
- 44 Jardine's Bazaar, Causeway Bay
  2895-5310

Very famous with locals for their wonton noodles.

Tsim Chai Kee Noodle .... 🏮 🏷️
- 153 Queen's Rd Central
  2581-3369
- G/F, 98 Wellington St, Central
  2850-6471

Prawn Noodle Shop .... 🏷️
- 2/F, Grand Millennium Plaza
  181 Queen's Rd Central
  3184-0505
- G/F, Rialto Bldg, 2 Landale St, Wan Chai
  2520-0268

Kau Kee .... 🏮 🏷️
G/F, 21 Gough St, Sheung Wan
2850-5967

This hole-in-the-wall noodle shop offers some of the best beef brisket noodles around. There's no English sign, but it's obvious at lunch time when you see the huge line-up to get in!

Kang Kee Noodles Ltd .... 🏮 🏷️
G/F, 4 Tai Wo St, Wan Chai
2572-8295

Law Fu Kee Noodle Shop .... 🏮 🏷️
- G/F, 140 Des Voeux Rd Central
  2541-3080
- G/F, Kimley Comm. Bldg
  142–146 Queen's Rd Central
  2543-3288
- G/F, 50 Lyndhurst Terrace, Central
  2850-6756

Wing Wah Noodle Shop ....🌙 🏮 🏷️
89 Hennessy Rd, Wan Chai
2527-7476

Ho Hung Kee .... 🏮 🏷️
2 Sharp St East, Causeway Bay
2577-6558

Lee Yuen Congee Noodles ....🌙 🏮 🏷️
539 Lockhart Rd, Causeway Bay
2832-4978

Tasty Congee & Noodle Wonton Shop .... 🏮 🏷️
21 King Kwong St, Happy Valley
2838-3922

Lotus Garden ....🌙 🏮 🏷️
51A Sing Wo Rd, Happy Valley
2891-5569

Sister Wah .... 🏮 🏷️
13A Electric Rd, Tin Hau
2807-0108

EVERYTHING FOOD & ENTERTAINMENT

I'M FEELING LIKE SOME GOOD OLD-FASHIONED
CONGEE. WHERE SHOULD I GO?

King's Palace Congee & Noodle Bar ....
L1, Festival Walk, 80 Tat Chee Ave, Kowloon Tong
2265-7777

King Lee Congee ....
G/F, 146 Wan Chai Rd, Wan Chai
2575-6181

Kin Mei Congee ....
39 Tang Lung St, Causeway Bay
2838-8358

Wai Kee Congee Shop ....
G/F, 82 Stanley St, Central
2551-5564

Sang Kee Congee Shop ....
G/F, 20 Hillier St, Sheung Wan
2541-1099

Lee Yuen Congee Noodles ....
539 Lockhart Rd, Causeway Bay
2832-4978

Tasty Congee & Noodle Wanton Shop ....
21 King Kwong St, Happy Valley
2838-3922

Lotus Garden ....
51A Sing Wo Rd, Happy Valley
2891-5569

IT'S COLD OUTSIDE AND A GOOD DOSE OF HOT POT
IS WHAT THE DOCTOR ORDERED. WHERE SHOULD
I GO?

Megan's Kitchen
5/F, Stanhope House, 165–171 Wan Chai Rd, Wan Chai
2866-8305
www.meganskitchen.com

Dong Lai Shun
B2, The Royal Garden Hotel
69 Mody Rd, East Tsim Sha Tsui
2733-2020
www.theroyalgardenhotel.com.hk

Tao Heung Super 88 ....
• 1/F, Sino Plaza
  255–257 Gloucester Rd, Causeway Bay
  2892-0988
• 2/F, Paradise Mall, 100 Shing Tai Rd, Heng Fa Chuen
  3520-1288
www.taoheung.com.hk
Various locations, see website.

Everfresh Seafood Restaurant ....
1/F, Elizabeth House
250 Gloucester Rd, Causeway Bay
2591-0363

FF Hot Pot ....
G/F, Paul Yee Mansion
340–344 Jaffe Rd, Wan Chai
2838-9392

Fai Seafood Hot Pot Restaurant ....
G/F, 82–84 Fuk Lo Tsun Rd, Kowloon City
2382-2000

Little Sheep .... 🔲
- 2/F, Causeway Bay Plaza 2
  463–483 Lockhart Rd, Causeway Bay
  2893-8318
- 1/F, 26 Kimberley Rd, Tsim Sha Tsui
  2722-7633
- G/F–4/F, 16 Argyle St, Mong Kok
  2396-8816
- 5/F, City Landmark 1
  68 Chung On St, Tsuen Wan, New Territories
  2940-7678
www.littlesheephotpot.com

Him Kee Hot Pot Restaurant .... *)🔲
1/F–2/F, Workingfield Comm. Bldg
408–412 Jaffe Rd, Causeway Bay
2838-6116

THE CHINESE ARE FAMOUS FOR THEIR **HERBAL TEA** AND **MEDICINAL DRINKS**. WHERE IS A GOOD PLACE TO TRY THESE?

Kung Lee Sugar Cane Drink .... 🔲
G/F, 60 Hollywood Rd, Central
2544-3571

Good Spring Co. Ltd .... 🔲
G/F, 8 Cochrane St, Central
2544-3518

Yip Heung Lau .... 🔲
104 Johnston Rd, Wan Chai
8202-7207

IT'S **ABOUT THE FOOD, NOT THE VENUE.** WHERE DO THE SERIOUS FOODIES GO?

Islam Food .... 🔲 🏷
- G/F, 1 Lung Kong Rd, Kowloon City
  2382-2822
- 33–35 Tak Ku Ling Rd, Kowloon City
  2382-1882
www.islamfood.biz.com.hk
Best veal/beef dumplings.

Yat Bun Dim Sum .... *)🔲 🏷
79 Woo Sung St, Yau Ma Tei
2783-0113
Dim sum at all hours of the night!

Aberdeen Seafood Restaurant .... 🔲 🏷
105 Woo Sung St, Yau Ma Tei
2384-3226
The speciality here is rice in clay pots with fresh seafood and meats.

Kau Kee .... 🔲 🏷
G/F, 21 Gough St, Sheung Wan
2850-5967

Sheung Hing Chiu Chow Restaurant .... 🔲 🏷
29 & 37–39 Queen's Rd West, Sheung Wan
2854-4570 / 2543-7794
This good value, no-frills restaurant is known for its tasty food and rich and famous clientele.

Chiu Yuen Chiu Chow Restaurant .... 🔲 🏷
G/F, 37 Spring Garden Lane, Wan Chai
2892-2322

Wing Hop Shing Restaurant .... ⊕ 🏷
G/F, 113–115 Jervois St, Sheung Wan
2850-5723
Open from 6am–4pm.

WHERE DO YOU SUGGEST I GO FOR A GREAT ASIAN LATE NIGHT SNACK?

Wah Nam Restaurant .... *)⊕ 🏷
G/F, 11 Thompson Rd, Wan Chai
2527-2478

Sun Kwong Chiu Chow Restaurant .... *) 🏷
G/F, Wah Fat Mansion
405–419 Lockhart Rd, Causeway Bay
2572-0830
Great, cheap Chiu Chow cuisine in a typical loud, vibrant setting.

Tsui Wah Restaurant .... *) 🏷
• G/F–2/F, 15–19 Wellington St, Central
  2525-6338
• G/F, 20–22 Cannon St, Causeway Bay
  2573-4338
• G/F, 483–499 Jaffe Rd, Causeway Bay
  2892-2633
• G/F, 77–83 Parkes St, Yau Ma Tei
  2384-8388
www.tsuiwahrestaurant.com
Asian comfort fast-food, greasy but very tasty, especially when you are hung over! Open 24 hours in the above locations, for more locations see website.

Keung Kee .... *)⊕ 🏷
Chuang's Enterprises Bldg
382 Lockhart Rd, Wan Chai
2572-5207

WHERE CAN I FIND THE BEST CHAR SIU AND BBQ MEATS?

Yung Kee
32–40 Wellington St, Central
2522-1624
www.yungkee.com.hk

Dynasty
1/F, Renaissance Harbour View Hotel
1 Harbour Rd, Wan Chai
2584-6971 / 2802-8888
www.marriott.com

Golden China Restaurant
G/F, 9 Jubilee St, 99 Queen's Rd Central
2545-1472

Tai Hing Restaurant .... *) 🏷
• 470–484 Jaffe Rd, Causeway Bay
  2577-7038
• 49–57 Lee Garden Rd, Causeway Bay
  2576-8961
www.taihingroast.com

Joy Hing Food Shop .... ⊕ 🏷
265–267 Hennessy Rd, Wan Chai
2519-6639
Renowned BBQ meat shop, specialising in char siu. Note: there is no English name/sign.

WHERE CAN I FIND THE BEST PEKING DUCK?

Lei Garden
See page 57
American Peking
G/F, 20 Lockhart Rd, Wan Chai
2527-7277
Peking Garden
• LG, Pacific Place, 88 Queensway, Admiralty
  2845-8452
• 3/F, Star House, Salisbury Rd, Tsim Sha Tsui
  2735-8211
Quan Ju De
• 4/F, China Resources Bldg, 26 Harbour Rd, Wan Chai
  2884-9088
• South Seas Centre, 75 Mody Rd, East Tsim Sha Tsui
  2845-8452
Spring Deer Restaurant
1/F, 42 Mody Rd, East Tsim Sha Tsui
2366-4012

HOW ABOUT HAI NAN CHICKEN RICE?

Singapore Hainan Chicken Rice
8/F, The Metropolis Mall
6 Metropolis Drive, Hung Hom
3162-8949
Koon Thai Hai Nan Chicken
• G/F, 4 Gilman's Bazaar, Central
  2881-8680
• G/F, 199–201 Johnston Rd, Wan Chai
  2770-0162
Nam Ah Restaurant 1964
G/F, 17–19 Leighton Rd, Causeway Bay
2187-3487

WHAT ABOUT CASUAL ASIAN RESTAURANTS THAT ARE COMFORTABLE, BUT WON'T BREAK THE BANK?

Bistro Manchu
G/F, 33 Elgin St, SoHo
2536-9218 / 2356-9996
Yi Jiang Nan
33–35 Staunton St, SoHo
2136-0886
Delicious food from Beijing, Shanghai, Hangzhou and Suzhou. Famous for its crisp roast deboned mutton, and beggar's chicken. Order in advance.
Pang's Kitchen
25 Yik Yam St, Happy Valley
2838-5462
Kin's Kitchen
9 Tsing Fung St, Tin Hau
2571-0913
Nha Trang Vietnamese Restaurant
• G/F, 88–90 Wellington St, Central
  2581-9992
• 2/F, Wu Chung House
  213 Queen's Rd East, Wan Chai
  2891-1177
www.nhatrang.com.hk

Xi Yan Sweets
G/F, 8 Wing Fung West St, Wan Chai
2833-6299
www.xiyan.com.hk

Café Siam
40–42 Lyndhurst Terrace, Central
2851-4803
www.cafesiam.com.hk

Macau Restaurant ....
G/F, Kornhill Plaza (North), 1 Kornhill Rd, Quarry Bay
2569-6820
Cheap, no-nonsense Macanese food. Portuguese-style egg tarts here are very delicious!

Tonkin Vietnamese Restaurant
G/F, Shun On Mansion, 3 Tai Yue Ave, Tai Koo
2569-7928

WHERE DO YOU SUGGEST I GO IN A **BIG GROUP** FOR THE **PRICE CONSCIOUS**?

Tung Po Kitchen ....
2/F, Municipal Bldg, Java Rd, North Point
2880-9399
Dai pai dong in a wet market that attracts locals, foreigners and recently known for celebrity sightings!

Box-Thai
1/F, Shiu King Court, 4–8 Arbuthnot Rd, Central
9123-6049
www.boxthai-moderneating.com
Reasonably priced modern Thai cuisine with large tables to share, or go with a big group.

The Bay ....
• UG/F, Beach Bldg, Island Rd, Deep Water Bay
  2812-2226
• 7 Mo Tat Wan, Lamma Island
  2328-2138
www.thebayhk.com
Overlooking the beach, these restaurants offer Mediterranean and French cuisine.

Red Pepper
7 Lan Fong Rd, Causeway Bay
2577-3811

Yung Kee
32–40 Wellington St, Central
2522-1624
www.yungkee.com.hk

Gi Kee ....
Wong Nai Chung Cooked Food Market
2 Yuk Sau St, Happy Valley
2574-9937

Chang Kee ....
Wong Nai Chung Cooked Food Market
2 Yuk Sau St, Happy Valley
2882-2994

Tandoor
1/F, Lyndhurst Terrace, 1 Lyndhurst St, Central
2845-2262

Nomads ....
G/F, 55 Kimberley Rd, Tsim Sha Tsui
2722-0733
www.igors.com

American Peking
G/F, 20 Lockhart Rd, Wan Chai
2527-7277
SML
11/F, Times Square
1 Matheson St, Causeway Bay
2577-3444
The Press Room Group's 5th restaurant serves up everything on the extensive menu in sizes small, medium and large, even the wine!

I'VE GOT **GUESTS IN TOWN.** WHERE SHOULD I TAKE THEM FOR AN **AUTHENTIC CHINESE FOOD EXPERIENCE**?

Fook Lam Moon
• 3/F, 35–45 Johnston Rd, Wan Chai
  2866-0663
• 53–59 Kimberley Rd, Tsim Sha Tsui
  2366-0286
www.fooklammoon-grp.com
Forum Restaurant
G/F, 485 Lockhart Rd, Causeway Bay
2891-2555
Seung Kei ....
3/F, Wong Nai Chung Market Complex
2 Yuk Sau St, Happy Valley
Yung Kee
32–40 Wellington St, Central
2522-1624
www.yungkee.com.hk
Known for its roast goose, this Hong Kong legend is great for a big group.
Luk Yu Tea House
24–26 Stanley St, Central
2523-1970
Sheung Hing Chiu Chow Restaurant ....
29 & 37–39 Queen's Rd West, Sheung Wan
2854-4570 / 2543-7794
Tak Kee Chiu Chow Restaurant ....
G/F, 533–537 Queen's Rd West, Sheung Wan
2819-5568

I AM ENTERTAINING **FRIENDS/CLIENTS.** WHERE CAN I TAKE THEM FOR AN **UPSCALE CHINESE MEAL WITH GREAT ATMOSPHERE**?

Island Tang
2/F, The Galleria, 9 Queen's Rd Central
2526-8798
www.islandtang.com
Lung King Heen
4/F, Four Seasons Hotel Hong Kong
8 Finance St, Central
3196-8880
Shang Palace
Lower Level 1, Kowloon Shangri-La
64 Mody Rd, East Tsim Sha Tsui
2733-8754
www.shangri-la.com

Summer Palace
5/F, Island Shangri-La Hotel, Pacific Place
Supreme Court Rd, Admiralty
2820-8552
www.shangri-la.com

T'ang Court
1/F, Langham Hotel, 8 Peking Rd, Tsim Sha Tsui
2375-1133 ext 2250
hongkong.langhamhotels.com

Golden Leaf
Lower Lobby, Conrad Hotel Hong Kong, Pacific Place
88 Queensway, Admiralty
www.conrad.com.hk
2822-8870

Ming Court
6/F, Langham Place Hotel, 555 Shanghai St, Mong Kok
3552-3300
hongkong.langhamplacehotels.com

Spring Moon
1/F, The Peninsula Hotel, Salisbury Rd, Tsim Sha Tsui
2315-3160
www.hongkong.peninsula.com

One Harbour Road
7/F–8/F, Grand Hyatt Hotel, 1 Harbour Rd, Wan Chai
2584-7722
www.hongkong.grand.hyatt.com
Hong Kong's most elegant Chinese restaurant.

I WANT TO GET AWAY FROM THE HUSTLE AND
BUSTLE. WHERE CAN I GO FOR **ASIAN FOOD OFF THE
BEATEN TRACK**?

SAI KUNG

Sai Kung Fishing Village ....
96–102 Man Nin St, Sai Kung, New Territories
2792-7453
*Seafood dominates this Cantonese style restaurant.
Specialities include pan-fried crab with garlic and spring
onion.*

Sampan Seafood Market ....
G/F, 138 Pak Sha Wan Centre, Pak Sha Wan Tsuen
Sai Kung, New Territories
2719-8886

Chuen Kee Seafood ....
• G/F, 87 Man Nin St, Sai Kung, New Territories
  2792-6938
• G/F, 53 Hoi Pong Rd, Sai Kung, New Territories
  2792-6183

Tin Tin Good Seafood Restaurant ....
G/F, 41 See Cheung St, Sai Kung, New Territories
2792-2819

Tung Kee Seafood Restaurant ....
G/F, Siu Yat House, Hoi Pong Square
Sai Kung, New Territories
2791-9886
Authentic Cantonese food on the beautiful promenade.

Dia Indian Restaurant
G/F, Saikung Bldg
42–56 Fuk Man Rd, Sai Kung, New Territories
2791-4466

LAMMA ISLAND, PO TOI ISLAND AND LEI YUE MUN

These are the places where you can find many seafood restaurants, similar to those in Sai Kung. Choose your own seafood and ask them to cook it for you!

Rainbow Seafood Restaurant
16–20 & 23–24 First St
Sok Kwu Wan, Lamma Island
2982-8100
www.rainbowrest.com.hk
They have a complimentary ferry shuttle from Hong Kong to Lamma for customers.

Ming Kee Seafood Restaurant
Po Toi Island
2849-7038
Only accessible by private boat or ferry service with very limited schedule from Stanley. For ferry information, call 2272-2022.

Han Lok Yuen (Pigeon Restaurant)
16–17 Hung Shing Yeh
Yung Shue Wan, Lamma Island
2982-0680
An institution in many people's eyes. Well worth the 15-minute walk from the Lamma pier.

OTHER AREAS

Shek O Chinese-Thai Seafood Restaurant
303 Shek O Village, Shek O
2809-4426

Saigon
2/F, Stanley Beach Villa
90 Stanley Main St, Stanley
2899-0999
www.chiram.com.hk

Chung Shing Thai Restaurant
G/F, 69 Tai Mei Tuk Village
Ting Kok Rd, Tai Po, New Territories
2664-5218
Tai Po's best Thai eats.

Po Lin Monastery
Ngong Ping, Lantau Island
2985-5248

Hoi Tin Garden Restaurant
5 Sam Sing St, Castle Peak Bay
Tuen Mun, New Territories
2450-6331
www.yp.com.hk/hoitingarden

Red Penny
G/F, 148 Kam Sheung Rd
Yuen Long, New Territories
2488-3263
Restaurant with a huge outdoor deck serving Thai-Vietnamese cuisine.

See also EVERYTHING STANLEY, pages 187–189.

EVERYTHING FOOD & ENTERTAINMENT

I NEED TO SPICE IT UP A BIT. WHERE ARE SOME
GOOD RESTAURANTS OFFERING **SPICY FOODS**?

CHINESE

Red Pepper
7 Lan Fong Rd, Causeway Bay
2577-3811
*Popular among tourists, but the food is undeniably
good. Fun, kitschy ambience.*
Chilli Fagara
G/F, 51A Graham St, SoHo
2893-3330
www.chillifagara.com
Shui Hu Ju
G/F, 68 Peel St, Central
2869-6927
Szechuan Lau
466 Lockhart Rd, Causeway Bay
2891-9027

THAI

Chili Club
1/F, 88 Lockhart Rd, Wan Chai
2527-2872
Café Siam
40–42 Lyndhurst Terrace, Central
2851-4803
www.cafesiam.com.hk
Chilli n Spice
- G/F, Miami Mansion
  13–15 Cleveland St, Causeway Bay
  2504-3930
- 1/F, The Westwood, 8 Belcher's St, Kennedy Town
  2542-7777
- L1, New Town Plaza, Phase 1
  Sha Tin Centre St, Sha Tin, New Territories
  2473-0168
- 1/F, Metro City, Phase 2
  Tseung Kwan O, New Territories
  3194-3823
- DD124 Lot 2289 Hung Shui Kui
  Tuen Mun, New Territories
  2473-0893
- G/F, Marina Magic Shopping Mall
  Gold Coast, Tuen Mun, New Territories
  3194-3823
Thai Pepper
G/F, Yen Kung Mansion, 1 Tai Mou Ave, Tai Koo
2886-4133
Thai Basil
LG, Pacific Place, 88 Queensway, Admiralty
2537-4682
www.maxconcepts.com.hk
Shek O Chinese-Thai Seafood Restaurant ....
303 Shek O Village, Shek O
2809-4426
Great for families.

Golden Orchid Thai Restaurant ....
12 Lung Kong Rd, Kowloon City
2383-3076

Sweet Basil Thai Cuisine
- 6/F, 99 Percival St, Causeway Bay
  2890-1993
- 3/F, Hang Lung Centre
  2–20 Paterson St, Causeway Bay
  2972-2272
- G/F, Site 4, Whampoa Garden, Hung Hom
  2356-1182

KOREAN

Kaya
6/F, 8 Russell St, Causeway Bay
2838-9550
www.yp.com.hk/kaya
Casual Korean food, great for lunch.

Myung Ga
13/F, wtc more, 280 Gloucester Rd, Causeway Bay
2882-5056
Higher-end Korean food. Known for their meat and barbecue dishes.

Secret Garden
G/F, Bank of America Tower, 12 Harcourt Rd, Central
2801-7990
Convenient location; good for a business lunch or dinner.

Sorabol
- 17/F, Lee Theatre Plaza, 99 Percival St, Causeway Bay
  2881-6823
- 4/F, Miramar Shopping Centre
  1 Kimberley Rd, Tsim Sha Tsui
  2375-2882
www.sorabol.com.hk
High-end Korean food. Koreans go for the jang ban kuk soo (noodle with vegetable) served at the end of the meal.

Arirang
- 11/F, Food Forum, Times Square
  1 Matheson St, Causeway Bay
  2506-3298
- G/F, Ocean Terminal, Harbour City
  Canton Rd, Tsim Sha Tsui
  2956-3288
www.arirang.com.hk

Pung Won .... *)
22–24 Prat Ave, Tsim Sha Tsui
2721-8730

INDIAN/PAKISTANI/NEPALESE

Bombay Dreams
1/F, Carfield Comm. Bldg
75–77 Wyndham St, Central
2971-0001
www.diningconcepts.com.hk

Jo Jo Indian Restaurant
2/F, David House, 37–39 Lockhart Rd, Wan Chai
2522-6209
www.jojofood.com
Ideal for a quick meal; casual and dependable.

Jo Jo Mess
U/F, 21 Man Nin St, Sai Kung, New Territories
2574-7477
www.jojofood.com

Tandoor
1/F, Lyndhurst Terrace, 1 Lyndhurst St, Central
2845-2262
Great food, great prices, private rooms available.

Duetto Italian & Indian Dining
2/F, Sun Hung Kai Centre, 30 Harbour Rd, Wan Chai
2598-1222 / 2827-7777
www.chiram.com.hk
Formerly The Viceroy, an institution, the food is always delicious.

Gaylord
1/F, Ashley Centre, 23–25 Ashley Rd, Tsim Sha Tsui
2376-1001

Jashan
1/F, Amber Lodge, 23 Hollywood Rd, Central
3105-5300 / 3105-5311
www.jashan.com.hk

Nepal Restaurant
G/F, 14 Staunton St, SoHo
2869-6212
www.nepalrestaurant.com.hk

INDONESIAN

Indonesian Restaurant 1968
G/F, 28 Leighton Rd, Causeway Bay
2577-9981
www.indonesianrestaurant1968.com

Warung Malang
2/F, Dragon Rise Bldg, 9–11 Pennington St, Causeway Bay
2915-7859
Authentic, casual Indonesian restaurant that also provides catering services.

Victor Sirait Indonesian Restaurant ....
19 Irving St, Causeway Bay
2576-5444
Offers great vegetarian options.

CRAB

Hee Kee Chilli Crab
392 Jaffe Rd, Wan Chai
2893-7565

Causeway Bay Spicy Crab
G/F, 440 Jaffe Rd, Causeway Bay
2572-6988

Under Bridge Spicy Crab ....
401–402 Lockhart Rd, Wan Chai
2834-6818

I'M LOOKING FOR SOMETHING MORE TRADITIONAL.
WHERE WOULD JAPANESE PEOPLE GO?

Agehan
2/F, Two Exchange Square, 8 Connaught Place, Central
2523-4332
Specialises in tempura. Good for lunch or dinner.

Inagiku
1/F, The Royal Garden, 69 Mody Rd, East Tsim Sha Tsui
2733-2933
www.rghk.com.hk

Kissho
1A Wong Nai Chung Rd, Happy Valley
2836-6992
An authentic restaurant where you will find Japanese and foreigners alike.

Sushi U
3/F, Century Square, 1–13 D'Aguilar St, Central
2537-9393
Extremely fresh fish and unique combinations.

WHAT ABOUT GOOD VALUE JAPANESE FOOD?

Azabusabo ....
- 1/F, Fashion Walk
  19 Great George St, Causeway Bay
  2882-1582
- 1/F, Hong Kong Pacific Centre
  28 Hankow Rd, Tsim Sha Tsui
  2736-5006
- G/F, Miramar Shopping Centre
  132 Nathan Rd, Tsim Sha Tsui
  2377-3780
www.azabusabo.com.hk
Good set lunch menu and Japanese desserts.

Sen-Ryo ....
- L3, IFC Mall, 8 Finance St, Central
  2234-7633
- 1/F, Cityplaza, Phase 1, 18 Taikoo Shing Rd, Tai Koo
  2967-5537
- 1/F, Elements Mall, 1 Austin Rd West, Kowloon
  2196-8209

Ha-Ne Sushi ....
G/F, 500 Jaffe Rd, Causeway Bay
3101-2821
www.hane-sushi.com
For more locations, see the website.

Yu Yu Sushi ....
3 Ship St, Wan Chai
2866-3322
Great value for some of the freshest fish in town.

Rokkaku ....
G/F, 6 Kwong Ming St, Wan Chai
2866-8166

Kiyotaki ....
G/F, 13 Gough St, Sheung Wan
2877-1772
Large variety of fresh fish and cooked items in this hidden little gem.

misocool ....
- 1/F, 11 Stanley St, Central
  2868-3738
- LG/F, Westlands Gardens
  2–10 Westlands Rd, Quarry Bay
  2565-1001
www.emperor.com.hk

Irori .... 🏷

- 4/F, Circle Plaza
  497 –499 Hennessy Rd, Wan Chai
  2838-5939
- 2/F, Bartlock Centre, 3 Yiu Wa St, Causeway Bay
  2838-5939

*This difficult-to-find restaurant, popular with Japanese
expats, offers a Japanese-only menu, although
waitresses speak all languages. Fresh seafood arrives
nightly from Japan by air.*

Sushi Hiro .... 🏷

- 10/F, Henry House
  42 Yun Ping Rd, Causeway Bay
  2882-8752
- 7/F, The Toy House, 100 Canton Rd, Tsim Sha Tsui
  2377-9877

www.sushihiro.com.hk
Good value set lunch and reasonable for group dinners.

Tonkichi .... 🏷

- P4, wtc more, 280 Gloucester Rd, Causeway Bay
  2577-6617
- G/F, 100 Canton Rd, Tsim Sha Tsui
  2314-2998

www.pokkacafe.com
*Casual family-style restaurants known for their tonkatsu
(pork cutlet).*

June Japanese Restaurant .... 🏷

G/F, 56 Electric Rd, Tin Hau
2234-6691

Sumibi .... 🏷

G/F, 5 Whitfield Rd, North Point
2510-8766
Specialises in Japanese beef.

Seigetsu Yakitori Restaurant .... 🏷

G/F, 9 & 11 St. Francis St, Wan Chai
2866-8802

Ha-Ne Sushi .... 🏷

G/F, 500 Jaffe Rd, Causeway Bay
3101-2821
www.hane-sushi.com
See website for more locations.

Itamae Sushi .... 🏷

- G/F, 24–26 East Point Rd, Causeway Bay
  2110-8504
- G/F, 14 Granville Rd, Tsim Sha Tsui
  3106-2846
- L1, Festival Walk, 80 Tat Chee Ave, Kowloon Tong
  2265-7722

itamae.com.hk
More locations throughout Hong Kong.

WHERE CAN I GO FOR A TASTE OF **VIETNAMESE FARE**?

Indochine 1929
2/F, California Tower, 30 –32 D'Aguilar St, Central
2869-7399

Song .... 🏷

LG/F, 75 Hollywood Rd, Central
2559-0997
A tiny chic restaurant with an innovative menu.

Café Annam
35 Elgin St, SoHo
2545-9966

Nha Trang Vietnamese Restaurant ....
See page 64
Good value. Excellent pho beef noodles.

Green Cottage ....
• 2/F, Cigna Tower, 482 Jaffe Rd, Causeway Bay
  2832-2863
• 6/F, Terminal 2, Hong Kong International Airport
  3197-9440
*You must try the beef pho, cold pork noodles, shrimp and
pork fresh rolls, as well as the best deep-fried chicken
wings in town.*

Lo Chiu ....
• G/F, 10 – 12 Hillwood Rd, Tsim Sha Tsui
  2314-7966
• 25 – 27 Man Yuen St, Jordan
  2384-2143
• 22 – 24 Parkes St, Jordan
  2314-7983

Café Locomotive
11 Wun Sha St, Tai Hang, Tin Hau
2882-8227
www.cafelocomotive.com

Sun Chuk Yuen Vietnamese Restaurant ....
• G/F & 1/F, Yat Chau Bldg
  262 Des Voeux Rd Central
  2815-8811
• 2 Landale St, Wan Chai
  2866-8871

Pho 26 ....
• G/F, 302 Queen's Rd Central, Sheung Wan
  2866-1888
• 2 Landale St, Wan Chai
  2628-3939
• 186 Electric Rd, North Point
  2806-8661
• G/F, Amoy Gardens, Phase 2, Kowloon Bay
  2333-8909
Kobe beef pho in a fragrant soup base.

Saigon ....
2/F, Stanley Beach Villa, 90 Stanley Main St, Stanley
2899-0999

WHERE DO I FIND THE BEST EGG TARTS AND
CHINESE DESSERTS IN TOWN?

Tai Cheong Bakery
G/F, 35 Lyndhurst Terrace, Central
2117-9825
*Recently re-opened at this new location, the queues are
usually long but move quickly at Chris Patten's favourite
egg tart place. Get them fresh out of the oven and buy at
least a box.*

Fresco Café
G/F, 99F Wellington St, Central
2581-1718

Yee Shun Milk Co. .... *) ⟨φ⟩
- G/F, Wah Hen Comm. Centre
  381 –383 Hennessy Rd, Wan Chai
  2576-1828
- G/F, 506 Lockhart Rd, Causeway Bay
  2591-1837
- G/F, 63 Pilkem St, Jordan
  2730-2799
- G/F, 513 Nathan Rd, Yau Ma Tei
  2332-2726
- G/F, 246 –248 Sai Yeung Choi St South, Mong Kok
  2393-3301

Honeymoon Dessert
L3, IFC Mall, 8 Finance St, Central
2868-9799
www.honeymoon-dessert.com
Many locations all over Hong Kong. See website for details.

Xi Yan Sweets
G/F, 8 Wing Fung West St, Wan Chai
2833-6299
www.xiyan.com.hk

Xi Yan Flavours
1/F, Elements Mall, 1 Austin Rd West, Kowloon
2628-3909
www.xiyan.com.hk

Yuen Kee Sweeten Food Experts Ltd .... ⟨φ⟩
32 Main St, Sai Ying Pun, Sai Wan
2548-8687

Man Shun Cheong .... ⟨φ⟩
MSC Bldg, 199 Wing Lok St West, Sheung Wan
2545-1190
www.msc-hk.com
Dried food, nuts, beans and snacks.

Tang Hoi Moon Kee .... ⟨φ⟩
G/F, 175 Wing Lok St, Sheung Wan
2544-6464
www.tang1968.com
Preserved plums and other kinds of dried fruit.

Kung Lee Sugar Cane Drink .... ⟨φ⟩
G/F, 60 Hollywood Rd, Central
2544-3571

North Point Hong Kong Style Waffle .... ⟨φ⟩
G/F, 492 King's Rd, North Point
2590-9726

Ching Ching Dessert .... ⟨φ⟩
G/F, 77 Electric Rd, Tin Hau
2578-6162

Hui Lau Shan .... *) ⟨φ⟩
- 2–6 Yee Wo St, Causeway Bay
  2972-2292
- G/F, Po Hon Bldg
  24 Percival St, Causeway Bay
  2574-6866
- G/F, Star House, 3 Salisbury Rd, Tsim Sha Tsui
  2377-9766
www.hkhls.com
More locations throughout Hong Kong.

HOW ABOUT ICE CREAM AND GELATO?

XTC on Ice
- 4/F, Food Court, The Landmark
  15 Queen's Rd Central
  2111-5634
- 45 Cochrane St, Central
  2541-0500
- 1/F, Vicwood Plaza
  199 Des Voeux Rd, Sheung Wan
  2544-8887
- G/F, Race View Apartments
  37 Wong Nai Chung Rd, Happy Valley
  2504-4282
- 1/F, Cityplaza, 18 Taikoo Shing Rd, Tai Koo
  3102-1908
- G/F, Star Ferry Pier, Tsim Sha Tsui
  2368-3602
- UG, Festival Walk, 80 Tat Chee Ave, Kowloon Tong
  2265-7300
www.xtc.com.hk
100% natural with over 40 flavours.

Gino's Gelato
- G/F, The Peak Tower, 128 Peak Rd, The Peak
  2849-8314
- G/F, Stanley Plaza, Cape Rd, Stanley
  2899-0314

I-Scream Gelato
- L1, IFC Mall, 8 Finance St, Central
  2234-7281
- Great Food Hall, LG, Pacific Place
  88 Queensway, Admiralty
  2918-0362
- 1/F, New Town Plaza, Phase 1
  Sha Tin Centre St, Sha Tin, New Territories
  2681-2902
www.iscream.biz

Ben & Jerry's
- G/F, Tak Woo House
  17–19 D'Aguilar St, Central
  2521-1622
- 7/F, Times Square, 1 Matheson St, Causeway Bay
  2506-1567
- L1, Festival Walk, 80 Tat Chee Ave, Kowloon Tong
  2265-8869
- G/F, Knutsford Terrace
  1 Kimberley Rd, Tsim Sha Tsui
  3798-0178
- L3, New Town Plaza, Phase 3
  Sha Tin Centre St, Sha Tin, New Territories
- L7, Departures East Hall, Terminal 1
  Hong Kong International Airport
  3171-1982
www.benjerry.com.hk
Very creamy premium ice cream in a multitude of unique flavours with great names.

Häagen Dazs
www.haagen-dazs.com.hk
Many locations in Hong Kong, Kowloon and New Territories. See website for details.

WHERE CAN I FIND A GOOD **FROZEN YOGHURT**?

Yo Mama ....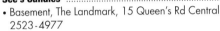
- L1, IFC Mall, 8 Finance St, Central
  2872-7000
- 16 Wing Fung St, Wan Chai
  2865-5600

Berrygood ....
G/F, 41 –43 Graham St, Central
2543-8393
www.berrygoodhk.com

Yogurtime ....
G/F, 46 Elgin St, SoHo
6165-4608
www.yogurtimehk.com

MY **SWEET TOOTH** HAS KICKED IN. WHERE CAN I
SATISFY THE CRAVING?

See's Candies ....
- Basement, The Landmark, 15 Queen's Rd Central
  2523-4977
- 2/F, Elements Mall, 1 Austin Rd West, Kowloon
  2376-0868
- G, Festival Walk, 80 Tat Chee Ave, Kowloon Tong
  2265-8199
www.sees.com

Chocolux ....
G/F, 57 Peel St, SoHo
2858-8760
www.chocoluxcafe.com
A chocoholic's dream café come true!

Antique Patisserie & Fine Chocolates
See page 33

agnès b. Délices
- L3, IFC Mall, 8 Finance St, Central
  2805-0678
- G/F, Fashion Walk, 27–47 Paterson St, Causeway Bay
  2577-0338
- 3/F, Times Square, 1 Matheson St, Causeway Bay
  2506-3323
- G/F, Gateway Arcade, Harbour City
  Canton Rd, Tsim Sha Tsui
  2956-0018
- Basement, The Sun Arcade
  28 Canton Rd, Tsim Sha Tsui
  2730-6628
- Concourse, APM, 418 Kwun Tong Rd, Kwun Tong
  3148-1318
www.agnesb-delices.com
Designer chocolates.

Epöch
- 12 – 14 Wing Fung St, Wan Chai
  3525-1570
- G/F, Taikoo Place, 12 Westlands Rd, Tai Koo
  2811-2140
www.epochdesserts.com

COCO
Lobby, The Mira Hotel, 118 Nathan Rd, Tsim Sha Tsui
2315-5566
www.themirahotel.com

Leonidas Chocolates
- L1, IFC Mall, 8 Finance St, Central
  2234-7343
- B2, SOGO, 555 Hennessy Rd, Causeway Bay
  2836-3695
- 3/F, Ocean Centre, Harbour City
  Canton Rd, Tsim Sha Tsui
  2317-7448
- L1, MegaBox, 38 Wang Chiu Rd, Kowloon Bay
  2506-1068
www.leonidas.com.hk

Vero
1/F, 1 Lung King St, Fenwick Pier, Wan Chai
2559-5882
www.verochocolates.com

WHERE CAN I BUY THE FINEST **EUROPEAN CHOCOLATES**?

La Maison du Chocolat
- L2, Pacific Place, 88 Queensway, Admiralty
  2522-2010
- 2/F, Elements Mall, 1 Austin Rd West, Kowloon
  2196-8333
www.lamaisonduchocolat.com/en
The best French chocolate ever with a price tag to match.

Teuscher Chocolates of Switzerland
L1, IFC Mall, 8 Finance St, Central
2462-6432
www.teuscher.com
Using absolutely no chemicals, additives or preservatives, these confections are made weekly and immediately flown in from Zurich, Switzerland.

Godiva Chocolates
L1, IFC Mall, 8 Finance St, Central
2805-0518
www.godiva.hk

COVA Pasticceria & Confetteria
- 1/F, Prince's Bldg, 10 Chater Rd, Central
  2869-8777
- 2/F, Alexandra House, 18 Chater Rd, Central
  2526-6033
- L3, Pacific Place, 88 Queensway, Admiralty
  2918-9643
- G/F, Lee Gardens, 33 Hysan Ave, Causeway Bay
  2907-3060
- G/F, wtc more, 280 Gloucester Rd, Causeway Bay
  2895-2368
- 1/F, Devon House, Taikoo Place
  979 King's Rd, Quarry Bay
  2811-9877
- G/F, Gateway Arcade, Harbour City
  Canton Rd, Tsim Sha Tsui
  2907-3881
- LG1, Festival Walk, 80 Tat Chee Ave, Kowloon Tong
  2265-8678
- L1, New Town Plaza, Phase 1
  Sha Tin Centre St, Sha Tin, New Territories
  2601-2106
www.cova.com.hk
Fine Italian chocolates from this popular café.

EVERYTHING FOOD & ENTERTAINMENT

Leonidas Chocolates
See page 78
Hand-made chocolates that are flown in weekly from Belgium.

WHICH **HOTELS** CARRY THE BEST **CHOCOLATES**?

The Boutique
Lobby Level, Four Seasons Hotel Hong Kong
8 Finance St, Central
3196-8690
www.fourseasons.com/hongkong
Dean & Deluca chocolates from New York.

The Peninsula Chocolatier
Basement, The Peninsula Hotel
Salisbury Rd, Tsim Sha Tsui
2315-3262
www.hongkong.peninsula.com

Chocolatier
G/F, Grand Hyatt Hotel
1 Harbour Rd, Wan Chai
2588-1234 ext 7298
www.hongkong.grand.hyatt.com

The Cake Shop
Mezzanine, Mandarin Oriental Hotel
5 Connaught Rd Central
2522-4008
www.mandarinoriental.com/hongkong
Try their line of chocolates, "Chocolate Therapy", created by their executive chefs in 40 unique flavours.

Island Gourmet
5/F, Island Shangri-La Hotel, Pacific Place
Supreme Court Rd, Admiralty
2820-8550
www.shangri-la.com

HOW ABOUT **OTHER TYPES OF FINE CHOCOLATES**?

Chocolux .... *)
G/F, 57 Peel St, SoHo
2858-8760
www.chocoluxcafe.com

Antique Patisserie & Fine Chocolates
See page 33
Fine chocolates and cakes that are beautifully presented in this new, upscale patisserie.

Monde
10/F, Horizon Plaza
2 Lee Wing St, Ap Lei Chau
2870-2988

agnès b. Délices
See page 77

See's Candies ....
See page 77

Royce Chocolates
Available at all city'super stores (see page 81).
Originating from Hokkaido, Japan, Royce has a loyal following like no other, and is reasonably priced in comparison. Try the Nama Chocolate that comes wrapped in a bag with an ice pack—simply divine.

Lucullus ....
- MTR Central Station, Central
  2530-9557
- G/F, 29 Wellington St, Central
  2810-4010
- MTR Admiralty Station, Admiralty
  2866-6393
- B2, SOGO, 555 Hennessy Rd, Causeway Bay
  2574-1318
- B2, Langham Place, 8 Argyle St, Mong Kok
  3514-4222
- MTR Kowloon Tong Station, Kowloon Tong
  2338-2775
- 1/F, New Town Plaza, Phase 1
  Sha Tin Centre St, Sha Tin, New Territories
  2367-1230

www.lucullus.com.hk

WHERE CAN I FIND THE BEST **HOT CHOCOLATE**?

Vero ....
1/F, 1 Lung King St, Fenwick Pier, Wan Chai
2559-5882
www.verochocolates.com

Caffè Vergnano 1882
- L2, IFC Mall, 8 Finance St, Central
  2234-7676
- 1/F, Lee Gardens Two, 28 Yun Ping Rd, Causeway Bay
  2907-3817
- 1/F, Elements Mall, 1 Austin Rd West, Kowloon
  2196-8340

www.caffevergnano.hk

Chocolux ....
G/F, 57 Peel St, SoHo
2858-8760
www.chocoluxcafe.com

HOW ABOUT ALTERNATIVE **COFFEE SHOPS**?

Caffè HABITU ....
See page 32

Uncle Russ Coffee
- 1/F, Central Pier 3, Central
  2501-0398
- 1 & 2 Lower Deck, Central Pier 6, Central
  2869-8339
- G/F, Citicorp Centre, 18 Whitfield Rd, North Point
  9356-1038
- G/F, Star Ferry Pier, Tsim Sha Tsui
  2110-9918
- G/F, Olympian City 2, 18 Hoi Ting Rd, Olympic
  2273-4013
- G/F, Discovery Bay Plaza
  Discovery Bay, Lantau Island
  2987-0068

www.unclerusscoffee.com

Caffè Vergnano 1882
See above

COVA Caffè-Ristorante
See page 33

Segafredo Zanetti Espresso Bar
U/G, The Loop, 33 Wellington St, Central
2523-2821
www.dolci.hk

Pascucci
- G/F, Block 2 & 3, The Zenith
  3 Wan Chai Rd, Wan Chai
  2976-4030
- L12, Langham Place, 8 Argyle St, Mong Kok
  3514-4171
www.pascucci.com.hk

Café Graham
51D Graham St, Central
2905-1768

Epöch
See page 77
Cool little coffee shop/café with amazing desserts.

Fuel Espresso
L3, IFC Mall, 8 Finance St, Central
www.fuelespresso.com

WHERE CAN I GO FOR A **CHEESE FIX**?

Classified The Cheese Room .... *)
G/F, 108 Hollywood Rd, Central
2525-3454
www.classifiedfoodshops.com.hk

Classified Mozzarella Bar .... *)
31 Wing Fung St, Wan Chai
2528-3454
www.classifiedfoodshops.com.hk

WHICH **GROCERY STORES** CARRY THE MOST
COMPREHENSIVE SELECTION OF **WESTERN FOODS**?

ThreeSixty ....
See page 35
*Look for Manager's Special items that change regularly
for discounted items throughout the store.*

Great Food Hall ....
LG, Pacific Place, 88 Queensway, Admiralty
2918-9986
www.greatfoodhall.com

Oliver's ....
2/F, Prince's Bldg, 10 Chater Rd, Central
2810-7710

city'super ....
- L1, IFC Mall, 8 Finance St, Central
  2234-7128
- B1, Times Square, 1 Matheson St, Causeway Bay
  2506-2888
- 3/F, Gateway Arcade, Harbour City
  Canton Rd, Tsim Sha Tsui
  2375-8222
- L2, New Town Plaza, Phase 1
  Sha Tin Centre St, Sha Tin, New Territories
  2603-3488
www.citysuper.com.hk

Park n Shop
www.parknshop.com
Check website for list of stores throughout Hong Kong.

TASK

- Basement & G/F, Hopewell Centre
  183 Queen's Rd East, Wan Chai
  2121-8346
- 2/F, Stanley Plaza, Ma Hang, Stanley
  2813-8520
- MTR Level, Festival Walk
  80 Tat Chee Ave, Kowloon Tong
  2265-8698
- G/F, Olympian City 2, 18 Hoi Ting Rd, Olympic
  2740-4159
- L4, Metroplaza
  223 Hing Fong Rd, Kwai Chung, New Territories
  2426-2604
- L2, East Point City
  8 Chung Wa Rd, Tseung Kwan O, New Territories
  3541-9573
- 3/F, Maritime Square
  33 Tsing King Rd, Tsing Yi, New Territories
  2434-5049
- 2/F, Tuen Mun Plaza, Phase 2
  3 Tuen Long St, Tuen Mun, New Territories
  2449-2404
- Basement, Citygate Outlets
  20 Tat Chung Rd, Tung Chung, Lantau Island
  2109-4500

www.aswatson.com

Park n Shop Superstores and TASTE stores offer a larger range of international grocery items, fresh and cooked food including live fish, fruit and vegetables and an in-store bakery.

Wellcome

www.wellcome.com.hk

Located throughout Hong Kong. One of the largest and most comprehensive stores catering to an international community.

Market Place by Jasons

- LG/F, Nexxus Bldg, 77 Des Voeux Rd Central
  3104-0652
- G/F, Hang Fung Bldg
  17–19 Wong Nai Chung Rd, Happy Valley
  2117-0525
- 1/F, 5 Perkins Rd, Jardine's Lookout
  2577-0185
- 100 Peak Rd, The Peak
  2849-7307
- 1/F, 33 Cloud View Rd, North Point
  2571-3656
- G/F, Repulse Bay Arcade
  109 Repulse Bay Rd, Repulse Bay
  2812-0340
- Surson Comm. Bldg
  140–142 Austin Rd, Tsim Sha Tsui
  3580-1325
- B2, Langham Place, 8 Argyle St, Mong Kok
  3580-8952
- Podium, Telford Plaza, 33 Wai Yip St, Kowloon Bay
  2117-4146
- G/F, Lot 1177, Razor Hill
  Clear Water Bay, Sai Kung, New Territories
  2358-0542

• G/F, Gold Coast Piazza, Gold Coast
  Tuen Mun, New Territories
  2430-7022
www.marketplacebyjasons.com

Jewish Community Centre Koshermart
70 Robinson Rd, Mid-Levels
2801-5440
www.jcc.org.hk
*Jewish Community Centre grocery store offers top quality
kosher products, meats and produce. Non-members
need to leave a $50 deposit upon entry.*

WHICH **GROCERY/FOOD STORES** HAVE GOOD AND
RELIABLE **ONLINE SHOPPING WEBSITES**?

Park n Shop
www.parknshop.com

Wellcome
www.wellcome.com.hk
*Park n Shop and Wellcome both offer extensive online
grocery shopping and home delivery for most items in
the stores, except for limited refrigerated food items.*

South Stream Seafoods Ltd
3/F, Mansfield Ind. Centre
19 Hong Yip St, Yuen Long, New Territories
2555-6200
www.south-stream-seafoods.com
*Home delivery (with $400 minimum purchase) of live
shellfish, fresh imported fish from New Zealand and
Australia, chilled meat (including organic), cheese and more.*

Online Limited
21/F, Nan Fung Centre
264–298 Castle Peak Rd
Tsuen Wan, New Territories
3595-0898
www.gourmet.com
*Offering a limited variety of everything from imported
meat to yoghurt and cheeses. Ask and they will try to
source certain things for home delivery.*

WHERE CAN I ORDER **STILL OR SPARKLING WATER**
FOR HOME DELIVERY?

Bonaqua Mineral Water
2210-3311
www.bonaqua.com.hk
Free delivery.

Watson's Water Centre
2660-7373
www.watsons-water.com.hk
Free delivery.

Natural Springs Australia (HK) Ltd
2484-1393 / 2484-1388
www.naturalsprings.hk

Aqua Pure Distilled Water Co. Ltd
2680-2888
www.aquapure.com.hk

Tip Top Water Group
2460-2663
www.tiptopwater.com.hk

I'M LOOKING TO BUY SOME GOOD QUALITY
CHINESE TEA. WHERE CAN I GO?

Lok Cha Tea Shop
- UG/F, 290B Queen's Rd Central, Sheung Wan
2805-1360
- Hong Kong Park, 19 Cotton Tree Drive, Admiralty
2801-7177

www.lockcha.com

Fook Ming Tong Tea Shop
L3, IFC Mall, 8 Finance St, Central
2295-0368
www.fookmingtong.com
Also many other locations around Hong Kong.

Lam Kie Yuen Tea Co. Ltd
105 Bonham Strand East, Sheung Wan
2543-7154

Ngan Ki Heung Teahouse
290 Queen's Rd Central, Sheung Wan
2544-1375

BESIDES THE BIG COFFEE CHAINS AND
GOURMET GROCERY STORES, WHERE CAN I GET
GOOD GROUND COFFEE?

Nespresso Boutique
- L1, IFC Mall, 8 Finance St, Central
2295-3395
- 2/F, Elements Mall, 1 Austin Rd West, Kowloon
2196-8313

www.nespresso.com
*You must have one of their coffee machines (worth the
investment); foolproof, excellent coffee for the home or
office.*

Coffee Assembly
Cockloft, 6 Elgin St, SoHo
2858-8153
www.coffeeassembly.com

WHERE CAN I FIND STORES THAT SELL WESTERN
BULK PROVISIONS?

Gateway Superstore
Basement, Golden Centre
188 Des Voeux Rd Central
2545-0338
*Everything under the sun when it comes to American
products in big-box sizes (dry/non-perishable goods
only). Great for cleaning and laundry supplies, food,
drinks and more.*

Prizemart
- G/F, 17 Li Yuen St West, Central
- G/F, Chun Wo Comm. Centre
23–29 Wing Wo St, Sheung Wan
- G/F, 203 Wan Chai Rd, Wan Chai
- G/F, Catic Plaza, 8 Causeway Rd, Causeway Bay
Hotline: 2406-8879
www.prizemart.hk
Various locations, see also website.

CAN YOU RECOMMEND A GOOD **BUTCHER**?

T.C. Deli Shop
G/F, 12B Hang Hau Village
Tseung Kwan O, New Territories
2358-2332
www.tcdeli.com
One of Hong Kong's best fresh/frozen meats suppliers,
carrying exclusively Australian meats, special cuts,
Angus beef, sausages, cheese, juice, sauces, and more.
They now deliver with two days' advance notice.

South Stream Seafoods Ltd
3/F, Mansfield Ind. Centre
19 Hong Yip St, Yuen Long, New Territories
2555-6200
www.south-stream-seafoods.com

Leo's Fine Food
8/F, Remex Centre, 42 Wong Chuk Hang Rd, Aberdeen
2814-0302
A full range of meat, fish, sausages and other grocery
items that can be pre-ordered and delivered to your home.

Tenderloin Fine Food
26/F, Universal Trade Centre
3–5 Arbuthnot Rd, Central
2877-2733
www.tenderloin.com.hk
Imported meat, poultry (including organic), seafood,
pet food, wine and caviar delivered to your home when
ordered one day in advance. Only home delivery.

Colorado Meats Co. Ltd
2523-9139
Large distribution centre. They carry Canadian,
Australian and New Zealand meat as well as seafood
and grocery items. Delivery only.

Pacific Gourmet Foods
12/F, Horizon Plaza, 2 Lee Wing St, Ap Lei Chau
2137-9985
www.pacificgourmet.com.hk
Imported meat, seafood, organic vegetables, and more
at wholesale prices. Check out their weekly specials and
discount food days.

I'VE SEEN MANY **LOCAL FROZEN MEAT SHOPS**. DO ANY
OF THEM CARRY QUALITY IMPORTED MEATS?

Woo Hing Hong (Frozen Meats) Ltd
G/F, Sung Lan Mansion, 37 Leighton Rd, Causeway Bay
2891-8215
www.yp.com.hk/woohinghong
Not as well-organised or well-packaged, but a good
source for inexpensive frozen, good quality meats,
including Canadian, Australian and New Zealand beef.
No home delivery. Cash only.

Shing Hing Frozen Meat Co. Ltd
• 15 Gage St, Central
  2544-3336
• G/F, Silvervale Mansion, 18 Cross St, Wan Chai
  2572-2159
Good local butcher, they also carry some imported
meats.

Brand One Concept ....
G/F, 1–3 Cheong Ming St, Happy Valley
2891-8966
*They also sell Japanese fruit, umai sake, gourmet cheese
and ham and delicate seafood.*

Yat Sing Food Company ....
G/F, Kam Shing Bldg
14–24 Stone Nullah Lane, Wan Chai
2838-0430
*Great source for reasonably priced imported meat,
poultry and seafood with free delivery over $500.*

WHERE CAN I ORDER A LARGE SELECTION
OF **IMPORTED SEAFOOD** TO BE DELIVERED TO MY
HOME?

South Stream Seafoods Ltd
3/F, Mansfield Ind. Centre
19 Hong Yip St, Yuen Long, New Territories
2555-6200
www.south-stream-seafoods.com

Tenderloin Fine Food
26/F, Universal Trade Centre
3–5 Arbuthnot Rd, Central
2877-2733
www.tenderloin.com.hk

Yat Sing Food Company
G/F, Kam Shing Bldg
14–24 Stone Nullah Lane, Wan Chai
2838-0430

ARE THERE ANY REPUTABLE **LOCAL SEAFOOD SHOPS**?

Fai Kee Seafood Ltd ....
59 Wan Chai Rd, Wan Chai
2575-5197
*For live fish and shellfish, this is the preferred choice of
well-heeled locals for the freshest seafood.*

ARE THERE ANY AUTHENTIC **ITALIAN DELICATESSENS**
IN HONG KONG?

il Bel Paese
• G/F, 85 Caine Rd, Mid-Levels
  2549-8893
• G/F, 25 Queen's Rd East, Wan Chai
  2804-2992
• 23 Sing Woo Rd, Happy Valley
  2868-2818
• 1/F, Peak Galleria, 118 Peak Rd, The Peak
  2849-2834
• Wilton Place, 68 Bonham Rd, Pok Fu Lam
  2858-2162
www.ilbelpaese.com.hk
They offer a good catering service as well.

Viva Italia
G/F, East Comm. Block
Paradise Mall, 100 Shing Tai Rd, Heng Fa Chuen
2849-2030
www.vita-italia.com.hk

Appetito
61 Yi Chun St, Sai Kung, New Territories
2791-5666
Castello del Vino
• 12/F, Century Square, 1–13 D'Aguilar St, Central
  2866-0577
• G/F, 12 Anton St, Wan Chai
  2866-0587
Specialising in Italian wines, this store also sells Italian cured meats, cheeses and dry goods.
Olala Charcuterie
G/F, 2 Star St, Wan Chai
2520-0931 / 9183-9351
Saporito Delicatessen
G/F, Sports Mansion
161 Wong Nai Chung Rd, Happy Valley
2895-4133 / 2895-1533

HOW ABOUT OTHER **GOURMET/SPECIALITY FOOD STORES**?

Monsieur Chatte
G/F, 121 Bonham Strand, Sheung Wan
3105-8077
www.mrchatte.com.hk
Fantastic French gourmet shop. The homemade foie gras terrine is a must-try!
Fenton's Gourmet
G/F, 151–153A Wong Nai Chung Rd, Happy Valley
3422-3411
www.fentonsgourmet.com
Pacific Gourmet Foods
12/F, Horizon Plaza, 2 Lee Wing St, Ap Lei Chau
2137-9985
www.pacificgourmet.com.hk
New Zealand Focus
G/F, Island Bldg
439–445 Hennessy Rd, Causeway Bay
2151-0652
www.nzfocus.com.hk
Gourmet
Basement, Lee Gardens, 33 Hysan Rd, Causeway Bay
3693-4101
www.aswatson.com
Euro Treat
G/F, 17B Old Bailey St, Central
2537-0207
www.eurotreat.com.hk
VOle'
G/F, Causeway Centre, 28 Harbour Rd, Wan Chai
2511-8473
www.vole.com.hk
Benson's
G/F, Yee Fat Mansion, 2 Min Fat St, Happy Valley
2893-1500
www.benson.com.hk
Percy's
G/F, 68 Catchick St, Kennedy Town
2855-1882
www.percys.hk
Delicious take-away menu and speciality food and wine.

Goodwell Gourmet Shop ....
- G/F, Siu On Mansion, 185 Hennessy Rd, Wan Chai
  3107-9150
- G/F, 122B Argyle St, Mong Kok
  2711-6324
- MTR Yuen Long Station, Yuen Long, New Territories
  2475-3308

www.italianfood.com.hk

This small gourmet shop offers a diverse range of imported products ranging from Italian pasta to canned fish and fruit, to all-natural raw nuts.

Bon Bon Bon
22 Pottinger St, Central
2523-6565

High-end food store offering an extensive range of exotic ingredients sourced directly by the owner.

Naturo Plus ....
G/F, 6 Sun St, Wan Chai
2865-0388
www.naturoplus.com.hk

Great Food Hall ....
LG, Pacific Place, 88 Queensway, Admiralty
2918-9986
www.greatfoodhall.com

city's super ....
See page 81

Oliver's ....
2/F, Prince's Bldg, 10 Chater Rd, Central
2810-7710

WHERE CAN I FIND A GOOD SELECTION OF ASIAN SPICES AND PROVISIONS?

The Indian Provision Store ....
- 18–20 Bowrington Rd, Wan Chai
  2891-8324
- Chungking Mansions, 36 Nathan Rd, Tsim Sha Tsui
  2891-8024/2891-8324/2891-8104

A good source for difficult-to-find spices and top quality ghee. Free delivery within Hong Kong, with minimum $200 purchase.

Shing Fat Coconut and Spices Ltd ....
G/F, 18 Spring Garden Lane, Wan Chai
2572-7725/9366-0394

A good source for fresh whole coconut, flesh and milk. You can also buy spices sold in bulk, less expensively than in grocery stores.

Cheong Thai Supermarket ....
G/F, 25–29 Kai Tak Rd, Kowloon City
2382-0095
www.cheongthai.com

One of the best Thai supply stores in Hong Kong.

Yu Kwen Yick ....
G/F, 8 Second St, Sai Ying Pun, Sai Wan
2568-8007
www.yukwenyick.com.hk

Kowloon Soy Co. Ltd ....
9 Graham St, Central
2544-3695
www.kowloonsoy.com

Bon Bon Bon
22 Pottinger St, Central
2523-6565

WHERE CAN I FIND A LARGE SELECTION OF
JAPANESE & KOREAN FOODS AND PROVISIONS?

Apita ....
B1–2/F, Cityplaza 2
18 Taikoo Shing Rd, Tai Koo
2885-0331
www.unyhk.com
JUSCO ....
• G/F–4/F, Kornhill Plaza (South)
  2 Kornhill Rd, Quarry Bay
  2884-6888
• B1 & G/F, Site 5–6M, Whampoa Garden, Hung Hom
  2627-6688
• 3/F, Lok Fu Shopping Centre 2, Junction Rd, Lok Fu
  2339-3888
• 1/F & 2/F, Zone B, Tai Po Mega Mall
  8–10 On Pong Rd, Tai Po, New Territories
  2662-8888
• UG/F & 1/F, Tuen Mun Town Plaza, Phase 1
  1 Tuen Shun St, Tuen Mun, New Territories
  2452-7333
www.jusco.com.hk
SOGO ....
• B2, 555 Hennessy Rd, Causeway Bay
  2833-8212
• B2, 12 Salisbury Rd, Tsim Sha Tsui
  3556-1840
www.sogo.com.hk
city'super ....
See page 81
New World Korean Supermarket ....
G/F, Phillip House
5 Kimberley St, Tsim Sha Tsui
2724-2414

WHERE CAN I ORDER FRESH MILK TO BE DELIVERED
TO MY HOME?

Farm Milk
78 Lui Kung Tin, Kap Lung Village
Shek Kong, New Territories
2832-9218

WHERE CAN I GET ORGANIC MEATS AND POULTRY
DELIVERED TO MY HOME?

South Stream Seafoods Ltd
3/F, Mansfield Ind. Centre
19 Hong Yip St, Yuen Long, New Territories
2555-6200
www.south-stream-seafoods.com
MeatMarket.hk
8135-1394
www.meatmarket.hk
They also carry organic meats that are halal accredited.

Tenderloin Fine Food
26/F, Universal Trade Centre
3–5 Arbuthnot Rd, Central
2877-2733
www.tenderloin.com.hk

WHERE CAN I ORDER **ORGANIC FRUITS AND VEGETABLES DELIVERED** TO MY HOME?

Aussie Organics ....
2293-2265
www.aussieorganics.com
They deliver a preset box every week with assorted fruits and vegetables, Australian guaranteed. Order online.

The Organic Farm ....
2483-9906
www.organic-farm.com / www.simply-organic.com.hk
Locally grown organic fruits and vegetables that you can have delivered to your door in 3kg packs weekly. Produce is chosen based on what is in season and freshest. You can also buy from their Veggie Van, in the parking lot of the Hong Kong Country Club every Thursday, and other locations weekly.

O2h ....
2981-2888
www.o2h.com.hk
They provide a weekly availability list so you can choose the exact amount of each item you would like delivered. In addition to fruits and vegetables, they carry organic herbs, cheese, tofu, juices and staple goods.

Life Café ....
G/F, 10 Shelley St, SoHo
2810-9043
www.lifecafe.com.hk
Organic shop. Can deliver OLife's Organic Box, seasonal fruit and veggies directly from Australia.

ARE THERE ANY **LOCAL ORGANIC PRODUCE** SHOPS OR STALLS?

Tung Ho Vegetable Stall ....
40 Wan Chai Rd, Wan Chai
This little vegetable stand carries pre-packaged local organic greens and other vegetables.

Oh My Farm Gourmet Greens Plus ....
G/F, Block 1, The Zenith, 3 Wanchai Rd, Wan Chai
2976-4100
www.hk.myblog.yahoo.com/ohmyfarm
A new shop carrying local organic vegetables and fruit.

OFarm ....
www.ofarmhk.com
Many locations, limited stock variety.

Vegetables Shop ....
127A, Caine Rd, Mid-Levels
2858-1288
This little shop offers fresh local organic vegetables daily in addition to organic dry goods, canned/bottled goods and beverages. Call to find out what is available. Free delivery in the Central/Mid-Levels area for orders over $100.

Bels Food Boutique .... 🄟
- 23 Mercury St, Tin Hau
  2570-7700
- 110 Nga Tsin Wai Rd, Kowloon City
  2382-6768

WHERE CAN I FIND A GROCERY STORE THAT
SELLS **ORGANIC FOODS**?

ThreeSixty .... ❦
See page 35
*Hong Kong's largest organic and natural food store,
carrying an extensive line of products ranging from meat
and produce to vitamins and supplements.*

Great Food Hall .... ❦
LG, Pacific Place, 88 Queensway, Admiralty
2918-9986
www.greatfoodhall.com

Oliver's .... ❦
2/F, Prince's Bldg, 10 Chater Rd, Central
2810-7710

city'super .... ❦
See page 81

Park n Shop .... ❦
www.parknshop.com

TASTE .... ❦
See page 82
*Most TASTE and Super Stores carry some organic foods
and dried goods. The Parkview and Stanley Plaza stores
are amongst those offering a good selection.*

Wellcome .... ❦
www.wellcome.com.hk

OFarm .... ❦
www.ofarmhk.com

WHAT ABOUT SMALLER **HEALTH AND ORGANIC FOOD
STORES**?

Green Concepts Health Shop .... ❦
2/F, Prosperous Comm. Bldg
54–58 Jardine's Bazaar, Causeway Bay
2882-4848
www.healthshop.com.hk

Organic Sense .... ❦
G/F, 34 Lyndhurst Terrace, Central
2581-2899
www.organicsense.com.hk

Health Gate .... ❦
8/F, Hung Tak Bldg, 106–108 Des Voeux Rd Central
2545-2289
www.health-gate.com

Nature's Blessing .... ❦
G/F, 60–62 Caine Rd, Mid-Levels
2517-2135
www.naturesblessing.com.hk

Simply Organic .... ❦
1/F, 21 Canal Rd West, Causeway Bay
2488-0138
www.simply-organic.com.hk
Many items, including fresh produce from the organic farm.

Organic MaMa .... ♥
8/F, Ming Tak Comm. Bldg
101–103 Wan Chai Rd, Wan Chai
2699-8837
www.organicmama.com.hk

Organic Land .... ♥
• 181 Hennessy Rd, Wan Chai
  2511-5628
• Underground L1, MTR Hong Kong Station (Near Exit E)
  3583-2016
www.organicland.com.hk
*Local and imported organic dry foods, and organic
toiletries, beverages and salad dressings. The store
at Wan Chai also has a small deli offering organic
sandwiches, salads, etc.*

Nutrition Centre .... ♥
11/F, Causeway Bay Comm. Bldg
1–13 Sugar St, Causeway Bay
2577-3663
www.nc-organic.com

Life Café .... ♥
G/F, 10 Shelley St, SoHo
2810-9043
www.lifecafe.com.hk

Hago .... ♥
3188-2461
www.hago-group.com/eng
*Online source for organic baby food, organic foods,
and supplements.*

Naturo Plus .... ♥
G/F, 6 Sun St, Wan Chai
2865-0388
www.naturoplus.com.hk

I'M LOOKING FOR GOOD QUALITY **IMPORTED
VITAMINS AND SUPPLEMENTS**. WHERE DO I GO?

Jireh International Health Limited .... ♥
2/F, Gee Chang Hong Centre
65 Wong Chuk Hang Rd, Aberdeen
2838-8902
www.jirehhealthhk.com

Hago .... ♥
3188-2461
www.hago-group.com/eng

GNC .... ♥
• 14–24 Wellington St, Central
  2528-6136
• MTR Admiralty Station, Admiralty
  2299-3388
• 1/F, Stanley Plaza, Stanley
  2299-3388
www.gnc.com
Throughout Hong Kong, see also website.

HOW ABOUT A GOOD **BAKERY FOR BREADS & PASTRIES**?

*For one-stop shopping visit any of the large grocery stores
for in-house bakeries. Alternatively, try any of the big hotels,
which all have delicious cake shops, or bake your own!*

Ali Oli Bakery ....
11 Sha Tsui Path, Sai Kung, New Territories
2792-2655
www.alioli.com.hk
Home delivery service available with minimum order $250.

Saffron Bakery ....
• 34 Hoi Kwong St, Quarry Bay
  2561-6695
• 1/F, Stanley Plaza, Stanley
  2813-0270
www.saffronbakery.com
Best bagels in town.

Le Salon de Thé de Joël Robuchon
3/F, The Landmark, 15 Queen's Rd Central
2166-9000
www.robuchon.hk

simplylife Bread & Wine
L1, IFC Mall, 8 Finance St, Central
2234-7356

Panash Limited ....
• G/F, Easey Comm. Bldg
  253–261 Hennessy Rd, Wan Chai
  2519-9367
• Apita, B1, Cityplaza 2
  18 Taikoo Shing Rd, Tai Koo
  2885-8012
• LG/F, The Westwood
  8 Belcher's St, Kennedy Town
  Bakery: 2542-7630 / Café: 2542-7652
• G/F, Ocean Terminal, Harbour City
  Canton Rd, Tsim Sha Tsui
  Bakery: 2730-1631 / Café: 2311-0411
• G/F, Chang Hing Square
  601 Nathan Rd, Mong Kok
  2385-8011
• G/F, 1 Soares Ave, Ho Man Tin
  2246-7831
• 1/F, Telford Plaza, 33 Wai Yip St, Kowloon Bay
  2750-2689
• 1/F, East Point City
  8 Chung Wa Rd, Tseung Kwan O, New Territories
  2628-6871

Pumpernickel ....
See page 37

Vanilla
• G/F, 33 Mosque St, Mid-Levels
  2530-4828
• 1/F, Lippo Centre, 89 Queensway, Admiralty
  2868-1711

agnès b. Café
See page 32

The Real Bread Company
G/F, 14 Shelley St, SoHo
2810-9326

Delifrance
2873-3893
www.delifrance.com.hk
Locations throughout Hong Kong. Great place for take-away baguettes, pastries and biscuits.

I NEED TO **ORDER A REALLY YUMMY CAKE**. WHERE SHOULD I GO?

Sweet Secrets ....
- G/F, 35 Graham St, Central
  2545-8886
- G/F, 28B Canal Rd East, Causeway Bay
  2575-6228

www.sweetsecrets.com.hk
They make delicious cakes for all occasions.

Cake-A-Licious ....
LG/F, 11 Lyndhurst Terrace, Central
2815-2218
www.cakealicious.com.hk
Very yummy, unique, personalised cakes.

Island Gourmet
5/F, Island Shangri-La Hotel, Pacific Place
Supreme Court Rd, Admiralty
2820-8550
For a seriously yummy chocolate fix, order the froufrou cake with the best crunchy bottom.

Baby Cakes ....
11/F, Horizon Plaza, 2 Lee Wing St, Ap Lei Chau
3175-8716
www.babycakesasia.com

Antique Patisserie & Fine Chocolates
See page 33
Delicious and visually beautiful cakes.

Sift ....
- G/F, 46 Graham St, Central
  2530-4288
- G/F, 51 Queen's Rd East, Wan Chai
  2528-0084
- 22/F, Horizon Plaza, 2 Lee Wing St, Ap Lei Chau
  2870-3887

www.siftdesserts.com
Try their delicious cupcakes and macaroons.

Vanilla
See page 93
This hidden little patisserie offers delectable cakes and treats. The lemon cheesecake is to die for!

Petits by Deschamps
2/F, Elements Mall, 1 Austin Rd West, Kowloon
2882-7477

Zoe Café
- G/F, J Residence, 60 Johnston Rd, Wan Chai
  2866-6885
- G/F, 7A Shan Kwong Rd, Happy Valley
  2892-1166
- G/F, Sunning Plaza, 10 Hysan Ave, Causeway Bay
  2234-7188

Vero ....
1/F, 1 Lung King St, Fenwick Pier, Wan Chai
2559-5882
www.verochocolates.com
In addition to regular cakes, they offer specialty shapes and themed cakes such as the "handbag" cake.

EVERYTHING FOOD & ENTERTAINMENT

WHO SPECIALISES IN CUSTOM-DESIGNED WEDDING CAKES?

Cake2
G/F, Victoria Court, 54 Hing Fat St, Tin Hau
2947-7575
www.cake2.com

Phoebe's
G/F, 25 Aberdeen St, Central
2815-8866
www.phoebes.com.hk

Antique Patisserie & Fine Chocolates
See page 33

Peninsula Boutique
Basement, East Wing, The Peninsula
Salisbury Rd, Tsim Sha Tsui
2315-3262
www.peninsula.com

Elayna Maria Cakes
6338-3646
www.elaynamariacakes.com

Eva Liu
White Bridal Couture, 17 Lyndhurst Terrace, Central
2376-4900
www.eva-liu.com

I WANT TO BAKE MY OWN CAKE. WHERE SHOULD I GO TO GET CAKE MOULDS, DECORATIONS AND TOOLS?

Complete Deelite ....
6/F, California Entertainment Bldg
34–36 D'Aguilar St, Central
3167-7022
www.completedeelite.com

I Love Cake
G/F, 388 Shanghai St, Yau Ma Tei
2671-2671
www.ilovecake.hk

city'super
See page 81

See also kitchenware, page 335–337.

WHERE CAN I FIND A GOOD WINE MERCHANT?

Berry Brothers & Rudd
3/F, Lee Gardens, 33 Hysan Ave, Causeway Bay
2907-2112
www.bbr.com.hk
One of the most respected wine merchants in Hong Kong. Berry Brothers can source "En Primeur" wines, arrange storage, set up a wedding wine registry, assist in building a personal wine portfolio and more.

Valdivia Ltd Shop
14/F, Sungib Ind. Centre
53 Wong Chuk Hang Rd, Aberdeen
2555-7431
Specialising in Italian wines, Valdivia offers a huge variety and home delivery.

Altaya Wines

28/F, Bank of America Tower, 12 Harcourt Rd, Central
2523-1945
www.altayawines.com
Wholesale and retail wine merchant, specialising in wines from France, Italy and other parts of Europe and the Americas. They offer an exceptional list of rare wines and can assist in building a personal wine portfolio, including an overseas direct purchasing service to avoid paying 80% duty and storage in the UK. An extensive list of vintage cigars is also available.

Galerie du Vin Ltd

- 73 Wellington St, Central
  2854-2987
- G/F, 313 Lockhart Rd, Wan Chai
  2591-9028

www.gdv.com.hk

Appellation

16/F, Wyndham Place, 40–44 Wyndham St, Central
2866-6335

WHERE CAN I FIND A REPUTABLE **WINE SHOP**
OFFERING A VARIETY OF QUALITY WINES?

Rare & Fine Wines Ltd

- G/F, The Putman
  202 Queen's Road Central, Sheung Wan
  2815-6000
- Lobby, The Bank of East Asia Bldg
  10 Des Voeux Rd Central
  2522-9797
- G/F, Hankow Centre, 5–15 Hankow Rd, Tsim Sha Tsui
  2311-1177

www.rarenfinewines.com.hk

Watson's Wine Cellar

- L3, IFC Mall, 8 Finance St, Central
  2530-5002
- LG/F, Century Square, 1–13 D'Aguilar St, Central
  2537-6998
- Great Food Hall, LG, Pacific Place
  88 Queensway, Admiralty
  2526-2832

www.watsonswine.com
Watson's Wine Cellar has huge buying power, offering competitive prices and a large range of good wines. Many outlets, but the location in Pacific Place is one of the best.

Ponti Food & Wine Cellar Ltd

- B1, Alexandra House, 18 Chater Rd, Central
  2810-1000
- G/F, 3 Yuen Yuen St, Happy Valley
  2972-2283
- G/F, The Mira, 118–130 Nathan Rd, Tsim Sha Tsui
  2730-1889
- 3/F, Telford Plaza 2, 33 Wai Yip St, Kowloon Bay
  2997-3008

www.ponti-fwc.com

Benson's

G/F, Yee Fat Mansion, 2 Min Fat St, Happy Valley
2893-1500
www.benson.com.hk

Bel Vino
248 Queen's Rd East, Wan Chai
2285-8989
www.belvino.com.hk
Specialising in Italian wines.

I'VE HEARD OF THESE NEW **BAR/WINE CELLARS**.
CAN YOU NAME A FEW?

Tastings .... *)
27 & 29 Wellington St, Central
2523-6282
They have 40 wines on tap and you can purchase wine by the shot, allowing the connoisseur the best of all worlds without purchasing an entire bottle. Closed Sundays.

Watson's Wine Cellar
See page 96

Force 8 Cellars
1/F, 42A Hollywood Rd, Central
2527-6217
www.force8wines.com

I AM HOSTING A LARGE PARTY. WHERE CAN I
SOURCE **WHOLESALE/WELL-PRICED WINE**?

Adelaide Cellar Door ....
10/F, Century Square, 1–13 D'Aguilar St, Central
2526-0151
www.adelaidecellardoor.com.hk
A wine outlet specialising in Australian and New Zealand wines from small family-owned wineries, priced well below equivalent wines sold through traditional retail shops. Delivery available.

Boutique Wines ....
16/F, Horizon Plaza, 2 Lee Wing St, Ap Lei Chau
2872-4234
www.boutiquewines.com.hk
A good selection of Australian, New Zealand and South African wines at warehouse prices. Delivery available at one case minimum.

Limestone Coast Wines ....
12/F, Horizon Plaza, 2 Lee Wing St, Ap Lei Chau
2817-1625
www.limestone-coast-wines.com
Hong Kong's first Australian "Unbranded Wine" company. Direct purchasing of unlabelled bottles from South Australian wineries keeps prices down. Personalised labels can be ordered for weddings and gifts (or bottles can be left unlabelled).

Margaret River Wine Shop ....
G/F, 3 St. Francis St, Wan Chai
2575-6770
www.mrwineshop.com

HOW ABOUT BUYING **WINE ONLINE WITH HOME DELIVERY** IN HONG KONG?

Berry Brothers & Rudd
3/F, Lee Gardens, 33 Hysan Ave, Causeway Bay
2907-2112
www.bbr.com.hk

My Wine Man
9673-3076
www.mywineman.com

Wineshop Hong Kong
5/F, Keen Hung Comm. Bldg
80 Queen's Rd East, Wan Chai
2528-4849
www.wineshop.hk
In addition to wine, they also offer beer, spirits, food, coffee and more.

Vinoteca HK
2895-6867
www.vinotecahk.com

Adelaide Cellar Door
10/F, Century Square, 1 – 13 D'Aguilar St, Central
2526-0151
www.adelaidecellardoor.com.hk

Cellarmasters Wine Club
9/F, Tin Fung Ind. Mansion
63 Wong Chuk Hang Rd, Aberdeen
2791-6332
www.cellarmasterwines.com

WHERE CAN I BUY A GOOD WINE FRIDGE FOR PROPER STORAGE?

Frigidaire
Stockist:
Gilman Home Appliances
• G/F, 52 Gilman St, Central
  2524-3554
• UG/F, Leighton Centre, 77 Leighton Rd, Causeway Bay
  2881-0055
• 3/F, Ocean Centre, Harbour City
  Canton Rd, Tsim Sha Tsui
  2730-6747
• 2/F, Grand Central Plaza
  138 Sha Tin Rural Committee Rd
  Sha Tin, New Territories
  2699-0345
www.gilman-group.com

Eu-Amex Wine Cellars Ltd
G/F, 159 Wong Nai Chung Rd, Happy Valley
2577-3181
www.eu-amex.com
Specialising in Nording Cave wine cellars. Check out www.nordingcave.com.

Alpha International Food Services
9/F, Chai Wan Ind. City, Phase 2
70 Wing Tai Rd, Chai Wan
2889-2123
www.eurocave-alpha.com

WHERE CAN I BUY WHOLESALE LIQUOR?

Leung Yick Co.
18/F, Eastern Harbour Centre, 28 Hoi Chak St, Quarry Bay
2598-8034
www.leungyick.com
A large variety of spirits and some wines and champagnes at wholesale prices with a minimum order.

Soho Wines and Spirits ....
49 Elgin St, SoHo
2525-0316
www.sohowines.hk
A good selection of wines and spirits at 10–20%
discount for wholesale orders (over $700).

WHERE IS A GOOD PLACE TO BUY **CIGARS**?

Cohiba Cigar Divan
G/F, East Lobby, Mandarin Oriental Hotel
5 Connaught Rd Central
2825-4074
www.pacificcigar.com
This outlet is a part of the Pacific Cigar Company, which
also has locations in the Sheraton Hotel, Cochrane St,
Carnarvon Rd and Elements Mall (see below).

Red Chamber Cigar Divan
G/F & Mezzanine, Pedder Bldg, 12 Pedder St, Central
2528-3966 / 2537-0977
www.pacificcigar.com

La Casa Del Habano
2/F, Sheraton Hong Kong Hotel and Towers
20 Nathan Rd, Tsim Sha Tsui
2123-9952
www.pacificcigar.com

Havana Express
• G/F, Cheung Fai Bldg, 45–47 Cochrane St, SoHo
  2110-9201
• G/F, 8A Carnarvon Rd, Tsim Sha Tsui
  2366-2537
www.pacificcigar.com

Cigar Emporium
2/F, Elements Mall, 1 Austin Rd West, Kowloon
2196-8366
www.pacificcigar.com

Cigarro Ltd
3/F, Pacific House, 20 Queen's Rd Central
2810-1883
www.cigarrohk.com

I NEED A **CATERER** FOR A **PRIVATE PARTY**, **RECEPTION**,
CORPORATE OR **THEMED EVENT**. WHO CAN I CONTACT?

Relish Kitchen
G/F, Hoi Sing Bldg, Block 2
128 Second St, Sai Ying Pun
3481-1979
www.relish-kitchen.com

Gingers Catering
LG/F, Hing Wah Mansions
2 Oaklands Path, Mid-Levels
2964-9160
www.gingers.com.hk

Go Gourmet
G/F, 17 Po Yan St, Sheung Wan
2530-3880
www.go-gourmet.com
They cater for all occasions, personal and corporate,
and also do "cooking parties".

UNWIND
www.unwindhk.com
Mobile bar/drinks catering for events of any size, anywhere in Hong Kong. They can provide their own equipment, personnel and uniformed waiters or bartenders.

Shamrock Catering Group
2547-8155
www.shamrock.com.hk
Large catering company that can do anything from corporate functions to platters for a junk.

Percy's
G/F, 68 Catchick St, Kennedy Town
2855-1882
www.percys.hk

Saporito Delicatessen
G/F, Sports Mansion
161 Wong Nai Chung Rd, Happy Valley
2895-4133 / 2895-1533

WHERE CAN I FIND SOMEONE TO **COME TO MY HOME AND COOK**?

Dine at Home
2813-7707
www.dine-athome.com
Dine at Home offers a range of options from full service dine-at-home to food on location for a boat party to catering a corporate event.

Love True Food Ltd
1 Pak Sze Lane, Central
2851-1650
www.lovetruefood.com
Lakshmi Harilela, a holistic chef and consultant, has opened her own private kitchen and also offers spa cooking classes.

Pat Soederberg
6687-7191
Pat will cook in your home or prepare and deliver a homemade Thai meal for minimum 6 people, $400/person.

I DON'T WANT TO EAT OUT, BUT I'M TOO LAZY TO COOK. WHERE DO YOU SUGGEST I GET SOME **GOOD TAKE-OUT ON MY WAY HOME**?

Chicken on the Run
LG/F, 1 Prince's Terrace, Central
2537-8285
www.chickenontherun.com

Soho Corner Shop
43 Staunton St, SoHo
2543-2632

Wang Fu
G/F, 98A Wellington St, Central
2121-8006
You can buy uncooked dumplings here and boil or steam them at home.

Duke's Deli .... 🍭
G/F, Two Chinachem Plaza
135 Des Voeux Rd Central
2544-7587
www.dukesdeli.com

Eat Right .... ❧
23 Staunton St, SoHo
2868-4832
www.eatright.com.hk

Life Café .... ❧
G/F, 10 Shelley St, SoHo
2810-9043
www.lifecafe.com.hk

Percy's
G/F, 68 Catchick St, Kennedy Town
2855-1882
www.percys.hk

Saporito Delicatessen
G/F, Sports Mansion
161 Wong Nai Chung Rd, Happy Valley
2895-4133 / 2895-1533

WHERE CAN I FIND A **GOOD RESTAURANT DELIVERY**
SERVICE THAT OFFERS A **LARGE SELECTION**?

Food by Fone
2868-6969
www.foodbyfone.net

Waiters on Wheels
2845-0000
www.waitersonwheels.com.hk

Ring-a-Dinner
3105-5310
www.ringadinner.com

Dial-A-Dinner
2598-1718
www.dialadinner.com.hk

Soho Delivery
2526-2029
www.sohodelivery.com.hk
*Food, beer, juice, soft drinks, cigarettes, convenience
store items and more.*

Food by Web
2805-1331
www.foodbyweb.com.hk

Cuisine Courier
2596-0000
www.cuisinecourier.com

Gourmet Express
2869-5050
www.diningconcepts.com.hk
*Orders for Capone's Pizza, Pizzeria Napoli and Jed's
Just Ribs Tennessee BBQ are done through Cuisine
Courier and Gourmet Express.*

Go Gourmet Delivers
2517-7077
www.gogourmetdelivers.com
*They have Rustic Organic Pizza Kitchen, Sprinkles
Cupcake Company, and Ragin' Cajun's.*

WHERE CAN I GET **GOOD HOME DELIVERY PIZZA?**

Pizzeria Italia
G/F, 1–7 Mosque St, Mid-Levels
2525-2519
Order through Food by Web (tel. 2805-1331,
www.foodbyweb.com.hk).

Capone's Pizza
G/F, 9 Possession St, Sheung Wan
2869-5050 / 2596-0000
Order through Cuisine Courier (tel. 2596-0000,
www.cuisinecourier.com) or Gourmet Express (tel.
2869-5050, www.diningconcepts.com.hk).

Wildfire
See page 45

Rustic Organic Pizza Kitchen
Order through Go Gourmet Delivers (tel. 2517-7077,
www.gogourmetdelivers.com).

EVERYTHING
FASHION
& SHOPPING

the trendiest shopping **SPOTS**	104
finding your **SIZE**	105
the **LOOK** for **LESS**	107
find the **LABEL** without the price	110
FANCY party dresses	114
DENIM you can't live without	117
if the **SHOE** fits	120
the **BARE** necessities	122
MEN need to look stylish too	126
custom **MAKE** it	129
world famous **TAILORS**	133
ALTER it to perfection	136
bags to **CARRY** around	137
clothes to **SWEAT** in	144
for the great **OUTDOORS**	147
blinded by **BLING**	149
BABIES a to z	160
TOYS for tots and big boys	165
KIDS' clothing that rocks	168
relax with a good **BOOK**	176
the lost art of **PRINT**	185
STANLEY for dummies	187
find your way in **SHAM SHUI PO**	189

WHERE CAN I FIND GOOD **SHOPPING AREAS** WITH SMALL OR INDEPENDENT BOUTIQUES OFFERING THE LATEST TRENDS?

SoHo

Elgin St, Staunton St, Old Bailey St, Graham St and Aberdeen St
Although the shops in SoHo are more spread out, this is a great neighbourhood offering some funky boutiques for clothing, bags and accessories.

Causeway Bay

Paterson St, Kingston St and Cleveland St
This is a fantastic area to buy the hippest and latest designer, street and casualwear in Hong Kong. Sizing is generally small and prices are not cheap.

Island Beverley
1 Great George St, Causeway Bay
A trendy fashion shopping centre filled with small boutiques and outlets selling young fashions and accessories, as well as some gifts and toys. Most of the clothing is designed locally and many of the shops deal in one-off items. Sizing is generally small, but in some cases can be custom ordered. Also explore the surrounding streets for hidden gems.

Wan Chai

Star St, Ship St and St. Francis St
A unique mix of restaurants and cafés interspersed with eclectic little shops carrying everything from fashion to homewares and curios.

Central

On Lan St, Wyndham St (between Fringe Club and On Lan St), Wellington St (up to Pottinger St) and Lyndhurst Terrace
From ultra-hip on On Lan St to funky boutiques, shoe stores and accessories.

WHAT ARE THE BEST **ONE-STOP MALLS** FOR ALL THE LATEST FASHIONS, SHOES AND ACCESSORIES?

Ocean Terminal / Ocean Centre / Gateway Arcade, Harbour City
Canton Rd, Tsim Sha Tsui
www.harbourcity.com.hk
Expansive connected malls that offer a huge selection of fashion and much more, including a great kids' zone; you'll find something for everyone here.

IFC Mall
8 Finance St, Central
www.ifc.com.hk

The Landmark
15 Queen's Rd Central

Prince's Bldg
10 Chater Rd, Central
www.centralhk.com

Pacific Place
88 Queensway, Admiralty
www.pacificplace.com.hk
Located within close proximity of each other, the above four high-end shopping destinations will offer you the absolute latest in fashion and style.

Langham Place
8 Argyle St, Mong Kok

Elements Mall
1 Austin Rd West, Kowloon
www.elementshk.com
*New mall catering to high-end and established brands,
with great dining options and even a skating rink.*

Cityplaza
18 Taikoo Shing Rd, Tai Koo
www.cityplaza.com.hk
*Very busy, expansive mall that attracts a large Japanese
and local clientele; offers everything under the sun.
Great place to combine shopping with kids' activities
(movies, skating, fun zone).*

Festival Walk
80 Tat Chee Ave, Kowloon Tong
www.festivalwalk.com.hk
*Popular with the local market, this mall offers a little bit
of everything, including a skating rink.*

WHERE CAN I FIND THE BEST **STREET MARKETS**
IN HONG KONG FOR INEXPENSIVE CLOTHING,
SHOES AND ACCESSORIES?

Stanley Market, Stanley
*Export overruns and seconds, great for Western-sized
casual wear, baby/kids' clothes, hip brands, ski wear
and gifts.*

Granville Rd, Tsim Sha Tsui
Trendy, export-branded clothing and accessories.

Li Yuen St East and West, Central
Clothing, shoes, handbags, accessories and gifts.

Fa Yuen St, Mong Kok
Between Argyle St and Prince Edward Rd West
*Cheap export overruns, including casual wear and
trendy looks.*

WHERE SHOULD I LOOK FOR STYLISH CLOTHING
STORES THAT CARRY **WESTERN SIZES**?

Amandarling
G/F, 32 Lyndhurst Terrace, Central
2581-0968
www.amandarling.com
*An extensive collection of contemporary cruise, resort
and swimwear. Great source for loose-fitting, long and
flowing tops for early pregnancy.*

D-mop
- G/F, 11–15 On Lan St, Central
  2840-0822
- Greenfield Mansion, Fashion Walk
  8 Kingston St, Causeway Bay
  2203-4130
- 4/F, Times Square, 1 Matheson St, Causeway Bay
  2175-4881
- 2/F, Silvercord, 30 Canton Rd, Tsim Sha Tsui
  2808-0825
- 2/F, Gateway Arcade, Harbour City
  Canton Rd, Tsim Sha Tsui
  3102-1317
- LCX, 3/F, Ocean Terminal, Harbour City
  Canton Rd, Tsim Sha Tsui
  3188-9396

- B1, The Sun Arcade, 28 Canton Rd, Tsim Sha Tsui
  2722-0072
- G/F, Miramar Shopping Centre
  132 Nathan Rd, Tsim Sha Tsui
  2736-6703
- L6, Langham Place, 8 Argyle St, Mong Kok
  3514-4308
- Upper Concourse, APM
  418 Kwun Tong Rd, Kwun Tong
  3148-1360
- L4, New Town Plaza, Phase 1
  Sha Tin Centre St, Sha Tin, New Territories
  2602-2625

www.d-mop.com.hk
Hip designer-brand clothing and street clothing.

Shine

- 1/F, Yuen Yick Bldg, 27–29 Wellington St, Central
  3426-9080
- G/F, Cleveland Mansion
  5–7 Cleveland St, Causeway Bay
  2890-8261

www.shinehongkong.com
Eclectic shop full of high-end men's and women's fashion, shoes and accessories from Europe and Japan.

Ranee K

2108-4068
www.raneek.com
Hip and vibrant everyday wear and cocktail dresses.

Tabla

Mezzanine, Prince's Bldg, 10 Chater Rd, Central
2525-5590 / 9755-6669
www.tabla.hk
Beautiful and feminine Indian-inspired clothing, wraps and accessories. Another great source for flowing, loose tops, ideal for early pregnancy.

Sanskrit

G/F, 48 Lyndhurst Terrace, Central
2545-2088
Modern Indian designer fashions. Fantastic for hand-embroidered or beaded tops, skirts and dresses, in addition to jewellery and accessories.

Indigo Designer Denim Bar & Contemporary Clothing

G/F, 32A Staunton St, SoHo
2147-3000
www.indigohongkong.com
Best for designer jeans with imported labels including Rock & Republic, Blue Cult, Kasil and more, with large sizes available. They also carry a fun range of women's clothing.

Addiction

1/F, 21–23 Lan Fong Rd, Causeway Bay
2869-4883
www.shopaddiction.com

Shanghai Tang

- G/F, Pedder Bldg, 12 Pedder St, Central
  2525-7333
- L2, Pacific Place, 88 Queensway, Admiralty
  2918-1505
- G/F & 1/F, House 1, 1881 Heritage
  2A Canton Rd, Tsim Sha Tsui
  2368-2932

- 1/F, InterContinental Hotel
  18 Salisbury Rd, Tsim Sha Tsui
  2723-1012
- 1/F, Elements Mall, 1 Austin Rd West, Kowloon
  2196-8200
- L7, Departures East Hall, Terminal 1
  Hong Kong International Airport
  2261-0606 / 2261-0318
- L5, Terminal 2, Hong Kong International Airport
  3559-1005

www.shanghaitang.com

Tiare
G/F, 53 Staunton St, SoHo
2540-3380
www.tiareboutique.com
Women's clothings, jewellery and accessories from LA's up-and-coming designers.

Marks & Spencer .... ♟ ⚘

- G/F, Central Tower, 28 Queen's Rd Central
  2921-8059
- 4/F, Times Square, 1 Matheson St, Causeway Bay
  2923-7970
- 1/F & 2/F, Cityplaza, 18 Taikoo Shing Rd, Tai Koo
  2922-7234
- 2/F & 3/F, Ocean Centre, Harbour City
  Canton Rd, Tsim Sha Tsui
  2926-3346
- LG1, Festival Walk, 80 Tat Chee Ave, Kowloon Tong
  2928-2213
- Telford Plaza, Phase 1, 33 Wai Yip St, Kowloon Bay
  2148-6012
- 1/F, Plaza Hollywood, 3 Lung Poon St, Diamond Hill
  2927-6494
- L4, New Town Plaza, Phase 1
  Sha Tin Centre St, Sha Tin, New Territories
  2929-4331

www.marksandspencer.com
Marks & Spencer has revamped its look to include some stylish basics and everyday wear.

See also Street Markets, page 105.

HOW ABOUT FASHION DIVAS WANTING **DESIGNER-LOOK CLOTHES WITHOUT THE DESIGNER PRICES**?

Zara .... 🍭 ⚘

- L1, IFC Mall, 8 Finance St, Central
  2234-7305
- L1, Pacific Place, 88 Queensway, Admiralty
  2918-1099
- 3/F, Times Square, 1 Matheson St, Causeway Bay
  2506-0070
- 2/F, Gateway Arcade, Harbour City
  Canton Rd, Tsim Sha Tsui
  2629-1858
- 1/F, Elements Mall, 1 Austin Rd West, Kowloon
  2196-8970
- L3, New Town Plaza, Phase 1
  Sha Tin Centre St, Sha Tin, New Territories
  2608-2272

www.zara.com.hk
Zara carries Western sizes up to European 44.

Mango .... ♟

- L1, IFC Mall, 8 Finance St, Central
  2295-3262
- L1, Pacific Place, 88 Queensway, Admiralty
  2918-9168
- 2/F, SOGO, 555 Hennessy Rd, Causeway Bay
  2831-8934
- 1/F, Cityplaza, 18 Taikoo Shing Rd, Tai Koo
  2513-8331 / 2513-6019
- 2/F, Gateway Arcade, Harbour City
  Canton Rd, Tsim Sha Tsui
  2314-7395
- LG1, Festival Walk, 80 Tat Chee Ave, Kowloon Tong
  2265-7137
- L5, Terminal 2, Hong Kong International Airport
  3197-9320

www.mango.es

H&M .... ♟♟

- 68 Queen's Rd Central
  2110-9546
- G/F & 1/F, Silvercord, 30 Canton Rd, Tsim Sha Tsui
  3521-1171
- L1, Langham Place, 8 Argyle St, Mong Kok
  3580-7621
- 1/F, Elements Mall, 1 Austin Rd West, Kowloon
  2196-8391
- L1, Festival Walk, 80 Tat Chee Ave, Kowloon Tong
  3106-6940

www.hm.com/hk_en

Club Monaco .... ♟

- L1, IFC Mall, 8 Finance St, Central
  3586-3045
- G/F, New World Tower 2
  16–18 Queen's Rd Central
  2118-2989
- 5/F, Times Square, 1 Matheson St, Causeway Bay
  2118-3515
- G/F, Fashion Walk
  24–47 Paterson St, Causeway Bay
  2895-0930
- 2/F, Gateway Arcade, Harbour City
  Canton Rd, Tsim Sha Tsui
  2118-5647
- LG1, Festival Walk, 80 Tat Chee Ave, Kowloon Tong
  2118-3512

www.clubmonaco.com

Massimo Dutti .... ♟

- L1, IFC Mall, 8 Finance St, Central
  2805-0588
- 3/F, Times Square, 1 Matheson St, Causeway Bay
  2506-0050
- 2/F, Gateway Arcade, Harbour City
  Canton Rd, Tsim Sha Tsui
  2175-0010

www.massimodutti.com

Calvin Klein Jeans .... ♟

- L1, IFC Mall, 8 Finance St, Central
  2295-3016
- Basement, The Landmark, 15 Queen's Rd Central
  2530-3632

- 5/F, Times Square, 1 Matheson St, Causeway Bay
  2506-9506
- 3/F, SOGO, 555 Hennessy Rd, Causeway Bay
  2833-8497
- Fashion Walk, 9 Kingston St, Causeway Bay
  2895-3979
- 2/F, Cityplaza, 18 Taikoo Shing Rd, Tai Koo
  2967-0840
- 2/F, Gateway Arcade, Harbour City
  Canton Rd, Tsim Sha Tsui
  2117-0070
- LCX, 3/F, Ocean Terminal, Harbour City
  Canton Rd, Tsim Sha Tsui
  2303-0656
- G/F, Miramar Shopping Centre
  132 Nathan Rd, Tsim Sha Tsui
  2730-9395
- B2, SOGO, 12 Salisbury Rd, Tsim Sha Tsui
  3556-1105
- Concourse, APM, 418 Kwun Tong Rd, Kwun Tong
  3148-1071
- YATA, L2 & L3, New Town Plaza, Phase 3
  Sha Tin Centre St, Sha Tin, New Territories
  2609-4608
- 1/F, Citygate Outlets
  20 Tat Tung Rd, Tung Chung, Lantau Island
  2109-0671

www.calvinklein.com

A|X Armani Exchange ....

- L1, IFC Mall, 8 Finance St, Central
  2234-7262
- G/F, Entertainment Bldg, 30 Queen's Rd Central
  2521-8422
- L1, Pacific Place, 88 Queensway, Admiralty
  2537-3118
- 4/F, Times Square, 1 Matheson St, Causeway Bay
  2506-1688
- G/F, Fashion Walk
  11–19 Great George St, Causeway Bay
  2881-8200
- 2/F, Cityplaza, 18 Taikoo Shing Rd, Tai Koo
  2967-6632
- G/F, Imperial Bldg, 54–66 Canton Rd, Tsim Sha Tsui
  2730-9682
- L1, Langham Place, 8 Argyle St, Mong Kok
  3514-4202
- 1/F, Elements Mall, 1 Austin Rd West, Kowloon
  2196-8272
- UG, Festival Walk, 80 Tat Chee Ave, Kowloon Tong
  2265-8233
- L3, New Town Plaza, Phase 1
  Sha Tin Centre St, Sha Tin, New Territories
  2681-0883

www.armaniexchange.com

Giordano Ladies

- G/F & 1/F, Lansing House, 43–45 Queen's Rd Central
  2921-2955
- 1/F, Man Yee Bldg, 60–68 Des Voeux Rd Central
  2922-6118
- Queensway Plaza, 93 Queensway, Admiralty
  2922-1090

- 1/F, Capitol Centre, Jardine's Crescent, Causeway Bay
  2923-7118
- 3/F, Cityplaza, 18 Taikoo Shing Rd, Tai Koo
  2922-7127
- 2/F, Gateway Arcade, Harbour City
  Canton Rd, Tsim Sha Tsui
  2926-3642
- 1/F, Manson House, 74–78 Nathan Rd, Tsim Sha Tsui
  2926-1331
- L1, Festival Walk, 80 Tat Chee Ave, Kowloon Tong
  2928-2208
- L3, New Town Plaza, Phase 1
  Sha Tin Centre St, Sha Tin, New Territories
  2929-4350
- L5, Terminal 2, Hong Kong International Airport
  2920-2175

www.giordanoladies.com

Mandarin Orange
3/F, Grand Progress Bldg
15–16 Lan Kwai Fong, Central
2525-8275
www.mandarinorangeclothing.com
Casual everyday clothes with a summer flair.

WHERE CAN I FIND SMALL BOUTIQUES/STORES
THAT CARRY **DESIGNER LABELS** WITHOUT THE
MATCHING PRICES?

Blum & Co.
10/F, Hang Lung Centre
2–20 Paterson St, Causeway Bay
2808-1027
Good for cocktail dresses and gowns; very well priced.

Button Hole
G/F, 58–60 Peel St, Central
2899-2069
*Unique clothing, bags, jewellery and accessories,
including well-known designer brands at discounted
prices. Visit often as stock turns over fast, with new
arrivals coming in every Monday.*

Brands Boutique
G/F, 41 Hollywood Rd, Central
2851-3111
*They carry overrun items by big designer labels as
well as lesser-known ones; their clothes are overruns
so sometimes you may have to be careful of irregular/
incorrect sizing.*

Betty Collections
- 12/F, Radiant Centre, 7 Cannon St, Causeway Bay
  2187-3883
- G/F, World Trust Tower, 50 Stanley St, Central
  3583-2882
- G/F, 22 Tai Yuen St, Wan Chai
  2147-1166

Candy Boutique
LG/F, 100 Caine Rd, Mid-Levels
2546-3331
Designer discount, small sizes only.

Fates 2H
6/F, Manning House, 38–48 Queen's Rd Central
6606-0186

All4U
- G/F, 3 Stanley St, Central
  2234-9138
- G/F, 30 Bonham Strand, Sheung Wan
  2544-1938

C&C
5/F, Thyrse House, 16 Pottinger St, Central
2147-2398
Designer discount.

Dress Code
4 Gresson St, Wan Chai
2819-3322

Faye Fashion ....
1/F, 40 Spring Garden Lane, Wan Chai
2836-6908

Magic Wardrobe
- G/F, Western Market
  323 Des Voeux Rd Central, Sheung Wan
  2545-8666
- 1/F, Admiralty Centre, Tower 2
  18 Harcourt Rd, Admiralty
  2529-2239
- G/F, 1E Sands St, Sai Wan
  2808-0366
- 1/F, Port Centre, Aberdeen
  2552-2209

Designer clothing at discount prices.

(No Name)
G/F, Hoi To Court, 273 Gloucester Rd, Causeway Bay
2117-1106
Shop has no name.

Apple Mall
Basement, 15–31 Hysan Ave, Causeway Bay
Stores to keep an eye out for when going to Apple Mall:
Deluca, Shop 2A; A-One Fashion, Shop 43; Rodeo,
Shop 42 & 42a; Pink Lady, Shop 21.

6/F–10/F, Hang Lung Centre
2–20 Paterson St, Causeway Bay
Five floors of outlet style, discounted brand-name clothing.

ARE THERE ANY **DISCOUNT DESIGNER** OUTLETS?

Citygate Outlets
20 Tat Tung Rd, Tung Chung, Lantau Island
2109-2933
www.citygateoutlets.com.hk
AIX Armani Exchange
Bally
Burberry
Benetton
Calvin Klein Underwear
Calvin Klein Jeans
DKNY @ Club 21
Esprit
Levi's
Nautica
Vivienne Tam
adidas
Puma
Quiksilver
And more…

Acetex Fashion Club
9/F, Far East Finance Centre, 16 Harcourt Rd, Admiralty
2868-6092
European designer clothing and footwear at discounted prices.

Extravaganza
• 1/F, Causeway Bay Plaza 1
  489 Hennessy Rd, Causeway Bay
  2915-0051
• LCX, 3/F, Ocean Terminal, Harbour City
  Canton Rd, Tsim Sha Tsui
  2576-0377
• 1/F, Miramar Shopping Centre
  132 Nathan Rd, Tsim Sha Tsui
  2730-0500
• L5, Langham Place, 8 Argyle St, Mong Kok
  3514-9141
• B1, Fashion World, Site 2
  Whampoa Garden, Hung Hom
  2954-0080
• 1/F, Kowloon City Plaza
  128 Carpenter Rd, Kowloon City
  2572-0990
• G/F, MegaBox, 38 Wang Chiu Rd, Kowloon Bay
  2796-6711 / 2796-6990
• G/F, Telford Plaza, Phase 1
  33 Wai Yip St, Kowloon Bay
  2757-1088
www.extravaganza.ws

Dickson Outlet
G/F, Citygate Outlets
20 Tat Tung Rd, Tung Chung, Lantau Island
2109-3700
www.dicksoncyber.com
Brands include S.T. Dupont, BCBGirl, Florsheim, Patrizia Pepe, Guess, D&G, Miss Sixty and more.

Esprit Outlet
• 3/F, Sun Yuen Long Centre
  8 Long Yat Rd, Yuen Long, New Territories
  2422-0282
• 2/F, Citygate Outlets
  20 Tat Tung Rd, Tung Chung, Lantau Island
  2109-3221
www.esprit.com.hk

I.T Sale Shop
3/F, Silvercord, 30 Canton Rd, Tsim Sha Tsui
2377-9466
www.ithk.com

Joyce Warehouse
21/F, Horizon Plaza, 2 Lee Wing St, Ap Lei Chau
2814-8313

Lane Crawford Warehouse
25/F, Horizon Plaza, 2 Lee Wing St, Ap Lei Chau
2118-3403
www.lanecrawford.com
Closed on Mondays.

Nike Outlet
G/F, Citygate Outlets
20 Tat Tung Rd, Tung Chung, Lantau Island
2707-9159
www.nike.com.hk

adidas Factory Outlet ....
7/F, Hong Kong Ind. Centre
489–491 Castle Peak Rd, Cheung Sha Wan
2959-0357
www.adidas.com.hk

Space
2/F, East Comm. Block, Marina Square
South Horizons, Ap Lei Chau
2814-9576
Prada, Miu Miu, Helmut Lang.

Armani Outlet
22/F, Horizon Plaza, 2 Lee Wing St, Ap Lei Chau
2552-9880

Fairton Labels Fashion Warehouse
19/F, Horizon Plaza, 2 Lee Wing St, Ap Lei Chau
2873-2230

MaxMara Fashion Group Warehouse
27/F, Horizon Plaza, 2 Lee Wing St, Ap Lei Chau
2553-7036

WHERE CAN I BUY **CHEAP AND CHEERFUL BASICS**?

Cotton On ....
• G/F, 2–10 D'Aguilar St, Central
  2537-4267
• G/F, Imperial Bldg, 54A–66 Canton Rd, Tsim Sha Tsui
  2314-3404
• G/F, 14–24 Sai Yeung Choi St, Mong Kok
  2359-7044
www.cottonon.com.au
Popular Australian brand that carries a line of up-to-date cotton clothes and staple necessities for the closet, recently available in Hong Kong. They also stock L and XL sizes.

Uniqlo ....
• 2/F, Lee Theatre Plaza
  99 Percival St, Causeway Bay 2577-5811
• P5, wtc more, 280 Gloucester Rd, Causeway Bay
  2881-5101
• 4/F, Cityplaza, 18 Taikoo Shing Rd, Tai Koo
  2907-0302
• 2/F, Miramar Shopping Centre
  132 Nathan Rd, Tsim Sha Tsui
  2314-8886
• L1, Festival Walk, 80 Tat Chee Ave, Kowloon Tong
  2265-8586
• 1/F, Telford Plaza, Phase 1, 33 Wai Yip St, Kowloon Bay
  2756-9010
• L2, New Town Plaza, Phase 1
  Sha Tin Centre St, Sha Tin, New Territories
  2606-1126
www.uniqlo.com.hk
See website for more outlets in Kowloon and New Territories.

Esprit ....
• G/F & 1/F, Loke Yew Bldg
  50–52 Queen's Rd Central
  2523-1900
• G/F & 1/F, Lee Theatre Plaza
  99 Percival St, Causeway Bay
  2890-4390

- G/F–2/F, 44–48 Yun Ping Rd, Causeway Bay
  2890-7809
- 6/F, SOGO, 555 Hennessy Rd, Causeway Bay
  2831-3932
- 2/F, Cityplaza, 18 Taikoo Shing Rd, Tai Koo
  2907-0022
- G/F, Miramar Shopping Centre
  132 Nathan Rd, Tsim Sha Tsui
  2957-8400
- G/F & UG/F, China Hong Kong City
  33 Canton Rd, Tsim Sha Tsui
  2730-2073
- G/F & Basement, Kaiseng Comm. Centre
  4–6 Hankow Rd, Tsim Sha Tsui
  2721-3318
- L1, Langham Place, 8 Argyle St, Mong Kok
  3514-4177
- Basement, Hollywood Plaza
  610 Nathan Rd, Mong Kok
  2388-0064
- G/F–2/F, Wai Fung Plaza
  664 Nathan Rd, Mong Kok
  2343-7077
- 2/F, Grand Century Plaza
  193 Prince Edward Rd West, Mong Kok
  2628-3223
- G/F & B1, Fashion World, Site 2
  Whampoa Garden, Hung Hom
  2334-2273
- L1, Festival Walk, 80 Tat Chee Ave, Kowloon Tong
  2265-8228
- L4, New Town Plaza, Phase 1
  Sha Tin Centre St, Sha Tin, New Territories
  2681-2286
- 2/F, Citygate Outlets
  20 Tat Tung Rd, Tung Chung, Lantau Island
  2109-3221

www.esprit.com
See website for more outlets in Kowloon and New Territories.

Giordano Ladies ....
See pages 109–110
See also EVERYTHING STANLEY, pages 187–189.

I'M LOOKING FOR A **UNIQUE DRESS/OUTFIT FOR A COCKTAIL PARTY**. ANY SUGGESTIONS?

Mint & Lemongrass
32 Staunton St, SoHo
2868-2380
Brands Boutique
G/F, 41 Hollywood Rd, Central
2851-3111
Ranee K
2108-4068
www.raneek.com
Shhhh
G/F, 14D–14F Elgin St, SoHo
2865-7235
www.shhhh.biz

Fang Fong
- G/F, 69 Peel St, SoHo
  3105-5557
- G/F, 47 Staunton St, SoHo
  2857-2057

Limited collection of dresses with unique fabrics and prints. They also make bespoke gowns for special occasions. You can find a casual dress from $1,000 up. Also carry vintage shoes, handbags, tops, skirts and accessories.

Trace
4/F, 9 On Lan St, Central
2526-6912

Hip fashion boutique stocked with designer clothes and handbags. Look here also for personal shopping.

Ben Yeung Ltd
8/F, Canton House, 54–56 Queen's Rd Central
2523-1319

WHERE CAN I BUY **EVENING WEAR** IN WESTERN SIZES?

Dorian Ho
- Lane Crawford
  L3, IFC Mall, 8 Finance St, Central
  2118-3388
- Lane Crawford
  Marco Polo Hongkong Hotel
  Harbour City, 3 Canton Rd, Tsim Sha Tsui
  2118-3428
- For custom-made gowns (by appointment only):
  2/F, Prince Ind. Bldg, 106 King Fuk St, San Po Kong
2882-7586
www.dorianho.net

Established designer offering everything from day-to-day wear, to bridal/evening couture. Dorian Ho has a line of ready-to-wear evening and cocktail dresses in US sizes 2–14.

Sparkle Fashion
6/F, Pedder Bldg, 12 Pedder St, Central
2524-2992

Cocktail and evening wear in sizes 4–16 imported from France, the US and Canada, starting from $2,000.

Evelyn B Fashion
3/F, Grand Progress Bldg
15–16 Lan Kwai Fong, Central
2523-9506

Imported ball gowns from New York, from $500 and up, with a good range in sizes up to 16 US.

Ruby Li
1/F, Vienna Mansion55 Paterson St, Causeway Bay
2882-9309
www.rubyli.com.hk

Uma Miy
1/F, Alfred House, 9 On Lan St, Central
2869-1269

Chic new boutique featuring quirky classic designs and fashion-forward pieces from local and international labels such as Among Strangers, Bliss Lau, Camilla Skovgaard, Tashkent and De La Luce.

Amours Antiques
G/F, 45 Staunton St, Central
2803-7877
This store has a wide range of vintage items dating back as early as the 1930s. You will find vintage clothes, hats, jewellery, ornaments, handbags and accessories.

Midwest ....
G/F, Victoria Centre, 15 Watson Rd, Fortress Hill
2802-6886
www.midwest-vintage.com
Specialising in casual vintage American clothing and accessories. The shop also has a full-time seamstress who can make transformations and alterations for custom-fitting and remodelling of old clothes.

Clover by Dilys Chan
58 Lyndhurst Terrace, Central
9462-1268
Stocking new and vintage fashions and accessories ranging from furs and dresses to hats, jewellery and handbags.

Select 18 ....
G/F, Grandview Garden, 18 Bridges St, SoHo
9310-6768
Great little treasure trove offering vintage clothing, shoes, bags, jewellery, menswear and retro eyeglasses (both new and used). They also accept consignment pieces if you have any vintage items you'd like to part with.

Vintage HK
G/F, 57–59 Hollywood Rd, Central
2545-9932
Although not entirely vintage, this shop also carries fairly new items that have character, including accessories, clothing, hats and jewellery.

Beatniks ....
G/F, 32 Graham St, Central
2881-7153
Offers 1960s and 1970s clothing for men and women.

Retrostone Used Clothes and Accessories
• 2/F, 1 Cannon St, Causeway Bay
   3107-9131
• 1/F, 504 Lockhart Rd, Causeway Bay
   2838-6419
• Trendy Zone, 580A Nathan Rd, Mong Kok
   2152-9697
This basic second-hand store offers jeans, T-shirts and nostalgic clothing sourced primarily from Thailand and Southeast Asia.

The 3rd Avenue Ltd
3/F, Pedder Bldg, 12 Pedder St, Central
2537-9168
www.3rd-ave.com.hk
In Place
4/F, Pedder Bldg, 12 Pedder St, Central
2808-1883

Milan Station
- G/F, 26 Wellington St, Central
  2736-3388
- G/F, Percival House
  77–83 Percival St, Causeway Bay
  2504-0128
- G/F, Cigna Tower, 482 Jaffe Rd, Causeway Bay
  2838-1618
- G/F, 46 Haiphong Rd, Tsim Sha Tsui
  2366-0332
- G/F, 81 Chatham Rd South, Tsim Sha Tsui
  2730-2528
- G/F, Pakpoleee Comm. Centre
  1A–1K Sai Yeung Choi St South, Mong Kok
  2782-0033
www.milanstation.com.hk
*See website for more outlets in Kowloon and New
Territories.*

**WHERE CAN I BUY THE LATEST STYLES IN
DESIGNER DENIM/HIP STREETWEAR?**

Indigo Designer Denim Bar & Contemporary Clothing
G/F, 32A Staunton St, SoHo
2147-3000
Addiction ....
1/F, 21–23 Lan Fong Rd, Causeway Bay
2869-4883
www.shopaddiction.com
The latest in stylish American must-haves.
Christian Audigier ....
- L3, IFC Mall, 8 Finance St, Central
  2801-4505
- 2/F, Gateway Arcade, Harbour City
  Canton Rd, Tsim Sha Tsui
  2375-4505
www.edhardy.hk/stores.php
Ultra-cool shirts, tees, jackets, hats and denim.
True Religion ....
- L3, IFC Mall, 8 Finance St, Central
  3101-0734
- 4/F, Harvey Nichols, The Landmark
  15 Queen's Rd Central
  3695-3502
- L1, Seibu, Pacific Place
  88 Queensway, Admiralty
  2971-3825
- Bauhaus, G/F–3/F, 2 Yiu Wa St, Causeway Bay
  2891-6811
- Club 8, 1/F, 19 Yun Ping Rd, Causeway Bay
  2972-2680
www.truereligionbrandjeans.com
7 For all Mankind ....
- L3, IFC Mall, 8 Finance St, Central
  2234-7742
- 3/F, Ocean Terminal, Harbour City
  Canton Rd, Tsim Sha Tsui
  2736-0202
www.7forallmankind.com

Deep Anger ....
2/F, 7 Lan Fong Rd, Causeway Bay
2869-8303
www.deepanger.com
*Locally designed streetwear meets slightly gothic
bikerwear, with a strong following of cool Hong Kong
urbanites.*

Replay ....
• 6/F, Times Square, 1 Matheson St, Causeway Bay
• 1/F, LCX, Fashion Walk, 9 Kingston St, Causeway Bay
• 2/F, Gateway Arcade, Harbour City
  Canton Rd, Tsim Sha Tsui
• LCX, 3/F, Ocean Terminal, Harbour City
  Canton Rd, Tsim Sha Tsui
2377-2665
www.replay.it

Lucky Brand ....
• L3, IFC Mall, 8 Finance St, Central
  2234-7473
• LCX, 3/F, Harbour City, Canton Rd, Tsim Sha Tsui
  2314-8278
• Sole Town, Hang Lung Centre
  2–20 Paterson St, Causeway Bay
  2577-8302
• 1/F, Elements Mall, 1 Austin Rd West, Kowloon
  2196-8202
www.luckybrand.com

Evisu ....
• L3, IFC Mall, 8 Finance St, Central
  2234-7266
• 3/F, Ocean Terminal, Harbour City
  Canton Rd, Tsim Sha Tsui
  2376-1955
• J-01, G/F, Miramar Shopping Centre
  132 Nathan Rd, Tsim Sha Tsui
  2375-7010
• J-01, G/F, Haywood Mansion
  Fashion Walk, 57 Paterson St, Causeway Bay
  2808-0501
• D-mop
  See pages 105–106
• Lane Crawford
  See page 120
www.evisu.com

Calvin Klein Jeans ....
See pages 108–109

Diesel ....
• G/F, Pacific House, 20 Queen's Rd Central
  2525-0540
• G/F, Vancouver Mansion, 6 Kingston St, Causeway Bay
  2895-1592
• 1/F, LCX, Fashion Walk, 9 Kingston St, Causeway Bay
  2521-2006
• 2/F, Gateway Arcade, Harbour City
  Canton Rd, Tsim Sha Tsui
  2117-0418
• 2/F, Elements Mall, 1 Austin Rd West, Kowloon
  2196-8445
• LG2, Festival Walk, 80 Tat Chee Ave, Kowloon Tong
  2265-8275
www.diesel.com

Miss Sixty ....
- 3/F, SOGO, 555 Hennessy Rd, Causeway Bay
  2831-8413
- G/F, Vienna Mansion, 55 Paterson St, Causeway Bay
  2892-0905
- LCX, 3/F, Ocean Terminal, Harbour City
  Canton Rd, Tsim Sha Tsui
  2377-0375
- 2/F, SOGO, 12 Salisbury Rd, Tsim Sha Tsui
  3556-1107
- L4, New Town Plaza, Phase 1
  Sha Tin Centre St, Sha Tin, New Territories
  2970-3069
www.misssixty.com

Bauhaus ....
- 6/F, Times Square, 1 Matheson St, Causeway Bay
  2506-9678
- G/F–3/F, 496–498 Lockhart Rd, Causeway Bay
  2838-6228
- G/F–3/F, 2 Yiu Wa St, Causeway Bay
  2891-6811
- G/F, Island Beverley, Causeway Bay
  2882-3551
- 1/F, Fashion Walk, 9 Kingston St, Causeway Bay
  2881-0817
- 2/F, Gateway Arcade, Harbour City
  Canton Rd, Tsim Sha Tsui
  2175-3002
- LCX, 3/F, Ocean Terminal, Harbour City
  Canton Rd, Tsim Sha Tsui
  2375-7890
- 2/F, Silvercord, Tower 1, 30 Canton Rd, Tsim Sha Tsui
  2375-6368
- G/F, 176 Nathan Rd, Tsim Sha Tsui
  2314-7515
- G/F, Ginza Plaza, 2A Sai Yeung Choi St, Mong Kok
  2332-0166
- L5, Langham Place, 8 Argyle St, Mong Kok
  3514-4331
- UG, Festival Walk, 80 Tat Chee Ave, Kowloon Tong
  2265-8066
- 2/F, Citygate Outlets
  20 Tat Tung Rd, Tung Chung, Lantau Island
  2109-4686
www.bauhaus.com.hk
Streetwear meets grunge; hip and popular with the
younger crowd. See website for other outlets in Kowloon
and New Territories.

Spy By Henry Lau ....
- G/F, 21 Staunton St, SoHo
  2530-3128
- G/F, 11 Sharp St East, Causeway Bay
  2893-7799
- 1/F, Cleveland Mansion, 5 Cleveland St, Causeway Bay
  2317-0806
- 4/F, Rise Comm. Bldg
  5–11 Granville Circuit, Tsim Sha Tsui
  2366-5866
www.spyhenrylau.com
Well-priced men's and women's limited-run hip
streetwear, with new lines/styles introduced regularly.

Dusty ....
- G/F, Tak Cheong Comm. Bldg
  215 Portland St, Mong Kok
  2789-2177
- 1/F, Allied Plaza, 760 Nathan Rd, Prince Edward
  2789-1178
- 3/F, Tuen Mun Town Plaza, Phase 1
  1 Tuen Shun St, Tuen Mun, New Territories
  3741-0579

www.dusty.com.hk

Lane Crawford ....
- L3, IFC Mall, 8 Finance St, Central
  2118-3388
- L1 & L2, Pacific Place, 88 Queensway, Admiralty
  2118-3668
- G/F–1/F, Times Square, 1 Matheson St, Causeway Bay
  2118-3638
- Marco Polo Hongkong Hotel, Harbour City
  3 Canton Rd, Tsim Sha Tsui
  2118-3428

www.lanecrawford.com

Jeanious ....
51 Staunton St, SoHo
2189-7148
A hip new men's store carrying stylish clothing and designer jeans, including True Religion jeans. Sizes up to 36" waist.

GAS Store LCX ....
3/F, Ocean Terminal, Harbour City
Canton Rd, Tsim Sha Tsui
2730-8288
Hip clothes for men, ladies and kids.

Ruby Li
1/F, Vienna Mansion, 55 Paterson St, Causeway Bay
2882-9309
www.rubyli.com.hk

Uma Miy
1/F, Alfred House, 9 On Lan St, Central
2869-1269

double-park ....
UG, Festival Walk, 80 Tat Chee Ave, Kowloon Tong
2265-8858

Charcoal Grey
L1, Festival Walk, 80 Tat Chee Ave, Kowloon Tong
3105-5931

8Five2 ....
2/F, United Success Comm. Centre
506–508 Jaffe Rd, Causeway Bay
2573-9872
www.8five2.com

I'M LOOKING FOR THE LATEST IN **HIP CASUAL/ SPORTS SHOES**. WHERE SHOULD I GO?

Camper ....
- 5/F, Times Square, 1 Matheson St, Causeway Bay
  2506-9051
- G/F, Fashion Walk, 9 Kingston St, Causeway Bay
  2882-7810

- 1/F, Silvercord, 30 Canton Rd, Tsim Sha Tsui
  2377-1021
- L3, Langham Place, 8 Argyle St, Mong Kok
  3514-4150
- UG, Festival Walk, 80 Tat Chee Ave, Kowloon Tong
  2265-8821
- Concourse, APM, 418 Kwun Tong Rd, Kwun Tong
  3148-1413
- L5, New Town Plaza, Phase 1
  Sha Tin Centre St, Sha Tin, New Territories
  2605-8661

shop.camper.com
*A Spanish shoe company that carries casual shoes,
sandals and boots.*

adidas ....

- 6 Kingston St, Causeway Bay
  2504-2186
- 3/F & 4/F, SOGO, 555 Hennessy Rd, Causeway Bay
  2831-4695 / 2831-8443
- 2/F, Sands Bldg, 17 Hankow Rd, Tsim Sha Tsui
  2730-0157 / 2730-0158
- 2/F, Gateway Arcade, Harbour City
  Canton Rd, Tsim Sha Tsui
  2730-6685 / 2175-3363
- 2/F, Ocean Terminal, Harbour City
  Canton Rd, Tsim Sha Tsui
  2736-7055
- B2, SOGO, 12 Salisbury Rd, Tsim Sha Tsui
  3556-1110
- 4/F, APM, 418 Kwun Tong Rd, Kwun Tong
  2950-0832
- L2, Festival Walk, 80 Tat Chee Ave, Kowloon Tong
  2328-6238

www.adidas.com.hk
*Also available at Gigasports and Marathon Sports (see
page 146). Visit their website for more details.*

Catalog ....

- 4/F, Cityplaza, 18 Taikoo Shing Rd, Tai Koo
  2907-0186
- UG, Festival Walk, 80 Tat Chee Ave, Kowloon Tong
  2265-8825

agnès b. ....

- L3, IFC Mall, 8 Finance St, Central
  2805-0678
- L1, Pacific Place, 88 Queensway, Admiralty
  2918-9830
- 3/F, Times Square, 1 Matheson St, Causeway Bay
  2506-3636
- 1/F, SOGO, 555 Hennessy Rd, Causeway Bay
  2831-8922
- P1, wtc more, 280 Gloucester Rd, Causeway Bay
  2882-9839 / 2890-2989
- G/F, Lee Gardens Two
  28 Yun Ping Rd, Causeway Bay
  2882-6865
- 2–4 Kingston St, Causeway Bay
  2881-9129
- 2/F, Cityplaza, 18 Taikoo Shing Rd, Tai Koo
  2885-9803

- LCX, 3/F, Ocean Terminal, Harbour City
  Canton Rd, Tsim Sha Tsui
  2375-1889
- 2/F, Ocean Centre, Harbour City
  Canton Rd, Tsim Sha Tsui
  2175-5221
- G/F, Miramar Shopping Centre
  132 Nathan Rd, Tsim Sha Tsui
  2735-2900
- B1, SOGO, 12 Salisbury Rd, Tsim Sha Tsui
  3556-1099
- G/F, The Sun Arcade, 28 Canton Rd, Tsim Sha Tsui
  2368-6116
- Concourse, APM, 418 Kwun Tong Rd, Kwun Tong
  3148-1303
- LG1, Festival Walk, 80 Tat Chee Ave, Kowloon Tong
  2265-7018
- L3, New Town Plaza, Phase 1
  Sha Tin Centre St, Sha Tin, New Territories
  2603-0268
- L6, Departures West Hall, Terminal 1
  Hong Kong International Airport
  2261-0877

www.agnesb.com

Roots
- 2/F, Cityplaza, 18 Taikoo Shing Rd, Tai Koo
  2560-8112
- 2/F, Gateway Arcade, Harbour City
  Canton Rd, Tsim Sha Tsui
  2992-0720
- LCX, 3/F, Ocean Terminal, Harbour City
  Canton Rd, Tsim Sha Tsui
  2992-0720
- G/F, Citygate Outlets
  20 Tat Tung Rd, Tung Chung, Lantau Island
  2109-2893

www.roots.com

Lane Crawford
See page 120

D-mop
See pages 105–106

Hogan
- L3, Pacific Place, 88 Queensway, Admiralty
  2918-0181
- G/F, Gateway Arcade, Harbour City
  Canton Rd, Tsim Sha Tsui
  2175-5121

www.hoganworld.com

WHERE CAN I BUY GOOD LINGERIE/UNDERWEAR?

Chasney Beauty
6/F, Pedder Bldg, 12 Pedder St, Central
2810-8831
www.chasneybeauty.com
Sexy, sophisticated and wearable lingerie in a romantic boudoir setting.

Private Shop
- 3/F, The Landmark, 15 Queen's Rd Central
  2877-5655

- L1, Seibu, Pacific Place, 88 Queensway, Admiralty
  2971-3860
- 5/F, Times Square, 1 Matheson St, Causeway Bay
  2506-1011
- 2/F, SOGO, 555 Hennessy Rd, Causeway Bay
  2833-2415
- 1/F, Cityplaza, 18 Taikoo Shing Rd, Tai Koo
  2560-5368
- L1, Festival Walk, 80 Tat Chee Ave, Kowloon Tong
  2265-8877

www.privateshop.com.hk

Present Lingerie
G/F, 41 Staunton St, SoHo
2522-9221

Secret Wardrobe
2/F, 15B Wellington St, Central
www.secret-wardrobe.com.hk

Lane Crawford ....
See page 120
*High-end lingerie labels including Agent Provocateur,
Dolce & Gabbana, DKNY and Prada.*

Forget Me Not
9/F, Vincent House, 513 Lockhart Rd, Causeway Bay
2882-3566

La Perla
- L3, Pacific Place, 88 Queensway, Admiralty
  2118-3977
- 2/F, Gateway Arcade, Harbour City
  Canton Rd, Tsim Sha Tsui
  2118-2312
- L6, Departures East Hall, Terminal 1
  Hong Kong International Airport
  2261-0226

www.laperla.com

Calvin Klein Underwear ....
- G/F, 62 Queen's Rd Central
  2526-6805
- G/F, Duke Wellington House, 18 Wellington St, Central
  2526-8113
- Seibu, L1, Pacific Place, 88 Queensway, Admiralty
  2918-1565
- 1/F, Queensway Plaza, 93 Queensway, Admiralty
  2865-4315
- 5/F, Times Square, 1 Matheson St, Causeway Bay
  2506-9126
- 2/F & 5/F, SOGO, 555 Hennessy Rd, Causeway Bay
  2831-8616 / 2831-8609
- 1/F, Lee Gardens Two, 28 Yun Ping Rd, Causeway Bay
  2577-5133
- G/F, Fashion Island, Causeway Bay
  2808-4699
- 1/F, Cityplaza, 18 Taikoo Shing Rd, Tai Koo
  2915-3230
- 2/F, Gateway Arcade, Harbour City
  Canton Rd, Tsim Sha Tsui
  2116-0602
- G/F, Silvercord, 30 Canton Rd, Tsim Sha Tsui
  2317-5365
- B1, SOGO, 12 Salisbury Rd, Tsim Sha Tsui
  3556-1012

- 1/F, Miramar Shopping Centre
  132 Nathan Rd, Tsim Sha Tsui
  2730-5771
- 1/F, Elements Mall, 1 Austin Rd West, Kowloon
  2196-8906
- L3, Langham Place, 8 Argyle St, Mong Kok
  3514-9022
- L1, Festival Walk
  80 Tat Chee Ave, Kowloon Tong
  2265-8891
- G/F, Telford Plaza 1
  33 Wai Yip St, Kowloon Bay
  2759-4225
- Upper Concourse, APM
  148 Kwun Tong Rd, Kwun Tong
  3148-1208
- YATA, L2 & L3, New Town Plaza, Phase 3
  Sha Tin Centre St, Sha Tin, New Territories
  2697-4720
- 2/F, Citygate Outlets
  20 Tat Tung Rd, Tung Chung, Lantau Island
  2109-3622
- L5, Terminal 2, Hong Kong International Airport
  3197-9460

www.calvinklein.com

Marks & Spencer
See page 107
A huge selection for every need, with styles ranging from the athletic and functional to the seductive.

Bralicious
9772-3864
www.bralicious.com.hk
Specialising in lingerie imported from New Zealand, Australia and around the world, their lines also include maternity and larger bust sizes.

Private Structure
6/F, Ko Wah Bldg
69 Percival St, Causeway Bay
2777-7917
www.privatestructure.hk
Fun, sexy, non-traditional and comfortable underwear for men and women. They also carry men's swimwear and gym wear.

Gentleman's Agreement
Mezzanine, 11E Aberdeen St, Central
2850-4666
www.g-agreement.com
Numerous men's underwear brands ranging from sexy and revealing to boyish and basic. They also carry seductive swimwear for men and boyish briefs for women.

WHERE IS A GOOD PLACE TO BUY HIGH-QUALITY CASHMERE IN FASHIONABLE STYLES?

Pearls & Cashmere
- Mezzanine, The Peninsula Hotel
  Salisbury Rd, Tsim Sha Tsui
  2723-8698
- Mezzanine, Mandarin Oriental Hotel
  5 Connaught Rd Central
  2525-6771

Cashmere & Seta
Mezzanine, The Peninsula Hotel
Salisbury Rd, Tsim Sha Tsui
2724-6585

Tabla
Mezzanine, Prince's Bldg, 10 Chater Rd, Central
2525-5590 / 9755-6669
www.tabla.hk

Dorfit
• 6/F, Pedder Bldg, 12 Pedder St, Central
  2501-0018
• 6/F, Mary Bldg, 71–77 Peking Rd, Tsim Sha Tsui
  2312-1013
www.dorfit.com.hk

Vica Moda Ltd
• 1/F, Bank of East Asia Bldg
  10 Des Voeux Rd Central
  2522-1331
• LG/F, Leighton Centre
  77 Leighton Rd, Causeway Bay
  2808-1482
• Basement, The Peninsula Hotel
  Salisbury Rd, Tsim Sha Tsui
  2723-8283
www.vicamoda.com.hk

Fable
4/F, Pedder Bldg, 12 Pedder St, Central
2530-5148

I'M A **FAN OF FUR**. WHERE DO YOU SUGGEST I LOOK
FOR FUR CLOTHING?

Siberian Fur Store Ltd
G/F, 29 Des Voeux Rd Central
2522-1380
*Specialising in top quality furs since 1935. The place to
go if you're serious about buying a fur coat.*

Fu Collection
6/F, Pedder Bldg, 12 Pedder St, Central
2524-2992 / 9871-2397

Fook Lee Fur & Fashion Co.
1/F, Melbourne Plaza, 33 Queen's Rd Central
2525-3654
www.yp.com.hk/fooklee
Ready and made-to-measure furs.

Twiggy
G/F, 9 On Lan St, Central
2882-1088
*A great source for reasonably priced fur jackets, wraps
and shawls. Also pashmina and embroidered cashmere
wraps and cover-ups.*

Casa de Jianette
G/F, Yee Fung Bldg, 1 Village Rd, Happy Valley
2838-7236

Vica Moda Ltd
See above
Inexpensive fur jackets, shawls and leather jackets.

Deep Winter Fur Co.
12/F, Valiant Comm. Bldg
22 Prat Ave, Tsim Sha Tsui
2739-6622

WHERE CAN I FIND **MEN'S CLOTHING** AND SHOPS
THAT CARRY WESTERN SIZING?

Brooks Brothers

- G/F & Mezzanine, Prince's Bldg
  10 Chater Rd, Central
  2523-3366
- L1, IFC Mall, 8 Finance St, Central
  2234-7088
- Seibu, L2, Pacific Place, 88 Queensway, Admiralty
  2918-1722
- 3/F, Times Square, 1 Matheson St, Causeway Bay
  2506-0833
- 1/F & 5/F, SOGO, 555 Hennessy Rd, Causeway Bay
  2834-7667 / 2882-6960
- 3/F, Ocean Terminal, Harbour City
  Canton Rd, Tsim Sha Tsui
  2175-4288
- Seibu, B3, Kowloon Hotel
  19–21 Nathan Rd, Tsim Sha Tsui
  2127-4718
- 2/F, Elements Mall, 1 Austin Rd West, Kowloon
  2196-8090
- LG2, Festival Walk, 80 Tat Chee Ave, Kowloon Tong
  2778-0200

www.brooksbrothers.com

5cm

- 51 Paterson St, Causeway Bay
  2890-9336
- LG, Festival Walk, 80 Tat Chee Ave, Kowloon Tong
  2265-7823

*Cool, affordable street clothes for men with sizes up to
large, or 36" waist.*

Chocoolate

- G/F, 537 Lockhart Rd, Causeway Bay
  2572-6687
- G/F, 100 Canton Rd, Tsim Sha Tsui
  2375-2126
- G/F, 63 Granville Rd, Tsim Sha Tsui
  2739-7798
- L6, Langham Place, 8 Argyle St, Mong Kok
  3514-9303
- G/F, 2A Sai Yeung Choi St South, Mong Kok
  2771-9048
- L1, Festival Walk, 80 Tat Chee Ave, Kowloon Tong
  2265-7521
- 2/F, APM, 418 Kwun Tong Rd, Kwun Tong
  3148-1120 / 3148-1223
- L4, New Town Plaza, Phase 1
  Sha Tin Centre St, Sha Tin, New Territories
  2696-3935
- 3/F, Tuen Mun Town Plaza
  1 Tuen Shun St, Tuen Mun, New Territories
  2441-9772

www.chocoolate.hk

The Black Store PUMA

L1, IFC Mall, 8 Finance St, Central
2234-7482
www.puma.com

adidas

See page 121

EVERYTHING FASHION & SHOPPING

MEN IT · ART IT · SEQUIN IT · DESIGN IT · SPORT IT · BABY IT · BARGAIN IT · CUSTOM IT · SHOE IT · SEW IT · MEND IT · FANCY IT

Nike ....
- G/F, 7 Pak Sha Rd, Causeway Bay
  2577-0703
- 4/F, SOGO, 555 Hennessy Rd, Causeway Bay
  2895-5668
- 2/F, Gateway Arcade, Harbour City
  Canton Rd, Tsim Sha Tsui
  2895-5912
- G/F, Silvercord, 30 Canton Rd, Tsim Sha Tsui
  2375-2175
www.nike.com.hk

Zara ....
See page 107

Y-3 ....
- L1, IFC Mall, 8 Finance St, Central
  2506-2071
- G/F, Vienna Mansion, Fashion Walk
  55 Paterson St, Causeway Bay
  2894-8368
- 3/F, Ocean Terminal, Harbour City
  Canton Rd, Tsim Sha Tsui
  2730-7115
www.adidas.com/campaigns/y-3
Also available at most D-mop outlets (see pages 105–106).

See also listings with ⬆ from stylish boutiques and designer-look clothes, pages 105–114.

I'M LOOKING FOR MEN'S DRESS AND CASUAL SHOES IN LARGE SIZES. WHERE SHOULD I START?

Church's ....
- L3, Pacific Place, 88 Queensway, Admiralty
  2918-1091
- G/F, Prince's Bldg, 10 Chater Rd, Central
  2536-0462
- 2/F, Elements Mall, 1 Austin Rd West, Kowloon
  2196-8452
www.church-footwear.com

Brooks Brothers ....
See page 126

Massimo Dutti ....
See page 108

Tassels Gentlemen's Shoe Store ....
2/F, 9 On Lan St, Central
2789-9911
www.tassels.com.hk
Exclusive top quality men's shoes.

Zara ....
See page 107

Cole Haan ....
- L2, IFC Mall, 8 Finance St, Central
  2234-7679
- LG1, Festival Walk, 80 Tat Chee Ave, Kowloon Tong
  2265-8386
www.colehaan.com

Moustache ....
31 Aberdeen St, Sheung Wan
2541-1955
www.moustachehongkong.com

WHERE CAN I FIND GOOD QUALITY MEN'S BOXER SHORTS AND SOCKS?

Marks & Spencer
See page 107

Brooks Brothers
See page 126

Massimo Dutti
See page 108

Zara
See page 107

Calvin Klein Underwear
See pages 123 – 124

HOW ABOUT SOME STYLISH AND FUN UNDERWEAR FOR MEN?

U&S Concept Shop
2/F, 13 Lee Garden Rd, Causeway Bay
2890-8675 / 6742-5888
www.toot-hk.com
U&S is the sole agent for Japanese underwear brand Toot which puts colour, style and fun into men's briefs. The store also carries Ginch Gonch from Vancouver and swimwear for men.

Private Structure
6/F, Ko Wah Bldg
69 Percival St, Causeway Bay
2777-7917
www.privatestructure.hk

Gentleman's Agreement
Mezzanine, 11E Aberdeen St, Central
2850-4666
www.g-agreement.com

WHERE CAN I FIND MEN'S CASUAL WEAR AT DISCOUNT PRICES?

Sun and Moon Fashion
• 18A – B Stanley Main St, Stanley
  2813-2723 / 2813-7829
• G/F, 15 – 19 Carnavon Rd, Tsim Sha Tsui
  2367-1636
Outlet store for casual/sportswear, and ski wear during the winter months.

Five Outlet (Hong Kong) Fashion Ltd
G/F, 52 – 56C Stanley Main St, Stanley
2899-0517
Men's casual clothes, including very large sizes.

Take it Easy
G/F, 5B Stanley Main St, Stanley
2899-0322
Abercrombie, surf and casual wear in Western sizes for men and women. Hip street clothes; sometimes you may find designer denim.

44 Stanley Main St, Stanley
2813-9777
Sells branded ski wear and surfwear, as well as casual clothes and shoes. You will also be able to find surfer flip-flops by Flojo for women.

WHERE CAN I FIND A DRESSMAKER/DESIGNER TO MAKE A GORGEOUS FROCK?

Soong Salon de Mode
2/F, Hanchung Mansion
8–10 Hankow Rd, Tsim Sha Tsui
2723-1400
Excellent workmanship. Especially good for executing your own designs or copying original pieces. By appointment only.

Kanchan Couture
2/F, 108–110 Wellington St, Central
2117-1782
www.kanchancouture.com
Bespoke dresses—expect 3 to 6 months for completion. Original designs inspired by a rich heritage including Indian, Chinese and Western influences.

Cecilia Yau Couture
UG/F, 168 Queen's Rd Central
(Entrance at Wellington St)
2851-7171
www.cecilia-yau.com
Cecilia Yau's award-winning designs are fresh and cutting-edge. She offers both wedding and evening wear.

Dorian Ho
See page 115

Margaret Court Tailoress Co.
8/F, Winner Bldg, 27–37 D'Aguilar St, Central
2525-5596
Specialising in ladies' dresses, gowns and bridal wear. Excellent finishes for that special piece.

Irene Fashions
3/F, Tung Chai Bldg, 86–90 Wellington St, Central
2850-5635
Reasonably priced tailor for women; known for her mastery in custom-fit clothing.

Siriporn
1/F, 28 Cochrane St, Central
2866-6668
Recommended for evening wear and bridesmaids' dresses.

Virginia Wong
6/F, Hung Kee Mansion, 5 Queen Victoria St, Central
2524-8397
Well-known tailor to the rich and famous. She can copy and make anything from evening to casual wear.

Ranee K
2108-4068
www.raneek.com

Long Kong Ladies' Tailors .... ☝
5 Sharp Street East, Causeway Bay
2891-8512
50s and 60s-style dresses. Prices start from $2,500. Take a translator with you.

ARE THERE ANY LOCAL UP-AND-COMING OR ESTABLISHED DESIGNERS YOU RECOMMEND FOR READY-MADE OR MADE-TO-MEASURE?

Kanchan Couture
See above
Dorian Ho
See page 115

Cecilia Yau Couture
UG/F, 168 Queen's Rd Central
2851-7171
www.cecilia-yau.com

BEA WORKSHOP Ltd
G/F, Block B, 58 & 60 Peel St, Central
2537-6292

Ranee K
2108-4068
www.raneek.com

Bonita Cheung
2/F, 85 Queen's Rd Central
2868-2820
www.bonitacheung.com
Evening wear, party separates and cocktail dresses.

The New Shop
G/F, 121 Wellington St, Central
2541-2881
Eclectic fabrics, hip designs and evening wear by Peter Lau and Nio Lam.

Ruby Li
1/F, Vienna Mansion, 55 Paterson St, Causeway Bay
2882-9309
www.rubyli.com.hk
Known for her stylish and funky line of women's clothing, accessories and jewellery. She has also undertaken bespoke costume design for famous Hong Kong performers and actresses.

IKA
8/F, Kam Hing Bldg, 20 Hillwood Rd, Tsim Sha Tsui
2724-1818
www.ikabutoni.com
Indonesian-born, Hong Kong-based designer who uses exotic styling, colours and embroidery in her collections. Also has a men's line.

Pristine Couture
1/F, InnoCentre, 72 Tat Chee Ave, Kowloon Tong
2523-2396
www.pristinehk.com
Designed by Ivy Ngan, Pristine Couture offers timeless and elegant evening wear. By appointment only.

I DON'T HAVE TIME TO TREK UP TO SHENZHEN. ARE THERE ANY **REASONABLY-PRICED DRESSMAKERS** IN HONG KONG?

Fung Ling Fashion
11/F, Winner Bldg, 27–37 D'Aguilar St, Central
2521-2133

Ah Wai Ladies Tailor
1/F, 108–110 Wellington St, Central
2524-6423

Aida Fashion Workshop
5/F, Commercial House, 35 Queen's Rd Central
2537-4836

Shing Yue Shanghai Tailor Co.
10/F, Yau Shing Bldg
120 Wing Lok St, Sheung Wan
3114-7527 / 6588-3488
Great for copying clothes you bring in. She is very cheap but doesn't speak English.

EVERYTHING FASHION & SHOPPING

WHERE DO I GO TO GET VINTAGE OR OLD DESIGNER **CLOTHING REDESIGNED**?

Gorgeous by Lydia
5/F, Yuen Yick Bldg, 27 Wellington St, Central
2522-5788 / 9101-7966
Beyond quality dressmaking, Lydia is excellent at revamping vintage clothing to look creative and fresh.

WHERE CAN I GET **CUSTOM-MADE FUR CLOTHING**?

Black & White
2/F, Melbourne Plaza, 33 Queen's Rd Central
2523-4380
Design your own fur coat and have it made here.

Fook Lee Fur & Fashion Co.
1/F, Melbourne Plaza, 33 Queen's Rd Central
2525-3654
www.yp.com.hk/fooklee

WHERE CAN I FIND A **STYLISH BRIDAL SALON**?

Marriage Maestros
8/F, 66 Wellington St, Central
2546-0049 / 2546-0085
www.marriagemaestros.com

Central Weddings and Occasions
35/F, Edinburgh Tower, The Landmark
15 Queen's Rd Central
2869-8666
www.centralweddings.com
A one-stop bridal destination for those wanting the absolute best. They can assist you with everything from wedding attire, flowers and styling, to photography. By appointment only.

Cecilia Yau Couture
UG/F, 168 Queen's Rd Central
(Entrance at Wellington St)
2851-7171

White Bridal Couture
G/F, 17 Lyndhurst Terrace, Central
2521-3288
www.whitebridal.com.hk

The Wedding Company
10/F, Ming Fat Bldg
74 Wellington St, Central
2869-4222
www.theweddingco.hk

The Wedding Shop
4/F, On Lan Centre
11 – 15 On Lan St, Central
2537-0322
www.theweddingshop.com.hk

Anaiss on Wedding
3/F, Tak Woo House
17 – 19 D'Aguilar St, Central
2522-2030
By appointment only.

Gianni Castelli Moda
G/F, 176 Wellington St, Central
2815-6028
www.giannicastelli.com

WHERE CAN I BUY A READY-TO-WEAR CHEONGSAM, OR GET ONE MADE?

Linva Tailors
G/F, 38 Cochrane St, Central
2544-2456

Shanghai Tang
See pages 106–107

Maymayking
Stockists:

- Sole Cultural Goods
  G/F, Dr Sun Yat-Sen Museum
  7 Castle Rd, Mid-Levels
  2899-2189
- LCX, 3/F, Ocean Terminal, Harbour City
  Canton Rd, Tsim Sha Tsui
  3102-3668
- Tai Yip Art Book Centre
  1/F, Hong Kong Museum of Art
  10 Salisbury Rd, Tsim Sha Tsui
  2732-2088
- Sole Cultural Goods
  G/F, Hong Kong Heritage Museum
  1 Man Lam Rd, Sha Tin, New Territories
  2699-3098

Enquiries: 2445-5655
www.maymayking.com
An eclectic mix of women's clothing, bags, shoes and accessories.

Barney Cheng Yenrabi Ltd
12/F, World Wide Comm. Bldg
34 Wyndham St, Central
2530-2829
www.barneycheng.com

Dorian Ho
See page 115

Blanc de Chine
- 2/F, Pedder Bldg, 12 Pedder St, Central
  2524-7875
- 2/F, The Landmark, 15 Queen's Rd Central
  2104-7934
www.blancdechine.com
Contemporary Chinese-inspired clothing with clean, simple lines.

Zeepha Couture
G/F, New Henry House, 10 Ice House St, Central
2523-2845
www.zeephacouture.com
Cheongsam maker.

Vogue Tailor
Basement, Starhouse Plaza, Star House
3 Salisbury Rd, Tsim Sha Tsui
2314-8016
www.voguetailor.com

Yue Hwa
301–309 Nathan Rd, Jordan
2522-2333
www.yuehwa.com

ARE THERE ANY TAILORS THAT SPECIALISE IN
TRADITIONAL INDIAN CLOTHING?

Shan Enterprises
1/F, Mirador Mansion, 58 Nathan Rd, Tsim Sha Tsui
2366-9602 / 6856-6645

WHERE CAN I GET A TOP QUALITY SUIT TAILORED?

William Cheng & Sons ....
8/F, Han Hing Mansion, 38 Hankow Rd, Tsim Sha Tsui
2739-7888
*Ideal for those who know what they want. Excellent
workmanship, reliable delivery time, a good selection of
fabrics and the best prices in town for a man's suit (but
no bargaining). Best for men's shirts and following any
design you can suggest. Ask for Sandy.*

Furama Tailor ....
1/F, Melbourne Plaza, 33 Queen's Rd Central
2521-6525 / 9525-9924
*A well-known, well-priced tailor who was in the Furama
Hotel before it was torn down.*

Collars & Cuffs ....
2/F, 9 Queen's Rd Central
2868-0488
They have been catering to a loyal clientele for 18 years.

Sam's Tailor ....
G/F, Burlington Arcade, 94 Nathan Rd, Tsim Sha Tsui
2367-9423
www.samstailor.com
*Tailor to the rich and famous, although they say the best
service is reserved for those who are rich and famous!*

A-Man Hing Cheong Co. Ltd ....
Mezzanine, Mandarin Oriental Hotel
5 Connaught Rd Central
2522-3336
*Famous Hong Kong tailoring institution. Top quality with
corresponding prices.*

Manesh Manolo Bespoke Tailoring ....
1/F, Wing Cheong House, 53 Queen's Rd Central
2523-5517 / 2524-8863
www.maneshmanolo.com
*They have a wide range of fabrics available, ranging
from affordable to exclusive; tailored suits start from
$1,200.*

William & Simon Tailor Co. ....
5/F, 12–16 Lyndhurst Terrace, Central
2525-6717
www.williamandsimon.com
*Men's and women's tailoring. They can also offer
competitive prices for making a boy's suit.*

Ascot Chang Co. Ltd ....
• 1/F, Prince's Bldg, 10 Chater Rd, Central
  2523-3663
• Mezzanine, The Peninsula Hotel
  Salisbury Rd, Tsim Sha Tsui
  2366-2398
• L2, IFC Mall, 8 Finance St, Central
  2295-3833
www.ascotchang.com
Well-known tailor, renowned for their men's dress shirts.

Loa Hai Shing ....
2/F, Tak Shing House, 20 Des Voeux Rd Central
2325-6167
www.lhshk.com.hk

Raja Fashions ....
• G/F, 34C Cameron Rd, Tsim Sha Tsui
  2311-1801 / 2366-1801
• UG/F, Wing On Plaza, 62 Mody Rd, Tsim Sha Tsui
  2366-1508
www.raja-fashions.com
This long-established tailor offers one of the largest in-house selections of fabrics.

Pursue ....
2/F, 13 Lan Kwai Fong, Central
2537-0993
www.pursuehk.com

W.W. Chan & Sons Tailor Ltd ....
2/F, Burlington House, 94 Nathan Rd, Tsim Sha Tsui
2366-9738 / 2366-2634
www.wwchan.com
Renowned tailor with excellent workmanship.

Gordon Yao ....
1/F, Royal Garden Hotel
69 Mody Rd, Tsim Sha Tsui East
2730-1545

WHERE CAN I **GET A KILT MADE**?

Yuen's Tailor ....
2/F, Escalator Link Alley, 80 Des Voeux Rd Central
2815-5388
Men's suits tailor that also specialises in handmade kilts, and carries a large selection of tartans.

I'M LOOKING FOR SOME **FABRIC TO TAKE TO MY TAILOR**. WHERE DO YOU SUGGEST I START?

Western Market
323 Des Voeux Rd Central, Sheung Wan
www.westernmarket.com.hk
On the first floor you will find many shops selling all kinds of practical fabrics for many uses, though nothing is very high-end.

Li Yuen St West, Central
Between Queen's Rd Central and Des Voeux Rd Central
In this well-known shopping lane, you will find a few fabric stores that are a convenient place to start.

Yau Shing Textile Co.
G/F, 208–220 Queen's Rd Central
2541-8033 / 2541-8041
See also EVERYTHING SHAM SHUI PO, page 189–191.

WHERE CAN I GO TO GET A SMALL QUANTITY OF **T-SHIRTS PRINTED**?

Jet T Technology
G/F, Lladro Centre, 72 Hoi Yuen Rd, Kwun Tong
2111-8161
www.jtt.hk

Whytecliff Trading
7A Tong Fuk, South Lantau Rd, Lantau Island
2987-5326 / 9153-2311
www.whytecliff.com

AND TO KEEP MY WARDROBE LOOKING GREAT,
WHERE CAN I BUY A HEAVY-DUTY **CLOTHES
STEAMER**?

Trade Style Ltd
7/F, Siu Wai Ind. Centre
29–33 Wing Hong St, Lai Chi Kok
2559-5533
www.tras-group.com
*A jiffy steamer from the US gives you professional-
looking results. This is what the steamer shops use.
Especially effective on knits and thinner fabrics that are
difficult to press using an iron. The J2 model sells for
around $1,300.*

WHERE CAN I BUY OR GET **FASHIONABLE WOMEN'S
SHOES** MADE?

LIII LIII
1/F, Admiralty Centre, Tower 2, 18 Harcourt Rd, Admiralty
2136-9739
*A high-end shoemaker who can replicate just about any
design you give them. Choose from their thousands of
samples and materials.*

JJ Partners
G/F, 173 Wong Nai Chung Rd, Happy Valley
2577-2383
*They can make shoes to match almost any dress colour.
They may be able to use fabric you provide.*

Perfect Shoes and Handbags
G/F, 3 Queen Victoria St, Central
2577-1771
*Affordable, simple shoes starting from $300. Also
carries larger sizes.*

GiGi (H.K.) Shoes & Handbags Co.
G/F, 171 Wong Nai Chung Rd, Happy Valley
2890-6260

Shoe Girl
G/F, 21 Yiu Wa St, Causeway Bay
2834-1023
www.shoegirl.com.hk
*Custom-made shoes and bags for brides, evening wear
and work. They are good at copying high fashion shoes
and their prices are reasonable.*

Edwina Shoes & Handbags
1/F, Admiralty Centre, Tower 1, 18 Harcourt Rd, Admiralty
2866-7183
*They can replicate from designs you provide and offer
ready-made options.*

Yue Wah Shoemaker
1 Tung Lo Wan Rd, Causeway Bay
2577-6658
Made-to-measure shoes in any style.

Cinderella Shoes & Bags
1/F, Admiralty Centre, Tower 1, 18 Harcourt Rd, Admiralty
2866-1190 / 2868-0900

WHERE CAN I BUY OR GET TOP QUALITY MEN'S SHOES MADE?

Mayer Shoes ....
Mezzanine, Mandarin Oriental Hotel
5 Connaught Rd Central
2524-3317
High-quality custom-made shoes and copies of originals in everything from crocodile to pony hair. They take a mould of your foot to make sure the fit is perfect. Also excellent for ladies' shoes, handbags, wallets and leather accessories.

Kow Hoo Shoe Co. ....
2/F, Prince's Bldg, 10 Chater Rd, Central
2523-0489
kowhoo.com.hk
Fine custom-made shoes for men, and some women's styles.

StyleMuster ....
25/F, Heng Shan Centre
145 Queen's Rd East, Wan Chai
2527-9338
www.stylemuster.com
Custom luxury European-style shoes for men, with options to purchase online. For those wanting to try before you buy, they can also arrange a fitting in the comfort of your own home. Free delivery in Hong Kong.

Tassels Gentlemen's Shoe Store ....
2/F, 9 On Lan St, Central
2789-9911
www.tassels.com.hk

WHERE CAN I GET EXPERT ALTERATIONS?

Ann & Bon (Perfect Dress Alteration Shop)
3/F, Melbourne Plaza, 33 Queen's Rd Central
2522-8838
They also do rush jobs; great for people who are not comfortable leaving their clothes with a tailor.

Thousand Bird Dress Alteration
1/F, Melbourne Plaza, 33 Queen's Rd Central
2523-4329
www.thousandbird.com.hk

Fashion Altering Co.
• 3/F, World-Wide House, 19 Des Voeux Rd Central
  2522-9657
• 2/F, Melbourne Plaza, 33 Queen's Rd Central
  2868-1713

Perfect Fashion Alteration Co.
3/F, World-Wide House, 19 Des Voeux Rd Central
2523-9816

Sincere Professional Fashion Alteration
Basement, President Shopping Centre
531 Jaffe Rd, Causeway Bay
2838-6523

Mitty Fashion Alteration
5/F, Kai Wah Bldg, 74 Wellington St, Central
2523-8786
Good-quality alterations at reasonable prices.

Wellfit Fashion Alteration Co.
2/F, World-Wide House, 19 Des Voeux Rd Central
2869-7587

Sincere Alteration
1/F, Melbourne Plaza, 33 Queen's Rd Central
2868-4133
Eva Alteration Tailor
2/F, World-Wide Plaza, 19 Des Voeux Rd Central
2523-5550
Million Fashion Altering Co.
2/F, World-Wide Plaza, 19 Des Voeux Rd Central
2526-3886

WHERE CAN I GET VERY CHEAP, **SIMPLE ALTERATIONS** DONE?

Pedder Lane
Outside Central MTR Exit D2
There are a few very reasonable alteration stalls along this lane.
Leung Kam Fat .... 💬
Pedder Lane, Central
2804-6639
Clothes mending and alteration.
Pottinger St
Between Queen's Rd Central and Stanley St, Central
There are a few good, cheap alteration stalls here as well.

I'M LOOKING FOR A **UNIQUE EVENING CLUTCH**. ANY SUGGESTIONS?

Kotur
2/F, Harvey Nichols, The Landmark, 15 Queen's Rd Central
3695-3388
www.koturltd.com
Exquisitely designed minaudires, clutches, vintage brocade clutches, shoulder bags, etc. A celebrity favourite. Also available online.

WHERE CAN I FIND **ACCESSORIES, HANDBAGS AND CLUTCHES WITH AN ASIAN FLAIR**?

Maymayking
See page 132
Tef Tef
Stockists:
• Lane Crawford, G/F & 1/F, Times Square
  1 Matheson St, Causeway Bay
  2118-3658
• The Green Lantern, G/F, 72 Peel St, SoHo
  2526-0777
• Melaine Living Arts, G/F, 37 Cochrane St, Central
  2815-7873
www.teftef.com.hk
Mischa Designs
Stockists:
• Fang Fong, G/F, 69 Peel St, SoHo
  3105-5557
• Fang Fong, G/F, 47 Staunton St, SoHo
  2857-2057
• Melaine Living Arts, G/F, 37 Cochrane St, Central
  2815-7873
• White Bridal Couture, G/F, 17 Lyndhurst Terrace, Central
  2521-3288

• HKTDC Design Gallery
  1/F, Hong Kong Convention and Exhibition Centre
  1 Harbour Rd, Wan Chai
  2584-4146 / 2584-4149
www.mischadesigns.com

Refine Designs
G/F, Fleet Arcade, 1 Lung King St, Wan Chai
2511-0021 / 9464-1941
*Christine can make to order unique purses using
Japanese fabrics and other Asian materials.*

Chako's Handmade Japanese Bags
Stockists:
• Kou Concept
  22/F, Fung House, 19–20 Connaught Rd Central
  2530-2234
• Sabina Swims, 1/F, 99F Wellington St, Central
  2115-9975
• Indigo Designer Denim Bar & Contemporary Clothing
  G/F, 32A Staunton St, SoHo
  2147-3000
• 9400-4971 (private viewing by appointment)
www.chakotokyo.com

Bez & Oho
Stockists:
• Chameleon Workshop
  2/F, Yan King Court
  119–121 Queen's Rd East, Wan Chai
  2527-2251
• Crafts (Just above Ali Oli Bakery)
  11 Sha Tsui Path, Sai Kung, New Territories
Enquiries: 9343-2362
www.bezandoho.com

Shanghai Tang
See pages 106–107

WHERE CAN I FIND **SNAKESKIN/EXOTIC HIDE HANDBAGS**?

Fiona's Collection
G/F, Amber Lodge, 23 Hollywood Rd, Central
2581-3968

Fabriano
• G/F, 81A Hollywood Rd, Central
  2736-8738
• L6, Departures East Hall, Terminal 1
  Hong Kong International Airport
www.fabriano-exotic.com

Piecco
1/F, 8 On Wo Lane, Central, Hong Kong
9431-8618

Kotur
2/F, Harvey Nichols, The Landmark, 15 Queen's Rd Central
3695-3388
www.koturltd.com

WHERE CAN I ORDER A **CUSTOM-MADE HANDBAG
WITH A PHOTO** ON IT?

Anya Hindmarch
• 2/F, Harvey Nichols, The Landmark
  15 Queen's Rd Central
  3693-4133

- 2/F, Lee Gardens, 33 Hysan Ave, Causeway Bay
  2808-0128
- 1/F, Ocean Centre, Harbour City
  Canton Rd, Tsim Sha Tsui
  2918-1689

www.anyahindmarch.com

Add any photo to a tote bag, wash bag, or top handle bag. Choose your own colour and material from their range to make an ideal gift or personalised bag for you.

Koji Bags & Accessories
2312-1591

www.kojibags.com

Available at Wing On Plaza (211 Des Voeux Rd Central), SOGO (555 Hennessy Rd, Causeway Bay) and JUSCO (2 Kornhill Rd, Quarry Bay).

WHERE CAN I BUY A PREVIOUSLY-OWNED DESIGNER HANDBAG?

Milan Station
See page 117

Paris Station
G/F, 60 Russell St, Causeway Bay
2369-3319

Fashion Line
G/F, 482 Jaffe Rd, Causeway Bay
2838-1618

Handbags in excellent condition (many new or nearly new), best brand names, current, recent and classic models that are in demand. Also a good place to trade in your designer handbags.

WHERE CAN I BUY NEW DESIGNER HANDBAGS AT MARKED DOWN PRICES?

ISA Boutique Ltd
- G/F, Alpha House, 29 Nathan Rd, Tsim Sha Tsui
  2366-5890
- LG/F, China Hong Kong City
  33 Canton Rd, Tsim Sha Tsui
  2366-5820
- 1/F, Imperial Bldg
  58 Canton Rd, Tsim Sha Tsui
  2366-5880
- B1, New World Centre
  20 Salisbury Rd, Tsim Sha Tsui
  2366-5023

www.isaboutique.com

Twist
- G/F, Wellington Place, 2–8 Wellington St, Central
  2577-9323
- P1, wtc more, 280 Gloucester Rd, Causeway Bay
  2970-2231
- Basement, The Sun Arcade, 28 Canton Rd, Tsim Sha Tsui
  2377-2880

www.twist.hk

Acetex Fashion Club
9/F, Far East Finance Centre, 16 Harcourt Rd, Admiralty
2868-6092

Milan Station
See page 117

Paris Station
G/F, 60 Russell St, Causeway Bay
2369-3319
*Although specialising in previously loved/used bags,
Milan Station and Paris Station also stock new designer
bags at below retail price.*

WHERE CAN I BUY **GOOD-QUALITY, DESIGNER-LOOK
HANDBAGS**?

Sam Wo Handbags Co.
5/F, 41–47 Queen's Rd Central
2524-0970 / 2524-1807 / 9430-4039
JJ Partners
G/F, 173 Wong Nai Chung Rd, Happy Valley
2577-2383
*In addition to handbags, they also sell and make good
quality designer-inspired shoes. There are a few more
similar shops in this area, but none quite as good as this.*
Cinderella Shoes & Bags
1/F, Admiralty Centre, Tower 1
18 Harcourt Rd, Admiralty
2866-1190 / 2868-0900

I'M ON MORE OF A BUDGET. WHERE CAN I BUY
FUN, **FASHIONABLE HANDBAGS** WITHOUT DESIGNER
PRICES?

Lianca Central
Basement, 27 Staunton St, SoHol
2139-2989
www.liancacentral.com
*Lianca makes her own fashionable handbags, wallets
and accessories. She also uses ostrich, snakeskin, pony
and other hides, and can do custom orders.*
Rabeanco
• 1/F, Man Yee Arcade, 68 Des Voeux Rd Central
  2259-5388
• Seibu, L1, Pacific Place, 88 Queensway, Admiralty
  2971-3842
• G/F, 11 Pak Sha Rd, Causeway Bay
  2890-7727
• G/F, 33 Sharp St East, Causeway Bay
  3586-0281
• SOGO, 12 Salisbury Rd, Tsim Sha Tsui
  2831-8964
• Seibu, B1, Kowloon Hotel
  19–21 Nathan Rd, Tsim Sha Tsui
  3514-9235
• G/F, Hong Kong Pacific Centre
  28 Hankow Rd, Tsim Sha Tsui
  2723-2516
• G/F, 26 Kimberley St, Tsim Sha Tsui
  2312-6098
• B1, Langham Place, 8 Argyle St, Mong Kok
  3514-4500
• Seibu, L2, Langham Place, 8 Argyle St, Mong Kok
  2269-1783
• 4/F, APM, 418 Kwun Tong Rd, Kwun Tong
  3148-9235

- YATA, L2 & L3, New Town Plaza, Phase 3
  Sha Tin Centre St, Sha Tin, New Territories
  2681-0989
- 1/F, Citygate Outlets
  20 Tat Tung Rd, Tung Chung, Lantau Island
  2109-0361
www.rabeanco.com

Kinta
G/F, 50 Staunton St, SoHo
2549-6698
www.kinta.hk

Petite Petite
G/F, 18 Aberdeen St, SoHo
2544-3604
Stylish handbags and accessories in leather, hides and more.

Refine Designs
G/F, Fleet Arcade, 1 Lung King St, Wan Chai
2511-0021 / 9464-1941

Art Cat
G/F, 8 Wong Ma Kok Rd, Stanley
2317-6227
A good range of fun handbags, scented candles, aromatherapy oils and more.

Coquette Hong Kong
www.coquettered.com
Online store for hip, fun handbags.

WHERE CAN I BUY A GOOD-LOOKING BUT
FUNCTIONAL **MURSE (MAN BAG)** OR PURSE?

Bally ....
- L2, IFC Mall, 8 Finance St, Central
  3586-2898
- L3, Pacific Place, 88 Queensway, Admiralty
  2522-8275
- SOGO, 555 Hennessy Rd, Causeway Bay
  2834-8872
- 2/F, Times Square, 1 Matheson St, Causeway Bay
  2506-3312
- G/F & Mezzanine, Prince's Bldg
  10 Chater Rd, Central
  2521-0606
- 2/F, Ocean Centre, Harbour City
  Canton Rd, Tsim Sha Tsui
  2736-8068
- Oterprise Square, 26 Nathan Rd, Tsim Sha Tsui
  2368-1041
- 90B Nathan Rd, Tsim Sha Tsui
  2366-2588
- Royal Garden Hotel, 69 Mody Rd, East Tsim Sha Tsui
  2723-0811
- LG2, Festival Walk, 80 Tat Chee Rd, Kowloon Tong
  2265-7100
experience.bally.com

Diesel ....
See page 118

Twist ....
See page 139

Dunhill .... ☂
- G/F, Prince's Bldg, 10 Chater Rd, Central
  2524-3663
- L3, Pacific Place, 88 Queensway, Admiralty
  2537-1009
- G/F, SOGO, 555 Hennessy Rd, Causeway Bay
  2893-1026
- 3/F, Times Square, 1 Matheson St, Causeway Bay
  2506-0886
- 2/F, Ocean Terminal, Harbour City
  Canton Rd, Tsim Sha Tsui
  2730-7608
- 2/F, Elements Mall, 1 Austin Rd West, Kowloon
  2196-8335
- LG, Festival Walk, 80 Tat Chee Ave, Kowloon Tong
  2265-7806
- L6, Departures East Hall, Terminal 1
  Hong Kong International Airport
  2261-0822
- L6, Departures Northwest Concourse, Terminal 1
  Hong Kong International Airport
  2383-1474
www.dunhill.com

Piquadro .... ☂
- L1, IFC Mall, 8 Finance St, Central
  2295-0933
- 3/F, Gateway Arcade, Harbour City
  Canton Rd, Tsim Sha Tsui
  2175-4833
- Basement, The Peninsula Hotel
  Salisbury Rd, Tsim Sha Tsui
  2369-3218
www.piquadro.com

Gucci .... ☂
- G/F, The Landmark, 15 Queen's Rd Central
  2524-4492
- L3, Pacific Place, 88 Queensway, Admiralty
  2524-0412
- G/F, Lee Gardens Two
  28 Yun Ping Rd, Causeway Bay
  2576-6918
- G/F, SOGO, 555 Hennessy Rd, Causeway Bay
  2893-4276
- 2/F, Times Square, 1 Matheson St, Causeway Bay
  2506-4262
- G/F, Gateway Arcade, Harbour City
  Canton Rd, Tsim Sha Tsui
  2199-7728
- 2/F, Elements Mall, 1 Austin Rd West, Kowloon
  2199-7728
- L6, Departures East Hall, Terminal 1
  Hong Kong International Airport
  2261-0538
- L6, Departures West Hall, Terminal 1
  Hong Kong International Airport
  2261-2082
www.gucci.com

agnès b. .... ☂
See pages 121 – 122

WHERE CAN I BUY **FORMAL AND FANCY HATS**?

Amours Antiques
G/F, 45 Staunton St, Central
2803-7877
They have a small selection of vintage hats, including fancy hats.

Clover by Dilys Chan
58 Lyndhurst Terrace, Central
9462-1268

Evelyn B Fashion
3/F, Grand Progress Bldg, 15–16 Lan Kwai Fong, Central
2523-9506
This ladies' formal wear shop also carries a small selection of hats.

WHERE CAN I FIND A GOOD ASSORTMENT OF **CASUAL HATS AND CAPS**?

Lids ....
- 1/F, Causeway Place
  2–10 Great George St, Causeway Bay
  3428-5686
- LCX, 3/F, Ocean Terminal, Harbour City
  Canton Rd, Tsim Sha Tsui
  3188-3948
- G/F, Park Hotel
  61–65 Chatham Rd South, Tsim Sha Tsui
  3523-0627
- L6, Langham Place, 8 Argyle St, Mong Kok
  3514-9109
- 2/F, Yuen Long Plaza
  249–251 Castle Peak Rd, Yuen Long, New Territories
  2475-6167
- UG/F, Citywalk, 1 Yeung Uk Rd
  Tsuen Wan, New Territories
  2410-0126
www.lids.com.hk
From sporty to funky to retro, you'll find a great selection here.

WHERE CAN I FIND THE BEST SHOPS FOR THE LATEST **STYLISH EYEWEAR**?

Eye'ni
- G/F, 63 Lee Garden Rd, Causeway Bay
  2882-2948
- Basement, Loke Yew Bldg, 50–52 Queen's Rd Central
  2522-1488
www.eyeni.com.hk

Berlin Optical
- L2, IFC Mall, 8 Finance St, Central
  2804-6318
- G/F, Sino Plaza
  255–257 Gloucester Rd, Causeway Bay
  2506-9368
- G/F, Park Lane Hotel
  310 Gloucester Rd, Causeway Bay
  2895-3535
www.berlinoptical.com

Alain Mikli
- G/F, 28 Wellington St, Central
  2523-0103
- L2, Pacific Place, 88 Queensway, Admiralty
  2523-0086
- LG2, Festival Walk, 80 Tat Chee Ave, Kowloon Tong
  2777-1186
www.mikli.com

The Red Lounge
11B, Aberdeen St, Central
2815-5799
www.dita.com

Bowan Optical Ltd
G/F, 45 Wellington St, Central
2868-0916
www.bowan.com.hk

WHERE CAN I FIND **DESIGNER GLASSES/SUNGLASSES AT DISCOUNTED PRICES**?

Wo Ping Optical
G/F, 278 King's Rd, North Point
2571-7810
Huge inventory of old and new designer specs, and non-big brand specs at fantastic prices. Worth the trip to North Point.

Fox Optical
G/F, Winning House, 12 Cochrane St, Central
2543-8633 / 2541-3018
Well-known source for great specs, speedy and reliable service, and good prices.

I NEED TO BUY **ATHLETIC CLOTHING, EXERCISE AND YOGA GEAR**. WHO HAS A GOOD SELECTION?

Rush
- G/F, Wyndham Mansion, 32 Wyndham St, Central
  2526-0620
- G/F, Discovery Bay Plaza
  Discovery Bay, Lantau Island
  3421-2010
www.rush.hk
Multi-brand store selling athletic, swim, yoga and footwear, including Running Bare, Wahine, Sea Folly, FitFlops, Havaianas, Crocs, Asics and more.

adidas
See page 121
adidas has just added a stylish line of women's performance active and swimwear designed by Stella McCartney.

Protrek
- 156–157 Connaught Rd Central, Sheung Wan
  2850-7900
- 46 Hennessy Rd, Wan Chai
  2529-6988
- 32 Leighton Rd, Causeway Bay
  2576-0833
- G/F, Metropole Bldg, King's Rd, North Point
  2590-7377
- G/F, Kornhill Plaza North, 1 Kornhill Rd, Tai Koo
  2885-3566

• 522 Nathan Rd, Yau Ma Tei
  2332-8699
www.protrek.com.hk
See website for more locations.

Pure Fitness
L3 & L4, IFC Mall, 8 Finance St, Central
8129-8000
www.pure-fit.com
Offers stylish yoga and athletic wear by lululemon from Canada. They also carry adidas and an assortment of yoga and sports gear.

Pure Yoga
• 16/F, The Centrium, 60 Wyndham St, Central
  2971-0055
• 25/F, Soundwill Plaza, 38 Russell St, Causeway Bay
  2970-2299
• 4/F, Lincoln House, Taikoo Place
  979 King's Rd, Quarry Bay
  8129-1188
• 14/F, The Peninsula, Office Tower
  18 Middle Rd, Tsim Sha Tsui
  8129-8800
• L7, Langham Place, Office Tower
  8 Argyle St, Mong Kok
  8129-2828
www.pure-yoga.com

Yoga 4 Yogi
3184-0841
www.yoga4yogi.com

Simply Yoga & Athletica
G/F, 14 Lyndhurst Terrace, Central
3154-9106
Specialising in yoga wear and gear.

Zobha
Stockist:
Posture Plus, 9/F, 10 Pottinger St, Central
2167-8801
www.zobha.com

Flex Yoga & Pilates Studio
1/F, Woodleigh House
80 Stanley Village Rd, Stanley
2813-2212
www.flexhk.com
Flex carries its own line of yoga wear called "Tuula".

10K Running Pro Shop ....
1/F, 169 Gloucester Rd, Wan Chai
2893-7990
www.10k.com.hk

Be Fit
1/F, Wing Fat Bldg, 3 Jervois St, Central
2815-4838
www.bfit.com.hk
Swimwear and brazilwear.

RC Outfitters ....
• 5/F & 6/F, Oriental House
  24–26 Argyle St, Mong Kok
  2390-0980
• 2/F, Kin Tak Fung Comm. Bldg
  467–473 Hennessy Rd, Causeway Bay
  2390-0020
www.alink.com.hk

Marathon Sports ....

- G/F, Yip Fung Bldg, 16 D'Aguilar St, Central
  2869-5020
- L1, Pacific Place, 88 Queensway, Admiralty
  2524-6992
- 6/F, Times Square, 1 Matheson St, Causeway Bay
  2506-3139
- G/F, 543 Lockhart Rd, Causeway Bay
  2831-9872
- G/F, Metropole Bldg
  416–426 King's Rd, North Point
  2516-9912
- Island Place, 500 King's Rd, North Point
  2805-5059
- LG/F, Fitfort, 560 King's Rd, North Point
  2590-0353
- G/F, Port Centre, 38 Cheng Tu Rd, Aberdeen
  2814-1208
- 1/F, New Jade Shopping Arcade
  233 Chai Wan Rd, Chai Wan
  2897-9095
- G/F, Marina Square, South Horizons, Ap Lei Chau
  2873-4220

www.imarathon.com
*Many other locations in Kowloon and New Territories;
see website for details.*

Gigasports ....

- L1, Pacific Place, 88 Queensway, Admiralty
  2918-9088
- 7/F, Times Square, 1 Matheson St, Causeway Bay
  2506-3300
- G/F, Cityplaza, 18 Taikoo Shing Rd, Taikoo Shing
  2915-3360
- 2/F, Ocean Terminal, Harbour City
  Canton Rd, Tsim Sha Tsui
  2115-9930
- L8, MegaBox, 38 Wang Chiu Rd, Kowloon Bay
  2629-5102
- 2/F, Discovery Park Shopping Centre
  398 Castle Peak Rd, Tsuen Wan, New Territories
  2940-0040
- 1/F, Metro City Plaza, Phase 2
  8 Mau Yip Rd, Po Lam, New Territories
  2918-0028

www.gigasports.com.hk

Tanka Sport Outlets ....

- G/F, 174 Hennessy Rd, Wan Chai
  2893-6389
- G/F, Home World, Provident Centre
  21–53 Wharf Rd, North Point
  2214-1088 / 2214-1718
- G/F, 75 Lion Rock Rd, Kowloon City
  2382-1281

Ozzie Cozzie Co ....
3/F, Grand Progress Bldg
15–16 Lan Kwai Fong, Central
2810-1356
www.ozziecozzieco.com
Swimwear.

WHERE CAN I BUY CHEAP, CASUAL **SURFER CLOTHES**?

A3 International Co. Ltd ....
29 Stanley Main St, Stanley
2813-2555 / 2813-8999

Quiksilver ....
• 1/F, 1–3 Pak Sha Rd, Causeway Bay
  2895-5028
• 3/F, SOGO, 555 Hennessy Rd, Causeway Bay
  2831-8439
• 2/F, Cityplaza, 18 Taikoo Shing Rd, Tai Koo
  2895-5398
• LCX, 3/F, Ocean Terminal, Harbour City
  Canton Rd, Tsim Sha Tsui
  2895-5128
www.quiksilver.hk
See website for more outlets in Kowloon and New Territories.

Surfer Girl
Stockist:
XGames, 1/F & 2/F, 10 Pak Sha Rd, Causeway Bay
2836-6073
www.xgamehk.com

Take it Easy ....
G/F, 5B Stanley Main St, Stanley
2899-0322

44 Stanley Main St, Stanley ....
2813-9777

WHERE CAN I BUY **COLD-WEATHER AND SKI CLOTHING AND ACCESSORIES** FOR MEN AND WOMEN?

Patagonia ....
• 7/F, Times Square, 1 Matheson St, Causeway Bay
  2506-0677
• 2/F, Ocean Terminal, Harbour City
  Canton Rd, Tsim Sha Tsui
  3188-2400
• L2, Festival Walk, 80 Tat Chee Ave, Kowloon Tong
  3105-1223
www.patagonia.com

Timberland ....
• L1, Pacific Place, 88 Queensway, Admiralty
  2868-0845
• 7/F, Times Square, 1 Matheson St, Causeway Bay
  2506-3808
• 3/F, SOGO, 555 Hennessy Rd, Causeway Bay
  2831-4641
• G/F, Cityplaza, 18 Taikoo Shing Rd, Tai Koo
  2907-0198
• G/F & 1/F, Granville Bldg
  12–16 Carnarvon Rd, Tsim Sha Tsui
  2366-1386
• Wai Fung Plaza, 664 Nathan Rd, Mong Kok
  2391-9838
• L5, New Town Plaza, Phase 1
  Sha Tin Centre St, Sha Tin, New Territories
  2698-9123
• Metroplaza, 223 Hing Fong Rd
  Kwai Fong, New Territories
  2423-6968

- 1/F, Citygate Outlets
  20 Tat Tung Rd, Tung Chung, Lantau Island
  2109-3629

www.timberland.com

Lok Wah Fashion Group ....

- G/F, CNT Tower
  338 Hennessy Rd, Causeway Bay
  2833-6770
- G/F, 11 Lee Garden Rd, Causeway Bay
  2504-5977
- G/F, 29 Granville Road, Tsim Sha Tsui
  2311-6890
- G/F, 193 Fa Yuen St, Mong Kok
  2789-9078

www.lokwah.com

See website for more outlets in Kowloon.

Five Outlet (Hong Kong) Fashion Ltd ....

G/F, 52–56C Stanley Main St, Stanley
2899-0517

Adult and children's ski wear at discount prices. Great ski-wear source for the whole family, only available from, roughly, October to March. Otherwise, throughout the year they carry a good selection of sportswear and casual clothing.

Eikowada ....

- 1/F, 173 Des Voeux Rd Central
  2851-8661
- 1/F, Wing On Centre
  211 Des Voeux Rd West, Sheung Wan
  2380-2690
- G/F, 357–359 Hennessy Rd, Causeway Bay
  2831-9862
- 4/F, SOGO, 555 Hennessy Rd, Causeway Bay
  2831-4858
- JUSCO, 1/F, Wing On Plaza South
  2 Kornhill Rd, Tai Koo
  2539-6106
- G/F, 301–309 Nathan Rd, Jordan
  2368-8965
- 3/F, Wing On Kowloon Centre
  345 Nathan Rd, Jordan
  2388-1906

www.eikowada.com.hk

See website for other outlets.

A3 International Co. Ltd ....

29 Stanley Main St, Stanley
2813-2555 / 2813-8999

Great finds for hip street/surf/skateboard clothes, bags and men's skiwear in the winter. Brands include Oakley, DAKINE, Dragon, Flojos and Caribbean Breeze.

Tai Chung Sporting Goods Co. ....

- G/F, Golden Era Plaza
  39–55 Sai Yee St, Mong Kok
  2385-8205
- G/F, 71 Sai Yee St, Mong Kok
  2787-2950
- G/F, 69 Shantung St, Mong Kok
  2385-8120

www.taichungsports.com.hk

Columbia cold-weather outerwear, clothing and shoes.

44 Stanley Main St, Stanley ....
2813-9777
Rossignol jackets and Vans board shoes.

Sun and Moon Fashion ....
- 18A – B Stanley Main St, Stanley
  2813-2723 / 2813-7829
- G/F, 15 – 19 Carnavon Rd, Tsim Sha Tsui
  2367-1636

WHERE CAN I BUY UNIQUE **DESIGNER JEWELLERY**,
INCLUDING THOSE MADE OF PRECIOUS AND
SEMI-PRECIOUS STONES?

Sandra D'Auriol
2526-0893
sandra@dauriol.com
*Sandra is one of the best-known designers of beautiful
Asian-inspired jewellery. All the influences of her life, her
upbringing between India and Ibiza and over 20 years
in Hong Kong are combined in her sculptural pieces,
including significant use of jade. She also designs
unique belts and accessories. Proceeds all go to charity.*

Joumana Achar & Sagiri Dayal
Joumana: achar@netvigator.com
Sagiri: lamba@netvigator.com
*Joumana and Sagiri use the influences of their diverse
backgrounds and the resources in the city they reside
in to create individual pieces of jewellery that are truly
unique. Hints of India, Morocco, Lebanon, Thailand and,
of course, China and Hong Kong can be found in their
jewellery.*

John Hardy ....
- L2, IFC Mall, 8 Finance St, Central
  2805-0652
- Lane Crawford
  See page 120
www.johnhardy.com

Youmna
8/F, Baskerville House, 22 Ice House St, Central
2521-6810 / 2104-3478
www.youmna.com.hk
*Born in Lebanon and raised in France, Youmna
reconciles elegance and fashion through her jewellery,
selling a luxurious individual look. Her multicultural
exposure has inspired her style-driven and progressive
sense of jewellery design. Contact her regarding private
sales or to commission a special piece.*

The Moja Jewellery
19/F, Dah Sing Life Bldg, 101 Des Voeux Rd Central
2525-1008
www.mojajewellery.com
*The designs are all original, and selected to make a
fashionable, artistic statement. They are suitable for
work, day-to-day wear, or for that very special occasion.*

David Yurman ....
- L2, IFC Mall, 8 Finance St, Central
  2295-0005
- L6, Departures East Hall, Terminal 1
  Hong Kong International Airport
  2261-2955
www.davidyurman.com

Clayton Exquisite
6333-0758
www.claytonx.com.hk
Sandrine Clayton uses a lot of unfinished stones and gems to give her pieces a mesmerising look. Her designs are untraditional yet still exquisite. All of her jewellery is hand-made in Hong Kong. Private viewings by appointment only.

Tayma
2/F, Prince's Bldg, 10 Chater Rd, Central
2525-5280
www.taymajewellery.com

Jan Logan
L2, IFC Mall, 8 Finance St, Central
2918-4212
www.janlogan.com

Janeth Weil Jewels Ltd
www.janethweil.com
Janeth's designs are funky, bohemian and mostly nature-inspired in sterling silver with semi-precious stones, occasionally in 18K gold. Look for new collections in Spring/Summer, Autumn/Winter and Holiday Season.

Trini Tambu
6110-4646
www.trinity-gems.com
Exquisite and unique one-off pieces, by commission only.

TiGa Creations
www.tigacreations.com
TiGa is the result of three talented Asian expat women joining forces to create a line of sophisticated modern jewellery at affordable prices. Great source for gifts.

Tasha D. Gioielli
9220-1905
www.tasha-d.com
A range of rich and diverse statement jewellery that will make you stand out. Well-priced necklaces, bold cuffs and more made from a variety of unique materials.

WHERE CAN I BUY FINE ANTIQUE JEWELLERY?

Christie's
22/F, Alexandra House, 18 Chater Rd, Central
2521-5396
www.christies.com
They hold bi-annual fine jewellery auctions in Hong Kong for exceptional jewellery and watches. Check their website calendar for upcoming auctions and locations.

Michael Youssoufian Ltd
18/F, Hing Wai Bldg, 36 Queen's Rd Central
2868-9093
www.youssoufian.com
With a family history in fine jewellery since 1865, Michael Youssoufian makes exquisite commissioned pieces of antique designer jewellery. He uses only the best quality gems available to custom-make pieces that suit the client's personality. Some of his creations can be seen at auction through Christie's and Sotheby's.

Sotheby's
31/F, One Pacific Place, 88 Queensway, Admiralty
2524-8121
www.sothebys.com
Check their website for regular auctions of fine jewellery.

WHERE CAN I BUY **FASHION ANTIQUE JEWELLERY**?

Amours Antiques
G/F, 45 Staunton St, Central
2803-7877
Vintage jewellery, among many other vintage offerings.

Victoria Antique Jewellery
12 Elgin St, Central
2858-2885

Select 18 .... 🔊
G/F, Grandview Garden, 18 Bridges St, SoHo
9310-6768

Evelyn Artwear
21 Aberdeen St, Central
2850-8906
Vintage jewellery and vintage-looking new jewellery.

True Colors
• G/F, 2–4 Gough St, Sheung Wan
  2544-0990
• 3/F, MTR Hong Kong Station
  2868-2552
• 1/F, The Excelsior
  281 Gloucester Rd, Causeway Bay
  2155-5055
• B1, The Elegance at Sheraton
  20 Nathan Rd, Tsim Sha Tsui
  2722-5522
• 1/F, Daily House
  35–37 Haiphong Rd, Tsim Sha Tsui
  2376-3377
www.truecolors.com.hk

I'M LOOKING FOR **UNIQUE CONTEMPORARY JADE JEWELLERY**. WHERE DO YOU SUGGEST?

Edward Chiu
L2, IFC Mall, 8 Finance St, Central
2525-2325
www.edwardchiu.com

Samuel Kung
L3, IFC Mall, 8 Finance St, Central
2295-0718
www.samuelkung.com

Chow Tai Fook
• G/F, Aon China Bldg, 29 Queen's Rd Central
  2523-7128
• 44–46 Queen's Rd Central
  2524-3374
• B2, Times Square, 1 Matheson St, Causeway Bay
  3102-9980
• Cameron Comm. Centre
  458–468 Hennessy Rd, Causeway Bay
  2832-9041
• 461 Hennessy Rd, Causeway Bay
  2893-2355
• 482A Hennessy Rd, Causeway Bay
  2573-3888
• G/F, Causeway Bay Plaza 1
  489 Hennessy Rd, Causeway Bay
  2838-6222

- 1/F, SOGO, 555 Hennessy Rd, Causeway Bay
  2836-3179
- G/F, Laforet Excelsior Plaza
  24−26 East Point Rd, Causeway Bay
  2882-4389
- 24−30 Paterson St, Causeway Bay
  2882-4422
- 367−373 King's Rd, North Point
  2571-8978
- G/F, Ocean Terminal, Harbour City
  Canton Rd, Tsim Sha Tsui
  3188-1381
- Holiday Inn Golden Mile
  50 Nathan Rd, Tsim Sha Tsui
  2368-0080
- 54−64B Nathan Rd, Tsim Sha Tsui
  2368-8232
- Majestic House, 80 Nathan Rd, Tsim Sha Tsui
  2721-0168
- Park Lane Shopper's Boulevard
  123 Nathan Rd, Tsim Sha Tsui
  2735-7966
- Telford Plaza, 33 Wai Yip St, Kowloon Bay
  2130-1618
- Concourse, APM, 418 Kwun Tong Rd, Kwun Tong
  3426-8483

www.chowtaifook.com
See website for other outlets.

WHERE CAN I BUY STYLISH IMITATION DIAMOND
AND **COSTUME JEWELLERY**?

CARAT
- 23 D'Aguilar St, Central
  2526-9688
- L3, IFC Mall, 8 Finance St, Central
  2234-7372
- Lane Crawford, L3, IFC Mall, 8 Finance St, Central
  2118-3388
- Seibu, L2, Pacific Place, 88 Queensway, Admiralty
  2971-3853
- Lane Crawford, G/F & 1/F, Times Square
  1 Matheson St, Causeway Bay
  3101-1590
- 2/F, Gateway Arcade, Harbour City
  Canton Rd, Tsim Sha Tsui
  3101-1510
- Lane Crawford
  Marco Polo Hongkong Hotel, Harbour City
  3 Canton Rd, Tsim Sha Tsui
  3101-1550

www.carat.cc
Arte Madrid
- L2, IFC Mall, 8 Finance St, Central
  2295-3980
- G/F, Yip Fung Bldg, 2−18 D'Aguilar St, Central
  3102-2022
- G/F, The Peak Tower, 128 Peak Rd, The Peak
  2849-6607
- Seibu, L2, Pacific Place, 88 Queensway, Admiralty
  2819-9281 / 2819-9382

- 1/F, Lee Gardens Two, 28 Yun Ping Rd, Causeway Bay
  2576-8782
- 1/F, SOGO, 555 Hennessy Rd, Causeway Bay
  2831-8943
- G/F, Style House, The Park Lane Hotel
  310 Gloucester Rd, Causeway Bay
  2805-6928
- B1, SOGO, 12 Salisbury Rd, Tsim Sha Tsui
  3556-1077
- 2/F, Gateway Arcade, Harbour City
  Canton Rd, Tsim Sha Tsui
  3101-9048

www.arte.com.hk
Excellent range of high quality synthetic gemstone pieces. Exotic and European designs at an affordable price, with a high-end look. See website for more locations.

WHERE CAN I BUY UNIQUE BEADED JEWELLERY THAT IS REASONABLY PRICED?

Chocolate Rain
G/F, 67 Peel St, SoHo
2975-8318
www.chocolaterain.com
Handmade beaded jewellery and accessories.

Jade Market
Junction of Kansu St and Battery St, Yau Ma Tei

Upper Lascar Row (Cat Alley)
Near Man Mo Temple, below Hollywood Rd, Central

Cherry Chung
Intersection of Wellington St and Cochrane St, Central
9126-8974 / 9040-2680
A hole-in-the-wall stall; Cherry sells a vast variety of beaded necklaces and bracelets. She can make a custom necklace for you using any of the beads that you like.

WHERE CAN I BUY STYLISH SILVER JEWELLERY?

Georg Jensen
- L2, IFC Mall, 8 Finance St, Central
  2234-7180
- 1/F, Prince's Bldg, 10 Chater Rd, Central
  2868-0707
- 2/F, Ocean Centre, Harbour City
  Canton Rd, Tsim Sha Tsui
  2302-0888
- LG2, Festival Walk
  80 Tat Chee Ave, Kowloon Tong
  2893-4050

www.georgjensen.com
Contemporary Scandinavian chic in silver.

Tous
- L1, IFC Mall, 8 Finance St, Central
  2295-0018
- 1/F, SOGO, 555 Hennessy Rd, Causeway Bay
  2831-8920
- 3/F, Gateway Arcade, Harbour City
  Canton Rd, Tsim Sha Tsui
  2175-5061

www.tous.com

Thomas Sabo ....

- L1, IFC Mall, 8 Finance St, Central
  2295-3585
- L2, Seibu, Pacific Place, 88 Queensway, Admiralty
  2918-1741
- 4/F, Times Square, 1 Matheson St, Causeway Bay
  2156-2836
- 1/F, SOGO, 555 Hennessy Rd, Causeway Bay
  2831-4622
- 2/F, Gateway Arcade, Harbour City
  Canton Rd, Tsim Sha Tsui
  2736-9585
- Basement & 1/F, SOGO
  12 Salisbury Rd, Tsim Sha Tsui
  3556-1383
- L3, Seibu, Langham Place, 8 Argyle St, Mong Kok
  3580-0339
- L4, New Town Plaza, Phase 1
  Sha Tin Centre St, Sha Tin, New Territories
  2424-5898
- G/F, Telford Plaza, Phase 1
  33 Wai Yip St, Kowloon Bay
  2155-9322

www.thomassabo.com

Links of London ....

- L1, IFC Mall, 8 Finance St, Central
  2295-3328
- 1/F, Prince's Bldg, 10 Chater Rd, Central
  2525-1598
- L1, Pacific Place, 88 Queensway, Admiralty
  2918-9727
- 1/F, Elements Mall, 1 Austin Rd West, Kowloon
  2196-8548
- LG2, Festival Walk, 80 Tat Chee Ave, Kowloon Tong
  2265-8982
- 3/F, Gateway Arcade, Harbour City
  Canton Rd, Tsim Sha Tsui
  2317-1613
- L6, Departures West Hall, Terminal 1
  Hong Kong International Airport
  2392-2802

www.linksoflondon.com

Tiffany & Co. ....

- L2, IFC Mall, 8 Finance St, Central
  2234-7163
- G/F, The Landmark, 15 Queen's Rd Central
  2845-9853
- L3, Pacific Place, 88 Queensway, Admiralty
  2918-9992
- G/F, SOGO, 555 Hennessy Rd, Causeway Bay
  2575-4263
- G/F, 1881 Heritage, 2A Canton Rd, Tsim Sha Tsui
  2301-2702
- DFS Galleria Sun Plaza, 28 Canton Rd, Tsim Sha Tsui
  2302-6888
- G/F, The Peninsula Hotel, Salisbury Rd, Tsim Sha Tsui
  2722-7691
- DFS Galleria Chinachem Plaza
  77 Mody Rd, East Tsim Sha Tsui
  2311-3813

- 1/F, Elements Mall, 1 Austin Rd West, Kowloon
  2196-8500
- L6, Departures East Hall, Terminal 1
  Hong Kong International Airport
  2261-0800

www.tiffany.com

John Hardy ....
See page 149

David Yurman ....
See page 149

MY HIP TEENAGER IS LOOKING FOR SOME
HARDCORE SILVER JEWELLERY. ANY SUGGESTIONS?

Silver Union
3/F, 8 Cameron Rd, Tsim Sha Tsui
2369-1808

Deep Anger ....
2/F, 7 Lan Fong Rd, Causeway Bay
2869-8303
www.deepanger.com

WHERE CAN I FIND REASONABLY PRICED SILVER JEWELLERY?

Saturn Essentials
1/F, 51 Wellington St, Central
2537-9335
www.saturnessentials.com
Regularly changing collection of silver.

Kwong Tai Silverware
G/F, Jordan Mansion, 37Q Jordan Rd, Jordan
2771-6893
www.ktsilver.com
This entire store is filled with silver jewellery including rings, bracelets, earrings, necklaces and more. They can also make silver jewellery for you from your own design. There are more silver shops like this one a few doors away.

Cheong Shing Jewellery ....
Kent Bldg, 39A Jordan Rd, Yau Ma Tei
2374-0093
Silver jewellery, silver clasps and balls.

President Jewellery ....
G/F, 527–539 Jaffe Rd, Causeway Bay
2893-2302
The three stalls next to this shop also carry inexpensive silver.

WHERE IS A GOOD CHEAP SOURCE FOR SOME
LAST-MINUTE JEWELLERY AND ACCESSORIES TO
COMPLETE AN OUTFIT?

Fang Fong
- G/F, 69 Peel St, SoHo
  3105-5557
- G/F, 47 Staunton St, SoHo
  2857-2057

H&M
See page 108

Cherry Chung
Intersection of Wellington St and Cochrane St, Central
9126-8974 / 9040-2680

X quisit
76 Wellington St, Central
2526-1660
Li Yuen St East, Central
Jardine's Bazaar, Causeway Bay
Fa Yuen St, Mong Kok
Temple St, Jordan

WHERE CAN I GET MY OLD JEWELLERY RESET/ REDESIGNED, OR NEW JEWELLERY MADE/COPIED?

Power Jewellers
G/F, Han Yee Mansion
19A Hankow Rd, Tsim Sha Tsui
2376-1782
Good at replicating from a picture and also offers unique design ideas. Ask for Jacqui, Christine or Harry.
Michael Youssoufian Ltd
18/F, Hing Wai Bldg, 36 Queen's Rd Central
2868-9093
www.youssoufian.com
Collector's Jewellery
G/F, 17 Yun Ping Rd, Causeway Bay
2805-6822
Good quality and prices. Can copy jewellery or create your designs.
Raj's Jewellery
14/F, Century Square, 1–13 D'Aguilar St, Central
9880-6988

WHERE DO YOU RECOMMEND I TAKE MY FINE JEWELLERY FOR REPAIR?

Power Jewellers
See above
Wah Hing Jewellery & Arts
LG/F, Silvercord, 30 Canton Rd, Tsim Sha Tsui
2366-8603
www.wahhingja.com

WHERE CAN I SELL MY OLD GOLD JEWELLERY?

Chow Tai Fook
See pages 151–152
Most large Chinese jewellery chains buy back old gold jewellery (18k and up), whether or not it was purchased from them. Some require you to purchase something new from them, while others like Chow Tai Fook will simply give you cash (for 24k gold only).
Chow Sang Sang
• 37 Queen's Rd Central
   3583-4150
• B2, Times Square, 1 Matheson St, Causeway Bay
   3101-0733
• G/F, Silvercord, 30 Canton Rd, Tsim Sha Tsui
   2735-4622
• Park Lane Shopper's Boulevard, Nathan Rd, Tsim Sha Tsui
   3105-9708
• 1/F, Elements Mall, 1 Austin Rd West, Kowloon
   2196-8680

EVERYTHING FASHION & SHOPPING

• LG2, Festival Walk, 80 Tat Chee Ave, Kowloon Tong
  2265-8322
www.chowsangsang.com
Many more outlets throughout Hong Kong.

WHERE DO YOU SUGGEST I GO TO FIND
INTERESTING PIECES OF **OLD JADE**?

Timmy Art Co. (Wholesale Jade Arts & Craft)
G/F, 220 Shanghai St, Yau Ma Tei
2770-2759
Chinese old jade, white jade and Burma jade.

A Jade
Stall 169, Jade Market, 437 Kansu St, Yau Ma Tei
9831-9127
*Sells interesting and inexpensive carved old jade pieces.
Ask for Mr Au.*

Jade Market
Junction of Kansu St and Battery St, Yau Ma Tei

Jade St
Canton St, Yau Ma Tei

WHERE CAN I FIND A REPUTABLE **DIAMOND WHOLESALER**?

Ornate Trading Co.
Taurus Bldg, 21A/B Granville Rd, Tsim Sha Tsui
2369-7519
*Leo Ng is a reputable jewellery wholesaler who
specialises in high-quality diamonds and pearls. He also
sells ready-made jewellery and can do custom designs.*

Peter Choi Gem & Jewellery
11/F, The Pinnacle, 8 Minden Ave, Tsim Sha Tsui
2317-6689
www.peterchoidiamond.com
*A professional gemologist since 1981; also deals with
loose stones (diamonds, rubies, sapphires, emeralds,
jade, pearls, topaz, aquamarine, etc.).*

WHERE IS A GOOD PLACE TO BUY INEXPENSIVE
PEARL JEWELLERY?

Sandra Pearls ....
Stalls 381 & 447, Jade Market
Kansu St, Yau Ma Tei
2456-9083
*Sandra carries a good selection of pearls and nice
ready-made pieces. She will also do custom design to
any style you can show her.*

Kum Fu Hoi Pearl Jewellery ....
Stalls 115–116, Jade Market
Kansu St, Yau Ma Tei
9686-4982
Cultured pearls, South Sea pearls and fresh water pearls.

Bao Quan Ornament Co. ....
G/F, 241 Ki Lung St, Sham Shui Po
2361-8586 / 9267-6746
www.baoquan.com.hk
*Sells handmade bead, jade, gem and crystal jewellery
and accessories. They also design and manufacture
jade, gold, silver, gem and crystal jewellery, accessories
and jewellery/gift boxes.*

WHERE DO YOU RECOMMEND I GO TO BUY **CRYSTAL AND SEMI-PRECIOUS BEADS**?

Him Shing Jade (All Jade Wholesaler) ....
G/F, 628 Canton Rd, Yau Ma Tei
6128-4074
For beading supplies, threads, rope, etc. They can also string your beads.

Yat Chow Pearls & Gems Co. ....
G/F, 620 Canton Rd, Yau Ma Tei
2374-5547
Lots of pearls, amethyst and jade for sale in strands.

M & D Gems ....
G/F, 586 Canton Rd, Jordan
2739-6178
Good source for choosing loose quartz and amethyst.

Ying Fung Beads Co. ....
G/F, 246 Yu Chau St, Sham Shui Po
2708-7623 / 2725-6066
They sell bulk beads by the bag, strands of sequins and beaded fabric.

Lik Ko Gem Co. ....
G/F, Wah Tang Bldg
127A Nam Cheong St, Sham Shui Po
2783-0273
Good source for strands of pearls and all types of crystal and semi-precious stone beads.

Siu Cheung Jewellery Factory ....
• G/F, 569 Canton Rd, Yau Ma Tei
  2771-7859
• G/F, Nam Cheong Centre
  89 Nam Cheong St, Sham Shui Po
  2729-3389
Good selection of crystal and other beads in all shapes and sizes.

James Antiques ....
G/F, 16 Tung St, Sheung Wan
2850-4988
Good source for antique and old beads.

Kin Shing Gem Co. ....
G/F, 222 Ki Lung St, Sham Shui Po
2958-9613
Beads and gems.

WHERE CAN I GET A **WELL-PRICED LEATHER JEWELLERY BOX** TO STORE ALL MY LITTLE TREASURES?

Grace Co.
G/F, 10 Aberdeen St, Central
2974-1870
Great little shop offering ready-made and custom-made jewellery/watch boxes. They have good leather and Plexiglas photo frames, also a good source for last-minute gifts.

WHERE CAN I FIND A REPUTABLE **MULTI-BRAND WATCH SHOP**?

Prince Jewellery & Watch Co.
2/F, Ocean Terminal, Harbour City
Canton Rd, Tsim Sha Tsui
2311-4432
www.princejewellerywatch.com
Ask for Jacky Chan.

King's Watch Co. Ltd
49 Queen's Rd Central
2522-3469 / 2522-4759

Carlson Watch
G/F, Aon China Bldg, 29 Queen's Rd Central
2525-5478

Cortina Watch HK Ltd
G/F, Wing Cheong House, 53 Queen's Rd Central
2522-0645
www.cortinawatch.com

Dickson Watch & Jewellery
• G/F, The Landmark, 15 Queen's Rd Central
  2521-4245
• 4/F, The Peninsula Hotel Shopping Arcade
  Salisbury Rd, Tsim Sha Tsui
  2369-8264

Elegant Watch Co.
• 4/F, Times Square, 1 Matheson St, Causeway Bay
  2506-3663
• 2/F, Ocean Terminal, Harbour City
  Canton Rd, Tsim Sha Tsui
  2735-8481
• 3/F, Ocean Centre, Harbour City
  Canton Rd, Tsim Sha Tsui
  2730-1211
www.elegantwatch.net

Eldorado Watch
G/F, Peter Bldg, 60 Queen's Rd Central
2522-7155 / 2526-6869

Kwai Yan Watch
• G/F, 14 Pennington St, Causeway Bay
  2808-1926
• G/F, Champagne Court, 16 Kimberley Rd, Tsim Sha Tsui
  2368-4687
• G/F, 19 Nelson St, Mong Kok
  2381-4311
• G/F, Yan Oi House
  237 Sha Tsui Rd, Tsuen Wan, New Territories
  2944-9222
www.kwaiyanwatch.com

WHERE CAN I BUY **HIGH-END PREVIOUSLY OWNED** JEWELLERY AND WATCHES?

Christie's
22/F, Alexandra House, 18 Chater Rd, Central
2521-5396
www.christies.com

Sotheby's
31/F, One Pacific Place, 88 Queensway, Admiralty
2524-8121
www.sothebys.com

Berne Horology
1/F, Peninsula Centre, 67 Mody Rd, East Tsim Sha Tsui
2576-8668 / 9725-4597
www.bernehorologytst.com
Treasure trove for vintage watches, clocks and timepieces.

WHERE CAN I GO TO REPLACE MY **WATCH BATTERY** OR BUY AN **INEXPENSIVE WATCH STRAP**?

Pedder Lane, Central
A couple of stalls here offer a wide range of straps and replace watch batteries.

WHERE CAN I GET MY **SWISS WATCH SERVICED**?

Eldorado Watch
G/F, Peter Bldg, 60 Queen's Rd Central
2522-7155 / 2526-6869
King's Watch Co. Ltd
49 Queen's Rd Central
2522-3469 / 2522-4759

I AM EXPECTING. WHERE CAN I FIND A SHOP OFFERING A GOOD SELECTION OF **SUPPLIES AND GEAR FOR NEW BABIES AND EXPECTANT MUMS**?

Bumps to Babes
• 5/F, Pedder Bldg, 12 Pedder St, Central
  2522-7112
• 21/F, Horizon Plaza, 2 Lee Wing St, Ap Lei Chau
  2552-5000
www.bumpstobabes.com
Great all-around superstore carrying a vast range of maternity, baby and kids' products, clothing, equipment, accessories and toys.

Organic Baby
1/F, Sun Fung Mansion
52–60 Lyndhurst Terrace, Central
2882-6008
www.organicbaby.com.hk
They specialise in furnishings, clothing, accessories and organic food.

Toys "R" Us
• G/F, Man Yee Bldg, 67 Queen's Rd Central
  2259-9166
• 7/F, Windsor House, 311 Gloucester Rd, Causeway Bay
  2881-1728
• 1/F, Cityplaza, 18 Taikoo Shing Rd, Tai Koo
  2569-2388
• 2/F, Aberdeen Centre Shopping Arcade, Site 2
  7–11 Nam Ning St, Aberdeen
  2518-7128
• G/F, Ocean Terminal, Harbour City
  Canton Rd, Tsim Sha Tsui
  2730-9462
• B2–G/F, Treasure World, Site 11
  Whampoa Garden, Hung Hom
  2356-2688
• L2, Festival Walk, 80 Tat Chee Ave, Kowloon Tong
  2265-7933

- L1, New Town Plaza, Phase 3
  Sha Tin Centre St, Sha Tin, New Territories
  2605-2225
- 1/F, Discovery Park Shopping Centre
  398 Castle Peak Rd, Tsuen Wan, New Territories
  2940-1968
- 1/F, Metro City Plaza, Phase 3
  8 Mau Yip Rd, Po Lam, New Territories
  3194-6399
- 2/F, Tuen Mun Town Plaza, Phase 1
  1 Tuen Shun St, Tuen Mun, New Territories
  2430-0268

www.toysrus.com.hk

Mothercare ....
- 3/F, Prince's Bldg, 10 Chater Rd, Central
  2523-5704
- 3/F, Lee Gardens Two
  28 Yun Ping Rd, Causeway Bay
  2504-1088
- G/F, Ocean Terminal, Harbour City
  Canton Rd, Tsim Sha Tsui
  2735-5738
- 5/F, Grand Century Place
  193 Prince Edward Rd West, Mong Kok
  2380-1832
- L9, MegaBox, 38 Wang Chiu Rd, Kowloon Bay
  2359-0018
- L1, New Town Plaza, Phase 3
  Sha Tin Centre St, Sha Tin, New Territories
  2698-5533

www.mothercare.com.hk
Maternity and baby products, equipment, clothing and baby toys.

Eugene Club Centre ....
- 4/F, Crawford House, 70 Queen's Rd Central
  2628-3777
- 6/F, Grand Century Place
  193 Prince Edward Rd West, Mong Kok
  2628-3228
- L7, MegaBox, 38 Wang Chiu Rd, Kowloon Bay
  2628-3880
- L1, New Town Plaza, Phase 3
  Sha Tin Centre St, Sha Tin, New Territories
  2628-3818
- 3/F, Discovery Park Shopping Centre
  398 Castle Peak Rd, Tsuen Wan, New Territories
  2628-3268
- 3/F, Sun Yuen Long Centre
  8 Long Yat Rd, Yuen Long, New Territories
  2628-3666

www.eugenegroup.com.hk
Another baby superstore carrying a large selection of baby equipment, supplies, toys, strollers and more. It specialises in Japanese baby products, including a good selection of strollers and car seats.

Honey Berrie ....
- G/F, Windsor House
  311 Gloucester Rd, Causeway Bay
  2506-0913 / 2576-6011
- 19/F, Horizon Plaza, 2 Lee Wing St, Ap Lei Chau
  2576-6011

- G/F, Ocean Terminal, Harbour City
  Canton Rd, Tsim Sha Tsui
  2957-8662
www.honeyberrie.com
Specialising in kids' furniture, bedding, babies' gifts, accessories and arts and crafts supplies.

Shop in HK .... ℗
2989-9147
www.shopinhk.com
Online store specialising in products for babies, as well as for expectant and new mums.

I'M LOOKING FOR A STYLISH **TOP-QUALITY STROLLER** OR A **SPECIALTY STROLLER** (DOUBLE, JOGGING, ETC.). WHERE SHOULD I LOOK?

Mothercare .... ℗
3/F, Prince's Bldg, 10 Chater Rd, Central
2523-5704
www.mothercare.com.hk
Great selection of many of the latest strollers available in Hong Kong. See website for other outlets.

Bumps to Babes .... ℗
See page 160

Eugene Club Centre .... ℗
See page 161

WHERE CAN I BUY TOP QUALITY **BABY TOILETRY ITEMS**?

Mustela .... ℗
9 Queen's Rd Central
2525-3591
www.mustela.com
Tested hypoallergenic products that address the specific needs of newborns, babies, children and expectant mothers. Great gift baskets with free delivery to all hospitals in Hong Kong.
See also baby superstores, pages 160–161.

I AM LOOKING FOR SOME **STYLISH MATERNITY CLOTHES**. WHERE SHOULD I START LOOKING?

Nine Months
7/F, V-Plus, 68–70 Wellington St, Central
2868-5988
www.ninemonthshk.com
Fashion forward designer maternity wear and lingerie set in a chic and comfortable living room setting.

Sono Vaso
22 Fifth St, Hong Lok Yuen
Tai Po, New Territories
2650-0262
www.sonovaso.com
Lifestyle maternity clothes.

Linea Negra
- 5/F, Pacific House, 20 Queen's Rd Central
  2522-7966
- 13/F, Chung Fung Comm. Bldg
  12 Canton Rd, Tsim Sha Tsui
  2730-7933
www.lineanegra.com.hk

H&M
See page 108
Zara
See page 107

DO YOU HAVE ANY OTHER SUGGESTIONS FOR
BASIC MATERNITY WEAR?

Bumps to Babes
See page 160
Twiggy Maternity Wear Co. Ltd
LG/F, Leighton Centre
77 Leighton Rd, Causeway Bay
2525-7688
Marks & Spencer
See page 107

ANY SUGGESTIONS ON WHERE TO BUY **CLOTHES
FOR THAT IN-BETWEEN STAGE** BEFORE NEEDING
ACTUAL MATERNITY CLOTHES?

Sanskrit
G/F, 48 Lyndhurst Terrace, Central
2545-2088
Tabla
Mezzanine, Prince's Bldg, 10 Chater Rd, Central
2525-5590/9755-6669
www.tabla.hk
Rush
See page 144
Giordano Ladies
See pages 109–110
*Reasonably priced and well-styled clothing with lots of
knits and stretchy fabrics that are ideal for early stages
of pregnancy.*
Esprit
See pages 113–114
Stanley Market, Stanley
See pages 187–189
Li Yuen St, Central

WHERE CAN I FIND **CLOTHING, EQUIPMENT AND
ACCESSORIES FOR NURSING?**

Bumps to Babes ....
See page 160
Mothercare ....
See page 161
BF Moms Nursing Wear & Acessories
8117-5082
www.hk-bfmoms.com
*Online store selling maternity wear and clothing for
nursing mothers.*
Frankie Maternity
2/F, Fairview Mansion, 51 Paterson St, Causeway Bay
2834-4122
Mother World ....
• G/F, 54–68 Lee Garden Rd, Causeway Bay
  2504-2737
• G/F, 117 Chatham Rd, Tsim Sha Tsui
  2992-0387

- UG/F, Hang Fung Centre, 228 Jordan Rd, Jordan
  2992-0325
- 5/F, Grand Century Place
  193 Prince Edward Rd West, Mong Kok
  2607-2610
- L9, MegaBox, 38 Wang Chiu Rd, Kowloon Bay
  2504-5735
- 3/F, Sha Tin Centre
  Sha Tin Centre St, Sha Tin, New Territories
  2604-5959
- 4/F, Tsuen Wan Plaza
  4–30 Tai Pa St, Tsuen Wan, New Territories
  2607-2010
- 2/F, Tuen Mun Town Plaza
  1 Tuen Shun St, Tuen Mun, New Territories
  2607-2163
- 2/F, Metro City Plaza 2
  8 Mau Yip Rd, Po Lam, New Territories
  2607-1111

www.motherworld.com.hk
Maternity/nursing clothing, support clothing and accessories.

WHERE CAN I BUY A **STYLISH DIAPER BAG**?

Smarty Pants ....
1/F, Sun Fung Mansion
52–60 Lyndhurst Terrace, Central
2544-2700
www.smartypants.com.hk
*Fantastic store for baby, toddler and expectant mums,
offering stylish clothing and accessories.*

Kate Spade
- 1/F, Elements Mall, 1 Austin Rd West, Kowloon
  2196 - 8499
- 2/F, Ocean Centre, Harbour City
  Canton Rd, Tsim Sha Tsui
  2110 - 3555
- L2, IFC Mall, 8 Finance St, Central
  3188 - 1928
- L2, Pacific Place, 88 Queensway, Admiralty
  2116 - 4998
- 1/F, SOGO, 555 Hennessy Rd, Causeway Bay
  2831 - 3948
- 3/F, Times Square, 1 Matheson St, Causeway Bay
  2506 - 2283

www.katespade.com

WHERE CAN I BUY A SENTIMENTAL OR **UNIQUE
BABY GIFT** FOR A GOOD FRIEND?

Saturn Essentials
1/F, 51 Wellington St, Central
2537-9335
www.saturnessentials.com

Baby Buddha Pumpkins ....
www.babybuddhapumpkins.com
*Specialising in organic baby products such as soft toys
and wooden toys, baby blankets, clothes and others.
Part of the proceeds go towards charities like UNICEF
and Habitat for Humanity.*

Tiffany & Co.
See pages 154–155
Kate Spade
See page 164
Links of London
See page 154
See also silver gift items, pages 334–335.

I'M LOOKING FOR UNIQUE GIFTS FOR A BABY OR KID'S BIRTHDAY. ANY SUGGESTIONS?

Smarty Pants ....
1/F, Sun Fung Mansion
52–60 Lyndhurst Terrace, Central
2544-2700
www.smartypants.com.hk
Organic Baby ....
1/F, Sun Fung Mansion
52–60 Lyndhurst Terrace, Central
2882-6008
www.organicbaby.com.hk
Offspring ....
The Repulse Bay, 109 Repulse Bay Rd, Repulse Bay
2812-2636
Great little shop on the South Side offering an eclectic mix of unique clothing, accessories, toys and more. They have a range of products for babies to teens.
Nuan Cashmere ....
9096-1645
www.nuancashmere.com
Customised baby and children's blankets in cashmere or lambswool.
smallprint ....
6050-5940 (Elisa) / 9381-5481 (Mandy)
Sunflower ....
9663-8982
Unique and personalised hand/footprint jewellery.
Kaloo ....
• 3/F, Prince's Bldg, 10 Chater Rd, Central
  2522-7770
• L6, Terminal 2, Hong Kong International Airport
  3197-9321
www.kaloo.com

MY CHILD IS GOING TO A BIRTHDAY PARTY. WHERE CAN I FIND A GOOD TOY STORE THAT OFFERS A LARGE SELECTION OF GIFTS FOR ALL AGES?

Toys "R" Us ....
See pages 160–161
Toys Club ....
• 13/F, 1 Duddell St, Central
  2167-8474
• 9/F, Horizon Plaza, 2 Lee Wing St, Ap Lei Chau
  2836-0875
www.itoysclub.com
A Barrel of Monkeys ....
G/F, EMAX, 1 Trademart Drive, Kowloon Bay
2234-0131

WHERE CAN I FIND A TOY STORE THAT CARRIES A GOOD RANGE OF **EDUCATIONAL TOYS**?

Wise Kids ....
- 3/F, Prince's Bldg, 10 Chater Rd, Central
  2377-9888
- L1, Pacific Place, 88 Queensway, Admiralty
  2868-0133
- G/F, 2 Sun Wui Rd, Causeway Bay
  2506-3328
- 1/F, Elements Mall, 1 Austin Rd West, Kowloon
  2613-8800
- 1/F, The Arcade, Cyberport, 100 Cyberport Rd
  2989-6298
www.wisekidstoys.com

Brick Shop ....
- 2/F, 12 Matheson St, Causeway Bay
  2882-1284
- 1/F, Sino Centre
  582–592 Nathan Rd, Mong Kok
  2771-2226
www.brickshop.com.hk
A great shop devoted to Lego, Playmobil and other quality brick or jigsaw toys.

ItsImagical ....
- G/F, Ocean Terminal, Harbour City
  Canton Rd, Tsim Sha Tsui
  2375-6020
- L1, New Town Plaza, Phase 3
  Sha Tin Centre St, Sha Tin, New Territories
  3148-1151
www.itsimagical.com.hk

Hobby Horse Toys ....
2/F, Prince's Bldg, 10 Chater Rd, Central
2523-3814 / 2523-6542
www.allinafamily.com

Baby Boom ....
12/F, CDW Bldg
388 Castle Peak Rd, Tsuen Wan, New Territories
2498-9101
www.babyboom.com.hk
Educational toys and teaching/learning materials.

Eugene Club Centre ....
See page 161

Bumps to Babes ....
See page 160

I'M LOOKING FOR **UNIQUE, HARD TO FIND, LIMITED EDITION TOY COLLECTIONS.** WHERE SHOULD I TRY?

CTMA Centre ....
1N Sai Yeung Choi St South, Mong Kok
This treasure trove for toy collectors/enthusiasts has two anchor stores—Superman Toys (Shop 222, tel. 2366-2396) and Toy Hunters (Shop 218, tel. 2388-4677)—in addition to several smaller shops.

Richmond Shopping Centre ....
111 Argyle St, Mong Kok
Another great source for toys. Many smaller shops all fighting for your business.

Toyzone 16 ....
16/F, Causeway Bay Comm. Bldg
3 Sugar St, Causeway Bay
2882-6850
www.toyzone.com.hk

Toy Museum ....
3/F, Prince's Bldg, 10 Chater Rd, Central
2869-1938

WHERE CAN I LOOK FOR **MODELS, TOYS AND COLLECTIBLE TOYS FOR BOYS** OF ALL AGES?

UML (Universal Model Ltd) ....
• 579 Nathan Rd, Mong Kok (Flagship Megastore)
  2771-1930
• G/F–3/F, 5 Pennington St, Causeway Bay
  2577-5594
• G/F, 63 Waterloo Rd, Kowloon
  2714-1268
• 1/F, Citywalk
  1 Yeung Uk Rd, Tsuen Wan, New Territories
  3665-0804
www.universal-models.com

C.I.C. Models & Toys Co. ....
G/F, 94 Queen's Rd East, Wan Chai
2529-6763

WHERE CAN I BUY A **GOOD QUALITY SCHOOL BAG**?

OldSkool ....
Stockists:
• X Game, 2/F, 10 Pak Sha Rd, Causeway Bay
  2881-8960
• X Game, L9, Langham Place
  8 Argyle St, Mong Kok
  2264-3088
• Offspring, G/F, Repulse Bay Arcade
  109 Repulse Bay Rd, Repulse Bay
  2812-2636
Enquiries: 2592-9886
www.o-skool.com
Designed by a HK mother in tune with the needs and desires of the young at heart, OldSkool offers hip, affordable, durable and functional school bags and accessories for boys and girls, aged 7 to teens.

Penny Scallan ....
31B Seabird Lane, Discovery Bay, Lantau Island
6105-4050
www.pennyscallan.biz
Catering to a younger clientele, pre-school to primary, Penny Scallan offers online orders for backpacks, lunch boxes, aprons, bibs, hats and more.

Allerhand ....
Seibu, L1, Pacific Place, 88 Queensway, Admiralty
2545-2645
www.allerhand.com
From Germany, Allerhand specialises in PVC-free bags in many sizes and styles including backpacks, messenger bags, matching lunch bags and pencil cases for kids.

Escapade
- 1/F, Yee Hing Bldg
  19 Leighton Rd, Causeway Bay
  2891-1855
- 1/F, Spa & Resort, Parkview
  88 Tai Tam Reservoir Rd, Tai Tam
  2812-3935
- G/F, Hong Kong Cricket Club
  137 Wong Nai Chung Gap Rd, Happy Valley
  2575-1861
www.escapade.com.hk

Lego Bags
6/F, SOGO, 555 Hennessy Rd, Causeway Bay
2666-0275
www.golddouble.hk
Lego-branded bags, gym bags, pencil cases and more for boys and girls aged 6 and under.

HOW ABOUT SOME **LABELS/BAG TAGS** FOR KIDS' CLOTHES AND GEAR?

Stuck On You
2549-2245
www.stuckonyou.biz/hongkong
Everything from vinyl labels to iron/sew-on labels, notepads and stickers that you can personalise with names, icons and colours for your children.

Kwik Tapes
10B Palm Court, 55 Robinson Rd, Mid-Levels
2147-3897
www.kwiktapes.com
Durable name tapes in iron-on or stick-on format.

Joseph Embroidering Enterprises Co. Ltd
2/F, Kwong Ah Bldg
114 Thomson Rd, Wan Chai
2573-3229 / 2575-0592
Offers sew-on embroidered clothing labels.

ARE THERE ANY **MALLS OR AREAS THAT SPECIALISE IN KIDS' CLOTHING, SHOES AND ACCESSORIES**?

3/F, Prince's Bldg
10 Chater Rd, Central

2/F–4/F (The In Square), Windsor House
311 Gloucester Rd, Causeway Bay
www.windsorhouse.hk

2/F, Lee Gardens Two
28 Yun Ping Rd, Causeway Bay
www.leegardens.com.hk

Stanley Market, Stanley
See pages 187–189

G/F, Ocean Terminal, Harbour City
Canton Rd, Tsim Sha Tsui
www.harbourcity.com.hk

2/F (above skating rink), Elements Mall
1 Austin Rd West, Kowloon
www.elementshk.com

WHERE CAN I BUY **HIP KIDS' CLOTHES** WITHOUT PAYING DESIGNER PRICES?

Zara .... 🍭
See page 107

H&M .... 🍭
See page 108

Kingkow .... 🍭
• G/F, Vicwood Plaza
  199 Des Voeux Rd Central, Sheung Wan
  2918-4288
• 1/F, Wing On Department Store
  211 Des Voeux Rd Central, Sheung Wan
  2545-8188
• 2/F, Lee Gardens Two, 28 Yun Ping Rd, Causeway Bay
  2576-0528
• 6/F, SOGO, 555 Hennessy Rd, Causeway Bay
  2831-4634
• 2/F, Cityplaza, 18 Taikoo Shing Rd, Tai Koo
  2535-9883
• Paradise Mall, 100 Shing Tai Rd, Heng Fa Chuen
  2889-4008
• G/F, Ocean Terminal, Harbour City
  Canton Rd, Tsim Sha Tsui
  2317-4088
• 4/F, Wing On Plus, 345 Nathan Rd, Jordan
  2780-8928
• Grand Century Place
  193 Prince Edward Rd West, Mong Kok
  2398-0488
• JUSCO, Site 5, Whampoa Garden, Hung Hom
  2954-0388
• L1, New Town Plaza, Phase 3
  Sha Tin Centre St, Sha Tin, New Territories
  2692-7188
• 2/F, Citygate Outlets
  20 Tat Tung Rd, Tung Chung, Lantau Island
  2882-7488
• L6, Terminal 2, Hong Kong International Airport
  3197-9323
www.kingkow.com
See website for more locations.

Baby Monster .... 🍭
• Basement, Windsor House
  311 Gloucester Rd, Causeway Bay
  2575-2821
• 6/F, SOGO, 555 Hennessy Rd, Causeway Bay
  2831-3983
www.babymonster.com.hk
Hip local brand for newborns to 8-year-olds.

Petit Bateau .... 🍭
G/F, Ocean Terminal, Harbour City
Canton Rd, Tsim Sha Tsui
3188-4051
www.petit-bateau.com

Smarty Pants .... 🍭
1/F, Sun Fung Mansion
52–60 Lyndhurst Terrace, Central
2544-2700
www.smartypants.com.hk

Seed ....

• Seibu, Pacific Place, 88 Queensway, Admiralty
  2918-4085
• 2/F, Lee Gardens Two
  28 Yun Ping Rd, Causeway Bay
  2577-0721
• G/F, The Repulse Bay
  109 Repulse Bay Rd, Repulse Bay
  2803-1677
www.seedchild.com.hk
Australian boutique offering clothes, shoes and accessories for kids 0– 10.

Ginger Bread Kids ....
G/F, Ocean Terminal, Harbour City
Canton Rd, Tsim Sha Tsui
3107-9097
www.gingerbread-kids.com

Dido Dido ....
G/F, 112 Queen's Rd East, Wan Chai
2865-1100
www.didodido.com.hk

WHAT ABOUT BUYING STYLISH, TOP QUALITY
KIDS' CLOTHES AND ACCESSORIES ONLINE OR THROUGH
TRUNK SALES, PRIVATE SALES OR BAZAARS?

Kuki Kids ....
26 Magazine Gap Rd, The Peak
9455-3410
www.kukikids.com
Bold, funky, quality clothes for babies and toddlers. The vibrant colours, bold prints and casual styling will definitely appeal to discerning little fashionistas.

Little Mercerie ....
6040-7893 / 6102-6032 / 6013-1439
www.little-mercerie.com
Quality, casual, French clothing collection for kids from 6 months to 10 years old.

I'M LOOKING FOR REALLY **HIP STREET CLOTHES FOR
KIDS**. ANY SUGGESTIONS?

Evisu ....
See page 118

Lucky Brand ....
See page 118

Juicy Couture ....
• L3, IFC Mall, 8 Finance St, Central
  3586-2017
• G/F, Gateway Arcade, Harbour City
  Canton Rd, Tsim Sha Tsui
  2118-2982
www.juicycouture.com

H&M ....
See page 108

Deep Anger ....
2/F, 7 Lan Fong Rd, Causeway Bay
2869-8303
www.deepanger.com
Designer denims and cool street clothes for tykes.

EVERYTHING FASHION & SHOPPING

WHERE CAN I BUY TOP QUALITY AND/OR **DESIGNER CLOTHES AND FORMAL WEAR FOR KIDS**?

Barocco ....
- 2/F, Lee Gardens Two, 28 Yun Ping Rd, Causeway Bay
  2577-7938
- G/F, Ocean Terminal, Harbour City
  Canton Rd, Tsim Sha Tsui
  2375-1137
- 1/F, Elements Mall, 1 Austin Rd West, Kowloon
  2196-8633
www.barocco.hk

Bonpoint ....
3/F, Prince's Bldg, 10 Chater Rd, Central
2526-9969
www.bonpoint.com
Simply sophisticated baby and children's clothing in timeless styles. High-quality natural fabrics and soft, muted colours are a hallmark of this French brand.

Nicholas & Bears ....
- 3/F, Prince's Bldg, 10 Chater Rd, Central
  2869-7698
- Seibu, L1, Pacific Place, 88 Queensway, Admiralty
  2918-1789
- 6/F, SOGO, 555 Hennessy Rd, Causeway Bay
  2831-3977
- 2/F, Lee Gardens Two, 28 Yun Ping Rd, Causeway Bay
  2890-9618
- 2/F, Cityplaza, 18 Taikoo Shing Rd, Tai Koo
  2907-0900
- G/F, Ocean Terminal, Harbour City
  Canton Rd, Tsim Sha Tsui
  2317-0628
- Basement, The Peninsula Hotel
  Salisbury Rd, Tsim Sha Tsui
  2739-8130
- 1/F, Elements Mall, 1 Austin Rd West, Kowloon
  2196-8000
- L2, Festival Walk, 80 Tat Chee Ave, Kowloon Tong
  2265-8148
www.nicholas-bears.com
See website for more outlets.

Marco & Mari ....
- 3/F, Prince's Bldg, 10 Chater Rd, Central
  2525-0337
- 2/F, The Peak Galleria, 118 Peak Rd, The Peak
  2849-8909
- 2/F, Lee Gardens Two, 28 Yun Ping Rd, Causeway Bay
  2881-1241
- 2/F, Cityplaza, 18 Taikoo Shing Rd, Tai Koo
  2569-0006
- Basement, New World Centre
  20 Salisbury Rd, Tsim Sha Tsui
  2721-0177
www.marcoandmari.com
See website for more outlets.

Jacadi ....
- 3/F, Prince's Bldg, 10 Chater Rd, Central
  2167-8339
- 2/F, Lee Gardens Two, 28 Yun Ping Rd, Causeway Bay
  2506-0099

• 6/F, SOGO, 555 Hennessy Rd, Causeway Bay
  2831-3988
www.jacadi.com
French fashion line for children from 0 to 12 years. It also offers shoes, nursery furniture and accessories.
Seed
See page 170
Comio boo
• 9/F, Times Square, 1 Matheson St, Causeway Bay
• 1/F, Elements Mall, 1 Austin Rd West, Kowloon
2886-0108

WHERE CAN I BUY INEXPENSIVE FORMAL WEAR OR PARTY CLOTHES FOR CHILDREN?

Smile Children Wear Co.
G/F, 4 Li Yuen St East, Central
2789-1663
Tuxedos for boys, princess dresses for girls, and all for just a few hundred dollars! On your left side as you head down Li Yuen St East from Queen's Rd Central.
Kids & Kids
19/F, Li Dong Bldg, 9 Li Yuen St East, Central
2869-6645
www.kidsandkids.com.hk

WHERE CAN I BUY INEXPENSIVE, BRAND-NAME CLOTHES FOR BABIES AND KIDS?

Central: **Lane markets on Li Yuen Streets East and West**
Mong Kok: **Ladies' Market on Fa Yuen St**
See also EVERYTHING STANLEY, pages 187–189.

WHERE CAN I FIND KIDS' UNDERWEAR AND BASICS?

Marks & Spencer
See page 107
Mothercare
See page 161
Kathy Children's Wear
30 Stanley Main St, Stanley
2813-0567
Inexpensive kids' underwear and cotton pyjamas.
Bumps to Babes
See page 160
H&M
See page 108
Giordano Ladies
See pages 109–110

HOW ABOUT SLEEPWEAR FOR BOTH KIDS/ADULTS?

Jimmi Jamms
6285-2564
www.jimmijamms.com
Denise Bergmark makes quality pyjamas for the whole family.
Marleen Molenaar Sleepwear
10/F, Winner Bldg, 27–39 D'Aguilar St, Central
2525-9872
www.marleenmolenaar.com

EVERYTHING FASHION & SHOPPING

WHERE CAN I RENT AN ELABORATE COSTUME?

House of Siren Productions ....
1/F, 18 Shelley St, Central
2530-2371
www.siren.com.hk
A wide range of exquisite costumes and accessories available for rental.

WHERE CAN I BUY DRESS-UP CLOTHES AND COSTUMES FOR CHILDREN?

Siu Wah Yuen Fashion Co. ....
15 Stanley New St, Stanley
2813-7123

Smile Children Wear Co. ....
G/F, 30 Stanley Main St, Stanley
2899-0238

Kids & Kids ....
19/F, Li Dong Bldg, 9 Li Yuen St East, Central
2869-6645
www.kidsandkids.com.hk

Pottinger St ....
Between Stanley St and Wellington St, Central

Toys "R" Us ....
See pages 160–161
A good selection of kids' costumes and dress-up clothes, especially around the Halloween season; however, they are of very average quality.

Bumps to Babes ....
See page 160

Remy Fashion ....
G/F, 24 Li Yuen St West, Central
2524-8847
www.remyfashion.com
Great place for costumes.

Partyland ....
Basement, 51 Wellington St, Central
2147–9283
See also EVERYTHING STANLEY, pages 187–189.

WHERE CAN I BUY KIDS' SKI CLOTHES?

Sun and Moon Fashion ....
• 18A–B Stanley Main St, Stanley
  2813-2723 / 2813-7829
• G/F, 15–19 Carnavon Rd, Tsim Sha Tsui
  2367-1636

Columbia Outlet Store ....
2/F, Citygate Outlets
20 Tat Tung Rd, Tung Chung, Lantau Island
2109-1373

Lafuma Outlet ....
2/F, Citygate Outlets
20 Tat Tung Rd, Tung Chung, Lantau Island
2109-1050

Eikowada ....
See page 148

RC Outfitters ....
See page 145

WHERE CAN I BUY **BALLET SHOES, DRESSES AND SUPPLIES**?

Paul's Ballet Supplies Centre ....
1/F, Admiralty Centre, 18 Harcourt Rd, Admiralty
2527-2867

Fonteyn Ballet Supplies Ltd ....
8 Thompson Rd, Wan Chai
2528-9399
www.yp.com.hk/fonteyn

Three Star Dancing Supply Co. ....
1/F, Prudential Centre, 216–228A Nathan Rd, Jordan
2385-5076

WHERE CAN I BUY **KIDS' TENNIS RACQUETS AND OTHER SPORTS EQUIPMENT**?

Gigasports ....
See page 146

Hong Kong Sports Institute ....
2 On Chun St, Ma On Shan, New Territories
2681-6888
www.hksi.org.hk
The sports shop at the Hong Kong Sports Institute usually carries a very good selection of all sorts of sports products for swimming, football, tennis, hiking, etc.

Escapade ....
See page 168
Check out their exclusive line of kids' tennis clothing.

Rose Sporting Goods ....
• G/F and Mezzanine
  432–436 Hennessy Rd, Causeway Bay
  2893-2801
• G/F, 33 Fa Yuen St, Mong Kok
  2781-1809

WHERE CAN I BUY **KIDS' TRICYCLES/BICYCLES AND ACCESSORIES**?

The Bicycle World ....
15 Wood Rd, Wan Chai
2892-2299
A good range of decent kids' bikes, some helmets and accessories.

Flying Ball Bicycle Co. ....
G/F, Por Yen Bldg, 478 Castle Peak Rd
Kwai Chung, New Territories
2381-5919 / 2381-3661
www.flyingball.com
Good-quality kids' bikes, helmets, gloves and accessories.

KHS Bicycles ....
201 Tung Choi St, Mong Kok
2723-7777
www.khsbicycles.com
A good selection of KHS kids' bikes.

Toys "R" Us ....
See pages 160–161

Wise Kids ....
See page 166

Cosmos Cycles ....
G/F, 32 Haven St, Causeway Bay
2882-2201

WHERE CAN I BUY **KIDS' SWIMWEAR, WETSUITS AND ACCESSORIES**?

Rush
See page 144
Multi-brand store that carries a great selection of kids' swimwear, swimshirts (rashies) and towels by Wahine and Rival, Havaiana flip-flops and more.

Escapade
See page 168
A good range of kids' swimwear, wetsuits, flotation devices, goggles, water toys and more.

Hong Kong Sports Institute
2 On Chun St, Ma On Shan, New Territories
2681-6888
www.hksi.org.hk

Kimley Co.
11A Stanley New St, Stanley
2813-9892
Cheap kids' swimwear, body suits, wetsuits and surfwear.

Bumps to Babes
See page 160

Gigasports
See page 146

Marathon Sports
See page 146

WHERE CAN I BUY **INEXPENSIVE SCHOOL BASICS** SUCH AS SHOES, CLOTHING AND SOCKS?

Li Yuen St East and Li Yuen St West, Central
These two lanes are packed with great bargains including several shops/stalls selling black school shoes, all-white running shoes, white cotton mock turtlenecks, tights, socks, backpacks, pencils and more.

Wan Chai Market
Cross St and Tai Yuen St, Wan Chai
Lots of bargain shops and stalls on these streets selling more of the same as above.

Jardine's Crescent, Causeway Bay
Also known as Jardine's Bazaar, but actually located on Jardine's Crescent
A small lane offering all kinds of bargains, including kids' supplies. Near the entrance of Jardine's Crescent is Good Lucky Shoes at 16 Kai Chiu Rd (2895-6283). They carry cheap kids' shoes, including school, leisure, sandals and fancy shoes.

Stanley Market
See pages 187–189

Mei Ah Hong
G/F, 140 Wellington St, Central
2815-6301
Cheap kids' shoes, ideal for those still growing quickly.

Po Shing Shoe Co. Ltd
G/F, 210 Prince Edward Rd, Prince Edward
2381-2442
While up at the Flower Market, detour to this great little shop for kids' school shoes. They also carry small men's sizes ideal for expat boys.

WHERE CAN I FIND **SPORTS SHOES FOR KIDS**?

Mr Keen Sports Goods ....
G/F, Aberdeen Centre, Site 2
7–11 Nam Ning St, Aberdeen
2873-0318
A great source for kids' sports shoes at reasonable prices.

Kong Kee ....
1C Stanley Main St, Stanley
2813-1925
Running shoes, sandals, water and hiking shoes.

Gigasports ....
See page 146

Marathon Sports ....
See page 146

WHERE CAN I FIND A GOOD SHOP OFFERING A **LARGE SELECTION OF KIDS' SHOES**?

Footstop ....
14/F, 10 Pottinger St, Central
2869-7922
They measure your child's foot including width. Shoes are more expensive but offer the proper fit and support.

Seibu ....
• L1 & L2, Pacific Place, 88 Queensway, Admiralty
  2971-3888
• Kowloon Hotel, 19–21 Nathan Rd, Tsim Sha Tsui
  3693-2388
• L1 & L2, Langham Place, 8 Argyle St, Mong Kok
  2269-1888
A good source for designer and well-made imported shoes for children, including Buckle My Shoe.

Shoe Box ....
• 2/F, Lee Gardens Two
  28 Yun Ping Rd, Causeway Bay
  2890-2329
• G/F, Ocean Terminal, Harbour City
  Canton Rd, Tsim Sha Tsui
  2736-1053
A huge shop dedicated to kids' shoes, with a variety of types and brands, including a large selection of sports shoes.

My Shop ....
2/F, Lee Gardens Two, 28 Yun Ping Rd, Causeway Bay
2894-9011
Another shop dedicated to kids' shoes.

WHERE CAN I FIND A GOOD **CHILDREN'S BOOKSTORE**?

Bookazine ....
• 3/F, Prince's Bldg, 10 Chater Rd, Central
  2525-0218 / 2525-0218
• Basement, Canton House, 54–56 Queen's Rd Central
  2521-1535 / 2521-1535
• 2/F, Winning House, 28 Hollywood Rd, Central
  2525-7792
• L3, IFC Mall, 8 Finance St, Central
  2295-3886
• Basement, Jardine House, 1 Connaught Place Central
  2501-5926

- 1/F, Central Pier 8, Central
  2167-8075
- 1/F, Central Pier 4, Central
  2530-9968
- Lippo Centre, Tower 2, 89 Queensway, Admiralty
  2866-7528
- Shui On Centre, 6–8 Harbour Rd, Wan Chai
  2802-4932
- 26 Nathan Rd, Tsim Sha Tsui
  2724-0431
- Discovery Bay Pier, Discovery Bay, Lantau Island
  2987-1373

www.bookazine.com.hk

Kelly & Walsh

- L2, Pacific Place, 88 Queensway, Admiralty
  2522-5743
- 3/F, One Exchange Square, Central
  2810-5128

www.kellyandwalsh.com

The Pacific Place location has an extensive selection of children's books.

Swindon

13–15 Lock Rd, Tsim Sha Tsui
2366-8001 / 2366-8033
www.swindonbooks.com

Hong Kong Book Centre

- Basement, On Lok Yuen Bldg
  25 Des Voeux Rd Central
  2522-7064 / 2522-7065
- 2/F, Cityplaza, 18 Taikoo Shing Rd, Tai Koo
  2539-6822

www.hongkongbookcentre.com

Dymocks

- L2, IFC Mall, 8 Finance St, Central
  2117-0360 / 2117-0362
- 1/F, Prince's Bldg, 10 Chater Rd, Central
  2826-9248
- G/F, Oriental Crystal Comm. Bldg
  46 Lyndhurst Terrace, Central
  2851-8030
- 1/F, Harbour Centre, 25 Harbour Rd, Wan Chai
  2511-8080
- 3/F, Hopewell Centre, 183 Queen's Rd East, Wan Chai
  3527-3560 / 3527-3561
- G/F, 1 Sing Woo Rd, Happy Valley
  2893-3824
- G/F, The Peak Galleria, 118 Peak Rd, The Peak
  2849-8782
- 1/F, Taikoo Place, 979 King's Rd, Quarry Bay
  2563-8230
- G/F, The Repulse Bay
  190 Repulse Bay Rd, Repulse Bay
  2803-1628
- G/F, 80 Stanley Main St, Stanley
  2813-8070
- 1/F, Discovery Bay Plaza, Discovery Bay, Lantau Island
  2987-8494

www.dymocks.com.hk

The outlet at Lyndhurst Terrace has a large selection of children's books.

BooKanZen ....
2/F, Lee Gardens Two, 28 Yun Ping Rd, Causeway Bay
8102-1011
A great little children's bookstore.

Pollux Books ....
• G/F, Hong Kong MTR Station
  2869-1498
• 21/F, Horizon Plaza, 2 Lee Wing St, Ap Lei Chau
  2873-6962
www.polluxbooks.com
Guaranteed 20–30% less than local bookstores on all
adult and children's books.

Naxos Book & Video ....
2/F, Fleet Arcade, 1 Lung King St, Wan Chai
2511-3611
Good prices for kids' books and DVDs.

WHERE CAN I **ORDER KIDS' BOOKS ONLINE**?

Shop in HK ....
2989-9147
www.shopinhk.com
A good online selection of books and DVDs for babies
and parents, with fast delivery service anywhere in
Hong Kong.

Paddyfield ....
2511-4211
www.paddyfield.com

WHERE ARE SOME OF THE BEST ENGLISH MEDIA
BOOKSHOP CHAINS IN HONG KONG?

Dymocks ....
See page 177
Convenient locations, great selection and variety of
books to suit everyone.

Bookazine ....
See pages 176–177
A well-established chain offering everything from books
to stationery and magazines.

Kelly & Walsh ....
See page 177
Extensive range of reference books on art, design,
literature and more.

Swindon Books ....
13–15 Lock Rd, Tsim Sha Tsui
2366-8001 / 2366-8033
www.swindonbooks.com

Page One ....
• 9/F, Times Square, 1 Matheson St, Causeway Bay
  2506-0381 / 2506-0382
• 3/F, Gateway Arcade, Harbour City
  Canton Rd, Tsim Sha Tsui
  2271-5200 / 2730-6080
• LG1, Festival Walk, 80 Tat Chee Ave, Kowloon Tong
  2778-2808
www.pageonegroup.com
Great for art and design books.

Pollux Books ....
See above

HOW ABOUT **CHINESE MEDIA** BOOKSTORES?

Commercial Press
- Causeway Bay Book Centre
  9 Yee Wo St, Causeway Bay
  2890-8028
- 395 King's Rd, North Point
  2562-0266
- 2/F, Kornhill Plaza North
  1 Kornhill Rd, Kornhill
  2560-0238
- 2/F, Miramar Shopping Centre Hotel Tower
  118–131 Nathan Rd, Tsim Sha Tsui
  2904-1988
- G/F, New Lucky House
  13 Jordan Rd, Yau Ma Tei
  2770-8881

www.commercialpress.com.hk
See website for more locations.

Joint Publishing
- G/F, 9 Queen Victoria St, Central
  2868-6844
- 141 Johnston Rd, Wan Chai
  2838-2081
- 1/F, The Westwood
  8 Belcher's St, Kennedy Town
  2258-9320
- 1/F, APM, 418 Kwun Tong Rd, Kwun Tong
  3148-1089
- 2/F, Plaza Hollywood
  3 Lung Poon St, Diamond Hill
  2955-5986

www.jointpublishing.com
See more locations on website.

WHERE CAN I ORDER **BOOKS ONLINE** IN HONG KONG?

Paddyfield ....
2511-4211
www.paddyfield.com

Yes Asia
www.yesasia.com
The Asian version of Amazon, this website offers books, CDs, DVDs, video games, toys and electronics.

Haven Books ....
www.havenbooksonline.com
A unique line-up of fiction and non-fiction books relevant to English-speakers in Hong Kong and Asia. Online, international and discounted bulk orders welcome.

WHERE IS THERE A **SECOND-HAND BOOK SHOP**?

Flow Community Bookshop
1/F, 40 Lyndhurst Terrace, Central
2964-9483
New/used books and CDs. Also, used VCDs and DVDs.

The Chapter House
10 Stanley Main St, Stanley
9268-9006

Leisure Bookstore
G/F, Block 1, Sai Kung Garden
Chan Man St, Sai Kung, New Territories
2791-9629
The Book Attic
7 – 17 Amoy St, Wan Chai
2259-3103
www.bookattic.info
Collectables
2/F, 11 Queen Victoria St, Central
2559-9562
Large selection of second-hand books and records.

WHERE CAN I FIND **RARE BOOKS**?

Old & Rare Books on Asia
1/F, 32 Lyndhurst Terrace, Central
2854-2853
The Bookshop
• SilverCentre, Silvermine Bay, Mui Wo, Lantau Island
  2984-9371
• 1/F, Discovery Bay Plaza
  Discovery Bay, Lantau Island
  2987-9372
*New books, second-hand books, as well as a good
selection of antiquarian books. This bookshop is great
and affordable if you're in the area. Open daily from
noon to 6pm.*
Lok Man Rare Books
192A Hollywood Rd, Sheung Wan
2868-1056
www.lokmanbooks.com

WHERE CAN I BUY **FRENCH-LANGUAGE BOOKS**?

Librairie Parenthèses
2/F, Duke of Wellington House
14 Wellington St, Central
2526-9215

WHERE CAN I FIND A GOOD SOURCE FOR
COMPUTER/COMPUTER SCIENCE BOOKS?

Duebase Computer Books
2/F, Wan Chai Computer Centre
130 Hennessy Rd, Wan Chai
2836-6990
*All types of computer books, including Chinese and
English text versions.*
HKU Swindon Book Co. Ltd
G/F, Run Run Shaw Bldg
University of Hong Kong, Pok Fu Lam
2546-8412
Man Yuen Books Co. Ltd
45 Parkes St, Jordan
2730-0594
Swindon Books
13 – 15 Lock Rd, Tsim Sha Tsui
2366-8001 / 2366-8033
www.swindonbooks.com

WHERE CAN I FIND A GOOD BOOKSTORE FOR
BUSINESS, LAW AND MEDICAL BOOKS?

Hong Kong Book Centre
- Basement, On Lok Yuen Bldg
  25 Des Voeux Rd Central
  2522-7064 / 2522-7065
- 2/F, Cityplaza, 18 Taikoo Shing Rd, Tai Koo
  2539-6822
www.hongkongbookcentre.com
*Tightly packed shelves of practically every book
category. An especially good source for medical and
business titles.*

Bloomsbury Books Ltd
1/F, Hutchison House
10 Harcourt Rd, Central
2110-9828 / 2526-5387
www.bloomsbury.com.hk
*Established in 1983, Bloomsbury is well-known for its
law and business titles.*

WHERE CAN I FIND A BOOKSTORE THAT SELLS
ART/DESIGN BOOKS?

Tai Yip Art Book Centre
- 1/F, Capitol Plaza
  2–10 Lyndhurst Terrace, Central
  2524-5963
- 1/F, Hong Kong Museum of Art
  10 Salisbury Rd, Tsim Sha Tsui
  2732-2088
- 1/F, Hong Kong Museum of History
  100 Chatham Rd South, Tsim Sha Tsui East
  2191-9188
www.taiyipart.com.hk
*Informative books, including bilingual, Chinese and
pictorial, for those interested in the world of art.*

Basheer Design Books
1/F, Island Bldg
439–441 Hennessy Rd, Causeway Bay
2126-7533
www.basheer.com.hk

Swindon Books ....
13–15 Lock Rd, Tsim Sha Tsui
2366-8001 / 2366-8033
www.swindonbooks.com

Page One ....
See page 178

Kelly & Walsh ....
See page 177

WHERE CAN I FIND A BOOKSTORE THAT
SPECIALISES IN **GAY AND LESBIAN TITLES**?

P.O.V. Bookstore
1/F, Hong Kong Mansion
137–147 Lockhart Rd, Wan Chai
2865-5116

EVERYTHING FASHION & SHOPPING

I WOULD LIKE TO ARRANGE HOME **NEWSPAPER DELIVERY**. WHO CAN I CALL?

Asia Times
2367-3715
www.atimes.com

The Wall Street Journal Asia
2573-7121
www.awsj.com

China Daily
2518-5111
www.chinadaily.com.cn

Financial Times
2845-3311
www.financialtimes.com

International Herald Tribune (HK) Ltd
2922-1171
www.iht.com

South China Morning Post
2680-8822 / 2565-2495 / 2680-8888
www.scmp.com

The Standard
3181-3355
www.thestandard.com.hk

USA Today
2730-6556
www.usatoday.com

WHERE CAN I ORDER **FOREIGN PAPERS AND MAGAZINES** FOR HOME DELIVERY?

International Newspaper & Magazine Subscription Services
2543-0162

Wilson Express
2811-4801

Kiu Yau Books & Magazines Services
2557-0121
Contact Ms Li.

Hong Kong & Foreign Magazine
2571-0554
Contact Mr Kok.

WHO SELLS **CHEAP MAGAZINES**?

Naxos Book & Video ....
2/F, Fleet Arcade, 1 Lung King St, Wan Chai
2511-3611

Chaip Coin Co. Ltd
2/F, World-Wide Plaza, 19 Des Voeux Rd Central
2523-3982
A good variety of English-language magazines at competitive prices.

WHERE DO YOU SUGGEST I GO TO BUY GOOD-QUALITY **PRINTED GIFT BOXES**?

Prints
• 2/F, Prince's Bldg, 10 Chater Rd, Central
  2523-9811
• 9/F, Times Square, 1 Matheson St, Causeway Bay
  2577-8221

- 3/F, Gateway Arcade, Harbour City
  Canton Rd, Tsim Sha Tsui
  2175-5018
- 2/F, Elements Mall, 1 Austin Rd West, Kowloon
  2196-8112

www.prints-international.com

In addition to beautiful gift boxes, Prints carries everything from greeting cards to photo albums to wrapping paper. Using vibrant colours and contemporary design, they offer unique stationery and accessories.

Papyrus
- L1, IFC Mall, 8 Finance St, Central
  2295-3313
- 2/F, Prince's Bldg, 10 Chater Rd, Central
  2869-8788
- 9/F, Times Square, 1 Matheson St, Causeway Bay
  2577-6212
- 3/F, Gateway Arcade, Harbour City
  Canton Rd, Tsim Sha Tsui
  2175-4888
- L2, Festival Walk, 80 Tat Chee Ave, Kowloon Tong
  2265-7088

www.papyrusonline.com

WHERE CAN I BUY INEXPENSIVE PAPER?

Winson Paper Co. Ltd ....
- G/F, 14 Gough St, Central
  2542-2393 / 2542-2009
- 6/F, Shing King Ind. Bldg, 45 Kut Shing St, Chai Wan
  2889-3312

Huge selection of paper, typically sold in reams.

Yat Cheong Paper Co. ....

G/F, 26 Lyndhurst Terrace, Central
2815-8466 / 2815-8408 / 2545-9719

Good selection of pre-packaged paper, envelopes and cards. Great source for DIY cards. Contact Benny Yuen.

WHERE CAN I BUY HAND-MADE GREETING CARDS?

Annie Mac Greeting Cards
6071-7290
Call Grace Wong for more details.

WHERE CAN I GO TO FIND A GOOD EVERYDAY STATIONERY SHOP?

Cosmos Book Shop
- Basement, 30 Johnston Rd, Wan Chai
  2866-1677
- 2/F, Manson House, 74 Nathan Rd, Tsim Sha Tsui
  2367-8699

www.cosmosbooks.com.hk

Reliance Stationery Centre
G/F, 17–19 Wing Wo St, Central
2522-4881

Wah Kwong Stationery Printing Co.
G/F, Waga Comm. Centre
99 Wellington St, Central
2523-0356

WHERE CAN I BUY **HIGH-QUALITY STATIONERY**?

Prints
- 2/F, Prince's Bldg, 10 Chater Rd, Central
  2523-9811
- 9/F, Times Square, 1 Matheson St, Causeway Bay
  2577-8221
- 3/F, Gateway Arcade, Harbour City
  Canton Rd, Tsim Sha Tsui
  2175-5018
- 2/F, Elements Mall, 1 Austin Rd West, Kowloon
  2196-8112

www.prints-international.com

Papyrus
- L1, IFC Mall, 8 Finance St, Central
  2295-3313
- 2/F, Prince's Bldg, 10 Chater Rd, Central
  2869-8788
- 9/F, Times Square, 1 Matheson St, Causeway Bay
  2577-6212
- 3/F, Gateway Arcade, Harbour City
  Canton Rd, Tsim Sha Tsui
  2175-4888
- L2, Festival Walk, 80 Tat Chee Ave, Kowloon Tong
  2265-7088

www.papyrusonline.com

The Artland Co. Ltd
3/F, Lockhart Centre
301–307 Lockhart Rd, Wan Chai
2511-4845
www.artland.com.hk

Hands Arts and Crafts
1/F, Po Wah Comm. Centre
226 Hennessy Rd, Wan Chai
2575-1836
www.hands1986.com
Well-stocked with art and craft stationery.

PaperArt
1/F, Tung Ming Bldg
40–42 Des Voeux Rd Central
2545-8985
www.hkpaperart.com
Rubber stamps, stationery, handmade paper, gift wrap and accessories. Personalised cards can be ordered using both Crane's and their own paper at a cheaper price.

HOW ABOUT AN **ONLINE STATIONERY STORE** THAT ALSO DELIVERS?

www.lyreco.com.hk
www.bigboxx.com

WHERE CAN I HIRE A **CALLIGRAPHER** FOR INVITATIONS AND CARDS IN ENGLISH?

Grafik Design Ltd
17/F, Toi Shan Association Bldg
167 Hennessy Rd, Wan Chai
2152-1019
www.grafikdesign.com.hk
Ask for Patrick Leung.

WHERE CAN I GET CHEAP **COLOUR PHOTOCOPIES**?

Leader's Fast Printing Co. ....
G/F, 107 Wellington St, Central
2541-8627

I'M LOOKING FOR A PRINTER WHO CAN DO **HOLIDAY CARDS, INVITATIONS, STATIONERY AND BUSINESS CARDS**. WHO DO YOU RECOMMEND?

Progressive Press ....
• UG/F, 174 Wellington St, Central
  2522-8778
• 4/F, 156 Wellington St, Central
  2522-2766
www.progressivepress.com.hk
Highly recommended, easy to deal with for foreigners, competitive pricing, heavy paper, embossing, raised and engraved lettering.

Co Card Printing
2/F, World-Wide House, 19 Des Voeux Rd Central
2522-3448
www.cocard.com
Popular, efficient and easy to work with.

Hang Sing Printing and Design
15/F, Derrick Ind. Bldg
49 Wong Chuk Hang Rd, Aberdeen
2554-6311
www.hangsingprinting.com
A full-service, reputable printer that is especially good for large and high-end orders.

H2 cards
G/F, 12A Tai Wong St East, Wan Chai
2542-2880
www.h2cards.com.hk

Huson Printing
7/F, Kong Long Bldg, 102 Jervois St, Sheung Wan
2542-1471
Contact Jean Lam for Christmas cards.

Keung Hing Printing Press
G/F, 19 Gough St, Central
2543-9316
Ask to speak with Deledda Tang.

Green Pagoda Press
13/F, Block A, Tong Chong Factory Bldg
655 King's Rd, Quarry Bay
2561-2324
www.gpp.com.hk

Good Day Cards ....
G/F, 15 Ship St, Wan Chai
2575-2412
www.goodday111.com

Lee Lok Man Chops and Printing
5 Man Wa Lane, Sheung Wan
2850-8599

Studio M
1/F, Tung Yiu Comm. Bldg, 31A Wyndham St, Central
2525-0765
www.studiomhk.com
Fresh, elegant and fashionable stationery, invitations and cards. Call for an appointment.

WHERE CAN I HAVE A **CHINESE WEDDING INVITATION** DONE IN A MORE CONTEMPORARY STYLE?

H2 Cards
G/F, 12A Tai Wong St East, Wan Chai
2542-2880
www.h2cards.com.hk
Contemporary Chinese wedding invitations and all types of quality printing and party favours.

Joys Card Ltd
• G/F, 29 Amoy St, Wan Chai
  2898-2850
• Basement, Golden Plaza
  745 Nathan Rd, Prince Edward
  2789-3931
www.joyscard.com

Progressive Press
See page 185

Co Card Printing
2/F, World-Wide House
19 Des Voeux Rd Central
2522-3448
www.cocard.com

Good Day Cards
G/F, 15 Ship St, Wan Chai
2575-2412
www.goodday111.com

Green Pagoda Press
13/F, Block A, Tong Chong Factory Bldg
655 King's Rd, Quarry Bay
2561-2324
www.gpp.com.hk

Studio M
1/F, Tung Yiu Comm. Bldg
31A Wyndham St, Central
2525-0765
www.studiomhk.com

WHERE CAN I GET FANCY **PAPER** TO DO MY OWN PRINTING?

Yat Cheong Paper Co. ....
G/F, 26 Lyndhurst Terrace, Central
2815-8466 / 2815-8408 / 2545-9719

Winson Paper Co. Ltd ....
• G/F, 14 Gough St, Central
  2542-2393 / 2542-2009
• 6/F, Shing King Ind. Bldg
  45 Kut Shing St, Chai Wan
  2889-3312

WHERE CAN I GET EXCEPTIONALLY **HIGH-END PRINTING FINISHES** FOR MY IMPORTANT INVITATIONS?

Wren Press
2547-1216
www.wrenpress.com
By appointment only.

For sportswear, kids' clothes, discounted labels and souvenirs, nothing beats a trip to Stanley. You can come away with piles of brand-name clothes at bargain prices.

Stanley Market is open Monday to Sunday: generally 10.30am to 6pm, although some stores open a bit earlier and close a bit later.

Weekends are extremely busy but still definitely worth the trek if you can't manage to get there on a weekday.

THE FOLLOWING IS A GOOD ROUTE TO TAKE TO MAKE SURE YOU DON'T MISS ANY GREAT SHOPS:

Start by walking down the slope of Stanley New St from the bus stop, pass the Watson's and turn **right** on the roundabout to Stanley Market St. On the left side of this street near the fruit stand there are four very good kids' clothing shops that sell Gap, Osh Kosh, Gymboree and more.

Continue along **Stanley Main St**, past the Salvation Army and turn **left** into the alley. This is marked Stanley Old St, with a small overhead sign. All the way down this alley on both sides you will find several shops carrying branded kids' clothes interspersed with a few kids' shoe shops and gift shops.

At the T-junction, turn left along Stanley Main St, where there are many notable shops worth visiting. Check out **Kwailin Shop** for contemporary Chinese-inspired jewellery as well as **Lung Sang Hong** for fashionable ladies' cashmere.

Continue down Stanley Main St and don't miss **Stanley Chinese Products** on the left, a great source for jewellery, gifts and souvenirs. Near the end (between shops no. 10 and 8) is an alley that turns uphill. Turn left here and take the next left soon after. At the end of this alley on the left side, you will find **Kathy Children's Wear Shop** (and its sister shop directly across from it). Great for European and American branded kids' clothes, costumes, formal wear and basics (pyjamas and underwear).

Exit Kathy's shop and immediately turn **left** down a narrow path (which doesn't seem like you are going the right way, but you are!) and **left** again down the path with a few steps. In a few more seconds, you will come to, on the left, a belt stall at the T-junction. Turn **right** going up the hill where there are several stalls carrying sportswear and casual clothes. Make your first left (a couple of shops up) down another alley. Along this alley on the **left** is a traditional "dai pai dong" style restaurant serving typical Cantonese fare. Across from this is a great shop that carries men's surf wear and denim.

Continue down this alley until you come to the T-junction which is **Stanley New St** again. When you come out of the alley, on your right and left are several gift/souvenir shops. By now you should be all shopped out! Time for a break and some lunch. Try **Lucy's Restaurant** (see page 21) for a sophisticated meal, or a quick snack at **Lucy's on the Front**, **Momentito** or **Grouchos**, all on the new Stanley waterfront, offering panoramic views of the bay.

Shu Zhai (see page 24) has ideal décor to experience an authentic Chinese meal in a tea house setting. Or try the myriad of restaurants along Stanley Main St and in the historic Murray House. See Food & Entertainment, pages 20–24, for more information.

Congratulations, you have survived!

SHOPS IN STANLEY TO KEEP IN MIND DURING YOUR RETAIL THERAPY TOUR:

Kwailin Shop
G/F, 10A Stanley Main St, Stanley
www.stanleymarket.com.hk
Jeweller.

Kong Kee
1C Stanley Main St, Stanley
2813-1925
Running shoes, sandals, water and hiking shoes for the whole family.

Tong's Sheets & Linen Co.
55–57 Stanley Main St, Stanley
2813-0337

Hoi Yuen Emporium
64 Stanley Main St, Stanley
2813-0470
Kids' and adults' cheongsams, Chinese velvet jackets and clothes.

Lung Sang Hong
45A Stanley Main St, Stanley
2577-6802 / 9323-2360
Cashmere.

Stanley's Silk & Linen
58 Stanley Main St, Stanley
2813-0147
Ladies' fashion made from linen and silk.

Winnie Toys
41 Stanley Main St, Stanley
2813-0086
Small toy store packed with a little bit of everything.

Smile
G/F, 30 Stanley Main St, Stanley
2899-0238
Baby/young kids' wear, costumes and formal wear.

Exclusive
Yau Wing House, 34–36 Stanley Main St
2813-2730
Toys and lifestyle shop.

Five Outlet (Hong Kong) Fashion Ltd
G/F, 52–56C Stanley Main St, Stanley
2899-0517

44 Stanley Main St, Stanley
2813-9777

Alice Sports Co.
23 Stanley Main St, Stanley
2813-9831
Everything-under-the-sun sports clothing.

A3 International Co. Ltd
29 Stanley Main St, Stanley
2813-2555 / 2813-8999

Far East Linen Co.
G/F, 9B Stanley Main St, Stanley
2813-9362

Ann G Fashion
9–11 Stanley Main St, Stanley
2813-5026
Linen fashions.

Stanley Chinese Products
22 Stanley Main St, Stanley
2813-0649
Souvenirs, gifts and jewellery, including pearls.

Sun and Moon Fashion
18A–B Stanley Main St, Stanley
2813-2723 / 2813-7829

Kathy Children's Wear
30 Stanley Main St, Stanley
2813-0567

Take It Easy
G/F, 5B Stanley Main St, Stanley
2899-0322

Lotus Village
• 2A Stanley Main St, Stanley
  2813-2012
• G/F, 17 Stanley Main St, Stanley
  2813-2012
www.lotusvillage.com.hk
Cheongsams, silk robes and gifts.

Children Wear & Costume Shop
G/F, 15 Stanley New St, Stanley
2813-7123

Siu Wah Yuen Fashion Co.
15 Stanley New St, Stanley
2813-7123

Kimley Co.
11A Stanley New St, Stanley
2813-9892

EVERYTHING SHAM SHUI PO

For the ultimate adventurer, exploring Sham Shui Po is a must. Wandering these truly Hong Kong streets, you will find everything from **textiles, notions**, "Do it Yourself" **(DIY)** projects, bargain **electronics, gifts, arts & crafts**, and **fashions**.

This area of interest is bounded by Lai Chi Kok Rd, Yen Chow St, Tai Po Rd and Boundary Rd. Within these boundaries the streets are grid-like, thus easy to navigate.

The area can generally be divided into four quadrants which are dissected by Cheung Sha Wan Rd (mainly wholesale clothing and businesses) and Nam Cheong St:

EVERYTHING FASHION & SHOPPING

Quadrant 1: (within Lai Chi Kok Rd, Nam Cheong St, Cheong Sha Wan Rd and Boundary St) Most of the area is inundated by textile shops, whilst Tai Nan St and Nam Cheong St are dominated by **ribbons**, **trims, buttons, sequin decals, feathers, zippers, fasteners**, etc.

Quadrant 2: (within Lai Chi Kok Rd, Yen Chow St, Cheung Sha Wan Rd and Nam Cheong St) Ap Liu St is "the" place to go for **cheap mobile phones, A/V equipment and computers**. However, be cautious of "bait-n-switch" tactics and phoney goods.

Mixed into this street are stalls carrying everything from headlights for hiking, to disco balls and great knick-knacks for kids' **loot bags**. On Yu Chau St, starting from Nam Cheong St, you will find everything to do with jewellery-making and beading. The rest of this quadrant offers a hodgepodge of clothing, accessories and wet/dry market-like shops and stalls.

Quadrant 3: (within Cheung Sha Wan Rd, Yen Chow St, Tai Po Rd and Nam Cheong St) If you're tired, hungry, and willing to try some local fare, look no farther than the restaurants on Un Chau St and Fuk Wing St for an eclectic mix of **Asian cuisine**. Check out Fuk Wing St, near Nam Cheong St, where you will find ladies' wholesale fashions and miscellaneous goods, in addition to toys and great loot bag items.

Quadrant 4: (within Nam Cheong St, Tai Po Rd and Cheung Sha Wan Rd) This quadrant is monopolised by wholesale clothing and accessories. For kids' wear, check out Wong Chuk St, and for ladies' fashions, Cheung Sha Wan Rd. For gentlemen who are brave enough to venture to Sham Shui Po, Fuk Wa St offers mostly **wholesale** and **retail men's casual clothing, denim, streetwear**, and a couple of shoe shops. Fuk Wing St offers a mix of **sportswear, toys** and **miscellaneous** finds.

FOR SPECIFIC OR HARD-TO-FIND NEEDS IN SHAM SHUI PO:

Upholstery

Although there are endless textile shops in Quadrant 1, upholstery fabric is hard to come by. It may be a bit "hit or miss" but try the following shops that generally carry fabrics suitable for upholstery and curtains. Note: non-bulk (not a full bolt) orders are usually accepted with a slightly higher per-yard cost. Typically you would order, and then pick up within a day or two.

Ruffle Co. ....
G/F, 168 Ki Lung St, Sham Shui Po
2381-3844
The only store known to carry exclusively upholstery fabrics. Lots of floral, brocade and busy patterns; however, occasionally you will find clean and simple fabrics ideal for your decorating needs.
Cheung Tai Piece Goods ....
G/F, 159 Tai Nan St, Sham Shui Po
2398-2805

EVERYTHING FASHION & SHOPPING

SHAM SHUI PO IT · ART IT · SEQUIN IT · FABRIC IT · DESIGN IT · SPORT IT · BABY IT · BARGAIN IT · CUSTOM IT · SHOE IT · SEW IT · MEND IT

Wing Lung Textile Co. ....
G/F, 172–174 Tai Nan St, Sham Shui Po
2395-2738

Yu Hing Piece Goods ....
G/F, 52 Yu Chau St, Sham Shui Po
2360-1078

Kan Fat Piece Goods Co. ....
G/F, 1 Shek Kip Mei St, Sham Shui Po
2392-0902 / 2392-1816

Onson Co. ....
G/F, 2D Wong Chuk St, Sham Shui Po
2787-4790

Leather, skins & furs

Cheong Hing Leather Co. Ltd ....
G/F, 200 Tai Nan St, Sham Shui Po
2787-3022
Leather/skins supplier.

Luen Cheong Co. ....
G/F, 173 Tai Nan St, Sham Shui Po
2393-5926

OTHER SHOPS TO KEEP IN MIND DURING YOUR SHAM SHUI PO ADVENTURE:

Practical International Trading Co. ....
• 14/F, Fashion Centre
  51 Wing Hong St, Lai Chi Kok
  2763-0350
• G/F, 72 Nam Cheong St, Sham Shui Po
  2393-0900
www.pitc.com.hk
Supplier of decorative and fashion materials, such as buttons, zippers, trimmings and ribbons.

Domo-Anna Ricci ....
G/F, Shun Tai Bldg, 4 Fuk Wa St, Sham Shui Po
2778-4841

Amass-Kidswear Wholesale ....
10–10A Wong Chuk St, Sham Shui Po
2778-6980

Toy Star ....
G/F, 30D Fuk Wing St, Sham Shui Po
2776-3136
www.hk-toystar.com

Ying Fung Beads Co. ....
G/F, 246 Yu Chau St, Sham Shui Po
2708-7623 / 2725-6066

Siu Cheung Jewellery Factory ....
See page 158

Bao Quan Ornament Co. ....
G/F, 241 Ki Lung St, Sham Shui Po
2361-8586 / 9267-6746
www.baoquan.com.hk

Yat Chow Pearls & Gems Co. ....
G/F, 620 Canton Rd, Yau Ma Tei
2374-5547

Kum Fu Hoi Pearl Jewellery ....
Stalls 115–116, Jade Market, Kansu St, Yau Ma Tei
9686-4982

EVERYTHING
LIFESTYLE
& WELL BEING

no pain, no gain, it's time to hit the **GYM**	194
SPORTS for all seasons	196
EQUIP yourself with the best	212
TRAVEL the world and the seven seas	219
EVENTS—is your name on the list?	223
ahoy matey, let's hit the **WATER**	225
a **PARTY** to remember	227
there's more to **KIDS'** parties than clowns	231
a **PHOTO** is worth a thousand words	236
don't mess with the **BRIDE**	238
MUSIC lessons for our inner Beethoven	252
ACTIVITIES to get the kids out of the house	257
only the best **SCHOOLS** for your children	266
what's up, **DOC**?	272
9 months and **BABY** makes 3	282
an **ALTERNATIVE** to western medicine	284
BEAUTY or the beast? it's all about maintenance	286
guys need to **PRIMP** too	296
restore, reverse, **REJUVENATE**	297

WHERE CAN I JOIN A **GYM WITH GOOD EQUIPMENT AND FACILITIES**?

Pure Fitness
- L3, IFC Mall 2, 8 Finance St, Central
  8129-8000
- 1–4/F, Kinwick Centre, 32 Hollywood Rd, Central
  2970-3366
- L7, Langham Place Office Tower, 8 Argyle St, Mong Kok
  8129-2828

www.pure-fit.com

Premier health and fitness facilities with state-of-the-art equipment, steam/sauna, group fitness studio, spinning studio, designated personal training studio, entertainment systems on all cardio equipment and an extensive DVD library.

Fitness First
- G/F–3/F, Cosco Tower, Grand Millennium Plaza
  181–83 Queen's Rd Central, Sheung Wan
- 5/F, PCCW Tower, Taikoo Place, Tai Koo
- 4/F, Olympia Palace, 255 King's Rd, North Point
- 6/F, Tower 6, Harbour City
  9 Canton Rd, Tsim Sha Tsui

Hotline: 3106-3000

www.fitnessfirst.com

Conveniently located, full-service gym.

Fitness First Plus
- 37/F, One Exchange Square, 8 Connaught Place, Central
  2525-2900
- 18/F, Sheraton Hotel Towers
  20 Nathan Rd, Tsim Sha Tsui
  2732-6801

Premier location, five-star facilities, for discerning clientele.

California Fitness
- 1 Wellington St, Central
  2522-5229
- 88 Gloucester Rd, Wan Chai
  2877-7070
- G/F, Lee Theatre Plaza, 99 Percival St, Causeway Bay
  2577-0004
- Parkvale, 1060 King's Rd, Quarry Bay
  2880-9660
- G/F, Grand Tower Arcade, 639 Nathan Rd, Mong Kok
  2522-1000
- Pakpolee Comm. Centre, Sai Yeung Choi St, Mong Kok
  2770-0188
- G/F–4/F, Prestige Tower
  23–25 Nathan Rd, Tsim Sha Tsui
  2366-8666
- G/F, Treasure World, Site 2
  Whampoa Garden, Hung Hom
  2622-2228
- 18/F, MegaBox, 38 Wang Chiu Rd, Kowloon Bay
  2250-5022
- 3/F, Tuen Mun Town Plaza, Phase 1
  1 Tuen Shun St, Tuen Mun, New Territories
  2618-3008

www.californiafitness.com

Multi-location full-service gym with a large number and selection of group exercise classes.

Lifestyle Fitness
2/F, 33 Sai Kung Tai St, Sai Kung, New Territories
2791-9220
www.lifestylefitness.com.hk
2,700-sq.-ft. fully equipped gym and aerobics studio on the water in old Sai Kung town.

Seasons Fitness
3/F, ICBC Tower, Citibank Plaza
3 Garden Rd, Central
2878-6288
www.seasonsfitness.com
Over 30,000 sq. ft. and more than three floors with facilities that include a 20-m indoor lap pool, a women-only fitness section and a 10,000-sq.-ft. gym.

YWCA
1/F, 1 Macdonnell Rd, Mid-Levels
3476-1330
www.ywca.org.hk
Convenient gym in the Mid-Levels with all the basics and a rooftop heated swimming pool.

I'M LOOKING FOR A MORE **PRIVATE HOTEL GYM WITH GOOD FACILITIES**. ARE THERE ANY THAT I CAN JOIN OR PAY TO USE?

The Marriott Hotel Gym
Marriott Hotel, Pacific Place, 88 Queensway, Admiralty
2810-8366

The Shangri-La Health Club
8/F, Island Shangri-La Hotel
Pacific Place, Supreme Court Rd, Admiralty
2820-8583
Minimum 3-month membership.

ARE THERE ANY **GYMS** THAT ARE **WOMEN ONLY**?

Seasons Fitness
See above

Curves
9/F, Pacific House, 20 Queen's Rd Central
2234-9000
www.curveshongkong.com
This women-only gym now has over 4 million members worldwide. It offers a complete cardio and strength training workout in just 30 minutes.

Club Siena
Discovery Bay, Lantau Island
2987-0772
www.dbrc.hk

Phillip Wain
- 4/F, Lee Gardens Two
  28 Yun Ping Rd, Causeway Bay
  2882-7880
- 2/F, Cityplaza 4, 18 Taikoo Shing Rd, Tai Koo
  2513-1333
- 5/F, Miramar Tower
  1–23 Kimberley Rd, Tsim Sha Tsui
  2377-3888
www.phillipwain.com
Women-only fitness and beauty club.

IT'S A RAINY DAY, ARE THERE ANY **PUBLIC INDOOR SPORTS CENTRES**?

Aberdeen UC Complex Indoor Games Hall
5/F–6/F, Aberdeen UC Complex
203 Aberdeen Main Rd, Aberdeen
2555-8909
www.lcsd.gov.hk

Chai Wan Indoor Games Hall
6 Yee Shun St, Chai Wan
2897-9144
www.lcsd.gov.hk

Harbour Road Sports Centre
27 Harbour Rd, Wan Chai
2827-9684
www.lcsd.gov.hk

Hong Kong Park Sports Centre
29 Cotton Tree Drive, Central
2521-5072
www.lcsd.gov.hk

Quarry Bay Indoor Games Hall
7/F, Quarry Bay Municipal Services Bldg
38 Quarry Bay St, Quarry Bay
2562-0374
www.lcsd.gov.hk

Sheung Wan Sports Centre
11/F, Sheung Wan Municipal Services Bldg
345 Queen's Rd Central, Sheung Wan
2853-2574
www.lcsd.gov.hk

South China Athletic Association
88 Caroline Hill Rd, Causeway Bay
2577-6932
www.scaa.org.hk

YMCA King's Park Centenary Centre
22 Gascoigne Rd, Yau Ma Tei
2782-6682
www.kpcchk.org

Stanley Sports Centre
UG/F, Stanley Municipal Services Bldg
6 Stanley Market Rd, Stanley
2813-5106
www.lcsd.gov.hk

WHERE CAN I TAKE **CLIMBING** LESSONS OR GO CLIMBING?

YMCA of Hong Kong
2/F, North Tower, 41 Salisbury Rd, Tsim Sha Tsui
2268-7000 ext 7138
Offers adult and children's courses and improver clinics. After completing an assessment course you will be given a card that then allows you to use the climbing facility. You can also learn rollerblading and other sports.

YMCA King's Park Centenary Centre
22 Gascoigne Rd, Yau Ma Tei
2782-6682
www.kpcchk.org

EVERYTHING LIFESTYLE & WELL BEING

WHERE CAN I FIND A FREELANCE HIGHLY-QUALIFIED **PERSONAL TRAINER**?

Optimum Performance Studio
2/F, World Trust Tower
50 Stanley St, Central
2868-5170
www.opstudiohk.com
Innovative training studio with the latest equipment, individualised training programmes and trainers specialising in Power Plate, Pilates, personal training and more. Most sessions can be done privately or in a small group.

Ross Eathorne Wellness
9833-7446
www.rosseathornewellness.com
With exceptional qualifications and certifications, Ross Eathorne offers personal training, nutrition and lifestyle appraisal, injury and posture correction, post-natal conditioning, sport performance, golf fitness and more. Ross was World Champion Mr Fitness in 2000.

Physical Harmony Personal Training Ltd
6086-0083
www.physicalharmony.com
Adam Menhennett has excellent credentials and is available for personal training and other sports and conditioning training.

Peter Lee
9232-4714
Peter is great at coaching running. Will work with you outdoors or at a gym.

N.I. Fitness
9379-8064 / 2292-2900
nifitness@netvigator.com
A formerly ranked Swedish boxer, Nike offers serious training for those who want results.

Louis Doctrove
9806-5155
louisdoctrove@hotmail.com
Louis specialises in body-building, strength-training, weight loss/gain and outdoor training. He is also a trainer with Bootcamp (see page 198).

Larry Sanders
9013-8344
Offers tennis classes at Hong Kong Tennis Centre, and personal training on Hong Kong Island.

Daniel Tang
Health Club, Conrad Hotel Hong Kong
Pacific Place, 88 Queensway, Admiralty
2521-3838
Former Mr Hong Kong. Offers training anywhere in Hong Kong.

Alley Tang
9096-2859
Offers training to help ladies recover their fitness. Comes to requested locations and brings equipment.
See also gyms, pages 194–195.

EVERYTHING LIFESTYLE & WELL BEING

I'M CONSIDERING A **TRIATHLON** OR **ADVENTURE RACE**. ARE THERE ANY COACHES/TRAINERS TO HELP ME PREPARE?

IHP Triathlon
Henry Fok Health & Fitness Complex
Stanley Ho Sports Centre, 10 Sha Wan Dr, Pok Fu Lam
2872-1205
www.eteamz.com/IHPTriathlon

Hong Kong Triathlon Association
10/F, Olympic House, 1 Stadium Path
So Kon Po, Causeway Bay
2504-8282
www.triathlon.com.hk
Training starting from age 8 and up for beginners and for all levels.

Asia Pacific Adventure
16/F, Gee Chang Hong Centre
65 Wong Chuk Hang Rd, Aberdeen
2792-7128
www.asiapacificadventure.com

I'M INTERESTED IN SOME SERIOUS **GROUP OUTDOOR TRAINING**. ANY SUGGESTIONS?

Bootcamp
2869-6883
www.bootcamp.com.hk
Kick-start your exercise regime with this results-based program that works on cardio, strength and muscle toning. Three different levels offering something for beginners to hardcore athletes. Contact Jackson Ip. Locations throughout Hong Kong and outlying areas. They also offer "Bootcamp chef" where individualised meals, designed to target your needs, are delivered to your home or office.

WHICH **TRACK FIELDS** CAN I USE FOR TRAINING?

Aberdeen Sports Ground
108 Wong Chuk Hang Rd, Aberdeen
2552-6043 / 2555-0103
Field closed Saturdays 8am to 12pm. Jogging times: 7am to 8am and 5:30pm to 10pm.

Wan Chai Sports Ground
20 Tonnochy Rd, Wan Chai
2827-6987 / 2879-5602
Field closed Saturdays; no jogging times for running track.

Causeway Bay Sports Ground
Causeway Rd, Causeway Bay
2890-5127 / 2879-5602
Field closed Mondays. Contact the staff for times the jogging track is open.

Sai Kung Tang Shiu Kin Sports Ground
41 Fuk Man Rd, Sai Kung, New Territories
2791-6410
Field closed Wednesdays. Jogging times: 6:30am to 10:30pm.

EVERYTHING LIFESTYLE & WELL BEING

I AM LOOKING FOR SOMEONE TO ORGANISE SOME **TEAM BUILDING** OR **ADVENTURE PROGRAMME FOR A GROUP**. WHO SHOULD I CONTACT?

Outward Bound Hong Kong
Tai Mong Tsai, Sai Kung, New Territories
2554-6067
www.outwardbound.org.hk

Dragonfly
12/F, Loon Kee Bldg, 267–275 Des Voeux Rd Central
2111-8917 / 2111-8918
Adventure sports organiser offering tailor-made outdoor adventure programmes.

HOW CAN I FIND OUT ABOUT **TRAIL RACES** TAKING PLACE IN HONG KONG?

Oxfam Trailwalker
2520-2525
www.oxfamtrailwalker.org.hk
This is the famous MacLehose, 100-km, four-person team race.

Green Power Hike
221 Queen's Rd East, Wan Chai
2893-2856
www.greenpower.org.hk
A 50-km trail race on the Wilson Trail.

Sowers Action Challenging 12 Hours Charity Marathon
2597-4739
www.challenging12hours.org

Raleigh International Hong Kong
G/F, Block J, Ming Wah Dai Ha
7A Kung Ngam Rd, Shau Kei Wan
8101-4622
www.raleigh.org.hk
www.wilsontrail.org
The organisation holds various orienteering and trail races, including its annual Raleigh Challenge on Wilson Trail, a 78-km race which lasts for two days.

Action Asia
3158-0251 / 3158-0250
www.actionasiaevents.com

King of the Hills Mountain Marathon
2812-0741 / 9034-6850
www.seyonasia.com

HK Marathon Pro .... ☎
2563-4422
www.ecotourism.org.hk/hkmp

Hong Kong Hiking Association .... ☎
www.hkha-china.org.hk

WHAT ABOUT **MARATHONS** AND **RUNNING RACES**?

Standard Chartered Hong Kong Marathon
2577-0800
www.hkmarathon.com

Standard Chartered: The Greatest Race on Earth
www.thegreatestrace.com
Four marathons in Nairobi, Singapore, Mumbai and Hong Kong. Teams of four or individual participants.

Hong Kong Runners
www.hkrunners.com
Athletic Veterans of Hong Kong
www.avohk.org
Hong Kong Distance Runners Club
www.hkdrc.org
Hong Kong Ladies Road Runners Club
www.hklrrc.org.hk
Sedan Chair Race
www.sedanchairace.org
Hong Kong ITU Triathlon Premium Asian Cup
www.hongkongitu.com
Hong Kong's very own annual triathlon.
Action Asia
www.actionasia.com/aae
Adventure races and sprint series. Multi-discipline, including trail running, open water swimming, trail and road biking, rope work, abseiling, orienteering and more.
marathon.HK
www.marathon.hk

HOW ABOUT OPEN WATER RACES?

Revolution Asia
22/F, Guangdong Finance Bldg
88 Connaught Rd West, Sheung Wan
6103-5514
www.revolution-asia.com
Multi-sport race organiser and event conceptualisation, design, implementation and management services. Revolution Asia organises a splash-and-dash aquathon series and an ocean swim series.

WHERE CAN I FIND GOOD PILATES CLASSES?

Flex Yoga & Pilates Studio
1/F, Woodleigh House, 80 Stanley Village Rd, Stanley
2813-2212
www.flexhk.com
Premier pilates and yoga studio, conveniently located in Stanley to serve Southside enthusiasts. Private, semi-private and group classes.
Iso Fit
8/F, California Tower, 30–32 D'Aguilar St, Central
2869-8630
www.isofit.com.hk
Pilates and gyrotonic exercise methods for group, private or semi-private and also pre/post-natal instruction.
B.E.T. Pilates Centre
24/F, World-Wide House, 19 Des Voeux Rd Central
2526-3706
www.betpilates.com
Biokinetik Exercise Technique (BET) is a rehabilitation approach employing corrective Pilates. Especially for people with injuries or muscle imbalance.
Physio Central
21/F, Universal Trade Centre
3–5 Arbuthnot Rd, Central
2801-4801
www.physio-central.com

One Pilates Studio
13/F, Li Dong Bldg, 9 Li Yuen St East, Central
2147-3318
www.onepilatesstudio.com
Private and group sessions. Training begins with a private assessment and instruction, followed by closely supervised group appointments.

Optimum Performance Studio
2/F, World Trust Tower, 50 Stanley St, Central
2868-5170
www.opstudiohk.com
Sally Adair's private, semi-private and mat pilates classes deliver excellent results.

Studio Sai Kung
1/F, 28 Man Nin St, Sai Kung, New Territories
2791-9705
www.thestudiosaikung.com

Bodywise Pilates
1C, Hooley Mansion
21 –23 Wong Nai Chung Rd, Happy Valley
2836-3166 / 2836-3186
www.bodywisepilateshk.com

WHERE CAN I FIND GOOD **YOGA CLASSES**?

Pure Yoga
- 16/F, The Centrium, 60 Wyndham St, Central
  2971-0055
- 25/F, Soundwill Plaza, 38 Russell St, Causeway Bay
  2970-2299
- 4/F, Lincoln House, Taikoo Place
  979 King's Rd, Quarry Bay
  8129-1188 / 3741-1480
- 14/F, The Peninsula Office Tower
  18 Middle Rd, Tsim Sha Tsui
  8129-8800
- L9, Langham Place Office Tower
  8 Argyle St, Mong Kok
  3691-3691 / 2186-8808
www.pure-yoga.com
Over 700 classes each week in a wide range of yoga practices, including hot and power yoga.

Yoga Limbs
33/F & 34/F, 69 Jervois St, Sheung Wan
2525-7415
www.yogalimbs.com
Yoga classes, Indian head massage and aromatherapy.

Yogasana
239 Jaffe Rd, Wan Chai
2511-8892
www.yogasana.com.hk

Yoga Central
4/F, Kai Kwong House, 13 Wyndham St, Central
2982-4308
www.yogacentral.com.hk

Planet Yoga
- 20/F, Silver Fortune Plaza, 1 Wellington St, Central
  2525-8288
- 12/F, Windsor House
  311 Gloucester Rd, Causeway Bay
  2525-8277

- 4/F, Sands Bldg, 17 Hankow Rd, Tsim Sha Tsui
  3165-8080
www.planetyoga.com.hk

Yoga For Life
1/F, Lot 1227, Heng Mei Deng, Clear Water Bay
Sai Kung, New Territories
2167-7401
www.yogaforlife.com.hk

Iyengar Yoga Centre of Hong Kong
4/F, New Victory House
93 – 103 Wing Lok St, Sheung Wan
2541-0401
www.iyengaryogahongkong.com

Yoga Kids
9861-6227
www.yogakids-asia.com

Anahata Yoga
18/F, One Lyndhurst Tower
1 Lyndhurst Terrace, Central
2905-1822
www.anahatayoga.com.hk
Various locations, see also website.

The Yoga Room
3/F, Xiu Ping Comm. Bldg
104 Jervois St, Sheung Wan
2544-8398
www.yogaroomhk.com

Life Management Yoga Centre
11/F, Kimberley House
35 Kimberley Rd, Tsim Sha Tsui
2191-9656
www.yoga.org.hk

Movement Improvement
3D Elegance Court, Discovery Bay, Lantau Island
2987-5852
www.movementimprovement.com.hk
*Pilates, yoga and fitness, including pre-natal, kids'
classes, privates and semi-privates.*

Flex Yoga & Pilates Studio
1/F, Woodleigh House, 80 Stanley Village Rd, Stanley
2813-2212
www.flexhk.com

Bodywise Pilates
1C Hooley Mansion
21 – 23 Wong Nai Chung Rd, Happy Valley
2836-3166 / 2836-3186
www.bodywisepilateshk.com

HOW ABOUT SOMEONE WHO OFFERS **PRIVATE
YOGA CLASSES**?

Tanya Boulton
6448-7310
www.tanya-b.com
*Tanya caters to your needs, whether it's healing an old
injury or a strong yoga session to tone your mind, body
and spirit.*

Movement Improvement
3D Elegance Court, Discovery Bay, Lantau Island
2987-5852
www.movementimprovement.com.hk

EVERYTHING LIFESTYLE & WELL BEING

MARTIAL ARTS IT . RACE I

PRIMP IT . RELAX IT . SPA IT . LEARN IT . IMPROVE IT . COACH IT . EXERCISE IT . HIGHLIGHT IT . SEE IT . READ IT . PLAN IT .

WHERE CAN I FIND GOOD **TAI-CHI CLASSES**?

Hong Kong Tai Chi School .... 🔆
3/F, Wing Shing Bldg
31 Clear Water Bay Rd, Sham Shui Po
2387-8256 / 2345-3239
www.taichihk.com

Practical Tai Chi
1/F, Cheung Hong Mansion
25–33 Johnston Rd, Wan Chai
www.taigik.com

Master Cheng Kam Yan
9480-2093

Master Edward Ho
9267-0143

Master Les Mcclure
2982-4775

Master Ng Kam Kee
9457-7540
www.hktaichi.com

Tai Chi with Raymond
9427-0851

WHAT ASSOCIATIONS AND LEARNING CENTRES
EXIST FOR **CONTACT SPORTS**?

International Karate-Do Goshin Kan Association
3/F, Anton Bldg, 1 Anton St, Wan Chai
9210-1310
www.goshinkan.org.hk

Hong Kong Chito Ryu Karate
www.chitoryu.hk

Judo Association of Hong Kong
2504-8360
www.hkjudo.org

Hong Kong Aikido Kan
2861-0191

Hong Kong Chong Do Taekwondo Association
9/F, 625 Nathan Rd, Mong Kok
2388-0707
www.chongdo.org.hk

Hong Kong Kendo Association
10/F, Olympic House, 1 Stadium Path, Causeway Bay
2504-8145
www.hongkongkendo.com

Ving Tsun Martial Arts Institute
4/F, Sun Hey Mansion, 68–76 Hennessy Rd, Wan Chai
2578-8928
www.vt.com.hk

Hong Kong Judo Kan
12/F, East Point Centre, 555 Hennessy Rd, Causeway Bay
2891-0851 / 2591-4570
www.hongkongjudokan.com
Classes are offered for both adults and children aged 6–16.

Gojuryu Karatedo Jinta-kan (HK) Dojos
2956-2868
www.karatehk.com

Hong Kong Aikido Association
2427-3540
www.aikido.com.hk

EVERYTHING LIFESTYLE & WELL BEING

WHERE CAN I FIND A **BOXING/MARTIAL ARTS GYM**?

Fightin' Fit
3/F, Peter Bldg, 56 – 62 Queen's Rd Central
2526-6648
www.fightinfit.com.hk
Martial arts and core fitness training. A full range of disciplines, classes and personal training options for beginner, advanced and professional levels.

DEF Boxing
15/F, The Pemberton
22 – 26 Bonham Strand East, Sheung Wan
2840-0162
www.def.com.hk
Hong Kong's first members-only boxing gym. Professional training for any age and experience level. Full-size boxing ring, heavy bags, speed bag, free weights and cable cross machines.

Kontact
9/F, LKF Tower, 33 Wyndham St, Central
2525-2400
www.kontact.hk

Jab Mixed Martial Arts Studio
5/F, Kimley Comm. Bldg,
142 – 146 Queen's Rd Central
2851-6684
www.jabmma.com
Highly recommended studio specialising in boxing, kick-boxing, Brazilian jiu jitsu and mixed martial arts. They also offer personal training and an excellent nutrition programme.

Impakt
2/F, Wing's Bldg, 110 – 116 Queen's Rd Central
2167-7218
www.impakt.hk

Philippine Martial Arts Federation
1/F, Seven Seas Shopping Centre
121 King's Rd, Fortress Hill
2565-0668
www.arnis.com.hk

Ving Tsun Martial Arts Institute
4/F, Sun Hey Mansion, 68 – 76 Hennessy Rd, Wan Chai
2578-8928
www.vt.com.hk

Hong Kong Wushu Union
10/F, Olympic House, 1 Stadium Path, Causeway Bay
2504-8226
www.hkwushuu.com.hk

Kick Start
26/F, Li Dong Bldg, 9 Li Yuen St East, Central
2167-8248
www.kickstart.hk

ARE THERE ANY **WEBSITES USEFUL FOR EQUESTRIANS**?

Hong Kong Equestrian Federation
www.hkef.org
The Hong Kong Jockey Club
www.hkjc.com

EVERYTHING LIFESTYLE & WELL BEING

WHERE CAN I GO **HORSE-BACK RIDING**?

Clearwater Bay Equestrian Centre ....
115 Mau Po, Clear Water Bay
Sai Kung, New Territories
6398-6241
www.ceec.hk

Lo Wu Saddle Club Ltd ....
STT 1408 (TP), Ho Sheung Heung, New Territories
2673-0066
www.lowusaddleclub.org

Pok Fu Lam Public Riding School ....
75 Pok Fu Lam Reservoir Rd, Pok Fu Lam
2550-1359
www.hkjcridingschools.com

Lei Yue Mun Public Riding School ....
Lei Yue Mun Park, 75 Chai Wan Rd, Chai Wan
2568-9776
www.hkjcridingschools.com

Tuen Mun Public Riding School ....
Lot 45, Lung Mun Rd, Tuen Mun, New Territories
2461-3338
www.hkjcridingschools.com

Beas River Riding School ....
Beas River Country Club, Sheung Shui, New Territories
2966-1990
This location is for the use of Hong Kong Jockey Club members.

WHERE CAN I DO **INLINE SKATING, HOCKEY AND SKATEBOARDING**?

YMCA King's Park Centenary Centre ....
22 Gascoigne Rd, Yau Ma Tei
2782-6682
www.kpcchk.org
KPCC is Hong Kong's first and only centre dedicated to extreme sports. It offers an inline hockey rink, Hong Kong's highest climbing wall (outdoor) and a skate park for skateboarders. Courses available for climbing, inline hockey, recreational and aggressive inline, skateboarding and tennis. They also have adult and youth inline hockey leagues.

Go Sport ....
9049-6292
maniagosk8@gmail.com
Donna Maniago runs a fantastic programme for kids who want to learn to inline skate. After they have mastered the basics, kids can join the inline hockey programme that she also runs.

Mei Foo Skate Park
Lai Chi Kok Park, Mei Foo Sun
Hong Kong's premier (by Hong Kong standards) skateboarding and BMX park. Not good for young children.

Chai Wan Skate Park ....
345 San Ha St, Chai Wan
Similar to the park above, but much smaller. Still worth going if you're in the neighbourhood or live nearby. This is a free skate park of approximately 630 sq. m.

WHERE CAN I GO TO **ICE-SKATE AND TAKE SKATING LESSONS**, TOO?

The Rink
G/F, Elements Mall, 1 Austin Rd West, Kowloon
2196-8016
www.rink.com.hk

Mega Ice
L10, MegaBox, 38 Wang Chiu Rd, Kowloon Bay
2709-4020
www.megaice.com.hk

Sky Rink
8/F, Dragon Centre, 37K Yen Chow St, Sham Shui Po
2307-9365
www.skyrinkhk.com
Ken Leung teaches hockey skating.

Cityplaza Ice Palace
1/F, Cityplaza, 18 Taikoo Shing Rd, Tai Koo
2844-8688
www.icepalace.com.hk

Festival Walk Glacier
UG, Festival Walk, 80 Tat Chee Ave, Kowloon Tong
2844-3588
www.glacier.com.hk

I AM LOOKING FOR PROFESSIONAL **KIDS' SOCCER COACHING**, WHO SHOULD I CONTACT?

Brazilian Soccer Schools
2/F, Chak Fung House
440–442 Nathan Rd, Yau Ma Tei
2385-9677
www.bss.com.hk

Hong Kong Football Academy
15/F, Ka Nin Wah Comm. Bldg
423–425 Hennessy Rd, Wan Chai
2866-7931
www.hkf-academy.com

I'D LIKE TO GET MY YOUNG CHILD INTO INTRODUCTORY **SOCCER LESSONS**, WHAT DO YOU RECOMMEND?

Socatots
2/F, Chak Fung House
440–442 Nathan Rd, Yau Ma Tei
2385-9033
www.socatots.com

Multi-Sport
8/F, Yien Yieh Bank Western Bldg
32–36 Des Voeux Rd West, Sheung Wan
2540-1257
www.multi-sport.com.hk

Play Sport
8/F, Wing Fu Bldg
18–20 Wing Kut St, Central
2818-9453
www.playsport.com.hk

EVERYTHING LIFESTYLE & WELL BEING

WHO CAN GIVE ME **PRIVATE SWIMMING LESSONS**?

Time to Swim – Karen Robertson ....
9419-3468
Ronald Chung ....
6491-1193
Multi-Sport ....
8/F, Yien Yieh Bank Western Bldg
32–36 Des Voeux Rd West, Sheung Wan
2540-1257
www.multi-sport.com.hk

ARE THERE ANY GOOD **PUBLIC SPLASHING POOLS** OR
WATER-PARK TYPE POOLS FOR KIDS?

Kowloon Park Swimming Pool
Kowloon Park, 22 Austin Rd, Tsim Sha Tsui
2724-3577
Tseung Kwan O Swimming Pool
Wan Lung Rd, Tseung Kwan O, New Territories
2706-7646
Kennedy Town Swimming Pool
12N Smithfield Rd, Kennedy Town
2817-7973
Victoria Park Swimming Pool
Victoria Park, Hing Fat St, Causeway Bay
2570-8347
Hammer Hill Rd Swimming Pool
30 Lung Cheung Rd, Wong Tai Sin
2350-6173

ARE THERE **PUBLIC POOLS** WHERE I CAN DO LAPS?

*Except for the last three listings, these are all 50-m
standard pools. Visit www.lcsd.gov.hk for more details.*
Pao Yue Kong Swimming Pool
2 Shum Wan Rd, Wong Chuk Hang
2553-3617 / 2555-0103
Kennedy Town Swimming Pool
12N Smithfield Rd, Kennedy Town
2817-7973
Morrison Hill Swimming Pool
7 Oi Kwan Rd, Wan Chai
2575-3028 / 2891-7335
Chai Wan Swimming Pool
345 San Ha St, Chai Wan
2558-3538 / 2564-2646
Victoria Park Swimming Pool
Victoria Park, Hing Fat St, Causeway Bay
2570-8347 / 2564-2646
Island East Swimming Pool
52 Lei King Rd, Sai Wan Ho
2151-4082
Sai Kung Swimming Pool
Wai Man Rd, Sai Kung, New Territories
2792-7285 / 2791-3100
*Here they have a main pool, a teaching pool, a fun/
leisure pool and a 450-seat spectator stand.*
Sham Shui Po Park Swimming Pool
733 Lai Chi Kok Rd, Sham Shui Po
2360-2329

EVERYTHING LIFESTYLE & WELL BEING

I'M KEEN ON **WATER SPORTS**, WHERE CAN I **KAYAK, WATERSKI, WINDSURF, WAKEBOARD,** ETC.?

Kayak-and-Hike Ltd
9300-5197
www.kayak-and-hike.com

Paradive
1/F, Cheong Ming Bldg, 88 Argyle St, Mong Kok
2355-7010
www.paradive.com.hk

Blue Sky Sports Club
12/F, Mow Shing Centre, 118 Bedford Rd, Tai Kok Tsui
2792-4938
www.bluesky-sc.com

Sea Dynamics
3/F, Sun Hey Mansion, 68–76 Hennessy Rd, Wan Chai
2604-4747
www.seadynamics.com

Cheung Chau Windsurfing Centre
1 Hak Pai Rd, Cheung Chau
2981-2772
www.ccwindc.com.hk

Jockey Club Wong Shek Water Sports Centre
Wong Shek Pier, Sai Kung, New Territories
2328-2311
www.lcsd.gov.hk/watersport/en/inde_jockey.php

WHERE CAN I BOOK A **PUBLIC TENNIS COURT**?

There are three ways to book your court:

1. Call Leisure Link to book any of the courts listed below: 2606-2111 / 2927-8080
2. Online via Leisure Link: registration required for Internet booking and payment:
   w1.leisurelink.lcsd.gov.hk/index/index.jsp
3. Call the tennis facility directly.

The following are just a few of the court venues available for booking:

Po Tsui Park, Yuk Nga Lane
Yuk Nga Lane, Tseung Kwan O, New Territories
2703-7231

Sai Kung Tennis Courts
Wai Man Rd, Sai Kung, New Territories
2792-6459 / 2792-4149

Chai Wan Park Tennis Courts
Tsui Wan St, Chai Wan
2898-7560

Quarry Bay Park
Hoi Chak St, Quarry Bay
2513-8499

Victoria Park Tennis Court
Causeway Rd, Causeway Bay
2570-6186

Kowloon Tsai Park
13 Inverness Rd, Kowloon City
2338-7748

Ho Man Tin Sports Centre
1 Chung Yee St, Ho Man Tin
2762-7837

Junction Rd Park
195 Junction Rd, Kowloon Tong
2336-4638
Ma Tau Wai Reservoir Playground
2A Sheung Wo St, Kowloon City
2713-7252
Tung Chau St Park
Tung Chau St, Sham Shui Po
2728-4888
Aberdeen Tennis & Squash Centre
1 Aberdeen Praya Rd, Aberdeen
2553-6130
Bowen Rd Tennis Court
2B Bowen Dr, Mid-Levels
2528-2983 / 2879-5602
Causeway Bay Sports Ground
Causeway Rd, Causeway Bay
2890-5127
Hong Kong Tennis Centre
Wong Nai Chung Gap Rd, Wan Chai
2574-9122
King's Park Recreation Ground
23 King's Park Rise, Yau Ma Tei
2385-8985

WHAT ASSOCIATIONS EXIST FOR **RACQUET SPORTS**?

Hong Kong Tennis Association
2504-8266
www.tennishk.org
Hong Kong Squash
2869-0229
www.hksquash.org.hk
Hong Kong Badminton Club
www.hkbadmintonclub.com

WHAT ASSOCIATIONS EXIST FOR **BALL AND PUCK SPORTS**?

Hong Kong Rugby Football Union
2332-7112
www.hkrugby.com
Hong Kong Invitational Cricket Festival
www.hkcricketfestival.com
Hong Kong Netball Association
Olympic House, 1 Stadium Path
So Kon Po, Causeway Bay
2504-8208
www.netball.org.hk
Hong Kong Tennis Association
2504-8266
www.tennishk.org
Hong Kong Cricket Association
2504-8102
www.cricket.com.hk
Hong Kong International Cricket Sixes
2543-8500
www.hksixes.com
Hong Kong Football Association
2712-9122
www.hkfa.com

Hong Kong Golf Association
2504-8659
www.hkga.com
Hong Kong Slo-Pitch Softball Association
8100-9922
www.hongkongsoftball.com
Handball Association of Hong Kong, China
2504-8119
www.handball.org.hk
Hong Kong Lacrosse Association
8107-6636
www.hklax.org
Hong Kong Hockey Association
2782-4932
www.hockey.org.hk
Hong Kong Typhoons Ice Hockey Club
2594-0165
www.hktyphoonsicehockey.org
Hong Kong Ice Hockey Association Ltd
2504-8189
www.hkiha.org
Hong Kong Amateur Ice Hockey Club
2863-4357
www.hkahc.com
Hong Kong Federation of Roller Sports
2504-8203
www.rollersports.org.hk
Hong Kong, China Inline Hockey Association Ltd
www.hkciha.com.hk

ANY **CYCLING SPORTS** ASSOCIATIONS?

Hong Kong Cycling Association
2504-8176
www.cycling.org.hk
Hong Kong Mountain Bike Association
www.hkmba.org
Unicycle Hong Kong
www.unihk.org

AND **WATER-SPORTS/SWIMMING** ASSOCIATIONS?

The Hong Kong Underwater Club
www.hkuc.org.hk
Splash Hong Kong
2792-4495
www.splashhk.com
Offers diving courses.
Hong Kong Amateur Swimming Association
2572-8594 / 2572-8524
www.hkasa.org.hk
Windsurfing Association of Hong Kong
2504-8255
www.windsurfing.org.hk
Hong Kong Sailing Federation
2504-8159
www.sailing.org.hk
Royal Hong Kong Yacht Club
Kellett Island, Causeway Bay
2832-2817
www.rhkyc.org.hk

Hebe Haven Yacht Club
2719-9682
www.hhyc.org.hk
Hong Kong Island Paddle Club
2812-2565
www.hkipc.com
Hong Kong Amateur Dragon Boat Association
8103-8233
www.dragonboat-hk.org
Hong Kong Dragon Boat Association
8106-8134
www.hkdba.com.hk
Stanley Dragon Boat Race Association
2813-0564
www.dragonboat.org.hk
Hong Kong Water Ski Association
2504-8168
www.waterski.org.hk

AND ASSOCIATIONS FOR **OTHER SPORTS AND ATHLETIC LEVELS**?

Hong Kong Dragons Triathlon Club
www.hktriclub.com
Hong Kong Ladies Road Runners Club
9139-3127
www.hklrrc.org.hk
Hong Kong Mountaineering Club ....
2504-8124 / 2504-8125
www.hkmu.org.hk
Hong Kong Parachute Association
Hong Kong Aviation Club
31 Sung Wong Toi Rd, Kowloon City
2713-5171
www.hkaviationclub.com.hk
Hong Kong Survival Game Association ....
8207-7232
www.survivalgame.org.hk
Hong Kong Shooting Association ....
2504-8138
www.hkshooting.org.hk
Orienteering Association of Hong Kong
www.oahk.org.hk
Hong Kong Paralympic Committee &
Sports Association for the Physically Disabled
2602-8232
www.hksap.org
Hong Kong Paragliding Association
9289-4157
www.hkpa.net
Hong Kong Street Skating Group ....
www.hkssg.org
Hong Kong Ultimate Players Association
www.hkupa.com
Hong Kong Amateur Athletic Association
2504-8215
www.hkaaa.com

EVERYTHING LIFESTYLE & WELL BEING

WHICH ARE **GOOD SPORTS SHOPPING AREAS** FOR FINDING SPORTSWEAR, SHOES AND EQUIPMENT?

Fa Yuen St, Mong Kok
Between Argyle St and Shantung St
This two-block area has more sports stores than you could ever imagine. Don't miss some of the big ones:
Wan Kee Co. Ltd
66 Fa Yuen St, Mong Kok
2388-3348 / 2787-5003
L.A. Sports Co.
97 Fa Yuen St, Mong Kok
2394-6738
Toronto Sports-Fusion
G/F, 80 Fa Yuen St, Mong Kok
2392-2498
www.torontosports.com.hk
Sportshouse
• 61 & 43B Fa Yuen St, Mong Kok
  2332-3099
• G/F, 64 –68 Fa Yuen St, Mong Kok
  2388-0190
www.sportshouse.com
Multiple locations, see also website.

WHERE ELSE CAN I FIND A GOOD SHOP FOR GENERAL **SPORTS EQUIPMENT AND GEAR**?

Gigasports ....
See page 146
Marathon Sports ....
See page 146
Hong Kong Sports Institute ....
2 On Chun St, Ma On Shan, New Territories
2681-6888
www.hksi.org.hk
Sports products for swimming, soccer, tennis, hiking, etc.
Rose Sporting Goods
Yan Wo Yuet Bldg, 436 Hennessy Rd, Causeway Bay
2893-2801
Escapade ....
See page 168
10K Running Pro Shop ....
1/F, 169 Gloucester Rd, Wan Chai
2893-7990
www.10k.com.hk
Popular one-stop destination for Hash House Harriers and runners for clothing, shoes, and accessories.
T.T. Sport
31 Johnston Rd, Wan Chai
2891-2997
Tanka Sport Outlets
See page 146
Biotrek
www.biotrek.com.hk
Yoga 4 Yogi
3184-0841
www.yoga4yogi.com

EVERYTHING LIFESTYLE & WELL BEING

WHERE CAN I BUY GOOD **EXERCISE EQUIPMENT** FOR A HOME GYM?

Life Fitness Asia Pacific Ltd
26/F, Miramar Tower, 132 Nathan Rd, Tsim Sha Tsui
2575-6262
One of the most well-known brands in commercial and home exercise and gym equipment.

Kettler
G/F, 112–113 Connaught Rd Central
2851-2816
www.kettler.com.hk

Asia Health Equipment
G/F, 155 Wong Nai Chung Rd, Happy Valley
2573-3389
www.ahe.com.hk

Oasis Fitness Engineering Co.
11/F, Pacific Trade Centre, 2 Kai Hing Rd, Kowloon Bay
2754-6868
www.oasis-fitness.com

Cheung Kee Sport Goods
G/F, 35 Hillier St, Sheung Wan
2543-8323

Movers and Shapers
12/F, The Centrium, 60 Wyndham St, Central
3621-0180

Wang Kei Sports
US Navy Fleet Arcade, Lung King St, Admiralty
2511-3079

WHERE CAN I BUY **YOGA ACCESSORIES AND CLOTHING**?

Rush ....
See page 144

Yoga 4 Yogi
3184-0841
www.yoga4yogi.com

Biotrek
www.biotrek.com.hk

lululemon
Stockists:
- L3, IFC Mall 2, 8 Finance St, Central
  8129-8000
- 14/F, Leighton Centre, 77 Leighton Rd, Causeway Bay
  2238-5555
- Pure Yoga
  See page 201
www.lululemon.com

I'M SERIOUS ABOUT BIKING. WHERE ARE THE BEST PLACES TO **BUY A BICYCLE**?

Flying Ball Bicycle Co. ....
G/F, Por Yen Bldg, 478 Castle Peak Rd
Kwai Chung, New Territories
2381-5919 / 2381-3661
www.flyingball.com

The Bicycle World ....
15 Wood Rd, Wan Chai
2892-2299

KHS Bicycles ....
201 Tung Choi St, Mong Kok
2723-7777
www.khsbicycles.com

Rodafixa
G/F, 12 On Wo Lane, Central
9090-9312
www.hkfixed.com
Fixed-gear bicycles with a cult-like following.

Shun Lee Bicycle Co. Ltd
• 2/F, Lucky Plaza Comm. Complex
  1 – 15 Wang Pok St, Sha Tin, New Territories
  2695-7195
• G/F, Fu Loy Garden, 7 Ma Wang Rd
  Yuen Long, New Territories
  2457-8390

Chung Yung Cycle Co.
G/F, 132 San Fung Ave, Sheung Shui, New Territories
2679-5602
www.hkbicycle.com

WHERE CAN I BUY **HOCKEY EQUIPMENT**?

Hong Kong Skate Co. ....
8/F, Dragon Centre, 37K Yen Chow St, Sham Shui Po
2386-2222
www.skateco-hkchina.com
*Established in 1982, this is Hong Kong's only true shop for
hockey equipment. They carry many major brands, but can
be limited in sizing, especially for children. You may want
to call Terrence Chin in advance to check size availability.*

C By Chickeeduck
1/F, Elements Mall, 1 Austin Rd West, Kowloon
2196-8703
www.chickeeduck.com.hk

Aberdeen Marina Club – Ice Rink Pro Shop
8 Shum Wan Rd, Aberdeen
2814-5484
Purchases only available through members' accounts.

WHERE CAN I BUY **ROLLERBLADES**?

King's Park Pro Shop ....
YMCA King's Park Centenary Centre
22 Gascoigne Rd, Yau Ma Tei
2782-6682

Alice Sports Co. ....
23 Stanley Main St, Stanley
2813-9831
*Rollerblades, clothes, wetsuits and sports shoes,
including kids' Converse running shoes.*

WHERE IS THE BEST PLACE TO BUY A **SKATEBOARD**
AND SKATEBOARD CLOTHING?

8FIVE2
2/F, United Success Comm. Centre
506 – 508 Jaffe Rd, Causeway Bay
2573-9872
www.8five2.com
Top brands for skateboards and high-end street clothing.

EVERYTHING LIFESTYLE & WELL BEING

WHO SELLS **SURFING, SKI AND SNOWBOARDING CLOTHES**?

Patagonia
See page 147
Ski and snowboarding clothes are sold here.
Wind N' Surf International Ltd
19–27 Wyndham St, Central
2536-9128
A good source for surfing clothes, flip-flops and accessories for men and women.

HOW ABOUT A PLACE WITH A **GOOD GOLF SIMULATOR**?

Golf Hideaway Ltd
5/F, Tung Chong Bldg
657–659 King's Rd, Quarry Bay
2561-2005
Real-time golf simulators and Thai massage therapy all under one roof.

WHERE ARE SOME OF THE BETTER **DRIVING RANGES**?

City Golf Club
8 Wui Cheung Rd, Jordan
2992-3333
www.citygolfclub.com
Hong Kong Jockey Club Golf Range
Sha Tin Racecourse, Sha Tin, New Territories
2966-6766
South China Athletic Association Golf Section
88 Caroline Hill Rd, Causeway Bay
2577-4437
www.scaa.org.hk
Tai Po Shuen Wan Golf Training Centre
70 Ting Kok Rd, Tai Po, New Territories
2660-9222
The Jockey Club Kau Sai Chau Public Golf Course
Kau Sai Chau, Sai Kung, New Territories
2791-3388
www.kscgolf.org.hk

WHERE CAN I BUY **GOLF EQUIPMENT AND ACCESSORIES**?

Taylor Made Golf
G/F, Sino Plaza
255–257 Gloucester Rd, Causeway Bay
2574-4706
www.taylormadegolf.com
ABC Golf Outlet
• G/F, Two Chinachem Plaza
  68 Connaught Rd Central
  2989-9122 / 2989-9133
• 1/F, Admiralty Centre
  18 Harcourt Rd, Admiralty
  2861-2163
• LG/F, Leighton Centre
  77 Leighton Rd, Causeway Bay
  2882-7282 / 2882-7286

Central Golf
G/F, Bank of America Tower, 12 Harcourt Rd, Central
2140-6633
www.centralgolf.com.hk
This golf centre has a well-stocked pro shop carrying all major brands and Hong Kong's largest variety of demonstration clubs. You can test them in one of their practice driving bays, and also look into selling your old clubs.

Improve Your Game Ltd
G/F, 56 Leighton Rd, Causeway Bay
2894-8338

Metro Golf
15/F, Melbourne Plaza, 33 Queen's Rd Central
2537-6217 / 8205-0568
www.metrogolf.com.hk

Queensway Golf International Ltd
2/F, Shun Tak Centre
168–200 Connaught Rd Central, Sheung Wan
2866-0306
www.queensway-golf.com.hk

WHERE CAN I GET TOP-QUALITY **BILLIARD SUPPLIES** AND **SNOOKER CUES**?

Snooker 147
4/F, Sang Woo Bldg
227–228 Gloucester Rd, Causeway Bay
2890-1815
www.snooker147.net

WHERE CAN I GET **OUTFITTED** FOR MY HIKING TRIPS?

Hong Kong Mountaineering Training Centre
1 Fa Yuen St, Mong Kok
2770-6746
www.hkmtc.com
Extensive shop selling packs, tents, camping accessories.

Karrimor Shop
G/F, 1K Fa Yuen St, Mong Kok
2770-7110
www.karrimor.com

Protrek
See pages 144–145

Mountain Services International
52–56 King's Rd, North Point
2541-8942
www.mshk.com.hk

Sun Mark Camping Equipment Co.
121 Wan Chai Rd, Wan Chai
2893-8553

RC Outfitters ....
See page 145

WHERE CAN I GET GENERAL INFORMATION ON HONG KONG'S **HIKING TRAILS**?

Map Publications Centre
23/F, North Point Government Offices
333 Java Rd, North Point
2231-3187
Maps of Hong Kong's best hiking areas can be bought here.

Hiker's Guide to Hong Kong
A book by Pete Spurrier from FormAsia
This best-selling, compact guidebook covers well-known trails in Hong Kong.

Above the City: Hiking Hong Kong Island
A book by Alicia M Kershaw and Ginger Thrash from Hong Kong University Press
Detailed routes, including distance and difficulty ratings for Hong Kong Island hiking trails, jogging trails and family walks.

Magic Walks
A book series by Kaarlo Schepel from Alternative Press
Titles for hikes on Hong Kong Island, Kowloon, Outlying Islands and the MacLehose Trail.

Hong Kong Pathfinder
A book by Dr Martin Williams from Asia 2000
A guide to day walks in Hong Kong by well-known freelance writer/photographer Dr Martin Williams who has a strong interest in wildlife, conservation issues and travel. See also his website www.drmartinwilliams.com.

Hong Kong Hikes: Twenty Best Walks in the Territory
A book by Christian Wright and Tinja Tsang from SCMP Publications
A well laid-out guide of twenty of Hong Kong's best hikes, including maps, taxi directions in Chinese and places to eat. Presented in binder format, each hike description is removable and can be taken along in the convenient plastic folder included. The book is out of print but you may still be able to find it in second-hand book shops (see pages 179–180).

Hong Kong Outdoors
www.hkoutdoors.com

Hong Kong Hikers Kiosk
www.hiking.com.hk

The Hong Kong Trampers
www.hktrampers.com

Hong Kong Adventurer
www.hkadventurer.com

WHO CAN HELP ME **ORGANISE A HIKING EXPEDITION**?

Kayak and Hike Ltd
9300-5197
www.kayak-and-hike.com
Paul Etherington organises kayaking, hiking, helicopter, powerboat, mountain biking (in any combination) adventure tours in Hong Kong.

WHAT FACILITIES DO **HONG KONG'S BEACHES** OFFER?

Deep Water Bay Beach
Island Rd, Deep Water Bay
2812-0228 / 2555-0103
Fast-food kiosk, barbecue area, changing room, shower facilities, toilet, raft, car park.

Repulse Bay Beach
Repulse Bay Beach Rd, Repulse Bay
2812-2483 / 2555-0103
Changing room, shower facilities, toilet, raft, car park, playground, beach volleyball court.

Middle Bay Beach ....
South Bay Rd, Repulse Bay
2812-2546 / 2555-0103
Light refreshment restaurant, barbecue area, changing room, shower facilities, toilet, bathing shed, raft.

South Bay Beach ....
South Bay Rd, Repulse Bay
2812-2468 / 2555-0103
Light refreshment restaurant, barbecue area, changing room, shower facilities, bathing shed, raft.

St. Stephen's Beach ....
Wong Ma Kok Path, Stanley
2813-1872 / 2555-0103
Light refreshment kiosk, barbecue area, changing room, shower facilities, toilet, raft.

Stanley Main Beach ....
Stanley Beach Rd, Stanley
2813-0217 / 2555-0103
Fast-food kiosk, barbecue area, changing room, shower facilities, toilet, bathing shed, raft.

Turtle Cove Beach ....
Tai Tam Rd, Stanley
2813-0386 / 2555-0103
Light refreshment kiosk, barbecue area, changing room, shower facilities, toilet, raft, playground.

Shek O Beach ....
Shek O Rd, Shek O
2809-4557 / 2555-0103
Light refreshment restaurant, barbecue area, changing room, shower facilities, toilet, raft, playground, car park, obstacle golf course.

Big Wave Bay Beach ....
Big Wave Rd, Shek O
2809-4558 / 2555-0103
Fast-food kiosk, barbecue area, changing room, shower facilities, toilet.

Hung Shing Yeh Beach ....
Yung Shue Wan, Lamma Island
2982-0352 / 2852-3220
Barbecue area, changing room, shower facilities, toilet.

Lo So Shing Beach ....
Sok Kwu Wan, Lamma Island
2982-8252 / 2852-3220
Barbecue area, changing room, shower facilities, toilet, raft.

Kwun Yam Beach ....
Hak Pai Rd, Cheung Chau
2981-8472 / 2852-3220
Refreshment kiosk, changing room, shower facilities, toilet, raft.

Cheung Chau Tung Wan Beach ....
Cheung Chau Beach Rd, Cheung Chau
2981-8389 / 2852-3220
Changing room, shower facilities, toilet, raft.

Trio Beach ....
Trio (Hebe Haven), Sai Kung, New Territories
2792-3672 / 2792-4149
Refreshment kiosk, barbecue area, changing room, shower facilities, toilet, raft, playground.

Silverstrand Beach .... 🍭
Silverstrand, Clear Water Bay Rd
Sai Kung, New Territories
2719-8230 / 2792-4149
Refreshment kiosk, barbecue area, changing room, shower facilities, toilet, raft.

Clear Water Bay First Beach .... 🍭
Tai Wan Tau, Clear Water Bay Rd
Sai Kung, New Territories
2719-8308 / 2792-4149
Barbecue area, changing/shower facilities, toilet, raft.

Clear Water Bay Second Beach .... 🍭
Tai O Mun Rd, Sai Kung, New Territories
2719-0351 / 2792-4149
Refreshment kiosk, changing room, shower facilities, toilet, raft.

WHERE CAN I FIND GOOD **TRAVEL AGENTS** FOR PERSONAL TRAVEL?

Charlotte Travel Ltd
10/F, 8 Hart Ave, Tsim Sha Tsui
2110-6070
Emergency number: 9385-6677
www.charlottetravel.hk
A reputable, reliable one-stop travel agent offering a variety of travel itineraries based on personal experiences worldwide. Check out their website for special deals and packages.

Rocksun Travel Agency
8/F, Yu To Sang Bldg, 37 Queen's Rd Central
2869-6838
Great for finding the best deals out there.

Wind Travel Ltd
5/F, Winway Bldg, 50 Wellington St, Central
2499-3380
www.windtravel.com
Speak to Connie or Angel for immediate answers to your booking questions and searching out good deals.

Concorde Travel
1/F & 7/F, Galuxe Bldg, 8–10 On Lan St, Central
2526-3391
www.concorde-travel.com

Emporium Travel Ltd
18/F, Winway Bldg, 50 Wellington St, Central
2530-3136
Reputable travel agent offering good service and recommendations for travel itineraries.

Farrington American Express Travel
17/F, Millennium City 6, 392 Kwun Tong Rd, Kwun Tong
2808-2828 / 3121-3121
www.amextravel.com.hk
Especially good for personal travel arrangements if you or your company also use them for corporate travel arrangements.

Oliver's Travel Ltd
10/F, Chung Seung Bldg, 9–10 Queen Victoria St, Central
2869-8823
Ask for Oliver Fung, who offers great package deals and seems to have good pull to get you on oversold flights.

Four Seasons Travel Service
5/F, Commercial House, 35 Queen's Rd Central
2868-0622

Aero International Ltd
6/F, Cheung Bldg,1–3 Wing Lok St, Sheung Wan
2545-6669

Travelex Hong Kong
9/F, Hong Kong Pacific Centre, 28 Hankow Rd, Tsim Sha Tsui
2270-7600
www.hktc.com.hk

Country Holidays
23/F, New World Tower 1, 18 Queen's Rd Central
2525-9199
www.countryholidays.com.hk

Tiglion Travel
9/F, Yue Xiu Bldg, 160–174 Lockhart Rd, Wan Chai
2511-7189
www.tiglion.com

I'M LOOKING FOR A **SPORTY OR ADVENTUROUS HOLIDAY**. ARE THERE ANY TRAVEL AGENCIES THAT SPECIALISE IN THIS?

China Golden Bridge Travel Service
6/F, Tak Woo House, 17–19 D'Aguilar St, Central
2801-5591
www.goldenbridge.net

Sun N Sea Holidays
9/F, May May Bldg, 683–685 Nathan Rd, Mong Kok
2926-1668
www.sunnseaholidays.com

Asia to Africa
17/F, Chinachem Hollywood Centre
1–13 Hollywood Rd, Central
2525-2776
www.atoasafaris.com

Fishtail Tours and Travel
1/F, Civic Comm. Bldg, 165 Woo Sung St, Yau Ma Tei
3104-8191
www.fishtail.org

The Travel Advisers
9/F, South Seas Centre, Tower 2
75 Mody Rd, East Tsim Sha Tsui
2368-5009
www.traveladvisers.com.hk

Diving Adventure Travel
2/F, Island Bldg, 439–445 Hennessy Rd, Causeway Bay
2572-2138
www.divinghk.com

I WANT TO PLAN A REALLY **UNIQUE HOLIDAY**. WHO CAN I FIND TO ORGANISE THIS?

Wanlilu Play Ltd
15/F, 1 Hysan Ave, Causeway Bay
3162-3729
www.wanliluplay.com
A professional leisure planning service offering what most travel agents have neither the time nor resources to do. They can organise every aspect of your holiday, offering you exceptional experiences abroad.

EVERYTHING LIFESTYLE & WELL BEING

WHICH REPUTABLE **ONLINE TRAVEL SERVICE** OFFERS CHEAP FLIGHTS AND HOLIDAY PACKAGES WORLDWIDE?

Zuji ....
28/F, Chinachem Leighton Plaza
29 Leighton Rd, Causeway Bay
2175-5786
www.zuji.com.hk
Online discount travel service offering flights, hotels and more.

Last Minute ....
G/F, Mirror Tower
61 Mody Rd, East Tsim Sha Tsui
2301-3188
www.lastminute.com.hk

WHERE CAN I GET ADVICE AND **VACCINATIONS** AGAINST TROPICAL DISEASES?

Dr John W Simon
The Central Medical Practice
15/F, Prince's Bldg, 10 Chater Rd, Central
2521-2567
Dr Simon is one of Hong Kong's leading specialists in tropical diseases. If you know exactly which jab you need, you can also drop by the Central Medical Practice during certain hours and have your vaccination given by a registered nurse without a consultation fee.

Vaccinations Travel Health Centre
• 18/F, Wu Chung House
  213 Queen's Rd East, Wan Chai
  2961-8840
• Department of Health
  1/F, Cheung Sha Wan Government Offices
  303 Cheung Sha Wan Rd, Sham Shui Po
  2150-7235
www.travelhealth.gov.hk

Prestige Vaccination Centre ....
21/F, Li Dong Bldg
9 Li Yuen St East, Central
3160-4886

I HAVE LIMITED VACATION TIME AND WOULD LOVE TO EXPERIENCE **HONG KONG'S COUNTRYSIDE**. WHAT WOULD YOU ADVISE?

Explore Sai Kung
G/F, 8 Tak Lung Back St
Sai Kung, New Territories
2243-1083
www.exploresaikung.com
This service promotes Sai Kung to visitors and explorers as a natural, peaceful haven from the high-energy pace of city life. In addition to the user-friendly website, they also put out an informative newsletter. Contact Judy Love-Eastham to discuss your next visit.

Kayak and Hike Ltd
9300-5197
www.kayak-and-hike.com
Offer adventure trips all over Hong Kong.

EVERYTHING LIFESTYLE & WELL BEING

WHERE CAN I BUY DEPENDABLE **LUGGAGE**?

Samsonite
- G/F, Man Yee Arcade
  68 Des Voeux Rd Central
  2259-9318
- L2, IFC Mall, 8 Finance St, Central
  2295-3055
- 2/F, Windsor House
  311 Gloucester Rd, Causeway Bay
  2736-936
www.samsonite.com
Various locations.

Tumi
- 1/F, Prince's Bldg, 10 Chater Rd, Central
  2869-7488
- 2/F, Elements Mall, 1 Austin Rd West, Kowloon
  2196-8158
- L6, Departures East Hall, Terminal 1
  Hong Kong International Airport
  2383-1474
- L5, Passenger Terminal 2
  Hong Kong International Airport
  3197-9072
intl.tumi.com
Various locations.

Victorinox
- L2, IFC Mall, 8 Finance St, Central
  2730-1847
- 7/F, Times Square, 1 Matheson St, Causeway Bay
  3101-2969
- 10/F, SOGO, 555 Hennessy Rd, Causeway Bay
  2836-3223
- 3/F, Gateway Arcade
  Harbour City, Canton Rd, Tsim Sha Tsui
  2175-5888
- 2/F, Elements Mall, 1 Austin Rd West, Kowloon
  2196-8531
- UG, Festival Walk, 80 Tat Chee Ave, Kowloon Tong
  2265-8000
- L6, New Town Plaza, Phase 1
  Sha Tin Centre St, Sha Tin, New Territories
  2286-8600
- L5, Terminal 2, Hong Kong International Airport
  2769-1382
www.victorinox.com.hk

WHERE CAN I GET GOOD **MAPS OF CHINA**?

Dymocks
See page 177
Maps of China in sheets or scrolls.

Commercial Press
See page 179
Detailed maps of China's provinces and cities, which cost from $15 to $40.

Page One
See page 178
They sell a user-friendly "China Touring Map" for $20.

EVERYTHING LIFESTYLE & WELL BEING

I HEAR THAT **AIRPORT CONCIERGE SERVICE** COMPANIES MAKE TRAVEL A BREEZE. WHERE CAN I FIND ONE?

Worldwide Flight Services
15/F, World-Wide House, 19 Des Voeux Rd Central
2261-2727
www.worldwideflight.com.hk
Packages available for their airport chaperone, porter, reception and shuttle services, wheelchair assistance, or even extra labour for setting up your convention stalls and the like.

WHAT IS THE **ULTIMATE GIFT FOR A HIGH-FLYER** WHO HAS EVERYTHING?

Quintessentially
2/F, Teda Bldg, 87 Wing Lok St, Sheung Wan
2540-8595
www.quintessentially.com
A membership in this private club, with its 24-hour global concierge service, is the ultimate gift of convenience. With an office in Hong Kong, they offer benefits such as practical assistance and special deals relating to travel, dining, art and music.

WHERE CAN I LOOK UP **LISTINGS OF ENTERTAINMENT EVENTS** TAKING PLACE AROUND TOWN?

CityLine / Urbtix
2111-5999
www.cityline.com.hk
Online booking for tickets to concerts, theatre, dance, musicals, circus, cinema and more, including performance information and seat selection.

Hong Kong Ticketing
3128-8288
hkticketing.hk
Online ticketing service for music, sports, dance, film, theatre and more through Urbtix. Also a booking service for UA Cinemas.

Hip Hong Kong
www.hiphongkong.com

HKClubbing
www.hkclubbing.com

Dim Sum and Then Some
www.dimsumandthensome.com.hk
See also EVERYTHING ONLINE, page 387.

WHERE CAN I BOOK **MOVIE TICKETS** ONLINE?

CityLine/UA Theatres
2317-6666
www.cityline.com.hk

Broadway Circuit
2388-0002
www.cinema.com.hk

AMC Cinemas
2265-8933
www.amccinemas.com.hk

MCL Cinemas
2418-8876
www.mclcinema.com

EVERYTHING LIFESTYLE & WELL BEING

IS THERE A LONG-STANDING **COMEDY CLUB** IN HONG KONG?

The Punchline Comedy Club
Duetto Italian & Indian Dining
2/F, Sun Hung Kai Centre, 30 Harbour Rd, Wan Chai
2598-1222 / 2827-7777
www.punchlinecomedy.com/hongkong

WHERE CAN I GO TO HEAR SOME **LIVE MUSIC** THIS WEEKEND?

Yumla
Lower Basement, Harilela House, 79 Wyndham St, Central
2147-2383
www.yumla.com
A "sound bar" established to promote alternative music. The front door opens into the upper terraces of Pottinger St Park, providing a tree-lined outdoor chill space. The exterior is periodically repainted by local artists.

Café Deco
1/F–2/F, Peak Galleria, 118 Peak Rd, The Peak
2848-5111
www.cafedecogroup.com
Live singer, Thu–Sat.

Insomnia
LG/F, Ho Lee Comm. Bldg, 38–44 D'Aguilar St, Central
2525-0957
www.liverockmusic247.com
Live band starts at 10:30pm nightly.

The Cavern
LG/F, LKF Tower, 55 D'Aguilar St, Central
2121-8969
www.igors.com

Fringe Club
2 Lower Albert St, Central
2521-7251
Live music on Friday and Saturday, 10:30pm to 1am.

Dusk Till Dawn
G/F, 76–84 Jaffe Rd, Wan Chai
2528-4689
www.liverockmusic247.com

Grappa's Country Restaurant
Basement, Jardine House, Connaught Rd Central
2521-2322
www.elgrande.com.hk
Jazz band from 8 to 11pm.

WHERE CAN I LOOK UP LISTINGS FOR **MUSIC EVENTS**?

MCB
www.mcb.com.hk
Hong Kong and international music news and reviews.

The Underground
www.undergroundhk.com
Lists local music acts playing in Hong Kong.

Hong Kong Ticketing
3128-8288
www.hkticketing.com
Online booking with seat selection for concerts, musicals, recitals and other entertainment events.

CityLine/Urbtix
2111-5999
www.cityline.com.hk

I WOULD LIKE TO **CHARTER A YACHT** AND CONSIDER BUYING. WHO SHOULD I CONTACT?

Simpson Marine Ltd
G/F, Aberdeen Marina Tower
8 Shum Wan Rd, Aberdeen
2555-8377
www.simpsonmarine.com
International charter of luxury boats and yachts can be arranged, in addition to buying or selling.

Asia Yacht Services
Gold Coast Yacht and Country Club
1 Castle Peak Rd, Castle Peak Bay
2815-0404
www.asiayachtservices.com

Saffron Marina
20/F, Teda Bldg, 87 Wing Lok St, Sheung Wan
3583-5234
www.saffron-marina.com

Saffron Cruises
20/F, Teda Bldg, 87 Wing Lok St, Sheung Wan
2857-1311
www.saffron-cruises.com
Offers fully catered private boat cruises and yacht charter.

I UNDERSTAND YOU NEED A **BOAT LICENCE** IN HONG KONG. WHERE CAN I TAKE A COURSE TO GET MY LICENCE OR JUST IMPROVE MY SKILLS?

The Marine Department
Harbour Bldg, 38 Pier Rd, Central
2852-4941
www.mardep.gov.hk

The Royal Hong Kong Yacht Club
Kellett Island, Causeway Bay
2832-2817
www.rhkyc.org.hk

Hong Kong Sailing Federation
2504-8159
www.sailing.org.hk

A YACHT IS OUT OF MY LEAGUE; WHERE SHOULD I LOOK FOR **SMALLER BOATS** AND TOYS?

Mustang Marine Co.
G/F, 146 Pak Sha Wan, Sai Kung, New Territories
2719-3391

Sea Dynamics
3/F, Sun Hey Mansion
68–76 Hennessy Rd, Wan Chai
2604-4747
www.seadynamics.com

Sai Sha Watersports
G/F, EMAX, 1 Trademart Drive, Kowloon Bay
2792-8307
www.sai-sha.com

WHERE CAN I FIND A RELIABLE SOURCE FOR
CHARTERING A JUNK?

Viking's Charters & Co. Ltd
13/F, Progress Comm. Bldg
7–17 Irving St, Causeway Bay
2576-8992 / 2814-9935
www.boatandboating.com
*Viking rents out everything from deluxe cruisers to junks
to speed boats. They offer boats in good condition and
their prices are good. Speak to Wendy Au or Mr Li.*

Standard Boat Agency
2/F, Seven Seas Comm. Bldg Centre
121 King's Rd, North Point
2570-1792 / 9233-2938
www.standardboat.com.hk
*Speak to Carmen Lee about renting a junk or boat and
make sure you ask for a good boat and price.*

Jaspas Party Junk
2792-6001
www.jaspasjunk.com

Saffron Cruises
20/F, Teda Bldg, 87 Wing Lok St, Sheung Wan
2857-1311
www.saffron-cruises.com

Duk Ling Chinese Sailing Junk
2573-5282
www.dukling.com.hk
Minimum charge of $9,000, for 2 hours.

Jumbo Charters
2871-0345

Laissez Faire
Mezzanine, Sino Centre, 582–592 Nathan Rd, Mong Kok
2770-8066
www.yp.com.hk/laissezfaire

I HAVE IMPORTANT GUESTS THAT I WANT TO
IMPRESS. WHERE CAN I **CHARTER A UNIQUE BOAT**?

Duk Ling Chinese Sailing Junk
See above
*One of the last authentic sailing junks in Hong Kong
offering a unique experience your guests will remember.
The Duk Ling holds up to 40 passengers. Catering must
be arranged separately; they provide only ice and water.*

Grand Cru
Grand Hyatt Hotel, 1 Harbour Rd, Wan Chai
2588-1234
*This spectacular yacht can be chartered for private
parties ranging from a sit-down dinner for up to 30 to
parties for up to 60+. All catering is done by the Grand
Hyatt. Contact the Catering Department for more details.*

Michelangelo
6111-3544
www.luxurysuperjunk.com
Ask for Ruby.

Jubilee International Tour Centre
23/F, Far East Consortium Bldg
121 Des Voeux Rd Central
2530-0530
www.jubilee.com.hk

EVERYTHING LIFESTYLE & WELL BEING

WHERE CAN I **CHARTER A LUXURY BOAT INTERNATIONALLY**?

Simpson Marine Ltd
G/F, Aberdeen Marina Tower
8 Shum Wan Rd, Aberdeen
2555-8377
www.simpsonmarine.com
International charter of luxury boats and yachts can be arranged, in addition to buying or selling.

I WANT TO GO OUT ON A JUNK/BOAT AND NOT
HAVE TO DEAL WITH ORGANISING FOOD. WHERE
CAN I HIRE A **JUNK/BOAT TRIP WITH FULL CATERING**?

Jaspas Party Junk
2792-6001
www.jaspasjunk.com
Jaspas Restaurant in Central and Sai Kung organise the food and drinks; you pay a flat fee per adult and child. The boats vary in size and standard, call this booking hotline for details.

Saffron Cruises
20/F, Teda Bldg, 87 Wing Lok St, Sheung Wan
2857-1311
www.saffron-cruises.com
Saffron has teamed up with Gingers to provide a fully catered boat cruise or just a hired boat, or anything in between. You can choose the food you want or select from pre-set menu suggestions.

WHERE CAN I FIND AN **EVENT PLANNER** FOR THE
ULTIMATE PARTY?

House of Siren Productions
1/F, 18 Shelley St, Central
2530-2371
www.siren.com.hk
For the ultimate party or event that no guest will forget.

Salon de Pigeon
3/F, Po Yick Bldg, 17–19 Hillier St, Sheung Wan
2544-5664
www.salondepigeon.com
A studio that provides creative event production, graphic design, photography, video and motion graphics.

What's Next
8 On Wo Lane, Sheung Wan
2234-5005 / 6628-0698
www.whatsnexthk.com
Rachel Plecas can help with both private and corporate event plannings.

WHERE CAN I **HIRE A DJ OR BAND** FOR A PARTY?

Double Happiness
3051-9992
www.doublehappiness.com.hk
Representing a wide repertoire of musicians for all types of music, Double Happiness can help you source the right musicians for a wedding, party or corporate function. They can also source DJs.

Mobile Disco DJ
2698-1718 / 2698-1719
Wedding Singers
2618-7444
www.weddingband.hk
Broham Entertainment
9496-8872
Specialist in sourcing a great DJ or band for all styles of music. Speak to Larry Hammond, the managing director.

WHERE CAN I FIND A **STRING QUARTET**?

Fermata
8101-6299
Strings, a woodwind quartet, live music, live bands and jazz bands available for hire. Speak to Charlotte.

WHERE CAN I FIND A **HARPIST**?

Music Academy of Zheng
1/F, Hoi Deen Court
276 Gloucester Rd, Causeway Bay
2833-6538 / 9103-0401
Ask for Ms Sze.

I WANT TO HOST A PARTY IN AN **UNUSUAL VENUE**, ANY SUGGESTIONS?

The Party Tram
Tram Depot, Connaught Rd West, Sai Wan
2118-6301
Party with your friends as the tram takes you through Hong Kong's lively streets.
Star Ferry
Star Ferry Pier, Tsim Sha Tsui
2118-6120
www.starferry.com.hk
Crown Wine Cellars
18 Deep Water Bay Dr, Shouson Hill
2580-6287
www.crownwinecellars.com
Béthanie
The Hong Kong Academy for Performing Arts
139 Pok Fu Lam Rd, Pok Fu Lam
www.hkapa.edu
The Grand Stage
2/F, Western Market
Des Voeux Rd Central, Sheung Wan
8202-2809
www.clubwedding.com.hk
Hong Kong Disneyland ....
Hong Kong Disneyland, Lantau Island
3510-6000
www.hongkongdisneyland.com
Aqua Luna
13/F, Times Square
1 Matheson St, Causeway Bay
2506-0009
www.aqua.com.hk
See also boat charter, pages 225–227, and alfresco dining options, pages 18–20.

HOW ABOUT **RESTAURANTS THAT OFFER A UNIQUE PARTY VENUE**?

Maison 1882
Tai Tam Reservoir Rd, Tai Tam
E-mail cocobay@biznetvigator.com for details.

The Box
L4, IFC Mall, 8 Finance St, Central
2234-7738
www.jcgroup.hk

Cococabana
UG/F, Beach Bldg, Island Rd, Deep Water Bay
2812-2226 / 2328-2138
www.toptables.com.hk

China Club
Old Bank of China Bldg, Bank St, Central
www.chinaclub.com.sg/aboutus_worldwide.html
Members only.

Domani
L4, Pacific Place, 88 Queensway, Admiralty
2111-1197
www.domani.hk

Watermark
Level P, Central Pier 7, Central
2167-7251
www.igors.com

Azure
29/F, Hotel LKF, 33 Wyndham St, Central
3518-9330
www.azure.hk

Cipriani
12/F, Old Bank of China Bldg, Bank St, Central
2501-0222
www.cipriani.com
Members only.

Isola Bar
L3, IFC Mall, 8 Finance St, Central
2383-8765
www.isolabarandgrill.com

Duetto Italian & Indian Dining
2/F, Sun Hung Kai Centre, 30 Harbour Rd, Wan Chai
2598-1222 / 2827-7777
www.chiram.com.hk

Top Deck
Top Floor, Jumbo Kingdom
Shum Wan Pier Drive, Wong Chuk Hang, Aberdeen
2552-3331
www.cafedecogroup.com

Ming Kee Seafood Restaurant
Po Toi Island
2849-7038

I AM ORGANISING A **CHEEKY HEN NIGHT**, ANY SUGGESTIONS FOR GIFT IDEAS?

Ann Devine
• 1/F, 2 Lan Kwai Fong, Central
  2522-0368
• G/F, Peninsula Centre, 67 Mody Rd, East Tsim Sha Tsui
  2722-0355
www.anndevine.com.hk

EVERYTHING LIFESTYLE & WELL BEING

Passionately Yours
9509-7871
www.feelpassionately.com
*This website is devoted to play-things for passionate
adults. They also offer highly recommended informative
group parties in your home, where a sales representative
shows and educates you and your guests on the
merchandise in a comfortable manner. Tyson is a well-
known male stripper that does parties and party grams.*

Secret Wardrobe
2/F, 15B Wellington St, Central
www.secret-wardrobe.com.hk

Gentleman's Agreement
Mezzanine, 11E Aberdeen St, Central
2850-4666
www.g-agreement.com

WHERE CAN I BUY A **DISCO BALL**?

Yuen Tung Co.
G/F, 36 Lyndhurst Terrace, Central
2851-6811
Cheap and cheerful shop that sells just about everything.
**See also street stalls in Ap Liu St, EVERYTHING SHAM SHUI PO,
pages 189–191.**

HOW CAN I GET **FIREWORKS AT MY PARTY**?

Major Moments
9/F, Parkes Comm. Centre, 2–8 Parkes St, Tsim Sha Tsui
2362-9238
www.major-momentspro.com

WHERE CAN I GET **CUPCAKES/CAKES FOR A PARTY**?

Baby Cakes
11/F, Horizon Plaza, 2 Lee Wing St, Ap Lei Chau
3175-8716
www.babycakesasia.com

Sweet Secrets
See page 94

Complete Deelite
6/F, California Entertainment Bldg
34–36 D'Aguilar St, Central
3167-7022
www.completedeelite.com

Cake-A-Licious
LG/F, 11 Lyndhurst Terrace, Central
2815-2218
www.cakealicious.com.hk

Sift
See page 94

HOW DO I ORDER LARGE QUANTITIES OF **ICE**?

Shiu Pong Ice Ltd
LG/F, Block 4, Yau Tong Ind. Bldg
18–20 Sze Shan St, Yau Tong
2340-0731 / 2340-0732
*Cube ice, dry ice, ice carvings, block ice; you can also
rent a freezer truck.*

EVERYTHING LIFESTYLE & WELL BEING

WHERE CAN I **RENT TABLES, CHAIRS AND TABLEWARE**?

Wilfred Catering Ltd
19/F, Grand Marine Ind. Bldg
3 Yue Fung St, Aberdeen
2870-0535
www.catering.com.hk
One-stop shop for everything you need to rent for a party from tables and chairs to glasses, tablecloths, napkins, cutlery, and serving dishes. They even deliver ice in cooler boxes. Transportation fee ranges from $400 to $500 depending where you live. Ask for Stella.
Joseph's Catering Services Ltd
5/F, 236 Aberdeen Main St, Aberdeen
2555-8022
www.jcatering.com
See also pages 336–337 for cheap purchase options.

WHERE DO I HIRE A **BARTENDER AND WAITER**?

Gingers Catering
LG/F, Hing Wah Mansions
2 Oaklands Path, Mid-Levels
2964-9160
www.gingers.com.hk
Ah Ping
9659-2319
He can source waiters/bartenders for your private parties.
Lewis
9848-0532
See also caterers, pages 99–100.

WHERE CAN I FIND A **VENUE** TO HOST A CHILDREN'S PARTY?

YWCA ....
1 Macdonnell Rd, Central
2877-3737 / 3476-1300
www.ywca.org.hk
They rent party rooms.
See also kid-friendly restaurants, pages 46–47.

WHERE CAN I FIND A COMPANY TO **HANDLE ALL ASPECTS OF MY KID'S BIRTHDAY PARTY**?

Party Animals ....
2/F, 48 Staunton St, SoHo
6253-2183
www.partyanimals.com.hk
They can plan and provide as little or as much as you want.

WHERE CAN I FIND A COMPANY THAT OFFERS A **VENUE AND ENTERTAINMENT FOR A KIDS' PARTY**?

Gymboree Play & Music ....
31/F, Universal Trade Centre
3–5 Arbuthnot Rd, Central
2899-2210
www.gymboree.com.hk

Panda Junction
20/F, Wyndham Place, 44 Wyndham St, Central
2855-0906 / 2855-0907
www.pandajunction.com

Complete Deelite
6/F, California Entertainment Bldg
34–36 D'Aguilar St, Central
3167-7022
www.completedeelite.com
Candy and cake-making birthday parties for 8-year-olds and up.

Colour My World
1/F, Aberdeen Marina Tower
8 Shum Wan Rd, Aberdeen
2580-5028
www.colour-my-world.com
A good place to host an organised children's party with an arts and crafts theme.

Hong Kong Disneyland
Hong Kong Disneyland, Lantau Island
3510-6000
www.hongkongdisneyland.com

My Gym
17/F, Coda Plaza, 51 Garden Rd, Central
2577-3322
www.mygymhk.com

Chameleon Workshop
2/F, Yan King Court
119–121 Queen's Rd East, Wan Chai
2527-2251 / 2527-2252
www.chameleonworkshop.com

Pizza Express
See page 45

Director's Club
5/F, Cityplaza, 18 Taikoo Shing Rd, Tai Koo
2567-3111

Baby Cakes
11/F, Horizon Plaza, 2 Lee Wing St, Ap Lei Chau
3175-8716
www.babycakesasia.com

I'M LOOKING FOR A **SPORTS-RELATED KID'S BIRTHDAY PARTY**. ANY SUGGESTIONS?

YMCA King's Park Centenary Centre
22 Gascoigne Rd, Yau Ma Tei
2782-6682
www.kpcchk.org

Mega Ice
L10, MegaBox, 38 Wang Chiu Rd, Kowloon Bay
2709-4020
www.megaice.com.hk

The Rink
G/F, Elements Mall, 1 Austin Rd West, Kowloon
2196-8016
www.rink.com.hk

Cityplaza Ice Palace
1/F, Cityplaza, 18 Taikoo Shing Rd, Tai Koo
2844-8688
www.icepalace.com.hk

Festival Walk Glacier ....
UG, Festival Walk, 80 Tat Chee Ave, Kowloon Tong
2844-3588
www.glacier.com.hk

Socatots ....
2/F, Chak Fung House
440–442 Nathan Rd, Yau Ma Tei
2385-9033
www.socatots.com

Multi-Sport ....
8/F, Yien Yieh Bank Western Bldg
32–36 Des Voeux Rd West, Sheung Wan
2540-1257
www.multi-sport.com.hk

Play Sport ....
8/F, Wing Fu Bldg, 18–20 Wing Kut St, Central
2818-9453
www.playsport.com.hk

WHICH **PRIVATE CLUBS OFFER GOOD VENUES FOR KIDS'
PARTIES**?

*The Private Clubs below offer several venues/
entertainment appropriate for children's parties,
ranging from indoor play zones, bowling alleys, to pool
facilities. Bookings must be done through a member, call
for more details.*

Aberdeen Mariner Club ....
8 Shum Wan Rd, Aberdeen
2555-8321
www.aberdeenmarinaclub.com

American Club ....
28 Tai Tam Rd, Tai Tam
2842-7400
www.americanclubhk.com

Hong Kong Cricket Club ....
137 Wong Nai Chung Gap Rd, Wong Nai Chung
3511-8668
www.hkcc.org

Hong Kong Football Club ....
3 Sports Rd, Happy Valley
2830-9500
www.hkfc.com.hk

Ladies Recreation Club ....
10 Old Peak Rd, The Peak
3199-3500
www.lrc.com.hk

Hong Kong Country Club ....
188 Wong Chuk Hang Rd, Deep Water Bay
2552-4165
www.countryclub.hk

HOW ABOUT **BIRTHDAY PARTY VENUES THAT WOULD
APPEAL TO BOTH BOYS AND BIG BOYS** (MY HUSBAND)?

Paintball Heaquarters ....
G/F, Po Lung Centre, 11 Wang Chiu Rd, Kowloon Bay
3106-0220
www.paintballhq.com.hk
Paintball war games.

MX Club
Tsiu Keng Tsuen, Sheung Shui, New Territories
www.mxclub.com.hk
Mini bike and dirt biking for big boys.

Sideways Driving Club
G/F, 1–2 Chancery Lane, Central
2523-0983
www.sideways-driving-club.com
High-end car racing simulators for big boys.

WHERE CAN I RENT A **BOUNCY CASTLE** OR OTHER INFLATABLE GAMES FOR A KIDS' PARTY?

Future Leisure
24/F, Hing Wai Centre, 7 Tin Wan Praya Rd, Aberdeen
2559-2995
www.future-leisure.com
Lasertag parties and games at South Island School's gymnasium. Inflatable games for children's parties or family fun days. Delivery and pick-up provided.

Jumpin' 4 Joy
9467-4545
www.jumpin-4-joy.tk
Bouncy castles, balloons, cakes. Ask for Kieron.

WHERE CAN I HIRE AN **ENTERTAINER** FOR A KIDS' PARTY?

Arabella's Party
2638-3174
www.arabellasparty.com
Experienced children's clowns and entertainers. They can email you a detailed information package.

Jan Preece
94 Ham Tin Kau Tsuen, Pui O, Lantau Island
2984-9224
Possibly the funniest male clown in town, enjoyed by both parents and kids.

Rachael's Fun House
2705-9556 / 2792-1124
www.funhousehk.com
Face painting, puppet shows, party games, balloon modelling, singing, dancing and much more. Barbie, clowns, fairies, princesses, disco divas are just a few of the characters Rachael and her team can provide.

Bead's Galore
2358-1452
www.beadsgalorehk.com
Call Julie about a jewellery-making party for your daughter.

WHERE CAN I GET A **KID'S BIRTHDAY CAKE** MADE?

Complete Deelite
6/F, California Entertainment Bldg
34–36 D'Aguilar St, Central
3167-7022
www.completedeelite.com
You can order a pre-made cake and decorate it yourself or a fully-made cake for all occasions.

Cake-A-Licious ....
LG/F, 11 Lyndhurst Terrace, Central
2815-2218
www.cakealicious.com.hk

Baby Cakes ....
11/F, Horizon Plaza, 2 Lee Wing St, Ap Lei Chau
3175-8716
www.babycakesasia.com

Rasma ....
2522-4844 / 9481-3445
For birthday, wedding, every occasion, and even 3D cakes.

WHERE CAN I BUY ASSORTED **PARTY PARAPHERNALIA**?

Party Caramba ....
11/F, Tung Chai Bldg
86–90 Wellington St, Central
2851-8320
www.partycaramba.com
One-stop shopping for all your party needs for children and adults.

Hobby Horse Toys ....
2/F, Prince's Bldg, 10 Chater Rd, Central
2523-3814 / 2523-6542
www.allinafamily.com
The one-stop party shop for all kinds of supplies and decorations.

Party & Toys ....
G/F, Dairy Farm Shopping Centre
39 Chung Hom Kok Rd, Chung Hom Kok
Great shop for themed partyware, helium balloons, party favours and toys.

WHERE CAN I GET GREAT **PARTY INVITATIONS** MADE?

See printers, pages 185–186.

WHERE CAN I GO FOR CHEAP **LOOT BAG** ITEMS?

JUSCO $10 Plaza
See page 339
This is a great source for loot bag items, where everything is $10.

Li Yuen St East and West, Central
This is a great place to find cheap loot bag items.

kidDcorner
G/F, Dragon Court, 28 Caine Rd, Mid-Levels
2810-1862
www.eshop.kiddcorner.com
Tons of things for loot bags.

Flower Market Rd, Mong Kok
Several stalls along Flower Market Rd sell individual clay-like eggs, filled with soil and a seed. All you need to do is cut off the top, add water and wait a week for it to start growing. You can buy plain ones that your child can paint that are great for Easter or birthday parties.
See also EVERYTHING SHAM SHUI PO, pages 189–191.

EVERYTHING LIFESTYLE & WELL BEING

WHERE CAN I FIND A GOOD **SPECIAL-EVENT PHOTOGRAPHER**?

Norm Yip
8/F, Block B, Hong Kong Ind. Bldg
26 Lee Chung St, Chai Wan
9257-1937 / 2540-6267
www.normyip.com

Olaf Mueller Photography
9470-0008 / 9747-8828
www.olafmueller.biz

Lisa B Photography
9/F, Kai Wah Bldg, 68–70 Wellington St, Central
9160-0453 / 2869-9732
www.lisabphotography.com
*An ex-model, Lisa branched out to express her creativity.
She is able to capture natural and candid moments.*

Simon Ng Photography
21/F, Eastern Centre, 1065 King's Rd, Quarry Bay
2880-5000
www.simon-ng-photo.com
Commercial, family and wedding photography.
See also wedding photographers, page 239–240.

I WANT TO GET SOME NATURAL **BABY AND FAMILY PHOTOS** DONE. WHO SPECIALISES IN THIS?

Amy K. Boyd Photography
9220-0404
www.amykboyd.com
*Amy brings freshness and expertise to her unique
portrayal of your family. She also specialises in
portraiture, commercial, architectural, art and
documentary photography.*

Rosa Tseng
10/F, Union Comm. Bldg
12 Lyndhurst Terrace, Central
2294-0481 / 9758-0119
www.rosatseng.com
*Rosa Tseng has excellent credentials, experience and
delivers natural and timeless result.*

Radhika Rao
9416-0972
www.radhikarao.com
Specialises in newborn, pregnancy and family photography.

Moments
G/F, Dairy Farm Shopping Centre
39 Chung Hom Kok Rd, Chung Hom Kok
2575-7117
www.momentsgallery.com
*Natural and timeless prints, capturing the beauty of
parenthood and childhood.*

Venture Photos
• 1/F Winway Bldg, 50 Wellington St, Central
  2885-6262
• LG/F, Henry House, 42 Yun Ping Rd, Causeway Bay
  2882-5858
• G/F, Ocean Terminal, Harbour City
  Canton Rd, Tsim Sha Tsui
  2377-4888
www.thisisventure.com.hk

EVERYTHING LIFESTYLE & WELL BEING

WHERE CAN I FIND A PHOTOGRAPHER WHO SPECIALISES IN **PORTRAITS**?

Craig Norris Photography
7/F, Cornell Centre, 50 Wing Tai Rd, Chai Wan
9810-4265
www.momentsbycraig.com
*Specialising in portraits, Craig also does weddings,
commercial photography and teaches a photography
workshop for beginners.*

Peter Inglis Photography
San Wai Bungalow, 4 Tai Po Rd
Tai Po Kau, New Territories
2528-4611
www.peteringlisphotography.com

Amy K. Boyd Photography
9220-0404
www.amykboyd.com

WHERE CAN I FIND A GOOD **CANDID PHOTOGRAPHER FOR A PARTY**?

Elvis Ho Photography Ltd
2633-6038 / 9431-7588
www.photoharmony.com.hk
*Elvis blends in well and is great for capturing the best
moments at a party.*

WHERE CAN I FIND A RELIABLE PLACE TO **DEVELOP MY EVERYDAY PHOTOS**?

Fotomax
G/F & Mezzanine, 4 Pottinger St, Central
2537-0992
www.fotomaxonline.com
*Many locations, including Pacific Place, Lippo Centre
and Times Square.*

Kodak Express Digital Solutions
• 1/F, World-Wide House, 19 Des Voeux Rd Central
  2869-1932
• L3, IFC Mall, 8 Finance St, Central
  2536-0899
• LG/F, Jardine House, 1 Connaught Place, Central
  2147-3188
• 1/F, Admiralty Centre, Tower 2
  18 Harcourt Rd , Admiralty
  3158-2829
www.kodakexpress.com.hk
*Branches throughout Hong Kong. Check the website for
your nearest branch.*

Tin Tin Photo Services
3/F, Stanley Plaza Shopping Centre, Carmel Rd, Stanley
2813-8060
www.tintinphoto.com
A good shop for photo developing and archiving.

SKYphoto
G/F, 345A Queen's Rd West, Sai Wan
2812-1163 / 2712-8803
www.skyphoto.com.hk
*Many locations, including World-Wide House and Times
Square. See website for details.*

WHERE CAN I GET **PROFESSIONAL PHOTO DEVELOPING** DONE FOR MY VERY BEST PHOTOS?

Robert Lam Color
- 43 Wellington St, Central
  2898-8418
- 78 Hennessy Rd, Wan Chai
  2898-8418

Color Six Laboratories Ltd
G/F, 28A Stanley St, Central
2526-0123
www.colorsix.com

WHERE CAN I BUY **PHOTOGRAPHY/VIDEO EQUIPMENT**?

See cameras and video equipment, pages 373–374 .

I WOULD LIKE TO HAVE **PERSONALISED ALBUMS** MADE. WHERE CAN I DO THIS?

Green Pagoda Press
13/F, Block A, Tong Chong Factory Bldg
655 King's Rd, Quarry Bay
2561-2324
www.gpp.com.hk
They offer large format, traditional albums that can be personalised on the binding or cover with gold leaf lettering.

HOW CAN I **MAKE MY OWN PHOTO ALBUMS**?

See arts and crafts supplies, page 250–251.

WHERE CAN I FIND A REPUTABLE **WEDDING PLANNER**?

The Wedding Company
10/F, Ming Fat Bldg, 74 Wellington St, Central
2869-4222
www.theweddingco.hk
Started by Michele Li and Caroline Shaw in 2003, the Wedding Company focuses purely on individual, tasteful and creative weddings. They can handle every aspect of your wedding from venue, entertainment, food and beverage to invitations. This one-stop service can help with overseas guests and even assist the groom with a ring, as Michele Li holds a gemology degree from the Gemologist Institute of America.

Coco Weddings
11/F, 113 Argyle St, Mong Kok
2537-8881
www.cocoweddings.com
A full range of services are offered for planning your whole wedding or just part of it.

My Dream Wedding
G/F, 49A–51 Kimberley Rd, Tsim Sha Tsui
2312-1908
www.mydreamwedding.hk

Bliss Creations
2982-0192
www.blisscreations.net
Specialises in luxury destination weddings.

Marriage Maestros Ltd
8/F, 66 Wellington St, Central
2546-0049 / 2546-0085
www.marriagemaestros.com
You can choose what level of wedding planning you would like: from a fully orchestrated event with a nine-month lead time required, to a one-month lead time where you have planned your own wedding and you now need someone to manage and coordinate all the aspects you have arranged.

Pink Inc.
2241-0172
www.pinkinc.com.hk
Offering unique and creative services, Pink can take care of every detail for a small, intimate and romantic wedding to a lavish party in a host of destinations. Contact Kimberly Johnson.

Plus One Weddings
3/F, Block B, Winner Bldg
8–6 Wing Wah Lane, Central
2697-3227
www.plusoneweddings.com
Plus One offers a range of à la carte services such as label printing, mailing and assembling invitations to complete wedding planning services. It is also the official representative of Tirtha Uluwatu, a 15-pavillion wedding complex on the cliffs of Southern Bali.

Base Weddings
16/F, Oriental Crystal Comm. Bldg
46 Lyndhurst Terrace, Central
2530-8164
www.basewedding.com

WHERE DO YOU RECOMMEND I GO TO FIND A GOOD **WEDDING PHOTOGRAPHER**?

Lisa B Photography
9/F, Kai Wah Bldg
68–70 Wellington St, Central
9160-0453 / 2869-9732
www.lisabphotography.com

Rosa Tseng
10/F, Union Comm. Bldg
12 Lyndhurst Terrace, Central
2294-0481 / 9758-0119
www.rosatseng.com

Norm Yip
8/F, Block B, Hong Kong Ind. Bldg
26 Lee Chung St, Chai Wan
9257-1937 / 2540-6267
www.normyip.com

OM Studio
5/F, Block A & B, How Ming Factory Bldg
99 How Ming St, Kwun Tong
2793-9333
www.omstudio.hk

Sean David Baylis
9277-1810
www.whitebox.hk

Melanie Adamson
9661-3234
www.melanie-adamson.com
CM Leung
4/F, 21 Cameron Rd, Tsim Sha Tsui
8334-1317
www.cmleung.com
Red Dog Studio
3 Sun St, Wan Chai
2865-3999
www.reddogstudio.com.hk

WHERE CAN I FIND A **VIDEOGRAPHER**?

One Shot Production
6/F, Mirage Tower, 13 – 15 Thompson Rd, Wan Chai
2851-1239
www.one100.com.hk
Award-winning videographer with a long list of credentials, Eric Suen now applies his trade to capturing weddings.
Charles Cheung
6476-4700
www.charlescheung.com.hk
Offering a journalistic and reportorial style, Charles Cheung offers a wide range of photographic and video-taking services.
Simon the Photo
9109-9665
www.blog.simonthephoto.com
Award-winning wedding photographer.
Johnny Productions
18/F, Professional Bldg
19 – 23 Tung Lo Wan Rd, Causeway Bay
8209-2808
www.johnnyproductions.com

WHERE CAN I CREATE A **WEBSITE** OF MY WEDDING?

Merry-me.com
6296-7867
www.merry-me.com
Contact Christine by phone or email to create a stylish website to share your beautiful memories with friends and family. Packages include a personalised domain name, a 5-minute movie, a welcome and thank-you page, 100 photos in the photo album, and more.
Happy Moments
3116-1508
www.happymoments.net
Also does photo and video.

WHERE CAN I GET HAIR AND **MAKEUP** DONE FOR MY WEDDING?

Fiona Jacob
9804-9222
Bridal packages starting from $2,500.
Nancy Kim
9387-9199
www.makeupnancy.com

EVERYTHING LIFESTYLE & WELL BEING

Liz Bohan
9759-3450
Qualified makeup artist at the London College of Fashion.

Aimee at the Shangri-La
8/F, Island Shangri-La Hotel
Pacific Place, Supreme Court Rd, Admiralty
2918-1339

WHERE CAN THE GROOM OR GROOMSMEN FIND
A **GOOD TAILOR** FOR THEIR WEDDING OUTFITS?

See tailors, pages 133–134.

WHERE CAN I BUY **WINE WITH PERSONALISED LABELS**?

Limestone Coast Wines
12/F, Horizon Plaza, 2 Lee Wing St, Ap Lei Chau
2817-1625
www.limestone-coast-wines.com
Buy South Australian unbranded wine and have your own labels put on the bottles.

Personalize Stuff
9023-6454
www.personalizestuff.com
Buy your wine from anywhere (see pages 95–99), then order personalised wine labels here and place them over top.

I'M GETTING MARRIED. CAN YOU MAKE SOME
SUGGESTIONS FOR **WEDDING FAVOURS**?

Vero
1/F, Fenwick Pier, 1 Lung King St, Wan Chai
2559-5882
www.verochocolates.com
With their factory in Hong Kong, Vero can make all types of chocolates and their packaging can be custom designed with anything you want. The chocolate is excellent. Ask for Roger.

Studio M
1/F, Tung Yiu Comm. Bldg
31A Wyndham St, Central
2525-0765
www.studiomhk.com
Wedding favours ranging from luggage tags to personalised custom boxes for sweets, trinkets, etc.

Limestone Coast Wines
See above

Personalize Stuff
See above

Grace Co.
G/F, 10 Aberdeen St, Central
2974-1870
Great source for photo frames, leather boxes and other items for wedding favours.

Double Happiness
3051-9992
www.doublehappiness.com.hk
Wedding favours and gift registry from over 70 well-known shops and services, combining your selections into a single gift list.

EVERYTHING LIFESTYLE & WELL BEING

I AM LOOKING FOR A **LIFE COACH** TO LEARN BETTER WAYS TO PLAN MY LIFE AND CAREER. WHO CAN I CONTACT?

Hong Kong Coaching Community
8/F, Two Exchange Square
8 Connaught Place, Central
2297-2466
www.coachinghk.org
A non-profit organisation for coaches and coaches in training. They offer a directory of coaches.

ID Life Coaching
4/F, Serene Court
2 Castle Lane, Mid-Levels
6102-5269
Personal, teenage and corporate coaching.

Mindsight
6/F, Cosmos Bldg, 8 Lan Kwai Fong, Central
www.mindsightasia.com
Offers life coaching and corporate training by an experienced ex-CEO and managing director of a global company.

The Rosenberg Group
11/F, Shing Hing Comm. Bldg
21–27 Wing Kut St, Central
2526-8801

Jaime Simpson
2987-2488
www.teensuccess.com.hk
Jaime Simpson offers professional life coaching for teenagers, families and parents.

Shape Your Life
9711-4961
Carol Gibb has been life coaching since 2001 and complements her work with her background in personal, fitness training, psychology and more.

The Masterminds
6/F, 38 Lok Ku Rd, Central
8208-2700
www.themastermindsgroup.com
Personal and corporate training and coaching.

WHERE CAN I TAKE A **MEDITATION COURSE**?

Simply Seeing Ltd
10/F, Kinwick Centre
32 Hollywood Rd, Central
www.simplyseeing.com
Dr Allen Dorcas, a spiritual guide and psychologist, uses no set method. The courses invite you to increase awareness of your own thought patterns, as many methods of meditation are simply extensions of thought.

WHERE CAN I TAKE A **FENG SHUI COURSE**?

Raymond Lo
12/F, Star House
3 Salisbury Rd, Tsim Sha Tsui
2736-9568 / 9024-9438
www.raymond-lo.com

EVERYTHING LIFESTYLE & WELL BEING

WHERE CAN I LEARN **FIRST AID**?

Asia Medical Services Ltd
1/F, Bonham Strand Trade Centre
135 Bonham Strand, Sheung Wan
2537-5924
www.asiamedicalservices.com
Courses for parents, helpers and other interested individuals. In addition to basic first aid and CPR courses, they also offer advanced training courses and emergency care drills for companies and institutions. Contact Peter Sommer.

Emergency Care Training
11/F, Wilson House, 19–27 Wyndham St, Central
2572-9651
www.ect-hk.com

St John's Ambulance
2 Macdonnell Rd, Central
2524-4888
www.stjohn.org.hk

WHERE CAN I FIND **TRAINING COURSES FOR MY HELPER**?

The Family Zone
A5, Alberose, 132–136 Pok Fu Lam Rd, Pok Fu Lam
9889-3235
www.thefamilyzone.hk
Practical workshops for training helpers in childcare.

Alison's Letterland Child Care Centre
1/F, Park View Centre, 7 Lau Li St, Tin Hau
2881-8717
www.letter-land.com
Offers childcare workshops.

Superhelper Ltd
36A Island Rd, Deep Water Bay
9199-0880
www.superhelper.goldphoria.com
Well-rounded courses for training your helper.

WHERE CAN I FIND BASIC **COOKING CLASSES FOR MY HELPER OR MYSELF**?

Towngas Cooking Centre
• Basement, Leighton Centre
 77 Leighton Rd, Causeway Bay
 2576-1535 / 2880-6988
• G/F, New World Centre
 20 Salisbury Rd, Tsim Sha Tsui
 2367-2707
www.towngas.com
A wide variety of courses and cuisines.

Six Senses Ltd
1/F, 12 Kai Yuen St, North Point
2838-9905
www.s6nses.com
Around $250–$350 per session.

Home Management Centre
10/F, Electric Centre, 28 City Garden Rd, North Point
2510-2828
www.heh.com

EVERYTHING LIFESTYLE & WELL BEING

YWCA English Speaking Members Department
1 Macdonnell Rd, Central
2877-3737 / 3476-1300
www.ywca.org.hk
Offering cooking lessons for domestics from dim sum to Indian barbecue to baking cookies and treats. There are also basic courses in English, table setting and health and hygiene in the kitchen.

Martha Sherpa's Cooking School
1/F, Lee Kwan Bldg, 40–46 Argyle St, Mong Kok
2381-0132
www.cookery.com.hk
No-frills cooking classes.

WHERE CAN I FIND **CHINESE COOKING CLASSES FOR MY HELPER OR MYSELF**?

Chinese Cuisine Training Institute
7/F, 145 Pok Fu Lam Rd, Pok Fu Lam
2538-2538
www.vtc.edu.hk

Chopsticks Cooking Cuisine
8A Soares Ave, Ho Man Tin
Cooking school opened by renowned cookbook author Cecilia Au Yeung, established in 1971.

WHERE CAN I **TAKE A COOKING COURSE WITH MY FRIENDS**?

Go Gourmet
G/F, 17 Po Yan St, Sheung Wan
2530-3880
www.go-gourmet.com
Two-hour demonstration classes with student participation for 3–4 course meals. From easy entertaining to elegant meals to Asian specialities. $300–$500 per course and students get to eat the dishes prepared after the class.

Corner Kitchen
G/F, 20 Po Hing Fong, Sheung Wan
2803-2822
www.corner-kitchen.com
Boutique cooking school run by talented New York chef and food stylist Vivian Herijanto. Private sessions available for groups.

Art-tastic Kitchen
3/F, Block A, Friend's House
4–6 Carnarvon Rd, Tsim Sha Tsui
2739-8681
www.art-tastichobbiescentre.com

ARE THERE ANY CLASSES THAT SPECIALISE IN **CAKES AND SWEETS**?

Complete Deelite
6/F, California Entertainment Bldg
34–36 D'Aguilar St, Central
3167-7022
www.completedeelite.com
Cake making and decorating courses for every level from the hobbyist to the professional decorator.

Coup Kitchen
8/F, Morecrown Comm. Bldg, 108 Electric Rd, Tin Hau
2508-0666
www.coup.com.hk

By Joanne Stylish Baking
5/F, Chang Pao Ching Bldg
417 Hennessy Rd, Wan Chai
2833-2066
www.byjoanne.com.hk

Vero
1/F, Fenwick Pier, 1 Lung King St, Wan Chai
2559-5882
www.verochocolates.com
Chocolate-making courses.

WHERE CAN I TAKE **GOURMET COOKING CLASSES**?

The Peninsula Academy
The Peninsula Hotel, Salisbury Rd, Tsim Sha Tsui
2315-3146
www.peninsula.com

Tour of Italy
Kowloon Shangri-La, 64 Mody Rd, East Tsim Sha Tsui
2733-8762
www.shangri-la.com
*Recently launched series with Angelini chef Vittorio
Lucariello.*

WHERE CAN I TAKE ENGLISH-LANGUAGE
COMPUTER COURSES?

Computer Academy
6A, Hua Chiao Comm. Centre
678 Nathan Rd, Mong Kok
2838-6687
www.computeracademy.com.hk
*Eric Ching offers excellent, specialised computer courses
in graphics, website design, MS Office and more.
Classes can be taught in English and in small groups, or
he can do one-on-one sessions.*

New Horizons
6/F, Sino Cheer Plaza, 23 Jordan Rd, Jordan
2155-1800
www.newhorizons.edu.hk
*A variety of private computer courses in English offered
on a one-on-one basis.*

WHERE CAN I FIND A GOOD **LANGUAGE SCHOOL** THAT
OFFERS A **VARIETY** OF LANGUAGES, **INCLUDING
CHINESE**?

Hong Kong Institute of Languages ....
6/F, Wellington Plaza, 56–58 Wellington St, Central
2877-6160
www.hklanguages.com
*Offering instruction in English, French, German, Spanish,
Mandarin, Cantonese and Japanese.*

Hong Kong Language Training Centre
28/F, Soundwill Plaza
38 Russell St, Causeway Bay
2834-2168
www.language.com.hk

EVERYTHING LIFESTYLE & WELL BEING

Berlitz Language Centre
8/F, Harcourt House, 39 Gloucester Rd, Wan Chai
2157-2277
www.berlitz.com
French, Spanish, English, German, Cantonese and Putonghua, focusing on speaking.

Pacific Language Centre
2/F, Dah Sing Life Bldg, 99 Des Voeux Rd Central
2388-9691
www.pacificlanguage.com

EDC Language
17/F, Tesbury Centre, 28 Queen's Rd East, Admiralty
2528-5200
www.hkedc.com

WHERE CAN I LEARN FRENCH?

Alliance Francaise
• 1/F–3/F, 123 Hennessy Rd, Wan Chai
  2527-7825
• G/F–3/F, 52 Jordan Rd, Jordan
  2730-3257
www.alliancefrancaise.com.hk
Committed to promoting French language and culture. Offers French language courses for adults and children, including diploma and certificate programmes.

Berlitz Language Centre
8/F, Harcourt House, 39 Gloucester Rd, Wan Chai
2157-2277
www.berlitz.com

F.F.F. Ltd (French for Foreigners)
6/F, Chang Pao Ching Bldg
427–429 Hennessy Rd, Wan Chai
2836-6701
www.fffltd.com.hk
Multi-level classes for adults and children. They also offer private and online classes.

WHERE CAN I STUDY CANTONESE AND MANDARIN?

Executive Mandarin
1/F, Wilson House, 19–27 Wyndham St, Central
2537-0835
www.execmandarin.com
Offers Mandarin and Cantonese courses.

Hong Kong Language Learning Centre
6/F, Emperor Group Centre
288 Hennessy Rd, Wan Chai
2572-6488
www.hkllc.com
Intensive Mandarin courses available.

New Concept Mandarin
2/F, Beautiful Group Tower
74–77 Connaught Rd Central
2850-4332
www.newconceptmandarin.com

Talking Mandarin Language Centre
8/F, Full View Bldg
140–142 Des Voeux Rd Central
2139-3226
www.talkingmandarin.com

Original Chinese Language Institute
4/F–5/F, Hong Kong Trade Centre
161–167 Des Voeux Rd Central
2121-8678
www.original-chinese.com

Moment and Future Educational Language Centre
2/F, Dah Sing Bldg
99 Des Voeux Rd Central
2633-3423

WHERE IS A GREAT PLACE TO STUDY MUSIC?

See piano/singing lessons, pages 252–253.

WHERE CAN I GO TO LEARN BALLROOM, LATIN AND FLAMENCO DANCING?

Champion Ballroom Dancing Academy
2/F, Capital Comm. Bldg
26 Leighton Rd, Causeway Bay
2882-3800
Offers private tango lessons for couples and singles.

Sunshine Dancing
22/F, 230 Wan Chai Rd, Wan Chai
9486-4984/9104-5307
www.sunshinedancing.com
Established in 1977, Sunshine and Keith teach group and private lessons from beginner to advanced.

Dansinn Dance Studios
21/F, 69 Jervois St, Sheung Wan
2581-1551
www.dansinn.com

YWCA English Speakers Department
1 Macdonnell Rd, Central
2877-3737 / 3476-1300
www.ywca.org.hk

Felah-Mengus Flamenco Workshop
12/F, Kam Chung Bldg, 54 Jaffe Rd, Wan Chai
2983-1692
www.felah-mengus.com
Hong Kong's first flamenco studio.

Herman Lam Studio
1/F, Kai Kwong House, 13 Wyndham St, Central
2320-3605
www.hermanlamdance.com

WHERE CAN I LEARN BELLY DANCING AND BOLLYWOOD DANCING?

Oasis Dance Centre
4/F, 1 Anton St, Wan Chai
2522-6698
www.oasis-dance-centre.com

Belly Princess
3/F, 528 Jaffe Rd, Causeway Bay
2575-5838
www.bellyprincess.com

Trio Spin Studio
7/F, 55 Hollywood Rd, Central
2521-2168
www.triospin.com

HOW ABOUT **POLE DANCING AND OTHER ALTERNATIVE DANCING**?

Pole Divas
6/F, Wai Hing Comm. Bldg
17–19 Wing Wo St, Central
2541-5157
www.poledivas-hk.com

Groove Dance Fitness Studio
15/F, Richmond Plaza, 496 Jaffe Rd, Causeway Bay
2833-2805
www.groove-dance2fit.com

WHERE CAN I LEARN **PHOTOGRAPHY**?

Alkira Technologies
7/F, Cornell Centre, 50 Wing Tai Rd, Chai Wan
9810-4265
www.craigsworkshop.com
Craig Norris is a highly regarded instructor. His beginner photography workshops cover exposure, metering, film and lenses, lighting and flash, composition and framing, portraiture and landscape, and more.

Hong Kong International Film Academy
13/F, Block B, Ming Pao Ind. Centre
18 Ka Yip St, Chai Wan
2897-7728 / 9107-7329
www.storyhongkong.com
Courses in film-making, photography, screenwriting, etc.

Hong Kong Photographic
www.hongkongphotographic.com

WHERE CAN I TAKE **PAINTING AND DRAWING CLASSES**?

Colour My World
1/F, Aberdeen Marina Tower
8 Shum Wan Rd, Aberdeen
2580-5028
www.colour-my-world.com
Workshops and short studio courses for adults in painting. Guidance in realising a personal art project. They also offer small creative parties (minimum 6) or one-off events where you as a group can choose your theme and medium.

Chameleon Workshop
2/F, Yan King Court
119–121 Queen's Rd East, Wan Chai
2527-2251 / 2527-2252
www.chameleonworkshop.com
Courses include mosaics, bookbinding, oil, acrylic, watercolour, sculpture, art nights and more.

Anastassia's Art House
• G/F, 5 Prince's Terrace, Mid-Levels
  2526-0882
• G/F, The Repulse Bay Shopping Arcade
  109 Repulse Bay Rd. Repulse Bay
  2812-6465
• Pacific Palisades, 1 Braemar Hill Rd, North Point
  2570-2316
• G/F, 9 Hoi Pong St, Sai Kung, New Territories
  2719-5533
www.arthouse-hk.com

Hong Kong Academy of Fine Arts
438 Nathan Rd, Jordan
2385-9929
www.gotoart.edu.hk
A solid foundation for serious learners. Classes in drawing, watercolour, oil, Chinese painting and calligraphy.

WHERE CAN I GO TO DO **PAINTING FOR FUN**?

Art Jamming
G/F, 123 Wellington St, Central
2541-8816
www.artjamming.com
Public sessions and private painting parties. You are provided with a canvas, paint brushes, paint and an apron; the rest is up to you. Parties with food, music and drink can also be arranged. Children's sessions are also available.

WHERE CAN I LEARN **GLASS ART**?

Selling Point
3/F, 65 Sha Po Old Village
Yung Shue Wan, Lamma Island
2982-4050
www.sellingpoint.com.hk
This workshop on Lamma Island offers classes teaching basic glass cutting, welding and polishing to enable you to start your own works of art. You can also frame glass with metal, colour glass, as well as make glass jewellery, wall-clock fixtures, stained-glass jewellery boxes and even a stained-glass kaleidoscope.

JaniQue
23/F, Cheung Tat Centre, 18 Cheung Lee St, Chai Wan
2894-8288
www.janique-art.com
Janice holds short courses in microwave fusing, glass fusing and slumping, and stained glass. The studio can also be rented by the hour for those who want to hone their skills.

WHERE CAN I TAKE A **VARIETY OF CRAFT CLASSES**?

Bookworks
12/F, 128 Wellington St, Central
2559-0175 / 2559-0175
www.bookworks.com.hk
Box-making and bookbinding courses.

WHERE CAN I TAKE **POTTERY** CLASSES?

The Pottery Workshop
Fringe Club, 2 Lower Albert Rd, Central
2525-7949
www.potteryworkshop.org
Classes in pottery, mould making, slip casting, throwing and designing with clay.

Hong Kong Arts Centre
2 Harbour Rd, Wan Chai
2582-0200
www.hkac.org.hk

EVERYTHING LIFESTYLE & WELL BEING

I Kiln
4/F, Goldfield Ind. Centre
1 Sui Wo Rd, Sha Tin, New Territories
2787-5544
www.i-kiln.org.hk

Klei Pottery Studio
2/F, 24 Hollywood Rd, Central
2526-8567
www.welcome.to/klei

WHERE CAN I LEARN HOW TO MAKE JEWELLERY?

Bibiana Fine Jewellery
7/F, Wing Lok St Trade Centre
235 Wing Lok St, Sheung Wan
2157-1970
www.bibianna.com
Beaded jewellery, Chinese knots, etc.

Chocolate Rain
G/F, 67 Peel St, SoHo
2975-8318
www.chocolaterain.com
Jewellery making classes. They also sell beaded jewellery and accessories.

Hong Kong Arts Centre
2 Harbour Rd, Wan Chai
2582-0200
www.hkac.org.hk

WHERE CAN I TAKE COURSES FOR ADULTS AND KIDS ON BOOKBINDING, SCRAP BOOKING, ETC?

Bookworks
12/F, 128 Wellington St, Central
2559-0175 / 2559-0175
www.bookworks.com.hk

HOW CAN I LEARN MORE ABOUT FINE ART?

Friends of the Art Museum
The Chinese University of Hong Kong
Sha Tin, New Territories
www.cuhk.edu.hk/ics/friends
Promotes the study and appreciation of Chinese art and culture. Lectures by resident and visiting experts and organised study groups and tours. Through its fundraising activities, the Friends provides scholarships and internships to fine arts students and augments the acquisition fund of the Art Museum at CUHK.

WHERE CAN I BUY ARTS AND CRAFTS SUPPLIES?

Spotlight
L5, MegaBox, 38 Wang Chiu Rd, Kowloon Bay
2359-0010
www.spotlight.hk

Tak Cheung
G/F, 124–126 Cheung Sha Wan Rd, Sham Shui Po
2788-0418
www.takcheung.com.hk

EVERYING LIFESTYLE & WELL BEING

The Artland Co. Ltd ....
3/F, Lockhart Centre
301–307 Lockhart Rd, Wan Chai
2511-4845
www.artland.com.hk
Hong Kong's largest arts and crafts materials shop. On Lockhart Rd between Stewart Rd and Tonnochy Rd.

Artsman Co.
2/F, Kiu Hong Mansion
3 Tin Lok Lane, Wan Chai
2573-8159
www.artsman.biz.com.hk
Well-priced, good quality local and imported art supplies.

Chung Nam Book & Stationery
G/F, 2Q Sai Yeung Choi St, Mong Kok
2384-2430
www.yp.com.hk/chungnamhk

I'M ON A D.I.Y. KICK, WHERE CAN I BUY KNITTING, CROCHETING, **NEEDLEWORK SUPPLIES AND YARN**?

Tailor & Alteration Needlework Club
14/F, Kin Tak Fung Comm. Bldg
467 Hennessy Rd, Causeway Bay
2525-9822
www.needleworkclub.com

Cheer Wool Co. Ltd
G/F, Shanghai Ind. Investment Bldg
48–62 Hennessy Rd, Wan Chai
2527-3901
www.cheerwool.com

GB Woollen
4/F, Cityplaza 2, 18 Taikoo Shing Rd, Tai Koo
2569-7638

Paris Lotion Singlets Co. Ltd
13 Pak Sha Rd, Causeway Bay
2577-1101

Mui Tong Wools Co. Ltd
1/F, 17 Jervois St, Sheung Wan
2544-2575

Filo Kilo
G/F, 167 Sai Yee St, Mong Kok
2392-9729

Spotlight ....
L5, MegaBox, 38 Wang Chiu Rd, Kowloon Bay
2359-0010
www.spotlight.hk

WHERE CAN I BUY **SUPPLIES FOR BEADING AND JEWELLERY MAKING**?

A&A Accessory
211 Yu Chau St, Sham Shui Po
2729-0398

Beadspro
5/F, 1065 King's Rd, Quarry Bay
8106-0079
www.beadspro.com
See EVERYTHING SHAM SHUI PO, pages 189–191.

EVERYTHING LIFESTYLE & WELL BEING

WHERE CAN I (OR MY CHILD) TAKE **PIANO LESSONS**?

Tom Lee Music Co.
• Heqdquarters:
  G/F–2/F, 1–9 Cameron Lane, Tsim Sha Tsui
  2723-9932
• 2/F, City Centre Bldg
  144–149 Gloucester Rd, Wan Chai
  2519-0238
• G/F–2/F, East South Bldg
  29 Percival St, Causeway Bay
  2893-8783
• Podium, Tien Sing Mansion, 1 Tai Wing Ave, Tai Koo
  2567-4363
• The Westwood, 8 Belcher's St, Kennedy Town
  2542-7077
• 2/F, Site 2, Aberdeen Centre
  7–11 Nam Ning St, Aberdeen
  2555-7808
• 4/F, Citylink Plaza, 1 Shatin Station Circuit
  Sha Tin, New Territories
  2602-3680
www.tomleemusic.com
See website for other locations.

Parsons Music
• 9/F, Times Square
  1 Matheson St, Causeway Bay
  2506-1383
• B1, Treasure World, Whampoa Garden, Hung Hom
  2365-7078
• L2, Festival Walk, 80 Tat Chee Ave, Kowloon Tong
  2265-7882
www.parsonsmusic.com
For more outlets, see website.

Do Rei Mi Music Studio
G/F, Universal Trade Centre
3–5 Arbuthnot Rd, Central
2522-7081
Sound-proof music rooms for private and group lessons.
Violin, flute, trumpet, singing, guitar, drum and more.

Grace Chan
9486-6713
Piano lessons by a US-trained trilingual teacher.

Perfect Pitch Music Centre
153 Wong Nai Chung Rd, Happy Valley
2894-9825

WHERE CAN I FIND A TEACHER WILLING TO GIVE
ME **PIANO LESSONS AT HOME**?

Irene Chan Piano Instructor
9853-3888
*Piano and theory from beginner to advanced. Irene
has an Honours Bachelor of Music education from a
Canadian university.*

Arturo
9484-9628
*Offers a fun yet disciplined teaching method where
children learn to play popular music quickly which
increases their confidence and interest.*

EVERYTHING LIFESTYLE & WELL BEING

WHERE CAN I (OR MY CHILD) TAKE **SINGING LESSONS**?

Katterwall ....
8/F, Arion Comm. Centre
2–12 Queen's Rd West, Sheung Wan
2575-3931
www.katterwall.com
Provides one-on-one lessons, workshops and year-round choirs. Singing, theory and listening classes are available for adults, in addition to one-on-one singing lessons for children aged 11 and up.

American Vocal Studio
5/F, Hang Lung House
184–192 Queen's Rd Central
6335-5590
www.americanvocalstudio.com
Voice lessons in a variety of styles of singing are offered by members of professional a cappella group Metro.

WHERE CAN I **BUY MUSICAL INSTRUMENTS**, ESPECIALLY A PIANO?

Tom Lee Music Co.
See page 252
Parsons Music
See page 252
Regent Piano Service Co.
25/F, Hing Wai Centre
7 Tin Wan Praya Rd, Aberdeen
2873-1077

ANY RECOMMENDATIONS ON WHERE CAN I **BUY ALTERNATIVE MUSIC**?

Green Music
8/F, East Asia Mansion
23–29 Hennessy Rd, Wan Chai
9849-7263
www.greenmusic.org
Thai-born composer and musician Chamras Saewataporn combines the sounds of nature with Oriental spiritual music. His CDs are ideal for relaxation, healing and meditation.

WHERE CAN I BOOK A **RECORDING STUDIO** TO MAKE A DEMO OF MY OWN MUSIC?

Touch Music
15/F, Max Trade Centre
23 Luk Hop St, San Po Kong
9225-0327
www.touchmusic.org
A well-equipped recording studio. They offer sessions at very reasonable rates. The engineers are also musicians and are very helpful.

Greenroom Studio
12/F, Asia Mansion
390 King's Rd, North Point
9258-4140
www.greenroom-studio.com

EVERYTHING LIFESTYLE & WELL BEING

WHERE CAN I GET **PROFESSIONAL ADVICE ABOUT PARENTING** MY YOUNG CHILD?

Early Years Network
www.early-years-network.com
A Canadian organisation that brings together early childhood specialists who provide education, mediation and consultation on parenting and childhood issues to English-speaking families.

Parent Effectiveness Training
9863-1744 (Claryss) / 9496-2048 (Katherine)
effectiveparent@biznetvigator.com
Popular course that teaches parents how to communicate more effectively with kids and resolve family conflicts. 7 classes, 4 hours each, that are taught throughout Hong Kong, or get a group together and form your own group.

I HEAR THAT PARENTS CAN USE **SIGN LANGUAGE** WITH THEIR BABIES. IS THERE ANYWHERE I CAN LEARN THIS IN HONG KONG?

Baby Signs
9633-3117
www.babysignshongkong.com

I'M LOOKING FOR **ACTIVITIES OR PLAYGROUPS FOR MY BABY**. ANY SUGGESTIONS?

Pekip
7/F, Ming Tak Bldg, 101 Wan Chai Road, Wan Chai
2573-6623
www.pekip.com.hk
Gives babies time to explore their bodies and express themselves.

My Kiddy Gym
10/F, Ming An Plaza
8 Sunning Rd, Causeway Bay
2759-8811
www.mykiddygym.com
Educational and developmental classes in English for ages 6 months to 5 years.

My Gym
17/F, Coda Plaza, 51 Garden Rd, Central
2577-3322
www.mygymhk.com

Kindyroo
16/F, Universal Trade Centre
3–5 Arbuthnot Rd, Central
2457-1510
www.kindyroo.com

Beansprouts Learning Centre
3/F, Tern Centre Tower 1
237 Queen's Road Central, Sheung Wan
2543-8182
www.beansprouts.com.hk

Kindermusik by Catherine
9/F, Universal Trade Centre
3–5 Arbuthnot Rd, Central
2518-4840
www.kateskids.com.hk

EVERYTHING LIFESTYLE & WELL BEING

PLAYGROUP IT · RACE IT

PRIMP IT · RELAX IT · SPA IT · LEARN IT · IMPROVE IT · COACH IT · EXERCISE IT · HIGHLIGHT IT · SEE IT · READ IT · PLAN IT

WHERE CAN I FIND A **PLAYGROUP** OFFERING A
LEARN-THROUGH-PLAY METHODOLOGY FOR MY
PRESCHOOLER?

My Gym ....
17/F, Coda Plaza
51 Garden Rd, Central
2577-3322
www.mygymhk.com

Kindyroo ....
16/F, Universal Trade Centre
3–5 Arbuthnot Rd, Central
2457-1510
www.kindyroo.com

Socatots ....
2/F, Chak Fung House
440–442 Nathan Rd, Yau Ma Tei
2385-9033
www.socatots.com

Panda Junction ....
20/F, Wyndham Place
44 Wyndham St, Central
2855-0906 / 2855-0907
www.pandajunction.com
For children from 8 weeks to 3+ years.

Gymboree Play & Music ....
31/F, Universal Trade Centre
3–5 Arbuthnot Rd, Central
2899-2210
www.gymboree.com.hk

My Kiddy Gym ....
10/F, Ming An Plaza
8 Sunning Rd, Causeway Bay
2759-8811
www.mykiddygym.com

Hong Kong Pre-School Playgroups Association (HKPPA)
Main office: 2523-2599
www.hkppa.org

- **Heng Fa Chuen Playgroup**
  G/F, West Carpark
  100 Shing Tai Rd, Heng Fa Chuen
  2898-2308

- **Hilltots Pre-School**
  Mezzanine, Fook Wah Mansion
  2–4 Tsing Fung St, Tin Hau
  2576-5859

- **Sai Kung International Pre-School**
  159 Che Keng Tuk Rd, Sai Kung, New Territories
  2791-7354

- **Leapfrog Kindergarten & Playgroup**
  11 Pak Tam Chung Village, Sai Kung Country Park
  2791-1540

- **City Kids Preschool**
  2/F, East Wing, 12 Borrett Rd, Mid-Levels
  5193-2044
  www.citykidshkppa.org

Beansprouts Learning Centre ....
3/F, Tern Centre Tower 1
237 Queen's Road Central, Sheung Wan
2543-8182
www.beansprouts.com.hk

EVERYTHING LIFESTYLE & WELL BEING

HOW CAN I NURTURE MY TODDLER'S **LOVE OF MUSIC**?

Kindermusik by Catherine
9/F, Universal Trade Centre
3–5 Arbuthnot Rd, Central
2518-4840
www.kateskids.com.hk
Developmentally-appropriate music and movement programmes for children from newborn to 7 years old.

My Musik Box
3/F, 1 Hysan Ave, Causeway Bay
2882-7601
www.mymusikbox.com
Age-appropriate music and drama programmes providing basic music concept and music theory to young children.

Baby Loves Disco
5133-8424
www.babylovesdisco.com.hk
Hip nightclubs are transformed during weekend days into child-proof discos for young kids.

WHERE CAN I FIND A **MANDARIN PLAYGROUP**?

Kids Land
23/F, 438 Hennessy Rd, Causeway Bay
6112-2675
www.kidslandhk.com
Dilys Hwang offers Mandarin playgroups for children from 18 months to 5 years. She takes a similar approach to typical English playgroups, except completely in Mandarin, offering play time, art time, singing time, snack time, circle time and more. She is excellent with kids and full of energy.

Hong Kong Institute of Languages
6/F, Wellington Plaza
56–58 Wellington St, Central
2877-6160
www.hklanguages.com
Playgroups/courses for kids from 3 to 17 in English, French, German, Spanish, Mandarin, Cantonese and Japanese.

Blossoms Early Mandarin
QQ Club, Lower Ground,
Maximall, City Garden
233 Electric Rd, North Point
2234-6677
www.earlymandarin.com
Learning Mandarin through play. Age groups: 18–36 months/3–5 years/5–7 years.

WHERE CAN I FIND AN **INDOOR PLAYGROUND/FACILITY** FOR KIDS?

Western Indoor Sports Centre
18 Eastern St North, Sai Ying Pun
2858-2493
When on the underpass, turn right at the traffic light just before the entrance to the Western Cross Harbour Tunnel.

Wong Nai Chung Sports Centre ....
4/F, 2 Yuk Sau St, Happy Valley
2891-8438
*Note that on the first Monday of each month, the
playroom is open only 3–8pm.*

Aberdeen Sports Centre ....
5/F, Aberdeen Municipal Services Bldg
203 Aberdeen Main Rd, Aberdeen
2555-8909

Smithfield Sports Centre ....
12K Smithfield Rd, Kennedy Town
2855-7321
*For more playrooms throughout Hong Kong, see also
website www.lcsd.gov.hk.*

Hong Kong Central Library Toy Library ....
2/F, 66 Causeway Rd, Causeway Bay
3150-1234
www.hkpl.gov.hk
*Offers 1,300 educational toys. Parents can also join
the play programmes and workshops for a fun and
enriching experience with kids.*

Wise Kids Playroom ....
L1, The Arcade, Cyberport
100 Cyberport Rd, Pok Fu Lam
2989-6298
www.wisekidstoys.com
*Eight dedicated play zones for kids 0–8, including a
baby/toddler room, art studio, construction zone and
DIY face painting. Entry is $100/child.*

PlayTown ....
Podium, The Westwood, 8 Belcher's St, Kennedy Town
2258-9558
www.playtown.com.hk

WHERE CAN I TAKE MY KIDS SO THEY CAN LEARN
TO APPRECIATE **NATURE AND THE ENVIRONMENT**?

Kadoorie Farm and Botanic Garden ....
Lam Kam Rd, Tai Po, New Territories
2483-7200
www.kfbg.org
*A real farm with a conservation and education centre
designed to increase awareness of our relationship with
the environment. A great place to take the kids for a
weekend outing. Book ahead for a parking spot.*

Hong Kong Wetland Park ....
Wetland Park Rd, Tin Shui Wai, New Territories
3152-2666 / 2708-8885
www.wetlandpark.com

WHERE CAN MY BUDDING **LITTLE CHEF** LEARN NEW
SKILLS?

Le Meridien Cyberport ....
100 Cyberport Rd, Pok Fu Lam
2980-7788
www.hongkong.lemeridien.com
*The hotel provides seasonal cooking classes for the
kids. Kids aged 4–12 learn how to cook heart-shaped
dumplings with a Chinese chef.*

PRIMP IT . RELAX IT . SPA IT . LEARN IT . **ACTIVITIES IT** . COACH IT . EXERCISE IT . HIGHLIGHT IT . SEE IT . READ IT . PLAN IT . PLAYGROUP IT . RACE IT

Complete Deelite
6/F, California Entertainment Bldg
34–36 D'Aguilar St, Central
3167-7022
www.completedeelite.com

Vero
1/F, Fenwick Pier, 1 Lung King St, Wan Chai
2559-5882
www.verochocolates.com
*They can organise chocolate-making classes for a
minimum of five kids and five accompanying adults.*

ANY IDEAS TO GET MY KIDS INTERESTED IN **SCIENCE**?

Active Kids Ltd (Science Adventure)
9178-7376
www.activekidshk.com
*Hands-on programmes for grades K3 to 6. They also
provide camps and activities.*

Hong Kong Science Museum
2 Science Museum Rd, East Tsim Sha Tsui
2732-3232
hk.scicence.museum

Hong Kong Space Museum
10 Salisbury Rd, Tsim Sha Tsui
2721-0226
hk.space.museum

Kadoorie Farm and Botanic Garden
Lam Kam Rd, Tai Po, New Territories
2483-7200
www.kfbg.org

Children's Technology Workshop
1/F, 151 Wong Nai Chung Rd, Happy Valley
2591-0100
www.ctworkshop.com.hk

Kids Sciences Education Centre
7/F, Redana Centre
25 Yiu Wa St, Causeway Bay
2851-1876
www.kidsciences.com
Hands-on science and math activity courses.

Little Brain Children Development Centre
31/F, Universal Trade Centre
3–5 Arbuthnot Rd, Central
2521-1617
www.littlebrain.hk
*They offer programmes for children between the ages
of 4–12 years old, including the Wide Eye Science
programme.*

WHAT ABOUT **ARTS AND CRAFTS** WORKSHOPS?

Kids' Gallery
• 21/F, Coda Plaza, 51 Garden Rd, Central
  2501-4842
• Club Bel-Air, Residence Bel-Air
  48 Bel-Air Ave, Island South
  2989-9000
• L8, The Metropolis Mall
  6 Metropolis Drive, Hung Hom
  2994-5111

- 28 Cumberland Rd, Kowloon Tong
  2337-1001
www.kidsgallery.com
Offering some of the most respected arts and crafts, speech and drama, Chinese calligraphy, painting, computer and ballet.

Chameleon Workshop ....
2/F, Yan King Court
119–121 Queen's Rd East, Wan Chai
2527-2251 / 2527-2252
www.chameleonworkshop.com
A wide range of arts and crafts courses for ages 3 and up.

Creative Kids - The Young Art Studio ....
- 12/F, Universal Trade Centre
  3–5 Arbuthnot Rd, Central
- G/F, 21A Caine Rd, Mid-Levels
2530-4336
www.creativekids.com.hk
Art and craft courses, ages 2½ to adult.

Colour My World ....
1/F, Aberdeen Marina Tower
8 Shum Wan Rd, Aberdeen
2580-5028
www.colour-my-world.com
Offer all kinds of art and drama courses.

Children's Own Workshop ....
5/F, One Hysan Ave, Causeway Bay
2530-4833 / 2504-4833
www.montessorihouse.com.hk
Reasonably priced, very small art classes.

JEMS ....
5/F, China Hong Kong Tower
8–12 Hennessy Rd, Wan Chai
3188-1516
www.jems.com.hk

WHERE CAN MY CHILD GET INVOLVED IN OR VIEW KIDS' **DRAMA AND SINGING**?

Faust International Youth Theatre ....
13/F, Fu Fai Comm. Centre
27 Hillier St, Sheung Wan
2547-9114
www.faustworld.com
Faust provides week-long programmes for various ages. Courses in drama, creative writing (ages 7–11), maths (P2 and up) and choir (ages 7–14).

Hullaballoo/Kassia Children's Choir ....
8/F, Arion Comm. Centre
2–12 Queen's Rd West, Sheung Wan
2575-3931
www.katterwall.com
Hullaballoo is Kassia's Children's Choir for kids aged 5–8. The choir meets weekly for practices, which culminate in an annual performance alongside Kassia's Women's and Men's Choir and other local Hong Kong choirs.

Kids' Gallery ....
See page 258–259

Colour My World ....
See above

Chunky Onion Productions Ltd ....
G/F, Effort Ind. Bldg, 2–8 Kung Yip St, Kwai Chung
2110-0014
www.chunkyonion.com
This is a theatre for kids, providing live interactive drama in English. They have programmes for schools. They also offer entertainment for birthday parties.

Fusion Academy of Performing Arts ....
2815-2298
www.fusionacademyglobal.com
Fusion is a new theatre school from Britain offering dance, drama and singing training for children. Classes are taught at Kennedy School in Pok Fu Lam and at Central Dance Studio in Central.

MY CHILD NEEDS TO IMPROVE HIS **ENGLISH LANGUAGE SKILLS**. WHO CAN HELP?

Dramatic English ....
6/F, Breakthrough Centre, 191 Woo Sung St, Jordan
2880-5085
www.dramaticenglish.org
Students learn English with theatre.

Canadian Workshop ....
6/F, Universal Trade Centre
3–5 Arbuthnot Rd, Central
2521-5000
www.canadianworkshop.com.hk
English workshops for children aged 2½ to 12.

Kidsedge ....
6/F & 8/F, Universal Trade Centre
3–5 Arbuthnot Rd, Central
2868-0636
www.kidsedgeonline.com
A full-service English learning centre, serving native and non-native English speakers.

The British Council ....
3 Supreme Court Rd, Admiralty
2913-5100
www.britishcouncil.org.hk
Quality English courses, professional examinations services, guidance for studying in Britain, scholarships for postgraduate studies, and innovative arts and science programmes.

I'D LIKE MY YOUNG CHILD TO LEARN **MANDARIN**. WHICH COURSES/PRE-SCHOOLS FOCUS ON THIS?

Tutor Time ....
• LG/F, Braemar Hill Shopping Centre
  45 Braemar Hill Rd, North Point
  2529-1833
• 1/F, Red Hill Plaza, 3 Red Hill Rd, Tai Tam
  2813-2008
• 1 Dorset Crescent, Kowloon Tong
  2337-0822
• 9 Suffolk Rd, Kowloon Tong
  2529-1188
www.tutortime.com.hk
This international nursery and kindergarten teaches children using English and Mandarin.
See also Mandarin/Cantonese schools, pages 268–269.

EVERYTHING LIFESTYLE & WELL BEING

WHERE CAN MY KIDS TAKE **CREATIVE WRITING** COURSES?

Faust International Youth Theatre ....
13/F, Fu Fai Comm. Centre
27 Hillier St, Sheung Wan
2547-9114
www.faustworld.com
Creative writing classes for age 7 and up.

Colour My World ....
1/F, Aberdeen Marina Tower
8 Shum Wan Rd, Aberdeen
2580-5028
www.colour-my-world.com

Kids' Gallery ....
See page 258–259

MY KIDS NEED SOME **EXTRA TUTORING FOR SCHOOL**. WHERE CAN I FIND THIS?

Sylvan Learning Center ....
6/F, Po Wah Comm. Centre
226 Hennessy Rd, Wan Chai
2873-0662
www.educate.com
Sylvan starts with an assessment of your child to identify their needs, then provides personalised lesson plans. They offer maths, literacy and creative writing tuition in small groups or as workshops during school breaks. Also located in Shum Wan, Aberdeen.

Kumon ....
5/F, 1 Hysan Ave, Causeway Bay
2881-6664
www.kumon.cn/KHK
Offering daily self-learning exercises in Maths. They also offer Chinese and English programmes. Various locations. See website for details.

ITS Tutorial School ....
3/F, Sun House, 181 Des Voeux Rd Central
2116-3916
www.tuition.com.hk
For students studying the IB–all subjects including EE and ToK. Contact Danny Harrington.

Kevin Harrison ....
2982-1996 / 9047-9548
www.mrkevin.com

WHAT ARE GOOD **EDUCATIONAL RESOURCES** TO HELP IN MY CHILD'S DEVELOPMENT?

Family Fitness Agency ....
427 Hennessy Rd, Causeway Bay
2886-3884 / 3579-5383
www.familyfitness.com.hk
Sell material on early fitness, early learning, sports, fitness, ergonomics, physiotherapy. They also sell learning material on maths, English and Mandarin.

EVERYTHING LIFESTYLE & WELL BEING

MY KIDS ARE OFF SCHOOL. ARE THERE GOOD **ACTIVITY DAY-CAMPS** MY KIDS CAN JOIN?

Kids' Gallery ....
See page 258–259
ESF Sports Department ....
5/F, Cigna Tower, 482 Jaffe Rd, Causeway Bay
2711-1280
www.esf.org.hk
ESF schools run regular camps for summer and Easter breaks. They also sell a range of kids' sports equipment.
Colour My World ....
1/F, Aberdeen Marina Tower
8 Shum Wan Rd, Aberdeen
2580-5028
www.colour-my-world.com

WHERE CAN MY CHILD LEARN **BALLET**?

DMR School of Ballet ....
1/F, Block C, Discovery Bay Plaza
Discovery Bay, Lantau Island
2987-4338
www.dmr-hk.com
Kids' Gallery ....
See page 258–259
Classes from 2 years and up.
Danse A Lili Ballet Academie ....
9/F, Lee Theatre Plaza, 99 Percival St, Causeway Bay
2970-2228
www.dansealili.com
Kinder Ballet classes begin from 12 months.
Lynne Ballet School ....
17/F, Universal Trade Centre
3–5 Arbuthnot Rd, Central
2808-1665
www.lynneballetschool.com
Lynne Charleston is a very experienced teacher with Royal Academy of Dance and Imperial Society of Teachers of Dancing qualifications. Classes are small (limited to 12), personal and all taught by Lynne. Classes start at age 3.
Jean M Wong Ballet ....
• 1/F, 18 Tanner Rd, North Point (headquarters)
  2886-3992
• 31/F, Universal Trade Centre, 3–5 Arbuthnot Rd, Central
  2869-6288
• 1/F, 139 Wong Nai Chung Rd, Happy Valley
  2577-2112
• 16/F, Telford House, 18 Wang Hoi Rd, Kowloon Bay
  2754-2277
• Podium, Telford Gardens, 33 Wai Yip St, Kowloon Bay
  2756-8226
www.jmwballet.org
See website for more locations.
Carol Bateman School of Dance ....
35 Garden Rd, Central
2525-3751
www.carolbatemanschool.com
Set in the colonial Helena May building with high ceilings and piano accompaniment. Classes from 3 years of age.

Hong Kong Ballet .... ✪
60 Blue Pool Rd, Happy Valley
2573-7398
www.hkballet.com
Better suited for more experienced ballet students.

Hong Kong Academy for Performing Arts .... ✪
1 Gloucester Rd, Wan Chai
2584-8500
www.hkapa.edu
Classes for ages 14–18 at all levels in contemporary and classical ballet.

HOW ABOUT **CONTEMPORARY DANCE** FOR KIDS?

Red Shoe Dance .... ✪
11/F, Chinachem Hollywood Centre
1–13 Hollywood Rd, Central
2117-9295 / 9813-0079
www.redshoedance.com
Classes ranging from hip-hop, classical jazz to cheerdance are offered at various venues in Hong Kong and Kowloon.

Island Dance .... ✪
Multi venue
2987-1571
www.islanddance.com.hk
A variety of classes ranging from classical ballet to funky freestyle disco.

WHO OFFERS COACHING IN A VARIETY OF **SPORTS ACTIVITIES** ALL OVER HONG KONG?

Multi-Sport .... ✪
8/F, Yien Yieh Bank Western Bldg
32–36 Des Voeux Rd West, Sheung Wan
2540-1257
www.multi-sport.com.hk

Play Sport .... ✪
8/F, Wing Fu Bldg, 18–20 Wing Kut St, Central
2818-9453
www.playsport.com.hk

I HEARD THAT **MARTIAL ARTS** TRAINING DOES WONDERS FOR A CHILD'S CONFIDENCE. ANY RECOMMENDATIONS?

ESF Sports Department .... ✪
5/F, Cigna Tower, 482 Jaffe Rd, Causeway Bay
2711-1280
www.esf.org.hk
ESF offers martial arts courses after school for children from any school, including judo, kung fu and karate.

Heng Yue Yen Long Kwon Modern Chinese Martial Art ..... ✪
10/F, 9 Morrison Hill Rd, Wan Chai
2511-8787
www.hyylkmartialarts.com
Classes are run by qualified black-belt instructors. Learning can be self-paced and instruction is in English. Lessons are fun and incorporate stretching and strengthening exercises. Obedience and co-operation are also cultivated.

EVERYTHING LIFESTYLE & WELL BEING

Hong Kong Judo Kan .... ◉
12/F, East Point Centre
555 Hennessy Rd, Causeway Bay
2891-0851 / 2591-4570
www.hongkongjudokan.com
South China Athletic Association .... ◉
88 Caroline Hill Rd, Causeway Bay
2577-6932
www.scaa.org.hk

I LOVE MY YOGA CLASS. IS THERE ANYWHERE
THAT I CAN LEARN TO **TEACH YOGA TO KIDS**?

Yoga Kids Asia .... ◉
9861-6227
www.yogakids-asia.com
*Workshops and training to teach kids yoga. Yoga Kids
also offers private parties, corporate parties, personal
pre-natal yoga in your home and more.*

WHERE CAN MY **KIDS DO YOGA**?

Pure Yoga .... ◉
See page 201
Yoga Limbs .... ◉
33/F & 34/F, 69 Jervois St, Sheung Wan
2525-7415
www.yogalimbs.com
Yoga Central .... ◉
4/F, Kai Kwong House, 13 Wyndham St, Central
2982-4308
www.yogacentral.com.hk
Planet Yoga .... ◉
See pages 201–202
Yoga For Life .... ◉
1/F, Lot 1227, Heng Mei Deng, Clear Water Bay
Sai Kung, New Territories
2167-7401
www.yogaforlife.com.hk
Yoga Kids .... ◉
9861-6227
www.yogakids-asia.com
Anahata Yoga .... ◉
18/F, One Lyndhurst Tower
1 Lyndhurst Terrace, Central
2905-1822
www.anahatayoga.com.hk
The Yoga Room .... ◉
3/F, Xiu Ping Comm. Bldg
104 Jervois St, Sheung Wan
2544-8398
www.yogaroomhk.com
Life Management Yoga Centre .... ◉
11/F, Kimberley House
35 Kimberley Rd, Tsim Sha Tsui
2191-9656
www.yoga.org.hk
Movement Improvement .... ◉
3D Elegance Court, Discovery Bay, Lantau Island
2987-5852
www.movementimprovement.com.hk

EVERYTHING LIFESTYLE & WELL BEING

KIDS SPORTS IT . RACE IT

PRIMP IT . RELAX IT . SPA IT . LEARN IT . IMPROVE IT . COACH IT . EXERCISE IT . HIGHLIGHT IT . SEE IT . READ IT . PLAN IT .

MY KIDS WANT TO PLAY **RUGBY**. WHERE SHOULD I TAKE THEM?

Mini Rugby ....
Hong Kong Rugby Football Union
2504-8300
www.hkrugby.com
There are over 15 active clubs, catering to boys and girls aged 4–12.

WHERE CAN MY KIDS LEARN HOW TO **SURF** IN HONG KONG?

China Coast Surf School ....
9017-5635
www.chinacoastsurf.com
Rex Lau, former pro surfer, offers private and group lessons at Big Wave Bay. Kids age 6 and up to adults.

Quiksilver Treasure Island Surf Camp ....
Pui O Beach, Lantau Island
2894-8711
www.treasureislandhk.com

WHERE CAN MY KIDS LEARN TO **SKATE**?

Mega Ice ....
L10, MegaBox, 38 Wang Chiu Rd, Kowloon Bay
2709-4020
www.megaice.com.hk
Hong Kong's only Olympic-sized rink offers both private and group figure skating and ice hockey lessons.

The Rink ....
G/F, Elements Mall, 1 Austin Rd West, Kowloon
2196-8016
www.rink.com.hk

Cityplaza Ice Palace ....
1/F, Cityplaza, 18 Taikoo Shing Rd, Tai Koo
2844-8688
www.icepalace.com.hk

Festival Walk Glacier ....
UG, Festival Walk, 80 Tat Chee Ave, Kowloon Tong
2844-3588
www.glacier.com.hk

Sky Rink ....
8/F, Dragon Centre, 37K Yen Chow St, Sham Shui Po
2307-9365
www.skyrinkhk.com

ARE THERE ANY **HOCKEY LEAGUES** FOR KIDS IN HONG KONG THAT OFFER COACHING AND TEAM PLAY?

Hong Kong Typhoons Ice Hockey Club ....
2594-0165
www.hktyphoonsicehockey.org
Hong Kong's largest youth hockey league is non-profit and primarily volunteer/parent run. The league offers kids age 5 and up an opportunity to practise and play with a team.

Bears Hockey Club ....
www.bearshockeyclub.com.hk

Hong Kong Amateur Hockey Club ....
www.hkahc.com

Hong Kong Academy of Ice Hockey (HKAIH) ....
2863-4368
www.hkaih.org

HKAIH with coach Barry Beck, former captain of the NY Rangers, offers beginner to advanced hockey coaching for children 4 to 12.

HOW ABOUT INLINE SKATING AND HOCKEY?

Go Sport ....
9049-6292
maniagosk8@gmail.com

Donna Maniago is passionate about hockey and skating and is wonderful with children. She offers classes ranging from learn to skate to advanced inline hockey at venues throughout Hong Kong.

I AM LOOKING AT SCHOOLS FOR MY CHILDREN. CAN YOU GIVE ME A GENERAL OVERVIEW OF WHAT IS AVAILABLE?

Pre-schools

Sunshine House ....
- 3/F, Peak Galleria, 118 Peak Rd, The Peak
  2849-7123
- 1/F, Redhill Plaza, 3 Red Hill Rd, Tai Tam
  2813-0713
- Pok Fu Lam Gardens, 180 Pok Fu Lam Rd, Pok Fu Lam
  2551-3213
- H1, Chi Fu Fa Yuen, Pok Fu Lam
  2551-3781
- 1/F, Discovery Bay Plaza
  Discovery Bay, Lantau Island
  2987-8143
- 2 Mei Tung St, Tung Chung, Lantau Island
  2109-3873
www.sunshinehouse.com.hk

Highgate House School ....
2/F, 100 Peak Rd, The Peak
2849-6336
www.highgatehouse.edu.hk

Woodland Pre-Schools ....
Main office: 2559-4855
- **Tai Tam Montessori Pre-School**
  G/F, Red Hill Plaza, 3 Red Hill Rd, Tai Tam
  2525-1655
- **Repulse Bay Montessori Pre-School**
  G/F, The Repulse Bay
  109 Repulse Bay Rd, Repulse Bay
  2803-1885
- **Mid-Levels Montessori Pre-School**
  119 Caine Rd, Mid-Levels
  2549-1211
- **The Peak Pre-School**
  81 Peak Rd, The Peak
  2849-6192

EVERYTHING LIFESTYLE & WELL BEING

PRIMP IT . RELAX IT . SPA IT . LEARN IT . IMPROVE IT . COACH IT . EXERCISE IT . HIGHLIGHT IT . SEE IT . READ IT . PLAN IT . SCHOOL IT . RACE IT

- **Happy Valley Pre-School**
  2 Hawthorne Rd, Happy Valley
  2575-0042
- **Pokfulam Pre-School**
  G/F, Comm. Complex
  Wah Fu 2, Wah Fu Rd, Pok Fu Lam
  2551-7177
- **Harbourside Pre-School**
  G/F, 3 Aberdeen Praya Rd, Aberdeen
  2559-1377
- **Woodland Tree House**
  G/F, Scenic Villas
  26–28 Scenic Villas Dr, Pok Fu Lam
  2872-6138
- **The Woodland Beachside Pre-School**
  2/F, 35 Beach Rd, Repulse Bay
  2812-0274
www.woodlandschools.com

ESF Kindergartens
Main office: 2574-2351
- **Sheung Wan Kindergarten**
  1/F & Mezzanine, Tung Fai Garden
  17 Po Yan St, Sheung Wan
  2540-0066
- **Tsing Yi Kindergarten**
  Maritime Square, 33 Tsing King Rd
  Tsing Yi, New Territories
  2436-3355
- **Wu Kai Sha Kindergarten**
  L1, 599 Sai Sha Rd, Sha Tin, New Territories
  2435-5291
www.esf.org.hk

Hong Kong Pre-School Playgroups Association (HKPPA)
See page 256

Small World
10 Borrett Rd, Mid-Levels
2525-0922
www.swck.edu.hk

Parkview International Pre-School (PIPS)
Tower 18, Parkview
88 Tai Tam Resevoir Rd, Repulse Bay
2812-6023
www.pips.edu.hk

Southside Kindergarten
G/F, The Repulse Bay
203 Repulse Bay Rd, Repulse Bay
2592-7527

The Montessori School of Hong Kong
2869-1811
www.montessori-edu.com

Carmel School of Hong Kong
4/F, One Robinson Place
70 Robinson Rd, Mid-Levels
2249-7600
www.carmel.edu.hk

Discovery Bay International School Kindergarten
Discovery Bay, Lantau Island
2914-2142
www.dbis.edu.hk

Mandarin/Cantonese or Bilingual Schools—Multi-level

Kiangsu & Chekiang School .... ⚲
30 Ching Wah St, North Point
2570-4594
www.kcis.edu.hk
This local school offers instruction in Mandarin (75%) and English (25%) with classes starting from two years of age.

Victoria Educational Organisation .... ⚲

- **Kornhill Victoria Nursery & Kindergarten**
  2/F, 18 Hong On St, Kornhill, Quarry Bay
  2885-1888

- **Victoria International Nursery & Kindergarten**
  2–8 Hong On St, Kornhill, Quarry Bay
  2885-3331

- **Causeway Bay Victoria Kindergarten & International Kindergarten**
  32 Hing Fat St, Causeway Bay
  2578-9998

- **Causeway Bay Victoria Nursery**
  Ko Fung Court, Harbour Heights
  5 Fook Yum Rd, North Point
  2571-3456

- **Victoria (South Horizons) International Nursery & Kindergarten**
  Podium, South Horizons, Phase 2, Ap Lei Chau
  2580-8633

- **Victoria (Belcher) International Nursery & Kindergarten**
  3/F, The Westwood, 8 Belcher's St, Kennedy Town
  2542-7001

- **Victoria (Homantin) International Nursery**
  1/F, Carmel-on-the-Hill
  9 Carmel Village St, Ho Man Tin
  2762-9130

- **Victoria (Harbour Green) Kindergarten & International Nursery**
  G/F, Harbour Green, 8 Sham Mong Rd, Kowloon
  2885-1928

www.victoria.edu.hk

International Montessori School .... ⚲

- G/F, Blocks 23–23A
  South Horizons, Phase 3, Ap Lei Chau
  2861-0339

- 4/F, 6 Salvation Army St, Wan Chai
  2156-9033

www.montessori.edu.hk

Lingnan Primary School and Kindergarten .... ⚲
www.lingnanp.edu.hk

- **Lingnan Kindergarten & Day Nursery**
  7 Tung Shan Terrace, Stubbs Rd, Wan Chai
  2893-2322

- **Lingnan Primary School & Kindergarten**
  15 Stubbs Rd, Wan Chai
  2572-9506

Tutor Time .... ⚲
See page 261

Independent Schools Foundation Academy .... ⚲
1 Kong Sin Wan Rd, Pok Fu Lam
2202-2000
www.isf.edu.hk

Chinese International School ....
1 Hau Yuen Path, Braemar Hill, North Point
2510-7288
www.cis.edu.hk

Singapore International School ....
www.singapore.edu.hk
- **Primary School**
  23 Nam Long Shan Rd, Aberdeen
  2872-0266
- **Secondary School**
  30 Oi Kwan Rd, Wan Chai
  2919-6966

Yew Chung International Schools ....
www.ycis-hk.com
- **Yew Chung Early Childhood Education**
  3 Somerset Rd, Kowloon Tong
  2338-0264
- **Yew Chung Primary School**
  2 Kent Rd, Kowloon Tong
  2336-7292
- **Yew Chung Secondary School**
  3 To Fuk Rd, Kowloon Tong
  2336-3443

International Primary and Secondary Schools

English Schools Foundation ....
Main office: 2574-2351
Primary Schools:
Beacon Hill School
23 Ede Rd, Kowloon Tong
2336-5221
Bradbury School
43C Stubbs Rd, Wan Chai
2574-8249
Clearwater Bay School
DD229, Lot 235,Clear Water Bay Rd
Clear Water Bay, Sai Kung, New Territories
2358-3221
Discovery College
38 Siena Ave, Discovery Bay, Lantau Island
3969-1000
Glenealy School
7 Hornsey Rd, Mid-Levels
2522-1919
Jockey Club Sarah Roe School
2B, Tin Kwong Rd, Ho Man Tin
2761-9893
Kennedy School
19 Sha Wan Dr, Pok Fu Lam
2855-0711
Kowloon Junior School
- 20 Perth St, Ho Man Tin
  2714-5279
- 4 Rose St, Yau Yat Chuen, Kowloon Tong
  2394-0687
Peak School
20 Plunketts Rd, The Peak
2849-7211

Quarry Bay School
6 Hau Yuen Path, Braemar Hill, Quarry Bay
2566-4242

Renaissance College
5 Hang Ming St, Ma On Shan
3556-3556

Sha Tin Junior School
Lai Wo Lane, Fo Tan, Sha Tin, New Territories
2692-2721

Secondary Schools:

Discovery College
38 Siena Ave, Discovery Bay, Lantau Island
3969-1000

Island School
20 Borrett Rd, Mid-Levels
2524-7135

Jockey Club Sarah Roe School
2B, Tin Kwong Rd, Ho Man Tin
2761-9893

King George V School
2 Tin Kwong Rd, Ho Man Tin
2711-3029

Renaissance College
5 Hang Ming St, Ma On Shan
3556-3556

Sha Tin College
Lai Wo Lane, Fo Tan, Sha Tin, New Territories
2692-2721

South Island School
50 Nam Fung Rd, Shouson Hill, Aberdeen
2555-9313

West Island School
250 Victoria Rd, Pok Fu Lam
2819-1962
www.esf.edu.hk

German Swiss International School
11 Guildford Rd, The Peak
2849-6216
www.gsis.edu.hk

Hong Kong International School
Main office: 3149-7001

• **Lower/Higher Primary School:**
  23 South Bay Coast, Repulse Bay
  2812-5000

• **Middle/High School:**
  1 Red Hill Rd, Tai Tam
  3149-7000
www.hkis.edu.hk

Kellett School
2 Wah Lok Path, Wah Fu, Pok Fu Lam
2551-8234
www.kellettschool.com

French International School
165 Blue Pool Rd, Happy Valley
2577-6217
www.fis.edu.hk

Canadian International School
2525-7088
www.cdnis.edu.hk

Hong Kong Academy ....
4/F, Chung On Hall, 15 Stubbs Rd, Wan Chai
2575-8282
www.hkacademy.edu.hk

Australian International School ....
3A Norfolk Rd, Kowloon Tong
2304-6078
www.aishk.edu.hk

Discovery Bay International School ....
Discovery Bay, Lantau Island
2987-7331
www.dbis.edu.hk

American International School ....
125 Waterloo Rd, Kowloon Tong
2336-3812
www.ais.edu.hk

Carmel School of Hong Kong ....
- **Elementary/Middle School:**
  10 Borrett Rd, Mid-Levels
  2964-1600
- **Elsa High School:**
  460 Shau Kei Wan Rd, Shau Kei Wan
  3665-5388
www.carmel.edu.hk

Delia School of Canada ....
Tai Fung Ave, Tai Koo
3658-0338
www.delia.edu.hk

Norwegian International School ....
170 Kam Shan Rd, Kam Shan Village
Tai Po, New Territories
2658-0341
www.nis.edu.hk

Japanese International School ....
4663 Tai Po Rd, Tai Po, New Territories
- **Primary Japanese Section:**
  2652-2313
- **Primary English Section:**
  2834-3531
www.jis.edu.hk

Hong Kong Japanese School ....
- **Primary School**
  157 Blue Pool Rd, Happy Valley
  2574-7135 / 2574-5479
- **Secondary School**
  9 Hau Yen Path, North Point
  2566-5311
www.hkjs.edu.hk

Korean International School ....
55 Lei King Rd, Sai Wan Ho
2569-5500
www.kis.edu.hk

WHERE DO I BUY, SELL OR LEASE A **SCHOOL DEBENTURE**?

Noblesse Membership Service
8/F, Chow Sang Sang Bldg, 229 Nathan Rd, Jordan
2366-9393 / 9639-4509
www.noblesse.com.hk
*Ask for Francis Cheng. They can also arrange club
memberships.*

Elite Membership Services Ltd
11/F, Perfect Comm. Bldg
28 Sharp St West, Causeway Bay
2838-3368
www.elitemembership.com.hk
Club memberships also arranged.

Amazing Membership Service
2890-4832
Club memberships also arranged.

Debenture Exchange
2810-4300

WE ARE CONSIDERING **BOARDING SCHOOL** FOR OUR
CHILD. WHO CAN HELP US CHOOSE THE RIGHT
ONE?

Academy Asia
20/F, Hang Lung Centre
2–20 Paterson St, Causeway Bay
2833-0919
www.academic-asia.com
*Hong Kong's largest and oldest UK boarding school
consultancy.*

Pathfinder Educational Consulting
6120-1248
www.pathfinderconsulting.com.hk
US college and boarding school consultancy.

I'VE JUST MOVED TO HONG KONG. WHERE ARE
THE KEY **PRIVATE/PUBLIC HOSPITALS**?

Hong Kong Adventist Hospital
40 Stubbs Rd, Happy Valley
2574-6211
www.hkah.org.hk

Matilda International Hospital
41 Mount Kellett Rd, The Peak
2849-0111
www.matilda.org

Hong Kong Sanatorium & Hospital
2 Village Rd, Happy Valley
2572-0211
www.hksh.com

Canossa Hospital
1 Old Peak Rd, Mid-Levels
2522-2181
www.canossahospital.org.hk

Ruttonjee Hospital
266 Queen's Rd East, Wan Chai
2291-2000
www.ha.org.hk

Queen Mary Hospital
102 Pok Fu Lam Rd, Pok Fu Lam
22855-3838
www.ha.org.hk/qmh

Pamela Youde Nethersole Eastern Hospital
3 Lok Man Rd, Chai Wan
2592-6111
www.ha.org.hk/pyneh

Hong Kong Baptist Hospital
222 Waterloo Rd, Kowloon Tong
2339-8888 / 2339-8801
www.hkbh.org.hk

Queen Elizabeth Hospital
30 Gascoigne Rd, Jordan
2958-8888
www.ha.org.hk/qeh

Prince of Wales Hospital
30–32 Ngan Shing St, Sha Tin, New Territories
2632-2211 / 2645-1222
www.ha.org.hk/pwh

WHAT WOULD YOU RECOMMEND AS AN
ESTABLISHED AND REPUTABLE **MULTI-SPECIALIST
MEDICAL PRACTICE** IN HONG KONG?

OT&P
- 5/F, Century Square
  1–13 D'Aguilar St, Central
  2521-3181
- 15/F, Shui On Centre
  8 Harbour Rd, Wan Chai
  2824-9112 / 7475-0107
- G/F, The Repulse Bay
  109 Repulse Bay Rd, Repulse Bay
  2813-1978
- 1/F, Razor Hill Dairy Farm Shopping Centre
  Clear Water Bay Rd, Pik Uk, New Territories
  2719-6366
www.otandp.com

Lucy Lord & Associates
- **Central Health Medical Practice**
  3/F, Baskerville House, 13 Duddell St, Central
  2824-0822
  www.centralhealth.com.hk
- **Southside Family Health Centre**
  1/F, 2H South Bay Rd, Repulse Bay
  2592-9000
  www.southside.com.hk
- **Island Health Family Practice**
  109A, Discovery Bay Plaza
  Discovery Bay, Lantau Island
  2987-7575
  www.islandhealth.com

Dr Nicholson & Associates
4/F, New World Tower, 18 Queen's Rd Central
2525-1251

Dr Lauren Bramley & Partners
9/F, Pacific House, 20 Queen's Rd Central
2877-6068
www.laurenbramley.com

Quality HealthCare Medical Centre
5/F, Prince's Bldg, 10 Chater Rd, Central
2523-8166
www.qhms.com
*Many additional locations throughout Hong Kong.
See website.*

HOW ABOUT A VERY REPUTABLE **DENTAL CLINIC**?

Bayley & Jackson Dental Surgeons
- 2/F, Jardine House, 1 Connaught Place, Central
  2526-1061 / 2524-8000
- G/F, Repulse Bay Shopping Arcade
  109 Repulse Bay Rd, Repulse Bay
  2812-2358
Hotline: 2525-2239
www.bjdental.com
See website for other locations in Tsim Sha Tsui, Mong Kok and Sha Tin.

Costello Brothers Dentistry
19/F, Coda Plaza, 51 Garden Rd, Mid-Levels
2877-9622
www.costellobrothersdentistry.com

Pacific Dental Care
4/F, Hing Wai Bldg, 36 Queen's Rd Central
2521-1663

Pacific Orthodontic Care
10/F, Grand Centre, 8 Humphreys Ave, Tsim Sha Tsui
2331-3238

Tam, Hulac & Partners Dental Ltd
- 15/F, World-Wide House, 19 Des Voeux Rd Central
  2868-1775
- G/F, The Repulse Bay, 109 Repulse Bay Rd, Repulse Bay
  2812-6337
www.thpdental.com

American Dental Group
5/F, Prince's Bldg, 10 Chater Rd, Central
2526-2288
www.adgl.com.hk

WHERE CAN I FIND A GOOD **PAEDIATRICIAN** OR **GP WHO IS GREAT WITH CHILDREN**?

Dr Tanpa Thondup
- Veritas Medical Practice
  29/F, Bank of America Tower, 12 Harcourt Rd, Central
  2877-3118
- Repulse Bay Medical Practice
  G/F, The Repulse Bay
  109 Repulse Bay Rd, Repulse Bay
  2812-2677
www.veritas-medical.com
Dr Thondup is a highly regarded, knowledgeable and popular paediatrician.

Dr Rulin Fuong, Dr Yvonne Ou, Dr Sarah Borwein
3/F, Baskerville House, 13 Duddell St, Central
2824-0822
www.centralhealth.com.hk

Dr Penny Nicolle, Dr Mark Chan
OT&P, 5/F, Century Square, 1–13 D'Aguilar St, Central
2521-3181
www.otandp.com

Dr Nichola Salmond, Dr Ken Chan
Dr Lauren Bramley & Partners
9/F, Pacific House, 20 Queen's Rd Central
2877-6068
www.laurenbramley.com

EVERYTHING LIFESTYLE & WELL BEING

WHERE CAN I FIND A **CHILDREN'S DENTIST** WHO WILL PUT MY CHILD AT EASE?

Dr Jennie Tsai ....
- 8/F, Hang Seng Bldg
  28 – 34 Yee Wo St, Causeway Bay
  2893-2386 / 2972-2686 / 9102-1205
- Costello Brothers Dentistry
  19/F, Coda Plaza, 51 Garden Rd, Mid-Levels
  2877-9622
  www.costellobrothersdentistry.com
Dr Jennie is a natural with kids, with plenty of tricks up her colourful sleeve.

Dr Denise L Giles ....
Dr Chan & Partners
14/F, Central Bldg, 1 – 3 Pedder St, Central
2525-3311 / 2523-6815
Dr Denise Giles comes highly recommended as a paediatric dentist.

Bayley & Jackson Dental Surgeons ....
See page 274
Dr Choo's patient manner is great for kids.

American Dental Group ....
5/F, Prince's Bldg
10 Chater Rd, Central
2526-2288
www.adgl.com.hk
Dr Peter Kwong is very knowledgeable, friendly and good with young children above toddler age.

Pacific Dental Care ....
4/F, Hing Wai Bldg
36 Queen's Rd Central
2521-1663
Dr Lee is gentle, patient and very good for young children.

WHERE CAN I FIND A GOOD **ORTHODONTIST** FOR MY CHILD?

Dr Martine Boisson ....
15/F, Prince's Bldg
10 Chater Rd, Central
2522-1996

Dr Alec K. Tam ....
6/F, Melbourne Plaza
33 Queen's Rd Central
2868-0218

Dr George Wang ....
20 Des Voeux Rd Central
2524-4275

Dr Winston Tong ....
Southside Dental Ltd
26/F, Bank of America Tower
12 Harcourt Rd, Central
2868-6992

Dr Ma Tsun ....
Bayley & Jackson Dental Surgeons
See page 274

Dr Louise Wong ....
Pacific Dental Care and Pacific Orthodontic Care
See page 274

EVERYTHING LIFESTYLE & WELL BEING

WHO IS A GOOD PLASTIC SURGEON FOR CHILDREN?

Dr Philip Hsieh
9/F, Tak Shing House
20 Des Voeux Rd Central
2521-8292
A respected surgeon who is great with kids and does expert stitching.

Dr Daniel Lee
5/F, Bank of America Tower
12 Harcourt Rd, Central
2526-6681
Highly regarded, precise and thorough plastic surgeon. Well-versed with mums who don't want their kids left with a big scar!

I WOULD LIKE MY CHILD'S EYES CHECKED FOR SIGHT AND COLOUR BLINDNESS. WHO CAN HELP?

Dr Susan Salnikov
• Matilda Health Centre
  Mount Kellett Rd, The Peak
  2849-1500
• OT&P, G/F, The Repulse Bay
  109 Repulse Bay Rd, Repulse Bay
  2813-1978
  www.otandp.com
Dr Salnikov specialises in eye tests for children, including tests for colour blindness.

WHERE CAN I BUY KIDS' UV SUNGLASSES?

LensCrafters
• UG/F, Century Square
  1–13 D'Aguilar St, Central
  2525-9861
• 2/F, Cityplaza 2
  18 Taikoo Shing Rd, Tai Koo
2886-4522 / 2866-4522
www.lenscrafters.com.hk
Many locations, see also website.

Fox Optical
G/F, Winning House
12 Cochrane St, Central
2543-8633 / 2541-3018

I'M WORRIED THAT MY CHILD IS NOT HEARING PROPERLY. WHERE CAN I GET HER HEARING CHECKED?

Phonak Hearing Centre
13/F, Albion Plaza
2–6 Granville Rd, Tsim Sha Tsui
2311-2828
www.phonak.com.hk
The technicians at Phonak are very good with hearing tests for children. A referral is recommended.

Widex Hong Kong
8/F, Crawford House
70 Queen's Rd Central
2111-8798
www.widexhongkong.com

EVERYTHING LIFESTYLE & WELL BEING

I THINK THAT MY CHILD MAY HAVE SOME **SPEECH ISSUES**. WHERE CAN I TAKE HIM FOR TESTING?

The Speech and Language Centre
23/F, 118 Connaught Rd West, Sheung Wan
2817-5450
www.slcentre.com
Helping anyone with communication, speech, language, learning and behavioural difficulties.

Hong Kong Speech & Swallowing Therapy Centre
• 11/F, Kornhill Plaza Office Bldg
  Kornhill Rd, Quarry Bay
  2568-2881
• 12/F, Hong Kong Pacific Centre
  28 Hankow Rd, Tsim Sha Tsui
  2311-6330
hkssc.com.hk
Helping children with misarticulation, language developmental delay and/or disorder, social communication disorder, neurological communication disorder, voice disorder, dysfluency and dyslexia.

Dr Jacqueline Gerard
Southside Family Health Centre
1/F, 2H South Bay Rd, Repulse Bay
2592-9000
www.southside.com.hk

WHERE CAN I TAKE MY CHILD TO BE TESTED FOR **ALLERGIES**?

Dr Adrian Wu
14/F, Prince's Bldg, 10 Chater Rd, Central
2818-0180
Allergy and immunology specialist.

HK BioTek
4/F, Universal Comm. House, 4 Shell St, Fortress Hill
2763-1488
www.hkbiotek.com

Dr Lynn Lim
OT&P, 5/F, Century Square, 1–13 D'Aguilar St, Central
2521-3181
www.otandp.com

I THINK MY CHILD MAY HAVE ALLERGIES AND/OR ASTHMA. WHERE CAN I GO FOR **NATURAL TREATMENT**?

The Body Group
17/F, 10 Pottinger St, Central
2167-7305
www.thebodygroup.com
They use a method founded on holistic principles that does not involve the use of medications to control or suppress allergic symptoms.

Integrated Medicine Institute
17/F, Kailey Tower, 16 Stanley St, Central
2523-7121
www.imi.com.hk
Australian qualified homeopath, naturopath and herbalist, specialising in the treatment of allergies, asthma and more.

ANY SUGGESTIONS FOR A **NUTRITIONIST/DIETICIAN**
TO ADVISE ON MY FAMILY'S DIET NEEDS?

Gabrielle Tuscher
OT&P, 5/F, Century Square, 1–13 D'Aguilar St, Central
2521-3181
www.otandp.com

Nicole Edwards
15/F, Shui On Centre, 8 Harbour Rd, Wan Chai
2824-9112 / 7475-0107
www.otandp.com

Denise Fair
• Central Health Medical Practice
• Southside Family Health Centre
See page 273

Dr Susan Jamieson & Associates
16/F, Hing Wai Bldg, 36 Queen's Rd Central
2523-8044
www.drjamieson.com

I THINK MY CHILD MAY HAVE **DYSLEXIA**. WHERE
CAN I FIND OUT MORE ABOUT THIS?

Dyslexia Association (Hong Kong) ....
10/F, Block 1, Victoria Gardens
301 Victoria Rd, Pok Fu Lam
2872-5489
www.dyslexia.org.hk
*Established by Hong Kong parents and others interested
in dyslexia, the association aims to raise levels of
awareness and to provide assistance and support for
people suffering from dyslexia. The website provides
useful information, books, education and more.*

F.O.C.U.S. Centre ....
CKK Comm. Centre, 289 Hennessy Rd, Wan Chai
2849-8218
www.focus.org.hk
*A non-profit organisation whose mission is to promote
public awareness of learning disorders and help
improve challenged children's education.*

WHO CAN HELP ME RECOVER FROM A MINOR
SPORTS INJURY?

Astretch Ltd (Stretch Flexibility Studio)
4/F, Winsome House, 73 Wyndham St, Central
2167-8686
www.stretchasia.com
*Specialising in postural conditioning using active
isolated stretching, neuromuscular therapy, soft-tissue
mobilisation and more. They help you prevent injuries,
not just treat them.*

Sports and Spinal Physiotherapy Centres
• 7/F, Jardine House, 1 Connaught Place, Central
   2715-4577
• 15/F, Winway Bldg, 50 Wellington St, Central
   2530-0073
www.physiohk.com

Byrne, Hickman & Partners
• 2/F, Dina House, Ruttonjee Centre, 11 Duddell St, Central
   2526-7533

- 1/F, Hutchison House, 10 Harcourt Rd, Central
  2521-3531
- G/F, The Repulse Bay, 109 Repulse Bay Rd, Repulse Bay
  2812-7231
- 8/F, Grand Centre, 8 Humphreys Ave, Tsim Sha Tsui
  2730-4437
- 6/F, Citylink Plaza
  1 Railway Circuit, Sha Tin, New Territories
  2604-4388

www.byrne-hickman.com
One of the best clinics for sports-related injuries.
All doctors and physiotherapists are expatriates or
internationally trained.

WHERE CAN I GO FOR A REMEDIAL MASSAGE?

The Body Group
17/F, 10 Pottinger St, Central
2167-7305
www.thebodygroup.com

WHERE DO I FIND A CHIROPRACTOR?

Cosman Health Group
5/F, Winway Bldg, 50 Wellington St, Central
2975-4114
Ask for Dr David Cosman. The Health Group also has a
trained osteopath and physiotherapist.

The Chiropractic Centre
6/F, Baskerville House, 13 Duddell St, Central
2973-0353
Ask for Dr Barry Decker.

Dr Russell Williams
5/F, Hing Tai Comm. Bldg, 114 Wing Lok St, Sheung Wan
2854-1234

WHERE DO I FIND A FOOT DOCTOR?

Karlyn Harfoot
Private clinics:
- 26/F, Matilda Medical Centre, Queen's Rd Central
  2877-1683
- Outpatient Department, Matilda Hospital
  41 Mount Kellett Rd, The Peak
  2849-1500
- 27 Cheung Sha Upper Village, Lantau Island
  2873-0868

Public hospitals/medical centres:
- Princess Margaret Hospital
  2–10 Princess Margaret Hospital Rd, Lai Chi Kok
- Caritas Medical Centre, 111 Wing Hong St, Sham Shui Po
  3408-7911

www.harfoot.com

Michael Leung
4/F, Eurasia Bldg, 6 Stanley St, Central
2137-9639

Dr Doug Horne
Dr Lauren Bramley & Partners
9/F, Pacific House, 20 Queen's Rd Central
2877-6068
www.laurenbramley.com

WHERE CAN I FIND A GOOD **OPTOMETRIST**?

Dr Ulrica Lai
12/F, Century Square
1–13 D'Aguilar St, Central
2522-8821
www.optometrist.com.hk
Full scope of optometric services including children's eye examinations.

Dr Lucia San
10/F, Melbourne Plaza, 33 Queen's Rd Central
2525-1733

WHAT ABOUT A QUICK AND RELIABLE **OPTICIAN**?

LensCrafters
See page 276
On-site optician and fast turnaround for prescription glasses.

Fox Optical
G/F, Winning House
12 Cochrane St, Central
2543-8633 / 2541-3018
Right under the Central escalator between Stanley St and Wellington St, Fox Optical offers eye testing, contact lenses, fitting for bifocal and Varilux lenses, good service, good selection, great prices, fast turnaround and even mail order.

I AM CONSIDERING LASIK **CORRECTIVE EYE SURGERY**. WHO SPECIALISES IN THIS?

Dr John Chang
Hong Kong Sanatorium & Hospital
2 Village Rd, Happy Valley
2835-8880
www.hksh.com

Dr Vincent Lee
Department of Ophthalmology & Visual Sciences
B7, Prince of Wales Hospital, Sha Tin, New Territories
2632-2878

Dr Norris Tsang
4/F, Hing Wai Bldg, 36 Queen's Rd Central
2525-0178

Hong Kong Ophthalmic Associates
• 10/F, New World Tower 2, 18 Queen's Rd Central
 2526-6198
• 3/F, Hang Seng Mong Kok Bldg
 677 Nathan Rd, Mong Kok
 2381-1614
www.eyehealth.com.hk
A 5,000-sq.-ft. facility including Hong Kong Eye Day Surgery Centre. Comprehensive eye-care specialists.

WHERE CAN I GO FOR **COUNSELLING** SERVICES?

David O'Rose
2547-1804
www.davidorose.com
Great with couples or on an individual basis, Dr O'Rose takes a down-to-earth approach to counselling.

Holistic Central
16/F, Hing Wai Bldg, 36 Queen's Rd Central
2523-8044
www.holistic-central.com
Dr Tommy Chan is a clinical psychologist who specialises in health and psychological problems in adults and children.

St. John's Counselling Service
7/F, On Hing Bldg, 1 On Hing Terrace, Central
2525-7207
www.stjohnscathedral.org.hk/counselling.html

Centre of Marriage & Child Guidance
7/F, Alliance Bldg, 130–136 Connaught Rd, Sheung Wan
2851-3460
www.cmcg.org.hk

Hong Kong Catholic Marriage Advisory Council
1/F, Grand Millennium Plaza
181 Queen's Rd West, Sheung Wan
2810-1104
www.cmac.org.hk

Laurene Man Counseling Service
9/F, Printing House, 6 Duddell St, Central
2868-3066
www.lmcounseling.com.hk

Mind Matters
2575-7707
www.mindmatters.com.hk

The Practice Psychological Services
10/F, On Hing Bldg, 1 On Hing Terrace, Central
2523-3941
www.practice.com.hk

Progression Psychological Practice
5/F, Season Comm. Bldg, 3 Humphreys Ave, Tsim Sha Tsui
2311-2512

Quality Family Education and Counselling Centre
13/F, CDW Bldg
388 Castle Peak Rd, Tsuen Wan, New Territories
2493-6763
www.qualitycounsel.biz.com.hk

ReSource: The Counselling Centre
23/F, Li Dong Bldg, 9 Li Yuen St East, Central
2523-8979
www.resourcecounselling.org

Cathy Tsang-Feign
10/F, Commercial House, 35 Queen's Rd Central
2122-9386
www.cathyfeign.com

Whole Person Development Institute
16/F, Chinachem Exchange Square 2
338 King's Rd, North Point
2881-8192
www.global-ican.net

HOW ABOUT SUPPORT FOR **ALCOHOL-RELATED ISSUES**?

Alcoholics Anonymous
Meetings at:
• 12 Borrett Rd, Mid-Levels
• St Joseph's Church, 37 Garden Rd, Mid-Levels
• St Anne's Church, 1/F, Stanley Village Rd, Stanley

- Sai Kung Sacred Heart Catholic Church
  Sai Kung, New Territories
- Castle Peak Hospital
  15 Tsing Chung Koon Rd, Tuen Mun, New Territories
- Discovery Bay, Lantau Island
- Lamma Island
  Hotline: 9073-6922
  www.aa-hk.org

WHERE CAN I FIND A DOCTOR WHO CAN ASSIST WITH **FERTILITY ISSUES?**

Dr Robert Stevenson
13/F, Century Square, 1–13 D'Aguilar St, Central
2537-7281
Fertility issues, including IVF.
Hong Kong Sexual Health Centre
21/F, Li Dong Bldg, 9 Li Yuen St East, Central
3162-0001
www.neohealth.com.hk
See also acupuncture, pages 284–285.

IS THERE A GOOD **OBSTETRICIAN-GYNAECOLOGIST**?

Veritas Medical Practice
29/F, Bank of America Tower, 12 Harcourt Rd, Central
2877-3118
www.veritas-medical.com
Dr Ghosh is a well-respected, professional and popular ob-gyn. He has a very caring personality and would be excellent for a first-time mum.
Dr Lucy Lord
Central Health Medical Practice
3/F, Baskerville House, 13 Duddell St, Central
2824-0822
www.centralhealth.com.hk
Dr Lucy Lord is well regarded as a highly experienced ob-gyn, including high risk pregnancies. She is very direct and professional, but not recommended for any (new) mums who need hand-holding. Dr Kathryn Weir is also highly regarded.
Dr Macor & Dr Lam
Hong Kong Prenatal Diagnosis Centre
31/ F, Henley Bldg, 5 Queen's Rd Central
2877-3280
www.hkpdc.net
Offering 3D-scanning and the latest equipment, Dr Lam is also a well-regarded ob-gyn with a gentle personality.
Dr Sally Ferguson
OT&P, 15/F, Shui On Centre, 8 Harbour Rd, Wan Chai
2824-9112 / 7475-0107
Professional and experienced ob-gyn with a loyal following.

WHERE CAN I HIRE A **MIDWIFE SERVICE** OR GET **ADVICE FOR NEW MOTHERS?**

Annerley Midwives
17/F, Tak Woo House, 17–19 D'Aguilar St, Central
2983-1558
www.annerley.com.hk
Ask for Hulda Thorey, the head midwife.

La Leche League
2987-7792 / 2817-7475 / 6331-5078
www.lllhk.org
Everdawn Midwives
11/F, Kiu Yin Comm. Bldg, 361 Lockhart Rd, Wan Chai
2705-9322

I NEED A **PROFESSIONAL NANNY** OR **MATERNITY NURSE**.

The Nanny Experts Ltd
2335-1127
www.thenannyexperts.com
*Recruitment organisation specialising in the placement
of nannies and maternity nurses internationally.*

I WANT TO HIRE A **HELPER** WHO IS EXPERIENCED
WITH NEWBORNS. WHERE DO I START?

See domestic helpers, pages 346–347.

WHERE CAN I FIND A **STEM CELL STORAGE** FACILITY?

Smart Cells (HK) Ltd
8/F, Double Bldg, 22 Stanley St, Central
2868-5046
www.smartcells.com
CryoLife
5/F, Delta House
3 On Yiu St, Siu Lek Yuen, Sha Tin, New Terriotries
2110-2121
www.cryolife.com.hk
*Offers expectant parents a once-in-a-lifetime option to
collect and store newborns' cord blood for reparative
and regenerative medicine.*

I'M HAVING A BABY IN HONG KONG FOR THE FIRST
TIME. WHERE CAN I GET SOME **GENERAL INFORMATION**?

Having Babies in Hong Kong:
A Guide to Pregnancy, Childbirth & Raising Kids in
Hong Kong
ihome.ust.hk/~lbcaplan/hkbb/hkbb.html
*Despite its ungainly URL, this is a useful webpage for
expectant mothers, especially if you are new to HK.*

WHERE CAN I FIND A **PHYSIOTHERAPIST** WHO IS
PARTICULARLY GOOD FOR WOMEN, INCLUDING
PREGNANT WOMEN?

The Body Group
17/F, 10 Pottinger St, Central
2167-7305
www.thebodygroup.com
*By combining cutting-edge manual therapy techniques
with traditional physiotherapy approaches, The Body
Group specialists focus on finding and removing the
underlying cause of a problem, instead of just treating its
symptoms. They have been particularly helpful and aware
of the needs of women, children, and pregnant women.*
Sports and Spinal Physiotherapy Centres
See page 278

EVERYTHING LIFESTYLE & WELL BEING

WHERE CAN I FIND AN INTEGRATED **HOLISTIC HEALTHCARE** CENTRE?

Holistic Central
16/F, Hing Wai Bldg, 36 Queen's Rd Central
2523-8044
www.holistic-central.com

The Body Group
17/F, 10 Pottinger St, Central
2167-7305
www.thebodygroup.com
Caroline Rhodes offers physiotherapy, homeopathy, massage therapy, craniosacral therapy, lymphatic drainage and more.

Optimum Health Centre
2/F, Prosperous Bldg, 54 Jardine's Bazaar, Causeway Bay
2577-3798
www.naturalhealing.com.hk

Balance (Asia) Ltd
27/F, Universal Trade Centre, 3–5 Arbuthnot Rd, Central
2530-3315
www.balancehealth.com.hk
With five expatriate specialists, the clinic offers acupuncture, physiotherapy, craniosacral therapy, homeopathy, manual therapy, osteopathy and specialised fitness instruction.

Integrated Medicine Institute
17/F, Kailey Tower, 16 Stanley St, Central
2523-7121
www.imi.com.hk
Graeme Bradshaw is a popular Australian-qualified homeopath, naturopath and herbalist specialising in treating allergies, digestive problems, asthma, hormonal problems and migraines.

WHERE CAN I FIND A SPECIALIST IN **CHINESE MEDICINE AND ACUPUNCTURE**?

Holistic Central
See above
Helen He is a Western-trained doctor who has been practising acupuncture her entire career.

The Vitality Center
8/F, Commercial House, 35 Queen's Rd Central
2537-1118
www.vitalitycenter.com.hk
Dr Celia The graduated with a medical degree from the Beijing University of Traditional Chinese Medicine.

Health-Wise Chinese Medicine Consultancy
10/F, Winway Bldg, 50 Wellington St, Central
2526-7908
Dr Troy Sing specialises in acupuncture and Chinese medicine.

Gianna Buonocore
Integrated Medicine Institute
17/F, Kailey Tower, 16 Stanley St, Central
2523-7121
www.imi.com.hk
In addition to acupuncture and Chinese medicine, Dr Buonocore specialises in obstetrics and gynaecology; she also treats addictions to tobacco, drugs, food and alcohol.

Brendt Reynolds
6149-2139
brendtreynolds@gmail.com
*Trained in Australia, China and Taiwan, Brendt
specialises in treating sport and yoga injuries,
immunodeficiency, depression and digestion problems
using a combination of acupuncture, moxibustion,
cupping and prescription of medicinal herbal formulas.*

WHO SPECIALISES IN CHINESE HEALING METHODS?

Lawrence Tse (Qigong healing consultant)
6055-5387
www.healingqigong.com
Uses effective Yin and Yang Qigong methods for healing.
Healing Fire
9501-0478
www.healingfire.com
Integrated Medicine Institute
17/F, Kailey Tower, 16 Stanley St, Central
2523-7121
www.imi.com.hk
*Tina Kalmar is knowledgeable in holistic medicine and
well trained in reiki, reflexology, aromatherapy, Swedish
massage and lymphatic drainage. Keven Duff has over
20 years' experience in the complementary health field,
specialising in reiki.*

WHERE CAN I FIND A REIKI MASTER?

Healing Fire
See above
*Offers reiki healing sessions, readings, courses with
a results-oriented approach. Chantal Phillips is a fully
certified Reiki Master Teacher and has practised in
Hong Kong since 1994.*
Integrated Medicine Institute
See above

WHERE CAN I FIND A REPUTABLE HYPNOTHERAPIST?

Dr Melanie Bryan
2575-7707
*Dr Bryan is a psychologist with over 20 years'
experience in using hypnosis to resolve smoking
addiction, public speaking fear, fear of flying, weight
issues, insomnia, stress and more.*
The Masterminds
6/F, 38 Lok Ku Rd, Central
8208-2700
www.themastermindsgroup.com

WHO CAN PROVIDE ALTERNATIVE HEALING SUPPORT?

New Age Shop
7 Old Bailey St, Central
2810-8694
www.newageshop.com.hk
*An excellent alternative resource centre, offering an
extensive range of books and products. Established
alternative practitioners (including mediums, psychics
and healers) work from the shop.*

WHERE CAN I GO FOR **ASTROLOGY PROFILING**?

Helene Liu
8202-2700

HOW ABOUT **COLONIC IRRIGATION** TREATMENT?

Hydrohealth Colon Hydrotherapy
• 9/F, South China Bldg, 1 Wyndham St, Central
  2530-9999
• 9/F, Mass Resources Development Bldg
  12 Humphrey's Ave, Tsim Sha Tsui
  2882-5533
www.hydrohealth.com.hk
Professional, dignified service in clean spa-like surroundings.

WHERE CAN I GET AN **EXPERT HAIRCUT** BY A TOP STYLIST?

The Hairdressers
• 7/F, Abdoolally House, 20 Stanley St, Central
  2973-0512
• 1/F Shama Place, 30 Hollywood Rd, Central
  2110-3123
Boutique full-service salon offering more moderate pricing. Ask for Darrin (Abdoolally House) and Chris (Shama Place).

Il Colpo
Mezzanine, Grand Hyatt Hotel, 1 Harbour Rd, Wan Chai
2802-0151
www.ilcolpo.com.hk
Prices range from $450 to $1,800. Special services include hair extensions and straightening.

Next
22/F, The Centrium, 60 Wyndham St, Central
3583-1002
Ask for Hervé, who is also great with colour.

Kim Robinson
1/F, Chater House, 8 Connaught Rd Central
2121-8484
www.kimrobinson.com
Hong Kong's pioneer and "hairstylist to the stars". Looking this good will cost you, but it's well worth the investment if you can afford it!

Headquarters
1/F & 2/F, Pacific House, 20 Queen's Rd Central
2868-9092
Jacky Choi is great with Asian hair.

Aimee at the Shangri-La
8/F, Island Shangri-La Hotel
Pacific Place, Supreme Court Rd, Admiralty
2918-1339
Experienced staff trained to style both Asian and Western hair.

Chandler
14/F, Tak Woo House, 17–19 D'Aguilar St, Central
2537-3737
Shane Chandler is a very in-demand stylist who started his own full-service salon.

Toni & Guy
- G/F, 15 Wyndham St, Central
  2801-7870
- 1/F, Lee Gardens Two
  28 Yun Ping Rd, Causeway Bay
  2890-1900
- InterContinental Hotel
  New World Centre
  20 Salisbury Rd, Tsim Sha Tsui
  2739-9988
www.toniandguy.com.hk
Moderately priced full-service chain. Ask for Sophie or Fernando; or Jess who is also great for blow-drying.

WHERE CAN I FIND SOMEONE WHO SPECIALISES IN **BLONDE HIGHLIGHTS**, AS WELL AS GREAT CUTS?

Triple Edge Salon
3/F, Century Square
1 – 13 D'Aguilar St, Central
3102-0238
Dingo does some of the most natural blonde high/low-lights in Hong Kong.

Hair Corner
1/F, Duke of Wellington House
24 Wellington St, Central
2522-3311
Lain Collinson is great for blonde highlights and reasonably priced.

Ken Qi
2/F, Central Bldg
1 –3 Pedder St, Central
2522-1112
www.psgroup.com.hk

Paul Gerrard
1/F & 2/F, Wah Hing House
35 Pottinger St, Central
2869-4408
www.paulgerrard.com
Ask for Robin, Paul or Catherine for blonde highlights.

WHO WOULD YOU RECOMMEND FOR **COLOURING BRUNETTE HAIR**?

The Colour Bar Salon
11/F, EuBank Plaza
9 Chiu Lung St, Central
2525-4228 / 2525-4229
www.thecolourbar.com.hk
Ian Lawlor has a long list of credentials and fans when it comes to colouring. He specialises in any colour for both men and women.

The Firm
15/F, The Centrium, 60 Wyndham St, Central
2525-6696
www.thefirm.com.hk
Bev Cappleman comes highly recommended for colouring.

WHERE CAN I GET A GOOD HAIRCUT AT A MODERATE PRICE?

Private I Salon
- L3, IFC Mall, 8 Finance St, Central
  2526-4488
- L6, Four Seasons Hotel Hong Kong
  8 Finance St, Central
  2521-0070
- 3/F, Tau Yau Plaza, 181 Johnston Rd, Wan Chai
  2234-0900
- 32/F, Soundwill Plaza, 38 Russell St, Causeway Bay
  2573-7100

www.psgroup.com.hk
Try Jones in the Causeway Bay location, who is great for Asian hair.

Philip George Salon
23/F, Chekiang First Bank Centre, 1 Duddell St, Central
2524-3143
Try Herbert or Shirley.

O2 Hair Studio
G/F, 38 Wyndham St, Central
2529-6289 / 2522-2884
www.o2hairstudio.com
Try Rudy.

La Coiffe
2/F, Yan Yan Court, 199 Queen's Rd East, Wan Chai
2866-1144
Specialises in various treatments from Japan.

Hipp.fish
LG/F, 32 Elgin St, SoHo
2815-3638
Try Keith.

The Hairdressers
See page 286

The Barbershop
1/F, 15B Wellington St, Central
2537-4292
www.thebarbershop.com.hk

WHERE DO I GO TO GET A TRIM, WASH AND BLOW DRY ON A BUDGET?

Mina Dev' Wil
- G/F, 28 Cochrane St, Central
  2121-0375
- 1/F, 16 Kai Chiu Rd, Causeway Bay
  2895-3797

www.minadevwil.com

Tommy Hair Design
73 Wellington St, Central
2543-6985 / 2544-1436
No-nonsense, good wash and blow dry starts at $58. Edmond is particularly good (off on Mondays).

Michel & Rene
30 Lyndhurst Terrace, Central
2544-2136
Great for shampoo and blow dry ($75) and deep conditioning.

Hair Magic
55 Wellington St, Central
2147-3311

Stanley Plaza Hair Dressers .... 🏷
3/F, Stanley Plaza, Carmel Rd, Stanley
2813-7808
Budget blow dry and styling outside Central.
Hair By Mike .... 🏷
1/F, Silverstrand Shopping Centre
7 Silverstrand Beach Rd, Clear Water Bay
2335-5018
This is a good place for kids and men's haircuts. Around $100/cut.
Hair Inn
G/F, 61 Queen's Rd East, Wan Chai
2866-2873

WHERE CAN I GET **HAIR EXTENSIONS**?

The Firm
15/F, The Centrium, 60 Wyndham St, Central
2525-6696
www.thefirm.com.hk
The Hairdressers
See page 286
Il Colpo
Mezzanine, Grand Hyatt Hotel, 1 Harbour Rd, Wan Chai
2802-0151
www.ilcolpo.com.hk
Chandler
14/F, Tak Woo House, 17–19 D'Aguilar St, Central
2537-3737

CAN YOU RECOMMEND A GREAT **DAY SPA**?

Bliss
72/F, W Hotel, 1 Austin Rd West, Kowloon
3717-2797
www.blissworld.com
Voted best spa of 2008. Offers their signature Triple Oxygen Treatment.
Plateau
Grand Hyatt, 1 Harbour Rd, Wan Chai
2584-7688 / 2588-1234
hongkong.grand.hyatt.com/hyatt/pure/spas
Elemis Day Spa
9/F, Century Square, 1–13 D'Aguilar St, Central
2521-6660
www.elemisdayspa.com.hk
The Oriental Spa
Landmark Mandarin Oriental Hotel
15 Queen's Rd Central
2132-0011
www.mandarinoriental.com/landmark/spa
21,000-sq.-ft. spa haven.
Chuan Spa
L41, Langham Place Hotel
555 Shanghai St, Mong Kok
3552-3510
www.chuanspa.com.hk
The Peninsula ESPA
Salisbury Rd, Tsim Sha Tsui
2315-3322
www.peninsula.com

Sense of Touch
- 83A Hollywood Rd, Central
  2517-0939
- 1/F–5/F, 52 D'Aguilar St, Central
  2526-6918
- LG/F, The Ovolo, 2 Arbuthnot Rd, Central
  2869-0939
- G/F, The Repulse Bay, 109 Repulse Bay Rd, Repulse Bay
  2592-9668
- 1/F, Block C, Discovery Bay Plaza
  Discovery Bay, Lantau Island
  2987-9198

www.senseoftouch.com.hk
Great aromatherapy massage.

Aveda Lifestyle Day Spa
2/F–3/F, The Loop, 33 Wellington St, Central
2868-9859

Feel Good Factor
2/F, Wyndham House, 73 Wyndham St, Central
2530-0610
www.feelgoodfactor.com.hk
Facials, massage and nail care.

Indulgence
33 Lyndhurst Terrace, Central
3115-7510 / 2815-6600
www.indulgence.hk
A cute little day spa that recently opened, offering skincare, facials, body treatments, hair, nail, make-up and image consultation.

DK Aromatherapy
G/F, 16A Staunton St, Central
2771-2847
www.aroma.com.hk

Paul Gerrard
1/F & 2/F, Wah Hing House, 35 Pottinger St, Central
2869-4408
www.paulgerrard.com

Body Zen
5/F, Hong Kong House, 17–19 Wellington St, Central
2770-6728
www.bodyzen.com.hk
Come here for all your home spa needs. You can also get massage treatments that leave you feeling centred with the universe. Meridians Circulation Therapy $780/60 mins.

Seasons Fitness
3/F, ICBC Tower, Citibank Plaza, 3 Garden Rd, Central
2878-6288
www.seasonsfitness.com
They also have spa treatments, massages, facials, for men and women. They also do waxing treatments for men and women.

Let's Spa
Basement, The Broadway, 54–62 Lockhart Rd, Wan Chai
2866-9221
www.letspa.hk

Angsana Spa
Blue Blue Club, Park Island
8 Pak Lai Rd, Ma Wan, New Territories
2296-4228
www.angsanaspa.com

EVERYTHING LIFESTYLE & WELL BEING

WHERE CAN I GO FOR A LEGITIMATE **MASSAGE** IF I AM **ON A BUDGET**?

Bua Hom Thai Massage ....
5/F, California Entertainment Bldg
34–36 D'Aguilar St, Central
2234-9322
Reasonably priced and great massages, usually bookable even last minute.

Sunny Paradise ....
341 Lockhart Rd, Wan Chai
They have separate floors for men and women; reputable, and reasonably priced.

Happy Foot ....
• 11/F, Jade Centre, 98–102 Wellington St, Central
  2544-1010
• 19/F, Century Square, 1–13 D'Aguilar St, Central
  2522-1151
• 1/F, 2–4 Tsoi Tak St, Happy Valley
  2573-3438
Happy Foot also does body massages but they are mainly known for their reflexology.

Thai Inn Massage
Mezzanine, Tung Shing Bldg
120 Queen's Rd East, Wan Chai
2520-0718
Well-priced ladies-only massage by trained Thai masseurs.

WHERE CAN I FIND A PLACE THAT SPECIALISES IN **CHILDREN'S SPA TREATMENTS** AND MASSAGES?

I-Spa at the InterContinental ....
3/F, 18 Salisbury Rd, Tsim Sha Tsui
2313-2306
www.hongkong-ic.intercontinental.com
Pure bliss for children's massage, $400/45 mins.

WHICH IS A GOOD SPA TO GO TO FOR A **GIRLS' GROUP PAMPERING** SESSION?

Beaute Par Zai ....
9/F, Queen's Place, 74 Queen's Rd Central
2524-1272
www.spabpz.com

Chuan Spa ....
L41, Langham Place Hotel, 555 Shanghai St, Mong Kok
3552-3510
www.chuanspa.com.hk

Paua Spa ....
3/F, CentreStage, Bridges St, Central
2522-3054

Bliss
72/F, W Hotel, 1 Austin Rd West, Kowloon
3717-2797
www.blissworld.com
Up to 3–4 people.

Feel Good Factor ....
2/F, Wyndham House, 73 Wyndham St, Central
2530-0610
www.feelgoodfactor.com.hk

Sense of Touch
See page 290
At home parties available for 3–8 people.

The Retreat at The Firm
15/F, The Centrium, 60 Wyndham St, Central
2525-6696
www.thefirm.com.hk
Hairdressing and holistic body treatments under one roof.

Let's Spa .... *)
Basement, The Broadway, 54–62 Lockhart Rd, Wan Chai
2866-9221
www.letspa.hk

WHERE CAN I GO FOR A GOOD **FOOT MASSAGE**?

Footy Footie
G/F, 33 Yik Yam St, Happy Valley
2893-8238

Happy Foot .... *) ✂
See page 291
Great foot massage and reflexology. Open till midnight.

Foot World Club
5/F, 118–120 Queen's Rd Central
2581-1323

FOOT Reflexology & Acupressure Ltd .... *)
8/F, Regent Centre, 88 Queen's Rd Central
2997-7138
www.foothk.com
Offers valet parking from 8pm.

Let's Spa .... *)
Basement, The Broadway
54–62 Lockhart Rd, Wan Chai
2866-9221
www.letspa.hk

Fun Feet .... *)
• 1/F, Winning Centre, 46–48 Wyndham St, Central
  2525-1101
• 1/F, Happy Court, 39E Sing Woo Rd, Happy Valley
  2838-3234
www.funfeet.com.hk

WHERE CAN I GET AN EXPERT **MANICURE AND PEDICURE**?

Mandarin Oriental Beauty Salon
24/F, Mandarin Oriental Hotel, 5 Connaught Rd Central
2528-4888
www.mandarinoriental.com/hongkong/spa
Samuel So, a medical pedicurist, can do wonders for your feet.

Feel Good Factor
2/F, Wyndham House, 73 Wyndham St, Central
2530-0610
www.feelgoodfactor.com.hk
Great manicures and pedicures, in addition to facials and massages.

Beyond The Fringe
20 On Lan St, Central
2530-1183
www.beyondthefringe.biz
Ask for Windy.

Susan's Nails
- 17/F, Shun Hei Causeway Bay Centre
  492 Lockhart Rd, Causeway Bay
  2838-8845
- Basement, Homeworld, Site 12
  Whampoa Garden, Hung Hom
  2333-9219

Gel nails, manicures and pedicures. They sell package deals to save money in the long run.

Nail Salon
22/F, The Loop, 33 Wellington St, Central
2104-7898
www.nailsalon.com.hk
They also do gel nails and eyelash extensions.

Sense of Touch
See page 290
Purchase 10, 20, or 30 manicures/pedicures in a package to receive a discount.

Nail Nail Studio by PS Group
- L3, IFC Mall, 8 Finance St, Central
  (inside Private-I salon)
  2295-3381
- 3/F, Lee Gardens Two
  28 Yun Ping Rd, Causeway Bay
  2882-4911
- 2/F, Miramar Shopping Centre
  132 Nathan Rd, Tsim Sha Tsui
  2377-2884
- Upper Level, Citylink Plaza
  1 Railway Circuit, Sha Tin, New Territories
  2688-0288

www.psgroup.com.hk

Beau Nail
L1, IFC Mall, 8 Finance St, Central
2234-7328
www.beau-nail.com

Nail Garden
9/F, United Success Centre, 506 Jaffe Rd, Causeway Bay
3748-9148

Suki Nail
- 1/F, 59 Percival St, Causeway Bay
  8208 6389
- 2/F, 5 Humphrey's Ave, Tsim Sha Tsui
  8208-6388

www.sukinail.com

WHERE CAN I GET A PROFESSIONAL **MEDICAL PEDICURE**?

Mandarin Oriental Beauty Salon
24/F, Mandarin Oriental Hotel
5 Connaught Rd Central
2528-4888
www.mandarinoriental.com/hongkong/spa
Ask for Mr So. Extremely sought after.

Happy Foot ....
See page 291
Kwan Sifu has been practising his trade for 50+ years. He can work miracles for those who suffer from ingrown toenails.

WHERE CAN I FIND SOMEONE TO DO MY **NAILS IN MY HOME**?

May
9801-1451

WHERE CAN I GO TO GET AN **EXPRESS MANICURE/ PEDICURE**?

Nail House
2/F, Santek Bldg, 78 Queen's Rd Central
2521-0986
They do an express manicure for $68 and an express pedicure for $128. They also do gel nails and express hand treatments involving a scrub and a massage.

City Nail
2/F, Mei Ling Bldg, 30–34 Cochrane St, Central
3145-1778
Express manicure from $108 and express pedicure from $198. They also do eyelash perming/extensions and gel nails.

HOW ABOUT CHEAP AND CHEERFUL **FACIALS**?

Mizu Mizu
2/F, Workingview Comm. Bldg
21 Yiu Wa St, Causeway Bay
2833-9188
www.mizumizuspa.com

Rainbow Beauty Salon
995 King's Rd, Quarry Bay
2561-4601

Renaissance Beauty Centre
14/F, Coda Plaza, 51 Garden Rd, Central
2868-5666

WHO OFFERS **GOOD-VALUE PACKAGES** FOR FACIALS AND BEAUTY TREATMENTS?

Rainbow Beauty Salon
See above

Renaissance Beauty Centre
See above
Facials, slimming and body massage treatments.

Secret Sense
10/F, Hon Kwok Jordan Centre
7 Hillwood Rd, Tsim Sha Tsui
2377-3220
www.secretsense.hk
Facial and massage package, 2½ hours for $698.

WHERE CAN I FIND SOMEONE GOOD TO COME TO MY **HOME** TO DO **BEAUTY TREATMENTS**?

Annie Ho
6178-9898
Facials and waxing.

Joanne Kwok
9789-3722
Professional facials, waxing and massage treatments (Swedish, deep tissue and acupressure) in your own home. Massage table provided.

EVERYTHING LIFESTYLE & WELL BEING

Shabnam
9561-2241
Waxing, threading, henna tattoos and more. She can also be hired to do henna tattoos for a small party.

WHERE ELSE CAN I GET **WAXING** DONE?

Sense of Touch
See page 290
Nude Waxing
9/F, VC House, 4–6 On Lan St, Central
3171-7100
www.nudewaxing.com.hk
As the name alludes, they also do Brazilian waxing as well as Swarovski crystal tattoos.

WHERE CAN I GO FOR AN EXPRESS **EYEBROW WAX/ SHAPE**?

Brow Bar
2/F, Ocean Terminal, Harbour City
Canton Rd, Tsim Sha Tsui
2110-3495
15 minutes—$150.

WHERE CAN I GET NATURAL LOOKING **EYELASH EXTENSIONS**?

Forget Me Not
8/F, Guangdong Centre, 18 Pennington St
Causeway Bay
2882-5468
Nail Salon
22/F, The Loop, 33 Wellington St, Central
2104-7898
www.nailsalon.com.hk
La Belle Salon
G/F, Glenealy Tower, 1 Glenealy, Central
2527-7178
www.la-belle-salon.com
They also do perms, ion hair straightening, artificial nail services and hair extensions by quotation.

WHAT ARE SOME GOOD **TANNING SALONS**?

California Beach Club
3/F, Jade Centre, 98 Wellington St, Central
2851-3357
www.californiabeachclub.net
California Super Tan
7/F, Workingview Comm. Bldg
21 Yiu Wa St, Causeway Bay
2573-0099
www.californiasupertan.com.hk
Elemis Day Spa
9/F, Century Square
1–13 D'Aguilar St, Central
2521-6660
www.elemisdayspa.com.hk
Sunergy Sun Fx
9686-2970
Ask for Jody.

EVERYTHING LIFESTYLE & WELL BEING

WHERE CAN I FIND AN **IMAGE CONSULTANT**?

Savvy Style
4/F, Baskerville House, 13 Duddell St, Central
2522-2592
www.savvystyle.com
Eve Roth Lindsay provides private and group consultation to improve your image from dress to cosmetics. You can even book her for a party for teenagers or big girls.

What's Next
See page 227
Rachel Plecas offers personal styling services, which she calls wardrobe recycling, in addition to image consultancy.

WHERE CAN **MEN** GO FOR SOME **GROOMING AND TREATMENTS**?

Bella Men's Skin Care Centre
17/F, New World Tower 1
16–18 Queen's Rd Central
2526-3855
www.menskincentre.com
Permanent laser hair removal, hair and skin analysis, and professional skin care.

Ziz Skincare For Men
5/F, Hang Shun Bldg
10–12 Wyndham St, Central
2111-2767
www.ziz.com.hk
Facial treatments, massage, body contouring and more.

Mence
- 13/F, Asia Pacific Centre
  8 Wyndham St, Central
  2117-8068
- 14/F, Eton Tower, 8 Hysan Ave, Causeway Bay
  2117-8038
- 10/F, 238 Bldg, 238 Nathan Rd, Jordan
  3106-3368
- 7/F, Futura Plaza
  111–113 How Ming St, Kwun Tong
  3106-3316
- 77–86 Kwai Sing Centre
  Wo Yi Hop Rd, Kwai Chung, New Territories
  2423-2667

www.mencebeauty.com.hk
Permanent hair removal, body toning, trimming and tightening through weight loss. They also do removal of freckles, pimples, warts, eye bags, double chins, and wrinkles. Free initial consultation.

WHERE CAN I FIND A GOOD DENTIST WHO ALSO SPECIALISES IN **WHITENING**?

Andrew Y.L. Kam
17/F, Century Square
1–13 D'Aguilar St, Central
2523-8993
www.dr-kam.com
English-speaking dentist, known for teeth whitening.

Costello Brothers Dentistry
19/F, Coda Plaza, 51 Garden Rd, Mid-Levels
2877-9622
www.costellobrothersdentistry.com

Dr David W.K. Tong
15/F, Winway Bldg, 50 Wellington St, Central
2810-1801
www.dr-tong.com
British-trained dentist.

Dr Adrian Seto
5/F, Manning House, 48 Queen's Rd Central
2522-2988
*Laser tooth whitening, laser gum surgery, recontouring/
depigmentation. Also has 24-hour emergency service.*

Dr Gregory Taylor
15/F, Tak Shing House, 20 Des Voeux Rd Central
2526-6866
American-trained dentist.

Dr Louise Wong
Pacific Dental Care and Pacific Orthodontic Care
See page 274
Cosmetic and implant dentistry, orthodontics.

Hong Kong Dental Lab
270 Queen's Rd Central
2854–4888
www.hkdentallab.com

Pacific Health Care
15/F, Tak Shing House, 20 Des Voeux Rd Central
2395-8883
www.pacifichealthcare.com.hk

Hong Kong Dental Association
www.hkda.org

Dental Council of Hong Kong
www.dchk.org.hk
Find a dentist near you with this easy to use website:
www.hkdentists.com.hk

WHERE CAN I GET **BOTOX** DONE?

Dr Stephen Chan
The Age Reversal Centre
3/F, Dairy Farm Shopping Centre
5 Perkins Rd, Jardine's Lookout
2881-8131
www.agereversalcentre.com

Dr Kenneth C W Hui
22/F, Bank of America Tower, 12 Harcourt Rd, Central
2523-7690
An established plastic surgeon.

Dr Otto Y T Au
4/F, New World Tower, 16–18 Queen's Rd Central
2522-9365
Also an established plastic surgeon.

Dr Lauren Bramley & Partners
9/F, Pacific House, 20 Queen's Rd Central
2877-6068
www.laurenbramley.com

Dr Ronald Leung
6/F, Tak Shing House, 20 Des Voeux Rd Central
2523-5995
Dermatologist.

Hong Kong IPL & Laser Institute
Sino Cheer Plaza, 23 Jordan Rd, Jordan
2191-6730

Neoface Clinic
4/F, Prince's Bldg, 10 Chater Rd, Central
2530-2338
www.neofaceclinic.com
Hair transplantation, laser, skin care and smile enhancement services.

Face Magic Haven
30/F, The Centrium, 60 Wyndham St, Central
2524-6882
www.facemagichaven.com

Skin Central Dermatology, Aesthetics & Lasers
- 12/F, Central Bldg, 1 Pedder St, Central
  2901-1281
- 1/F, 2H South Bay Rd, Repulse Bay
  2869-6509
- 7/F, Prestige Tower, 23–25 Nathan Rd, Tsim Sha Tsui
  2368-0816
www.skincentral.com

WHO IS GOOD FOR ADVANCED SKIN TREATMENTS?

Skin Central Dermatology, Aesthetics & Lasers
See above
Ask for Dr Tinny Ho. A wide range of professional skin treatments: Botox, AHA peels, dermal fillers, Intense Pulsed Light, laser hair removal, laser skin rejuvenation, etc.

Henry Chan
Hong Kong Dermatology and Laser Centre
12/F–13/F, Club Lusitano, 16 Ice House St, Central
2109-9999
www.hhlchan.com

Dr Ronald Leung
6/F, Tak Shing House, 20 Des Voeux Rd Central
2523-5995

WHERE CAN I GET A TATTOO?

Cubist Tattoo
2/F, 1 Pak Sha Rd, Causeway Bay
2881-6234
www.cubisttattoo.com

Chinese Tattoos
1/F, James Lee Mansion
33–35 Carnarvon Rd, Tsim Sha Tsui
2368-3621
Tattoos and body piercing by Mr Wong.

Jimmy Ho
1/F, 99 Parkes St, Jordan
2783-7011
www.tattoo-centre.com

Tattoo Temple
3/F, 30 Stanley St, Central
6386-4668
tattootemple.hk

Star Crossed Tattoo
2/F, 57 Granville Rd, Tsim Sha Tsui
6256-0217 / 3427-3820
www.starcrossedtattoo.com

SZE C Tattoo
1/F, 170 Wellington St, Central
8207-6920
www.szectattoo.hk

WHERE CAN I GET A TATTOO **REMOVED**?

Bioscor
23/F, Crawford House, 70 Queen's Rd Central
2810-9018
www.bioscor.com.au
Neoface Clinic
4/F, Prince's Bldg, 10 Chater Rd, Central
2530-2338
www.neofaceclinic.com

WHERE CAN I GO TO FIND **REHABILITATION AND MEDICAL SUPPLIES**?

Medimart
• G/F, 2 Johnston Rd, Wan Chai
  2866-8608
• G/F, Eastern Centre, 1065 King's Rd, Tai Koo
  2127-4125
• G/F, 14–16 Jordan Rd, Jordan
  2375-2322
• G/F, Yan On Bldg, 1 Kwong Wa St, Mong Kok
  3151-7622
• 2/F, MetroCity 1, The Metropolis
  Tseung Kwan O, New Territories
  3194-6880
www.medimart.com.hk

WHERE CAN I GO TO PURCHASE **HEALTH AND PERFORMANCE SUPPLEMENTS**?

Nature's Village ....
• G/F, 38 Lyndhurst Terrace, Central
  2121-1637
• 1/F, Tai Yau Plaza, 181 Johnston Rd, Wan Chai
  2111-0683
• 4/F, Kornhill Plaza South
  1 Kornhill Rd, Tai Koo
  2117-2373
• G/F, Elizabeth House
  250 Gloucester Rd, Causeway Bay
  2575-0188
• 1/F, The Elegance at Sheraton
  Nathan Rd, Tsim Sha Tsui
  2770-5098
• G/F, Yan On Bldg, 1 Kwong Wa St, Mong Kok
  3188-5183
• G/F, Concord Square
  88 Cheung Long St, Tsuen Wan, New Territories
  3586-2123
• Citylink Plaza
  1 Shatin Station Circuit, Sha Tin, New Territories
  3188-5918
www.naturesvillage.com.hk

GNC .... ♥
- 14–24 Wellington St, Central
  2521-6136
- 3/F, Prince's Bldg, 10 Chater Rd, Central
  2525-3732
- MTR Admiralty Station, Admiralty
  2865-7716
- G/F, 6 Matheson St, Causeway Bay
  2506-1938
- 29 Sing Woo Rd, Happy Valley
  2295-6719
- 20–20C Carnavon Rd, Tsim Sha Tsui
  2367-1393
- East Tsim Sha Tsui MTR Station, East Tsim Sha Tsui
  2311-3763
- 1/F, Discovery Bay Plaza
  Discovery Bay, Lantau Island
  2987-9331

www.gnc.com
See website for more outlets.

Little Giant .... ♥
15/F, Chung Wai Comm. Bldg
447 –449 Lockhart Rd, Causeway Bay
2573-3610
www.littlegianthk.com
Supplements store.

WHERE CAN I GO TO PURCHASE **ORGANIC FACE AND BODY CARE** PRODUCTS?

Natural Living
G/F, 385 Lockhart Rd, Wan Chai
2847-3378

Body Wize
- 18–20 Sing Woo Rd, Happy Valley
  2838-5808
- Body Wize Retreat, 16 Sing Woo Rd, Happy Valley
  2838-5808

www.bodywize.com.hk
Massage treatments, waxing, and couples sessions.

WHERE CAN I BUY **AROMATHERAPY PRODUCTS**?

Who's Aromist
- 1/F, Queensway Plaza, 93 Queensway, Admiralty
  2333-7303
- G/F, wtc more, 280 Gloucester Rd, Causeway Bay
  2404-0919
- 1/F, Paradise Mall, Hang Fa Chuen, Chai Wan
  2576-2803
- 3/F, Telford Plaza 2, 33 Wai Yip St, Kowloon Bay
  2886-0287
- 1/F, East Point City, Tsueng Kwan O, New Territories
  2706-0660

www.whosgroup.com

Aroma Culture
6/F, One Capital Place, 18 Luard Rd, Wan Chai
8200-2689
www.aromaculture.com.hk

Asia-Pacific Aromatherapy
12/F, Unicorn Trade Centre
127–131 Des Voeux Rd Central
2882-2444
www.aromatherapyapa.com

DK Aromatherapy
G/F, 16A Staunton St, Central
2771-2847
www.aroma.com.hk

EVERYTHING
HOUSE &
HOME

there's a **PICASSO** for all of us   304

timeless **TREASURES**   310

FURNITURE a to z   312

make it **NEW** again   318

dim the **LIGHTS**   320

kingdom for **KIDS**   322

SLEEPING in style   324

ACCESSORIES to add that final touch   328

everyone ends up in the **KITCHEN**   335

satisfy your home **APPLIANCE** needs   337

CLEANLINESS is godliness   340

DOMESTIC divas and caregivers   346

the grass is always **GREENER**   348

man's **BEST FRIEND**   353

i need some help: **DESIGN** for dummies   359

who's **HANDY** with a hammer?   362

FLAT hunting 101   366

book a **ROOM** for out-of-towners   370

there's a **TECH** geek in all of us   373

what has four wheels and goes **VROOM**   379

don't worry, it's a **RENTAL**   380

DELIVER it fast   381

consult the **EXPERTS**   382

EVERYTHING HOUSE & HOME

WHERE CAN I BUY ARTISTIC & OLD PHOTOGRAPHS OF HONG KONG?

Laurence Lai Gallery
- L1, Peak Galleria, 118 Peak Rd, The Peak
  2849-6183
- G/F, Peak Galleria, 118 Peak Rd, The Peak
  2849-6173
- 1/F, Star Ferry Pier, Tsim Sha Tsui
  2367-7810
- 9/F, Manning Ind. Bldg
  116–118 How Ming St, Kwun Tong
  2191-2097

www.laurencelaigallery.com
See below as well for vintage photographs.

HOW ABOUT OTHER NOSTALGIC MEMORABILIA, SUCH AS ANTIQUE MAPS & PHOTOS?

Picture This
- Gallery & Office:
  13/F, 9 Queen's Rd Central
  2525-2820
- Shop:
  2/F, Prince's Bldg, 10 Chater Rd, Central
  2525-2803

www.picturethiscollection.com
Antique maps dating from the late 1500s to WWII, old movie posters, vintage advertisement prints, antique books, old photos of Hong Kong and other nostalgic memorabilia.

Altfield Gallery
- Gallery:
  2/F, Prince's Bldg, 10 Chater Rd, Central
  2537-6370
- Annex:
  9/F, Gee Chang Hong Centre
  65 Wong Chuk Hang Rd, Happy Valley
  2552-1968

www.altfield.com.hk

Brian Seed Fine Art
P.O. Box 106, Cheung Chau
2981-3777
www.brianseed.com
One of the largest collections of historical maps in Hong Kong. Online gallery only.

Wattis Fine Art
2/F, 20 Hollywood Rd, Central
2524-5302
www.wattis.com.hk
One of the best sources for antique maps. Also specialising in European paintings and work by contemporary Hong Kong artists.

WHERE CAN I SOURCE TRADITIONAL & ANTIQUE ASIAN ARTWORK, COSTUMES & TEXTILES?

Teresa Coleman Fine Arts Ltd
G/F, 79 Wyndham St, Central
2526-2450
www.teresacoleman.com
Hong Kong's premier specialist in Chinese and Asian robes, textiles and Tibetan art.

Yan Gallery
1/F, Oriental Crystal Comm. Bldg
46 Lyndhurst Terrace, Central
2139-2345
www.yangallery.com
Exclusively representing artists from China, Yan Gallery is also a good source for Chinese calligraphy and can arrange commissioned paintings.

The Tibetan Gallery
G/F, 55 Wyndham St, Central
2530-4863
www.thetibetangallery.com
Specialising in antique Tibetan art, rugs and furniture.

WHERE CAN I FIND SOMEONE TO HELP ME ACQUIRE **FINE ASIAN ART**?

Canvasia Ltd
7/F, 80 Gloucester Rd, Wan Chai
9152-7881
www.canvasia.com
Amber Boswell specialises in helping individuals and corporations acquire an Asian art collection.

WHERE CAN I LOOK FOR GALLERIES SPECIALISING IN **CONTEMPORARY, CUTTING EDGE ASIAN ART**?

Ooi Botos Gallery
G/F, 5 Gresson St, Wan Chai (Near Queen's Rd East)
2527-9733
www.ooibotos.com
Leading avant-garde gallery specialising in photography, digital media, video and installation.

Contemporary by Angela Li
G/F, 90–92 Hollywood Rd, Central
3571-8200
www.cbal.com.hk
Very contemporary and modern Chinese art.

Connoisseur Art Gallery
G/F, Chinachem Hollywood Centre, 1 Hollywood Rd, Central
2868-5358
www.connoisseur-art.com

agnès b. Librairie Galerie
1/F, 18 Wing Fung St, Wan Chai
2869-5505
www.agnesb.com

HanArt TZ Gallery
2/F, Henley Bldg, 5 Queen's Rd Central
2526-9019
www.hanart.com
HanArt is a great source for contemporary Chinese art, including Communist and Chinese pop art.

Zee Stone Gallery
G/F, Yu Yuet Lai Bldg, 43–55 Wyndham St, Central
2810-5895
www.zeestone.com
A beautiful gallery and a great source for contemporary art from China, Vietnam and Burma.

Wellington Gallery
G/F, 36 Wyndham St, Central
2804-6688
www.wellingtongallery.com.hk

Schoeni Art Gallery
- G/F, 21–31 Old Bailey St, Central
  2869-8802
- G/F, 27 Hollywood Rd, Central
  2542-3143

www.schoeni.com.hk

Arguably one of Hong Kong's best sources for contemporary art from China, including Chinese avant-garde and pop art.

Plum Blossoms Gallery
G/F, 1 Hollywood Rd, Central

2521-2189

www.plumblossoms.com

One of the top contemporary Asian art galleries, specialising in artists from China, Hong Kong and Vietnam, including Zhu Wei, one of China's supreme contemporary artists.

CAIS Gallery
UG/F, 54 Hollywood Rd, Central

2527-7798

www.caisgallery.com

Featuring contemporary Korean artists.

Kwai Fung Hin Art Gallery
- G/F, 20 Ice House St, Central
- 2/F & 5/F, HK Diamond Exchange Bldg
  8 Duddell St, Central

2580-0058 / 2577-1232

www.kwaifunghin.com

A good source for European and Chinese paintings and sculptures. They also offer art consultancy services for hotels, restaurants, offices and private residences.

82 Republic
9/F, Parekh House, 63 Wyndham St, Central

3521-0300

www.82republic.com

Art Beatus Gallery
G/F, Kar Ho Bldg, 35–39 Graham St, Central

2526-0818

www.artbeatus.com

EDGE Gallery
G/F, 60C Leighton Rd, Causeway Bay

2887-0313

www.edge-gallery.com

ARE THERE ANY GALLERIES THAT SPECIALISE IN SOUTHEAST ASIAN, INDIAN AND ABORIGINAL ART?

Sin Sin Fine Art
- G/F, 1 Prince's Terrace, Mid-Levels
  2858-5072
- Sin Sin Annex, 52–53 Sai St, Central

www.sinsin.com.hk

Sin Sin has a strong focus on Southeast Asian contemporary art, promoting both established and upcoming artists from Hong Kong, China, USA, France, Thailand and Indonesia.

Damina Gallery
2/F, 65–65A Peel St, SoHo

2549-7711

www.daminagallery.com

Specialising in Vietnamese art.

MOVE IT . BUILD IT . FIX IT . LEASE IT . DESIGN IT . PARTY IT . CLEAN IT . PICTURE IT . DISCOUNT IT . HOUSE IT . PICASSO IT . FURNISH IT

Asia Fine Art Ltd
14 Sik On St, 99 Queen's Rd East, Wan Chai
2522-0405
www.asia-fineart.com
Formed as an Internet company, they are committed to promoting emerging artists from Asia, including Vietnam, China and Hong Kong. They are a great source of affordable Vietnamese art in all media.

Hong Kong Fine Art
11/F, Century Square, 1–13 D'Aguilar St, Central
2537-7322
www.hkfineart.com
Specialising in original contemporary art, Manisha Khemka has one of the largest collections of paintings from Vietnam. She also has a range of Indian art.

Southern Exchange
House 2, 8 Deep Water Bay Rd
Deep Water Bay
9221-2598
www.southernexchange.com.au
Contact Georgie Bruce for South African and Aboriginal art from Australia. See website for upcoming exhibits.

Aryan Art Gallery
5/F, Glenealy Tower 1, Glenealy, Central
2525-5898
www.aryanartgallery.com
Specialising in Indian contemporary art.

WHERE ARE SOME OF THE MOST PROMINENT ART GALLERIES IN HONG KONG SPECIALISING IN **INTERNATIONAL ARTISTS**?

The Cat Street Gallery
• Gallery:
  G/F, 222 Hollywood Rd, Sheung Wan
  2291-0006
• Annex:
  14/F, 38 Lok Ku Rd, Sheung Wan
  2544-6223
www.thecatstreetgallery.com
Specialising in renowned and up-and-coming international contemporary artists, with new exhibits bi-monthly.

10 Chancery Lane Gallery
G/F, 10 Chancery Lane, SoHo
2810-0065
www.10chancerylanegallery.com
Specialising in contemporary work by both emerging and established artists from around the world, with a good selection of work by Australian artists.

Sundaram Tagore Gallery
G/F, 57–59 Hollywood Rd, Central
2581-9678
www.sundaramtagore.com

Opera Gallery
G2/F, M88, 2–8 Wellington St, Central
2810-1208
www.operagallery.com
With galleries in Paris, London, New York, Miami, Singapore and Hong Kong, the Opera Gallery is a source for high-end decorative art and American pop art.

Amelia Johnson Contemporary
G/F, 6–10 Shin Hing St, Central
2548-2286
www.ajc-art.com

Art Statements Gallery
G/F, 5 Mee Lun St, Central
2122-9657
www.artstatements.com

Fabrik Contemporary Art
4/F, Yip Fung Bldg
2–18 D'Aguilar St, Central
2525-4911
www.fabrik-gallery.com

ARE THERE ANY GALLERIES SPECIALISING IN GLASS?

Gaffer Studio Glass
17/F, Hing Wai Centre
7 Tin Wan Praya Rd, Aberdeen
2521-1770
www.gafferstudioglass.com
High-end gallery specialising in studio glass art by innovative artists from around the world.

Galerie Vee
2/F, Prince's Bldg, 10 Chater Rd, Central
2522-3166 / 2522-1677
www.galerievee.com
Beautiful studio glass art and ceramics made by established artists from around the world.

LiuliGongFang
- G/F, Tak Shing House
  20 Des Voeux Rd Central
  2973-0820
- L1, Pacific Place, 88 Queensway, Admiralty
  2918-9115
- 2/F, Elements Mall
  1 Austin Rd West, Kowloon
  2882-0541
- G, Festival Walk
  80 Tat Chee Ave, Kowloon Tong
  2265-7188
www.liuli.com

WHERE CAN I GET MADE-TO-ORDER ORIGINAL CONTEMPORARY ART?

Tanja Ocena Sek
2661-2130 / 6344-2413
www.to-artworks.com

WHERE CAN I BUY REASONABLY PRICED PRINTS AND ORIGINAL ART?

Schoeni Art Gallery
See page 306

Art Collection House ....
5/F, Block B, Mai Hing Ind. Bldg
16–18 Hing Yip St, Kwun Tong
8102-0286
www.ach.com.hk
Specialising in volume prints, and framing.

EVERYTHING HOUSE & HOME

I AM LOOKING FOR A GOOD RELIABLE FRAMING SHOP. WHO SHOULD I TRUST?

Zetter Picture Framer
G/F, Wing On Bldg, 40 Hollywood Rd, Central
2542-4269
www.zetterpictureframer.hk
Used by many high-end galleries and art dealers for quality and craftsmanship. Speak to Gordon.

Galerie du Monde
1/F, Ruttonjee Centre, 11 Duddell St, Central
2525-0529
www.galeriedumonde.com
Excellent quality, expensive framing shop recommended for your very best pieces.

Lee Wah Glass & Frames
G/F, 59 Wellington St, Central
2525-9416
A husband-and-wife team that previously did framing for Altfield Interiors. Excellent craftsmanship, reasonable prices and a good selection of frames. Jeannie has a good eye to assist you in choosing your frame.

Man Fong Picture Frame Co. Ltd
G/F, 1–7 Lyndhurst Terrace, Central
2522-6923
They use acid-free wood for stretching canvases. They offer excellent quality and craftsmanship and are highly regarded and used by many galleries.

Wong's Art Ltd
G/F, 59 Stanley Main St, Stanley
2813-0881
A good quality framing shop located in Stanley.

Po Sang Glass & Framing Co. ....
1/F, 61 Wellington St, Central
2523-1374 / 2523-6258
If you know what you want, Po Sang can be a good, inexpensive place to do your framing.

WHO CAN HELP ME RESTORE A PAINTING?

Wan Hong Lau Conservation Centre & Mounting Studio
8/F, Central Mansion, 270–276 Queen's Rd Central
2851-6692

Cham Yin Hin Chinese Mounting Art Design ....
4/F, Flat C, Tung Kin Factory Bldg
196–198 Tsat Tsz Mui Rd, Quarry Bay
2397-3500

PHOTOGRAPHIC CANVAS ART SEEMS TO BE ALL THE RAGE. WHERE IN HONG KONG CAN I GET MY OWN PHOTOGRAPHS TRANSFERRED TO CANVAS?

Color Six Laboratories Ltd
G/F, 28A Stanley St, Central
2526-0123
www.colorsix.com

O-Live Décor
10/F, Fuk Wo Ind. Bldg, 5 Sheung Hei St, San Po Kong
8105-2588
www.giclee.com.hk
Make an appointment before visit.

Digital Force
7/F, Wah Ha Factory Bldg
8 Shipyard Lane, Quarry Bay
2573-0730

WHICH **AUCTION HOUSES** SHOULD I LOOK AT TO ADD
TO A SERIOUS ART COLLECTION?

Sotheby's
31/F, One Pacific Place, 88 Queensway, Admiralty
2524-8121
www.sothebys.com

Christie's
22/F, Alexandra House, 18 Chater Rd, Central
2521-5396
www.christies.com

The Sovereign Art Foundation – Charity Auction
16/F, Kinwick Centre
32 Hollywood Rd, Central
2542-1177
www.sovereignartfoundation.com
*The coveted Sovereign Art Prize, held annually, attracts
established and up-and-coming artists primarily from
Asia. Works other than the first prize are auctioned off
at an annual charity event. See website for details.*

WHO CAN I TRUST TO **TRANSPORT AND HANG** MY
ARTWORK?

Simon Lung
9132-1631
*Simon is recommended for local art transportation (pick-
up and delivery). He can collect your purchased pieces,
deliver and hang them for you.*

WHO WOULD YOU RECOMMEND I USE FOR
SHIPPING ARTWORK WORLDWIDE?

Eagle Logistics
5/F, World Trade Square
21 On Lok Mun St
Fanling, New Territories
2677-8813 / 2683-1999
www.eaglelogistics-hk.com.hk
*Experienced and offer competitive pricing for
shipping artwork from Hong Kong to most worldwide
destinations.*

WHERE CAN I SOURCE **CHINESE ANTIQUE FURNITURE**
AND DECORATIVE ART?

Oi Ling Fine Chinese Antiques
• Main Gallery:
  G/F, 52 Hollywood Rd, Central
• Warehouse by appointment only:
  6/F, Harbour Ind. Centre, 10 Lee Hing St, Ap Lei Chau
2815-9422
www.oilingantiques.com
*Oi Ling is a highly regarded expert on Chinese antiques
with regular columns in Culture Hong Kong magazine.*

EVERYTHING HOUSE & HOME

MOVE IT · BUILD IT · FIX IT · LEASE IT · DESIGN IT · PARTY IT · CLEAN IT · PICTURE IT · DISCOUNT IT · HOUSE IT · **TREASURE IT** · FURNISH IT

Honeychurch Antiques
G/F, 29 Hollywood Rd, Central
2543-2433
www.honeychurch.com
Established in 1963. Glenn and Lucille Vessa are reputable antique dealers, specialising in Chinese export silver. Be sure to look in all the cabinets as there are pieces tucked everywhere. Also a good collection of old books.

Altfield Gallery
See page 304
One of the first antique dealers to focus on Chinese furniture. It also offers a good selection of Southeast Asian sculpture, Chinese and Tibetan carpets and decorative arts from Asia.

Arch Angel Antiques
G/F, 53–55 Hollywood Rd, Central
2851-6848
www.archangelgalleries.com
One of Hollywood Road's largest shops for Asian antiques, including antique ceramics, furniture, figurines, terracotta and collectibles. Every antique piece is accompanied by a detailed certificate of authenticity.

Dragon Culture
G/F, 184 & 231 Hollywood Rd, Central
2545-8098
www.dragonculture.com.hk
One of the largest dealers of Chinese antiques. Victor Choi has 25 years of experience in the business and is one of Hong Kong's most respected authorities on Chinese antique collecting.

Wonder Dragon Ltd
G/F, Al-Aqmar House, 30 Hollywood Rd, Central
2526-8863
They offer a good collection of antique telephones, binoculars and other interesting collectibles.

Chine Gallery
G/F, 42A Hollywood Rd, Central
2543-0023
www.chinegallery.com
Reputable source for antique furniture and rugs from China.

Zitan Oriental Antiques
G/F, 52 Graham St, Central
2523-7584
Antique furniture and furnishings from China.

The Red Cabinet
31/F, Universal Trade Centre
3–5 Arbuthnot Rd, Central
2536-0123 / 2868-0681
www.red-cabinet.com.hk
Antique and reproduction Chinese furniture.

Koko Nor Gallery
23/F, Hing Wai Centre, 7 Tin Wan Praya Rd, Aberdeen
2873-3281
Specialising in antique Tibetan chests and cabinets. This high-end gallery also carries pieces from China, Mongolia, Thailand and Burma. All furniture is offered in original, unrestored condition. A restoration service is available.

The Tibetan Gallery
G/F, 55 Wyndham St, Central
2530-4863
www.thetibetangallery.com

Interpret
G/F, 5 St. Francis St, Wan Chai
2838-3408
www.interpret.hk

WHERE CAN I FIND **EUROPEAN ANTIQUE, ART DECO** & **VINTAGE FURNITURE**?

Manks Ltd
2 Kennedy Terrace, Mid-Levels
2522-2115
www.manks.com
20th-century European antiques, Scandinavian furniture and design items, lighting, china, glass, silver and decorative arts. This is really a hidden gem.

chen mi ji
G/F, 4 Sun St, Wan Chai
2549-8800
www.chenmiji.com
Great source for well-priced retro/vintage furniture and decorative items.

Mooi Shop
G/F, 7 Chun St, Tin Hau
2882-1384
www.mooishophk.blogspot.com
Two-storey treasure trove for European furniture and accessories from the '50s to '70s.

D'Objets
1/F, Hau Fu Comm. Bldg
111 Queen's Rd West, Sheung Wan
2151-1238
www.dobjets.com
Art deco, Chinese antique furniture, and accessories.

WHERE DO I FIND **CONTEMPORARY AND ASIAN INSPIRED FURNITURE** PIECES?

Joineur Family Store Ltd
• G/F, Dominion Centre
  43–49 Queen's Rd East, Wan Chai
  2866-6733
• 11/F, Horizon Plaza, 2 Lee Wing St, Ap Lei Chau
  3542-5771
• 5/F, Premier Home Forum, HITEC
  1 Trademart Drive, Kowloon Bay
  3168-2700
• L1, Home Square
  138 Sha Tin Rural Committee Rd
  Sha Tin, New Territories
  2688-0727
www.joineur.com
Contemporary Chinese furniture.

HC28
16/F, Horizon Plaza, 2 Lee Wing St, Ap Lei Chau
2552-8002
www.hc28.com.hk
Simple, modern design with Asian influences.

EVERYTHING HOUSE & HOME

Tree
- G/F, 22 Elgin St, SoHo
  2841-8844
- 28/F, Horizon Plaza, 2 Lee Wing St, Ap Lei Chau
  2870-1582 / 2870-1583
www.tree.com.hk
Contemporary furniture.

Ginger Lily Days Trading Co. Ltd
10/F, Horizon Plaza, 2 Lee Wing St, Ap Lei Chau
2518-3588
Imaginative design for coffee tables, cabinets and sofas.
Natural materials like rattan and interesting woods are used.

Indigo Living
- 2/F, Prince's Bldg, 10 Chater Rd, Central
  2523-5561
- G/F, The Repulse Bay
  109 Repulse Bay Rd, Repulse Bay
  2592-8721
- 6/F & 18/F, Horizon Plaza
  2 Lee Wing St, Ap Lei Chau
  2555-0540 / 2552-0545
- 1/F, Grand Central Plaza
  138 Sha Tin Rural Committee Rd
  Sha Tin, New Territories
  2634-1618
www.indigo-living.com
A furniture, home and lifestyle shop offering stylish and
versatile products.

Out of Stock
- G/F, 12 On Wo Lane, Central
  2369-6008
- 14/F, Wah Yiu Ind. Centre
  30–32 Au Pui Wan St, Fo Tan, New Territories
  2690-4442
www.outofstock.com.hk
Out of Stock reproduces a great line of vintage classic
furniture.

WHERE IS A GOOD PLACE TO LOOK FOR **ULTRA-MODERN FURNITURE AND ACCESSORIES**?

Lane Crawford
- L3, IFC Mall, 8 Finance St, Central
  2118-3388
- L1 & L2, Pacific Place, 88 Queensway, Admiralty
  2118-3668
- G/F–1/F, Times Square, 1 Matheson St, Causeway Bay
  2118-3638
- Marco Polo Hongkong Hotel, Harbour City
  3 Canton Rd, Tsim Sha Tsui
  2118-3428
www.lanecrawford.com
A visit to the Pacific Place store is a must if you're looking
for stylish home and lifestyle accessories.

Aluminium
- G/F, 1 Lyndhurst Terrace, Central
  2546-5904
- G/F & Basement, Queen's Centre
  58–64 Queen's Rd East, Wan Chai
  2577-4066 / 2577-4099
www.hk-aluminium.com
See website for more locations.

Dentro
- G/F, Winway Bldg, 50 Wellington St, Central
  2801-7608
- G/F, Wilson House, 19–27 Wyndham St, Central
  2866-8829

www.dentro.com.hk
Dentro offers high-end imported furniture and lighting.

Minotti By Andante
G/F, The Design Showcase, Ruttonjee Centre
11 Duddell St, Central
2537-9688
www.andante.com.hk

Ligne Roset
- G/F, Guardian House
  32 Oi Kwan Rd, Causeway Bay
  3106-3221
- G/F, 16 Blue Pool Rd, Happy Valley
  2891-0913

www.ligne-roset.com

Ovo Home
G/F, 16 Queen's Rd East, Wan Chai
2526-7226
www.ovohome.com.hk
A modern lifestyle shopping experience. Ready-made and custom furniture.

Ovo Studio
G/F, 60 Johnston Rd, Wan Chai
2529-6060
www.ovostudio.com.hk

Nuconcepts
G/F, Ruttonjee Centre, 11 Duddell St, Central
2525-2121

Desideri Lifestyle
7/F, Oriental Crystal Comm. Bldg
46 Lyndhurst Terrace, Central
2950-4026
www.desideri.com.hk
Unique designs, including modern furniture, lighting and fashion.

Via
- 1/F, Ruttonjee Centre, 11 Duddell St, Central
  2507-3232
- G/F, 3–11 Wing Fung St, Wan Chai
  3102-3189
- G/F, 1 Electric St / Star St, Wan Chai
  3102-0808

www.viahk.biz
For lighting, small furniture, and bathroom furnishings.

Ulferts of Sweden (Far East) Ltd
- G/F, Cityplaza 2, 18 Taikoo Shing Rd, Tai Koo
  2567-8370
- B1, New World Centre, 20 Salisbury Rd, Tsim Sha Tsui
  2628-3355
- G/F, Whampoa Gardens, Hung Hom
  2333-6281
- 1/F, Grand Central Plaza
  138 Sha Tin Rural Committee Rd
  Sha Tin, New Territories
  2634-1318

www.ulferts.com.hk

EVERYTHING HOUSE & HOME

IS THERE ANY PLACE THAT SPECIALISES IN
CONTEMPORARY/ART DECO CHAIRS?

Bfelix Furniture
192A Hollywood Rd, Sheung Wan
2367-1735
www.bfelix.com
Art deco and classic leather club chairs.

Axis Collections
G/F, 47 Gough St, Central
2858-6919
www.axiscollections.com
Good source for stylish, modern and funky chairs.

Sol y Luna Lifestyle
16/F, Horizon Plaza, 2 Lee Wing St, Ap Lei Chau
2814-0203
*Modern furniture, chairs and accessories including the
Mies van der Rohe and Boa chairs. Contemporary lines,
including Minotti from Italy, are also available.*

Out of Stock
See page 313

WHERE CAN I FIND A **LEATHER DESK, CHAIR** OR
LEATHER ACCESSORIES?

Melandas
• 8/F, Lee Theatre Plaza, 99 Percival St, Causeway Bay
  2881-6198
• 2/F, Grand Central Plaza
  138 Sha Tin Rural Committee Rd
  Sha Tin, New Territories
*Well-made, nicely-designed leather L-shaped office
desks with white stitching starting from $16,800.
Matching leather swivel chairs starting from $3,800,
and assorted leather desk accessories.*

Grace Co.
G/F, 10 Aberdeen St, Central
2974-1870
*Great source for faux leather boxes, desk accessories,
waste paper baskets and more, made on the premises to
your specifications.*

WHERE CAN I BUY A **BEAN BAG** CHAIR?

The In Place
G/F, 22–24 Fuk Man Rd, Sai Kung, New Territories
2792-9445
www.theinplace.com
*Leather, faux leather, and faux fur bean bags available
from $600. You can buy just the filling and make your
own. This lifestyle shop accepts online orders and also
sells candles, gift items, handbags, sheepskin rugs, etc.*

G.O.D.
• G/F & 1/F, 48 Hollywood Rd, Central
  2805-1876
• 2/F, Peak Galleria, 118 Peak Rd, The Peak
  2778-3331
• Leighton Centre, 77 Leighton Rd, Causeway Bay
  2890-5555
• Basement, Silvercord, 30 Canton Rd, Tsim Sha Tsui
  2784-5555
www.god.com.hk

EVERYTHING HOUSE & HOME

WHERE CAN I GET **FURNITURE CUSTOM-MADE**?

Art Deco Furniture Collection Ltd ....
• G/F, 240 Queen's Rd East, Wan Chai
  2834-6203
• G/F, Ocean Terminal, Harbour City
  Canton Rd, Tsim Sha Tsui
  2366-9987
www.artdecofurniture.com.hk
*They are good at replicating wooden, hand-painted
furniture from photos and do a very good job making
baby and children's furniture.*

Tony Sofa Co. ....
G/F, 29A Haven St, Causeway Bay
2895-3291
*A good, reasonably priced sofa maker who can work
from any photo you provide. You need to source your
own fabric.*

Ficus
G/F, Tung Hei Bldg
20 Queen's Rd East, Wan Chai
2527-2893 / 2527-2941
www.arturaficus.com
*Ready-made designs or they can produce your own
design or copy from a photo (having measurements
really helps). Good quality at reasonable prices.*

Giormani
G/F, Tung Shing Bldg
138–144 Queen's Rd East, Wan Chai
2362-3869
www.giormani.com
*Specialising in plush sofas, fabric or leather. Can custom
make sofas.*

Fresh Design (Kurt Wong / Wai Ming) ....
9039-8525
fdesign2@yahoo.com.hk
*Reasonably well-priced carpenter who can make any
type of basic furniture.*

Attitude
7/F, Horizon Plaza
2 Lee Wing St, Ap Lei Chau
2375-4705
*A reliable source for furniture, beds with fabric
headboards, curtains and more. Speak with Esther.*

Ovo Home
G/F, 16 Queen's Rd East, Wan Chai
2526-7226
www.ovohome.com.hk

Artura
15/F & 18/F, Horizon Plaza
2 Lee Wing St, Ap Lei Chau
3105-3903 / 3105-3908
www.arturaficus.com
Sister shop to Ficus and similar in offerings and style.

Alyssa Liang Furniture Ltd
10/F, Horizon Plaza
2 Lee Wing St, Ap Lei Chau
2526-6310
www.alyssaliang.com
Specialising in Chinese furniture.

Wai Wing Upholstery & Curtain
G/F, 17 Sun Chun St, Tai Hang, Causeway Bay
2890-3814 / 9013-6162
Mr Siu can design or copy all types of sofas, chairs, cushions, curtains or blinds. He is especially good at Roman blinds. He can show you his fabric samples or you can provide your own. He is also good with reupholstering.

L & K Furniture & Decoration Co. Ltd
10/F, Nan Fung Centre
264–298 Castle Peak Rd, Tsuen Wan, New Territories
2402-9970
L & K make all types of sofas, either from their own design or you can provide a picture for them to copy. Their quality and prices are very good. They can also make other types of furniture and furnishings.

Wing Sun Upholstery
13/F, Harbour Ind. Centre, 116 Lee Nam Rd, Ap Lei Chau
2871-9293
Mr Kwan is very experienced and produces high-quality work. He can design or copy any type of soft furnishing including sofas, chairs, cushions, curtains or blinds and can show you a catalogue of sofas that he can copy. No showroom.

Rimba Rhyme
5/F, Horizon Plaza
2 Lee Wing St, Ap Lei Chau
2870-0389 / 8330-8100
www.rimbarhyme.com
They specialise in aged wood (recycled wood) or government-approved and regulated plantation wood. Can be custom-made.

WHERE CAN I FIND **WALL STICKERS** OR GET A **MURAL PAINTED** FOR MY KID'S BEDROOM?

Marguerite & Gribouilli
19/F, Shun Pont Comm. Bldg
5–11 Thomson Rd, Wan Chai
2520-0075
www.marguerite-gribouilli.com
High-end exquisite wall stickers that can be custom-made to fit any décor.

IKEA
• Basement, Park Lane Hotel
  310 Gloucester Rd, Causeway Bay
• 3/F, Telford Plaza 2, 33 Wai Yip St, Kowloon Bay
• 3/F & 5/F, Grand Central Plaza
  138 Sha Tin Rural Committee Rd
  Sha Tin, New Territories
• 1/F & 2/F, Jumbo Plaza
  6 Choi Fai St, Sheung Shui, New Territories
3125-0888
www.ikea.com.hk

Walls of the Wild
www.wallsofthewild.net
Based in Poughkeepsie, New York; however they deliver to Hong Kong.

Elizabeth Art
9655-7924
elizabethart@netvigator.com
Murals, paint finishing, furniture painting and more.

EVERYTHING HOUSE & HOME

WHERE CAN I ORDER **WALL PANELS** FOR MY HOME?

2 Magpies
15/F, Guardian House, 32 Oi Kwan Rd, Wan Chai
2572-9028
www.2magpies.com.hk
*Eco-friendly Cushini wall panels from Scotland for visual
and lighting effects, acoustic and insulation benefits, or
pinboard and display possibilities. By appointment only.*

WHERE CAN I FIND SOMEONE TO **FIX OR RESTORE**
ANTIQUE FURNITURE?

Antique Doctor (T.S. Chan)
3/F, YYC Ind. Bldg, 20 Wang Hoi Rd, Kowloon Bay
2759-1133
www.antique-doctor.com
*Mr Chan comes well-recommended for fixing or
restoring your precious antique pieces.*

Taprobane Antique Restoration
48 Des Voeux Rd Central
6233-6029

The Birdcage
16/F, Horizon Plaza, 2 Lee Wing St, Ap Lei Chau
2580-5822
*Specialising in Chinese furniture, The Birdcage can pick
up, repair and deliver your furniture back to you.*

WHERE CAN I FIND SOMEONE WHO WILL COME
TO MY HOME TO DO **FURNITURE REPAIR**?

Eddy Chuek's Workshop
13/F, Block 2, Kingley Ind. Bldg
33–35 Yip Kan St, Wong Chuk Hang
2570-9772 / 9272-7533 (Wendy)
*Reliable in-home furniture repairs and handyman service.
Eddy also has a portfolio of wooden furniture he can or
has built. Call Wendy who speaks English to arrange.*

Bricks & Stones
G/F, 97 Queen's Rd East, Wan Chai
2520-0577
*A quotation can be provided based on a photo of the
damaged piece of furniture. Home repairs can be done
if the damage is minor.*

Casey Workshop
21/F, Block 2, Kingley Ind. Bldg
33–35 Yip Kan St, Aberdeen
2552-1999
*They do minor furniture repairs at home, depending on
the extent of the damage.*

Simon Lung
9132-1631
*Simon will come to your home to repair most types of
furniture, except sofas.*

Teo Cheow Seng
13/F, West Tower, Shun Tak Centre
200 Connaught Rd Central
2548-4196
www.cheowseng.com
*High quality industrial fasteners, nuts, bolts, screws,
rivets, washers, etc.*

EVERYTHING HOUSE & HOME

WHERE CAN I GET MY **SOFA REUPHOLSTERED**?

Tony Sofa Co. ....
G/F, 29A Haven St, Causeway Bay
2895-3291

Attitude
7/F, Horizon Plaza, 2 Lee Wing St, Ap Lei Chau
2375-4705

MCV Asia
5/F, Capitol Plaza, 2–10 Lyndhurst Terrace, Central
2189-7068
www.mcvasia.com

WHERE CAN I GET **MADE-TO-ORDER CURTAINS AND BLINDS**?

Sun Sun Interiors ....
G/F, 24 Fleming Rd, Wan Chai
2511-2008 / 2511-3046

Bedford Interiors
G/F, 101 Queen's Rd East, Wan Chai
2529-0472

New Bedford Interiors ....
G/F, 67 Queen's Rd East, Wan Chai
2520-0330
Reasonably priced, they can make just about anything.

Cetec
18/F, Printing House, 6 Duddell St, Central
www.cetec.com.hk
Offer fine imported fabrics that can be made into curtains.

Cotton Tree Interiors
G/F, 92 Queen's Rd East, Wan Chai
2866-6921
For sofas, curtains and rugs.

Millennium Fabrics International
• G/F, 2 Blue Pool Rd, Happy Valley
  2834-4555
• G/F, 1–2 Kwai Fong St, Happy Valley
  2834-4428
www.mefabrics.com

Sheryia Curtain Co.
G/F, 1 Lyndhurst Terrace, Central
2525-6596
www.fabricworld.com.hk
Conveniently located, Sheryia has a good selection of fabrics for curtains and all types of upholstery.

Curtain Suppliers ....
1/F, 117 Queen's Rd East, Wan Chai
2529-2727
A good place that makes cheap, simple curtains.

Anthony Chao
LG/F, Ivy House, 20 Wyndham St, Central
2971-0338
www.anthonychao.com

Sun Beauty Curtain
1/F, On Hing Mansion
156 Queen's Rd East, Wan Chai
2866-8069
www.sunbeauty.com.hk

Ornaments
G/F, 50 Junction Rd, Kowloon City
2383-3712
www.ornaments.com.hk

Colourful Piece Goods & Curtains Co.
1/F, Siu Kwan Mansion
120 Old Main St, Aberdeen
2554-6199
www.colourfulcurtain.com.hk

WHERE CAN I BUY QUALITY IMPORTED UPHOLSTERY & CURTAIN FABRICS?

Altfield Interiors
11/F, 9 Queen's Rd Central
2525-2738 / 2524-4867
www.altfield.com.hk
A wide range of European fabrics.

Kinsan Collections
G/F, 59 Wyndham St, Central
2526-2309
www.kinsanhk.com

Cetec
18/F, Printing House, 6 Duddell St, Central
www.cetec.com.hk
Great source for high-end upholstery and curtain fabric, with great designs and including leather and skins.

WHERE CAN I BUY VINTAGE OR RETRO FABRIC?

Morn Creations
G/F, 62A Peel St, SoHo
2869-7021
www.morn.com.hk
Vintage fabrics from $120 per yard. Ideal for cushion covers, lampshades, bags, etc.
See also EVERYTHING SHAM SHUI PO, pages 189–191.

WHERE CAN I LOOK FOR MODERN LIGHTING FIXTURES?

Lumino Collection
G/F, 72 Wellington St, Central
2577-1288
Modern lighting, lamp shades and home accessories.

Flos
G/F, Winway Bldg, 50 Wellington St, Central
2801-7007
www.flos.com

Zodiac
G/F, Tak On Mansion
32–34 Morrison Hill Rd, Wan Chai
2832-9987
www.zodiaclighting.com

Artemide
1/F, Ruttonjee Centre, 11 Duddell St, Central
2523-0333
www.artemide.com

Andante
G/F, The Design Showcase, Ruttonjee Centre
11 Duddell St, Central
2537-9688
www.andante.com.hk

Apartment
G/F, 62 Leighton Rd, Causeway Bay
2882-2198

Kartell Hong Kong
1/F, Ruttonjee Centre, 11 Duddell St, Central
2810-0408
www.kartell.it

Décor en Folie
6/F, Fuk Wo Ind. Bldg, 5 Sheung Hei St, San Po Kong
3580-0598
www.decorenfolie.com
Lifestyle/homeware shop that carries modern natural wood lamps and shades.

Lampada
G/F, 54 Morrison Hill Rd, Wan Chai
2893-5050
See also ultra-modern furniture, pages 313-314.

WHERE CAN I BUY OR CUSTOM MAKE GOOD QUALITY **LAMP SHADES**?

Soong Arts Lampshades
G/F, 6 Square St, Sheung Wan
2549-0615
You can design your own and provide the fabric.

WHICH AREA HAS A WIDE RANGE OF **LIGHTING SHOPS**?

Morrison Hill Rd, Causeway Bay
Between Wan Chai Rd and Leighton Rd

Lockhart Rd, Wan Chai
Near Fleming Rd

Shanghai St, Mong Kok
Between Argyle St and Shantung St
While you're there, don't miss these good ones:

Lampada
G/F, 54 Morrison Hill Rd, Wan Chai
2893-5050

Hoking Lighting Design
G/F, 9 Morrison Hill Rd, Wan Chai
2572-9003

Faddy Lighting
G/F, 637 Shanghai St, Mong Kok
2392-3808

Element Lighting Design
G/F, 629 Shanghai St, Mong Kok
2390-3228

Future Lighting Collection
G/F, 647–651 Shanghai St, Mong Kok
3540-5486

Zoom Lightings Ltd
G/F, 627 Shanghai St, Mong Kok
2399-7130

PLC Lighting
- G/F, 210–212 Lockhart Rd, Wan Chai
  2519-6275
- G/F, 50 Morrison Hill Rd, Causeway Bay
  2836-3839
- 1/F, 8C Mong Kok Rd, Mong Kok
  2798-2226

Good source for a large range of lighting fixtures and styles.

EVERYTHING HOUSE & HOME

WHERE CAN I BUY **INEXPENSIVE CRYSTAL CHANDELIERS**?

absoluconcept
3/F, Yau Tong Ind. City, 17 Ko Fai Rd, Yau Tong
2763-7622
www.absoluconcept.com

WHERE CAN I GET A **CHANDELIER MADE**?

Hong Kong Lighting Ltd
2881-8968
*Send a picture of what you want made for a quotation.
Call and speak with Ms Vian for details.*

WHERE CAN I BUY **A CEILING FAN**?

Life's a Breeze
16/F, Horizon Plaza, 2 Lee Wing St, Ap Lei Chau
2572-4000
www.lifesabreezehk.com
*Offer ceiling fans in modern and contemporary designs
using wood, chrome and brass, priced from $1,400 to
$5,000. A range of outdoor-use fans is also available.*
Elegant Ceiling Fan
G/F, 14 Merlin St, North Point
2887-6638
home.netvigator.com/~alanenco
*This showroom is part of Alan Engineering Company.
Fortress Hill MTR, exit A.*

WHERE CAN I BUY **KIDS'/INFANTS' BEDDING**?

Kids by Red Cabinet
31/F, Universal Trade Centre
3–5 Arbuthnot Rd, Central
2536-0123 / 2868-0681
www.kidsbyredcabinet.com
*Affordable, quality kids' bedding in 100% cotton;
matching table lamps also available.*
IKEA
See page 317
Inside
• 2/F, Prince's Bldg, 10 Chater Rd, Central
  2537-6298
• G/F, The Repulse Bay, 109 Repulse Bay Rd, Repulse Bay
  2812-6685
• 12/F, Horizon Plaza, 2 Lee Wing St, Ap Lei Chau
  2873-1795
www.inside.com.hk
Far East Linen Co.
G/F, 9B Stanley Main St, Stanley
2813-9362
Contemporary and embroidered bed sets for kids.
Bumps to Babes
See page 160
Mothercare
See page 161

EVERYTHING HOUSE & HOME

WHERE CAN I BUY **READY-MADE CHILDREN'S FURNITURE**?

Indigo Living ....
See page 313

Kids by Red Cabinet ....
31/F, Universal Trade Centre
3–5 Arbuthnot Rd, Central
2536-0123 / 2868-0681
www.kidsbyredcabinet.com

Modern Baby ....
UG/F, Winway Bldg
50 Wellington St, Central
2525-3711
www.modernbabyhk.com

Bedazzle! ....
10/F, Century Square
1–13 D'Aguilar St, Central
2869-7990
www.stokke.com
They sell the Stokke children's collection.

IKEA ....
See page 317

Honey Berrie ....
See pages 161–162
*A good source for baby and kids' furniture, toys,
equipment and products.*

Colors ....
G/F, 137 Queen's Rd East, Wan Chai
2866-6138
www.colors.com.hk

Bumps to Babes ....
See page 160

Eugene Club Centre ....
See page 161

WHERE CAN I GET **KIDS' FURNITURE CUSTOM MADE**?

Art Deco Furniture Collection Ltd ....
See page 316
*Browse through their extensive portfolio of pictures
or bring your own design/photo. Art Deco offers
imaginative custom-made kids' furniture using only lead-
free paint.*

Kids by Red Cabinet ....
31/F, Universal Trade Centre
3–5 Arbuthnot Rd, Central
2536-0123 / 2868-0681
www.kidsbyredcabinet.com
*In addition to their ready-made kids' furniture, this shop
also offers custom-made designs including reproduction
Chinese antique furniture in kids' sizes.*

Top Carpenter Furniture Ltd ....
G/F, Kensington House
68–74 Junction Rd, Kowloon City
2383-3518
*This shop is very good at making character or themed
children's furniture, and can copy just about anything.*

EVERYTHING HOUSE & HOME

WHERE CAN I FIND **INEXPENSIVE BUNK BEDS** FOR MY KIDS' ROOM?

IKEA ....
See page 317
Jade Rattan ....
- G/F & 1/F, 181 Wan Chai Rd, Wan Chai
  2866-6087
- Sofa City, Mezzanine, United Bldg
  145 King's Rd, Fortress Hill
  2503-0881
- G/F, 243 Shau Kei Wan Rd, Shau Kei Wan
  2567-9602
- G/F, Sang Cheong Bldg
  427–437 Queen's Rd West, Sai Wan
  2872-8978
- G/F, 181 Sai Yee St, Mong Kok
  2499-6759
- 4/F, Dragon Centre, 37K Yen Chow St, Sham Shui Po
  2720-3028
- G/F, Whampoa Garden, Hung Hom
  2333-0481
- G/F, Bo Shek Mansion
  328 Sha Tsui Rd, Tsuen Wan, New Territories
  2439-9566
- G/F, 117 Kwong Fuk Rd, Tai Po, New Territories
  2653-0617
- G/F & Cockloft, Park Court
  41 Tak Ching Court, Tuen Mun, New Territories
  2440-4311
- G/F, Hung Yip Bldg
  253–263 Castle Peak Rd, Yuen Long, New Territories
  2470-0889
www.jaderattan.com
Great source for inexpensive pine bunkbeds and furniture. Can also customise sizes.

WHERE CAN I BUY A GOOD **MATTRESS**?

Simmons
- 2/F, Man Yee Bldg, 67 Queen's Rd Central
  2506-1100
- G/F, Windsor House
  311 Gloucester Rd, Causeway Bay
  3693-4569
- Basement, New World Centre
  20 Salisbury Rd, Tsim Sha Tsui
  2736-5583
- 6/F, Grand Century Place
  193 Prince Edward Rd West, Mong Kok
  2628-3591
- L3, MegaBox, 38 Wang Chiu Rd, Kowloon Bay
  2723-3009
- 2/F, Grand Central Plaza
  138 Sha Tin Rural Committee Rd
  Sha Tin, New Territories
  2696-9226
- 5/F, Tsuen Wan Plaza
  4–30 Tai Pa St, Tsuen Wan, New Territories
  2525-5220

EVERYTHING HOUSE & HOME

- 2/F, Tuen Mun Town Plaza
  1 Tuen Shun St, Tuen Mun, New Territories
  2618-0109
www.simmons.hk

SOGO
- 555 Hennessy Rd, Causeway Bay
  2833-8338
- 12 Salisbury Rd, Tsim Sha Tsui
  3556-1212
www.sogo.com.hk/en/home.html

Wing On Department Store
- 211 Des Voeux Rd Central, Sheung Wan
  2852-1888
- Cityplaza, 18 Taikoo Shing Rd, Tai Koo
  2885-7588
- Wing On Kowloon Centre, 345 Nathan Rd, Mong Kok
  2710-6288
- Wing On Plaza, 62 Mody Rd, Tsim Sha Tsui East
  2196-1388
- Block C, Discovery Bay Plaza
  Discovery Bay, Lantau Island
  2987-9268
www.wingonet.com

Lavital ....
10/F, Horizon Plaza, 2 Lee Wing St, Ap Lei Chau
3741-1828
www.lavitalasia.com
Imported luxury, sustainable, organic, handcrafted mattresses and boxsprings.

Suzuranbed
- G/F, Citywalk
  1 Yeung Uk Rd, Tsuen Wan, New Territories
- 4/F, Leighton Centre
  77 Leighton Rd, Causeway Bay
- 6/F, Grand Century Place
  193 Prince Edward Rd West, Mong Kok
2408-7078
www.suzuranbed.com.hk

Magazzini
- 1/F, Ruttonjee Centre, 11 Duddell St, Central
  2521-3282
- 9/F, Horizon Plaza, 2 Lee Wing St, Ap Lei Chau
  2814-1663
www.magazzini-vivace.com

Okooko
27/F, Horizon Plaza, 2 Lee Wing St, Ap Lei Chau
2870-1132
www.okooko.com

Dunlopillo
- 6/F, Grand Century Place
  193 Prince Edward Rd West, Mong Kok
  2628-9868
- Basement, New World Centre
  20 Salisbury Rd, Tsim Sha Tsui
  2301-3338
- 2/F, Grand Central Plaza
  138 Sha Tin Rural Committee Rd
  Sha Tin, New Territories
  2634-1288
www.dunlopilloworld.com

JUSCO
- Kornhill Plaza (South), 2 Kornhill Rd, Quarry Bay
2884-6888
- G/F & B1, Site 5 & 6, Whampoa Garden, Hung Hom
2627-6688
- Lok Fu Shopping Centre, 100 Junction Rd, Lok Fu
2339-3388
- 1–4/F, Tsuen Wan Plaza
4–30 Tai Pa St, Tsuen Wan, New Territories
2414-8686
- UG & 1/F, Tuen Mun Town Plaza, Phase 1
1 Tuen Shun St, Tuen Mun, New Territories
2542-7333
- 1–2/F, Zone B, Tai Po Mega Mall
8–10 On Pong Rd, Tai Po, New Territories
2662-8888
www.jusco.com.hk

WHERE CAN I FIND A GOOD **BEDDING SHOP**?

Bed & Bath
- 2/F, Prince's Bldg, 10 Chater Rd, Central
2522-5151
- 1/F, Elements Mall, 1 Austin Rd West, Kowloon
2196-8583
www.bednbath.com.hk

Natural Home
2/F, Kornhill Plaza, Kornhill Rd, Quarry Bay
2506-1289
Bedsheets, down-filled comforters, pillows and more.

SOGO
See page 325

Lane Crawford
See page 313

Kokoon Beds & Bedding
11/F, Horizon Plaza, 2 Lee Wing St, Ap Lei Chau
2518-8382
www.kokoon.biz

Into Home
9/F, Horizon Plaza, 2 Lee Wing St, Ap Lei Chau
2814-7413
*Large range of Margaret Muir furniture and colourful
bedding including kids' designs.*

WHERE CAN I BUY GOOD QUALITY, **REASONABLY-
PRICED BED LINENS**?

IKEA
See page 317

G.O.D.
See page 315

MUJI
- P4, wtc more, 280 Gloucester Rd, Causeway Bay
3971-3118
- 3/F, Lee Theatre Plaza, 99 Percival St, Causeway Bay
3971-3120
- 4/F, Ocean Centre, Harbour City, Canton Rd, Tsim Sha Tsui
3971-3101
- 3/F, Miramar Shopping Centre
132 Nathan Rd, Tsim Sha Tsui
3971-3160

EVERYTHING HOUSE & HOME

- L7, Langham Place, 8 Argyle St, Mong Kok
  3971-3140
- 2/F, APM, 418 Kwun Tong Rd, Kwun Tong
  3971-3150
- 3/F, New Town Plaza, Phase 3
  Sha Tin Centre St, Sha Tin, New Territories
  3971-3130
- L6, Departures Northwest Concourse, Terminal 1
  Hong Kong International Airport
  2261-0711

www.muji.com.hk

Inside ....

See page 322

Hong Kong Arts & Crafts Co.

11A–13 Stanley Main St, Stanley

2813-9887

Embroidered table linens, cushion covers, duvet covers, night gowns and bedsheets.

Tong's Sheets & Linen Co. ....

55–57 Stanley Main St, Stanley

2813-0337

Same type of stock as the above shop.

Far East Linen Co. ....

G/F, 9B Stanley Main St, Stanley

2813-9362

More contemporary tablecloths and sheets.

Okooko

27/F, Horizon Plaza, 2 Lee Wing St, Ap Lei Chau

2870-1132

www.okooko.com

A-Fontane ....

3/F, Pioneer Centre, 750 Nathan Rd, Mong Kok

2406-0635

www.a-fontane.com.hk

Popular with the local market, this store offers an extensive range. See website for more details.

WHERE CAN I GO TO BUY **DECENT-QUALITY INEXPENSIVE TOWELS**?

Towel Shop ....

1/F, Kelly House, 6–14 Gresson St, Wan Chai

2865-6378

This hole-in-the-wall warehouse shop sells towels at discount prices. It is a hit-or-miss shop in terms of stock availability. Press Floor 1, Unit 2 on the buzzer at entrance.

WHERE CAN I BUY **HOTEL-QUALITY BED LINENS, PILLOWS** AND **DUVETS ONLINE**?

Sleep Naked!

www.sleepnaked.hk

WHERE CAN I GET **EMBROIDERING OR MONOGRAMMING** DONE ON MY LINENS?

Marika Linen

6/F, Yau Shun Bldg, 50 D'Aguilar St, Central

2868-3308

You can have your napkins, tablecloths, towels and more monogrammed here.

Ching Mei Computer Embroidery Factory
12/F, Block U, Everest Ind. Centre
396 Kwun Tong Rd, Kwun Tong
2763-0043
www.ching-mei.com
*Offering all types of embroidery and monogramming,
but only on large quantity orders. Contact Mr Dilly Chau.*

Joseph Embroidering Enterprises Co. Ltd
2/F, Kwong Ah Bldg, 114 Thomson Rd, Wan Chai
2573-3229 / 2575-0592
*They can embroider names and simple logos. Generally
only accept larger orders.*

WHERE CAN I GET **CLOTHING** OR **LINENS**
PROFESSIONALLY DYED?

Chi Ko Dyeing Factory
11/F, 13 Yai Yip St, Shui On Ind. Bldg, Kwun Tong
2793-9078

I'M LOOKING TO BUY A **PERSIAN RUG**. WHERE DO I
START?

Carpet Buyer
G/F, Horizon Plaza, 2 Lee Wing St, Ap Lei Chau
2850-5508
www.carpetbuyer.com

Tai Ping Carpets
2/F, Prince's Bldg, 10 Chater Rd, Central
2522-7138
www.taipingcarpets.com

WHERE CAN I GET A **REASONABLY PRICED RUG** MADE?

Yarns Wool Carpets ....
1/F, Kam Man Fung Factory Bldg
6 Hong Man St, Chai Wan
2833-2886
www.yarns-ltd.com

Sun Sun Interiors
G/F, 24 Fleming Rd, Wan Chai
2511-2008 / 2511-3046

New Bedford Interiors
G/F, 67 Queen's Rd East, Wan Chai
2520-0330

Cotton Tree Interiors
G/F, 92 Queen's Rd East, Wan Chai
2866-6921

WHERE CAN I LOOK FOR **GENUINE AND FAUX FUR
ACCESSORIES**?

Faux Home
3/F, Harbour Ind. Centre, 10 Lee Hing St, Ap Lei Chau
2851-4040
www.faux-home.com

Hidestyle
10/F, Time Centre, 53–55 Hollywood Rd, Central
2790-3801 / 8191-3948
www.cowhiderugs.hk
Exotic cowhide rugs.

EVERYITHING HOUSE & HOME

WHERE CAN I FIND A GOOD SELECTION OF CANDLES?

The Candle Company
G/F, 11 Lyndhurst Terrace, Central
2545-0099
www.candles.hk
*High-quality, non-drip candles in all shapes, sizes
and colours, in addition to candleholders, stands,
candelabras, aromatherapy products and incense.*

Healing Plants Ltd
13/F, Capitol Plaza, 2–10 Lyndhurst Terrace, Central
2815-9448
*Come here for your Votivo candles; they are all the
rage in the US. These are long burning candles that
offer lovely lasting scents that make your entire house
fragrant. They are a great gift (not cheap, but worth it).
Try the scent called "Clean, Crisp, White".*

Abode
11/F, Kai Centre, 36 Hung To Rd, Kwun Tong
3426-3634
www.abode.com.hk
Candles and home accessories.

AT Scent
• G/F, 27 Lyndhurst Terrace, Central
  2543-7980
• Sai Kung Villa, Fuk Man Rd, Sai Kung, New Territories
  2791-2793
Candles, aromatherapy products and accessories.

IKEA ....
See page 317
*Great selection of inexpensive candles, including
floating candles.*

Spotlight ....
L5, MegaBox, 38 Wang Chiu Rd, Kowloon Bay
2359-0010
www.spotlight.hk
Good for craft supplies and DIY home interior projects.

Jo Malone
Stockists:
• Lane Crawford, L3, IFC Mall, 8 Finance St, Central
  2118-5720
• Lane Crawford, Times Square
  1 Matheson St, Causeway Bay
  2118-6182
www.jomalone.com
*Fantastic fragrances from Jo Malone, now available in
Hong Kong. Custom-made fragrances available.*

WHERE CAN I FIND THE WIDEST VARIETY OF REPRODUCTION CHINESE CERAMICS?

Wah Tung China Arts Ltd ....
• 7/F, Lee Roy Comm. Bldg
  57–59 Hollywood Rd, Central
  2543-2823
• 14–17/F, Grand Marine Ind. Bldg
  3 Yue Fung St, Tin Wan, Aberdeen
  2520-5933
www.wahtungchina.com
*World's largest supplier of hand-decorated ceramic
collectibles, with over 18,000 Chinese/European designs.*

EVERYTHING HOUSE & HOME

WHERE DO I PICK UP STYLISH **ASIAN HOME AND LIFESTYLE ACCESSORIES**?

Shanghai Tang
See pages 106–107
Fantastic lifestyle shop, specialising in Chinese-inspired clothing accessories and gifts. Great source for unique and hip gifts from Hong Kong.

Asian Artworks Gallery
G/F, The Repulse Bay, 109 Repulse Bay Rd, Repulse Bay
2812-0850
www.asianartworks.com.hk
Myriad of unique things from all over Asia, all under one roof. One friend describes the shop as carrying all those things and more that you've seen in your travels and wished you'd bought, but didn't. This is not a place for bargains, but it's convenient one-stop shopping.

Good Laque Gift Gallery
• G/F, 40–42D, Stanley Market
  Stanley Main St, Stanley
  2899-0632
• 16/F, Horizon Plaza, 2 Lee Wing St, Ap Lei Chau
  3106-0163
www.goodlaque.com
A good selection of lacquerware, home décor items, lanterns and gifts, mostly imported from Vietnam.

Tao
1/F, Hollywood Comm. Bldg
3–5 Old Bailey St, Central
2521-1223

Hutu
58B Peel St, Central
2530-2102
A bright little store carrying an array of reasonably priced Asian-inspired homeware, cushions, clothing and accessories.

Indigo Living
See page 313

I NEED SOME **BASICS** FOR MY NEW FLAT. WHAT **LIFESTYLE/HOMEWARE STORES** OFFER AN EXTENSIVE RANGE?

IKEA ....
See page 317
A great place for cheap and stylish homeware.

Indigo Living
See page 313

Muji
See pages 326–327
Stylish, clean designs of all the basics.

Francfranc
• 2/F, Hang Lung Centre, 2–20 Paterson St, Causeway Bay
  3427-3366
• G, Festival Walk, 80 Tat Chee Ave, Kowloon Tong
  3106-8958
www.francfranc.com

Bals Tokyo
1/F, Elements Mall, 1 Austin Rd West, Kowloon
2302-1961
www.balstokyo.com

I & D Home Concept
G/F & 1/F, Wing Cheung Mansion
78 Morrison Hill Rd, Wan Chai
3422-3338
G.O.D.
See page 315
Wing On Department Store
See page 325
SOGO
See page 325

I'M LOOKING FOR **CONTEMPORARY HOME ACCESSORIES**.
WHERE SHOULD I START?

Inside ....
See page 322
*Contemporary bathroom accessories, towels, pyjamas,
loungewear, clothing, slippers and more.*
White Contemporary Homewares
• 2/F, Prince's Bldg, 10 Chater Rd, Central
  2526-8482
• G/F, 156–165 Queen's Rd East, Wan Chai
  2907-5338
• 1/F, Grand Central Plaza
  138 Sha Tin Rural Committee Rd
  Sha Tin, New Territories
  2691-0933
Allure Living Co.
G/F, 109B Caine Rd, Mid-Levels
2153-1022

HOW ABOUT SOMETHING **UNIQUE AND TRENDY IN
HOME ACCESSORIES**?

Homeless
• G/F, 29 Gough St, Central
  2581-1880
• Wun Ying Collection, G/F, 7 Gough St, Central
  2581-1110
• 1/F, 17 Yun Ping Rd, Causeway Bay
  2890-8789
• Xplus, LCX, 3/F, Ocean Terminal, Harbour City
  Canton Rd, Tsim Sha Tsui
  2780-1138
• 1/F Grand Central Plaza
  138 Sha Tin Rural Committee Rd
  Sha Tin, New Territories
  2691-1981 / 2691-1980
www.homeless.hk
All kinds of unique and funky things for your home.
Azona
• G/F, Pearl City, 22–36 Paterson St, Causeway Bay
  2808-0606
• LCX, 3/F, Ocean Terminal, Harbour City
  Canton Rd, Tsim Sha Tsui
  2377-0202
• L5, New Town Plaza, Phase 1
  Sha Tin Centre St, Sha Tin, New Territories
  2698-3362
www.azona.com.hk

G.O.D.
See page 315
Morn Creations
G/F, 62A Peel St, SoHo
2869-7021
www.morn.com.hk

CAN YOU RECOMMEND ANY LIFESTYLE STORES
THAT ARE A GOOD SOURCE FOR **GIFTS AND KNICK-
KNACKS**?

Melaine
G/F, 37 Cochrane St, Central
2815-7873
www.melaine.com.hk
Kapok
G/F, 5 St. Francis Yard, Wan Chai
2549-9254
www.ka-pok.com
*Eclectic collection of "hand-picked" products
showcasing the founder Arnault Castell's frequent
shopping trips abroad. Also, homegrown talent abounds
with products including clothing, jewellery, small
furniture items and accessories.*
Sonjia
G/F, 1–2 Sun St, Wan Chai
2529-6223
www.sonjiaonline.com
*In addition to her own line of clothing, designer Sonjia
Norman also carries unique home accessories from
around the world.*
Campo Marzio
3/F, Gateway Arcade, Harbour City
Canton Rd, Tsim Sha Tsui
3579-2030
www.campomarziodesign.it
*An Italian design company offering fine home and
personal accessories such as wallets, pens, handcrafted
boxes, and watches.*
Fiori
G/F, 4 Lyndhurst Terrace, Central
2890-8448
Morn Creations
See above
*An eclectic store with ornaments, lampshades, fabrics,
bags, clothing and other accessories.*
Francfranc
See page 330
Amours Antiques
G/F, 45 Staunton St, Central
2803-7877
ECOLS ....
G/F, 8 & 10 Gough St, Central
3106-4918
www.ecols.biz
*They sell modern furniture and accessories made from
recycled materials.*
Addiction
G/F, 15 Gough St, Central
2581-2779

EVERYTHING HOUSE & HOME

I NEED A **FEATURE DECORATIVE PIECE** TO ADD THAT FINAL TOUCH. WHERE SHOULD I LOOK?

Ovo Home
G/F, 16 Queen's Rd East, Wan Chai
2526-7226
www.ovohome.com.hk
A good source for special sculptures.

Galerie Vee
2/F, Prince's Bldg, 10 Chater Rd, Central
2522-3166 / 2522-1677
www.galerievee.com

Gaffer Studio Glass
17/F, Hing Wai Centre, 7 Tin Wan Praya Rd, Aberdeen
2521-1770
www.gafferstudioglass.com

Honeychurch Antiques
G/F, 29 Hollywood Rd, Central
2543-2433
www.honeychurch.com
Charming, unique silver decorative pieces.

Wing Wah Porcelain Painting Factory ....
G/F, 40 Elgin St, Central
2524-8241
A ceramics treasure trove filled with colourful old and new ceramics, including communist-inspired figurines. Hit-or-miss shop that seems a bit tacky, but imagine what the piece will look like out of the shop.

HOW ABOUT A REPRODUCTION **VENETIAN MIRROR**?

Blupool
26/F, Horizon Plaza, 2 Lee Wing St, Ap Lei Chau
3527-3826
Reproduction Venetian etched mirrors in all shapes and sizes. Custom sizes available.

I'M LOOKING FOR FINE **CHINA, TABLEWARE AND CRYSTAL**. WHERE CAN I GO THAT ALSO OFFERS A GIFT REGISTRY OPTION?

Pavillion Christofle
1/F, Prince's Bldg, 10 Chater Rd, Central
2869-7311
www.christofle.com

Villeroy & Boch Tableware
7/F, SOGO, 555 Hennessy Rd, Causeway Bay
2831-4636
www.villeroy-boch.com

Exclusivités
• Basement–3/F, 1 Duddell St, Central
 2259-6630 / 2521-8626
• 1/F, Prince's Bldg, 10 Chater Rd, Central
 2877-2815
• 7/F, SOGO, 555 Hennessy Rd, Causeway Bay
 2893-0703
• 3/F, Gateway Arcade, Harbour City
 Canton Rd, Tsim Sha Tsui
 2735-0579
www.shiamas.com
Multi-brands, all high-end and elegant.

Tiffany & Co.
See pages 154–155

Town House
• 2/F, Prince's Bldg, 10 Chater Rd, Central
2845-0633
• UG, Festival Walk, 80 Tat Chee Ave, Kowloon Tong
2375-0002
High-end homeware, including wine glasses, decanters, silver frames and gift items.

WHERE CAN I BUY SILVER HOME ACCESSORIES AND GIFT ITEMS?

Argento
2/F, Prince's Bldg, 10 Chater Rd, Central
2869-6233

Luciana's Silver ....
2/F, Fleet Arcade, Lung King St, Wan Chai
2511-2178
Reasonably priced silver-plated tableware and gift items.

Nugget Ltd
2/F, Prince's Bldg, 10 Chater Rd, Central
2523-5281

Links of London
See page 154
A wide variety of silver accessories, jewellery, men's gifts and picture frames, both sterling silver and silver-plated.

Town House
See above

Fink
• G/F, 155 Queen's Rd East, Wan Chai
2866-7884
• G/F, 28 Hollywood Rd, Central
2127-4886
Large selection of silver-plated home and gift items.

WHERE CAN I GET SILVER ENGRAVING DONE?

The Grand Co.
G/F, Melbourne Plaza, 33 Queen's Rd Central
2525-4291
Engraving done using templates. Ask for Mr Shum.

HOW ABOUT A GOOD SOURCE FOR REASONABLY PRICED TABLECLOTHS AND NAPKINS?

Chun Sang Trading Co.
G/F, Block B, 3–4 Glenealy, Central
2522-9246
Never-ending supply of tablecloths and napkins, ranging from everyday to fine hand-embroidered pieces. Ask if you want to see the good stuff.

Hong Kong Arts & Crafts Co.
11A–13 Stanley Main St, Stanley
2813-9887

Tong's Sheets & Linen Co.
55–57 Stanley Main St, Stanley
2813-0337

Far East Linen Co.
G/F, 9B Stanley Main St, Stanley
2813-9362

EVERYTHING HOUSE & HOME

I WANT TO DESIGN MY **OWN PATTERN FOR PLATES AND DISHES**. WHERE CAN I HAVE THESE MADE?

Yuet Tung China Works
3/F, Kowloon Bay Ind. Centre
15 Wang Hoi Rd, Kowloon Bay
2796-1127 / 2796-1125
www.porcelainware.com.hk
This large porcelain manufacturer can make your own design of dishes with minimum quantities. They also sell a large range of ready-made dinnerware, decorative items, gift items and accessories.

WHERE IS THERE A GOOD PLACE TO BUY **PLAIN DISHES, GLASSES AND SERVING PIECES**?

Ichi Ni San Shop
G/F, 16A Elgin St, SoHo
2525-6649
A good source for reasonably priced, simple and stylish basic dishes, glasses and serving pieces.

IKEA
See page 317

Spotlight
L5, MegaBox, 38 Wang Chiu Rd, Kowloon Bay
2359-0010
www.spotlight.hk

G.O.D.
See page 315

King Tak Hong Porcelain Co. Ltd
G/F, 128 Queen's Rd East, Wan Chai
3118-2422 / 3118-2423
www.kingtakhong.com
Everything from cooking utensils, glasses, bamboo steamers, dishes and rattan baskets, to glass vases. This shop has it all, both Western and Asian and at very good prices. A great source for setting up your new kitchen or planning that big party. You can buy glasses/ dishes here for what it costs to rent them twice!

HOW ABOUT **TOP-QUALITY KITCHENWARE, POTS AND PANS**?

Pantry Magic
G/F, 25 Lok Ku Rd, Central
2504-0688
www.pantry-magic.com

Pan Handler
3/F, Prince's Bldg, 10 Chater Rd, Central
2523-1672
www.thepanhandler.biz
The best selection of top-quality kitchenware including pots/pans, blenders, knives, serving dishes, etc. If money is no object and you simply want the best, look no further when it comes to Western kitchenware.

I Love Kitchen
- G/F, 1 Leighton Rd, Causeway Bay
  2572-0009
- G/F, 2 Hillier St, Sheung Wan
  2815-6332
- G/F, 2 Humphreys Ave, Tsim Sha Tsui
  2723-9303

- L3, MegaBox, 38 Wang Chiu Rd, Kowloon Bay
  2629-5098
www.ilovekitchen.com

Le Creuset Boutique
LG/F, Hoisenee House, 69 Wyndham St, Central
2790-1808
www.lecreuset.co.uk
*Offering the famous Le Creuset range of cast iron pots,
pans and kitchen equipment, in addition to the Screwpull
brand of premium corkscrews and accessories.*

WHERE CAN I BUY REASONABLY PRICED BASIC KITCHENWARE?

Gourmet Kitchen
3/F, Gateway Arcade, Harbour City
Canton Rd, Tsim Sha Tsui
2175-0098
www.gourmetkitchen.com.hk

IKEA
See page 317

King Tak Hong Porcelain Co. Ltd
G/F, 128 Queen's Rd East, Wan Chai
3118-2422 / 3118-2423
www.kingtakhong.com

Japan Home Centre
- G/F, 128 Wellington St, Central
  2815-0434
- LG/F, Cheong Ip Bldg
  350–354 Hennessy Rd, Wan Chai
  2572-1420
- Cockloft, 5 Sharp St East, Causeway Bay
  2576-1041
- G/F, Provident Centre, 53 Wharf Rd, North Point
  2562-5130
- G/F, 29 & 31 Des Voeux Rd West, Sai Wan
  2291-6146
- 4/F, Shopping Centre, Stanley Plaza, Stanley
  2813-8571
www.japanhome.com.hk
Many locations. Great for home and kitchen supplies.

Man Fung
13/F, Coda Plaza, 51 Garden Rd, Mid-Levels
2571-4027

Wing On Department Store
See page 325
*Reasonably priced home and kitchenware items. Large
items can be delivered.*

SOGO
See page 325

WHO SELLS TOP-QUALITY TABLEWARE AT WHOLESALE PRICES?

Pacific Rim Trading Ltd
9/F, Kowloon Centre, 29–39 Ashley Rd, Tsim Sha Tsui
2838-8977
www.prt.com.hk
Unparalleled selection of table linens.

EVERYTHING HOUSE & HOME

Equip Asia Ltd
9/F, Kowloon Centre
29–39 Ashley Rd, Tsim Sha Tsui
2838-8989
www.equipasia.com
A leading hotel/restaurant supplies company in Hong Kong, offering top European, Australian, American and Asian designer brands. Glassware, chinaware, cutlery, hollowware, and a wide variety of table accessories at wholesale prices. Good when ordering large quantities.

WHERE CAN I BUY **KITCHENWARE IN BULK** FOR CATERING A LARGE PARTY?

Sharp Arrow Ltd
Yau On Court, 322 Shanghai St, Yau Ma Tei
Hotel and restaurant supplier of stainless steel kitchen equipment, including trays, serving platters, buffet trays, industrial meat slicers, blenders and more.

Cosmos Stainless Steel Engineering
G/F, 327A Shanghai St, Yau Ma Tei
2384-4328 / 2771-2501
www.cosmos.hk
Trays, pots, cleavers, strainers and more.

Kwong Wing Food Ind. Stainless Steel Engineering Ltd
G/F, 312–314 Shanghai St, Yau Ma Tei
2332-2463
Cheap, large, oval stainless steel platters, baking utensils and more.

Kam Lee
G/F, Kam Court Bldg
60–62 Bonham Strand, Sheung Wan
2543-8921 / 2543-8627

Man Kee Chopping Board
G/F, 342 Shanghai St, Yau Ma Tei
2332-2784
www.mankee.hk
Chopping boards, knives, etc.

Chan Chi Kee Cutlery Co. Ltd
G/F, 316–318 Shanghai St, Yau Ma Tei
2385-0317 / 2384-7515
www.chanchikee.com

WHERE CAN I GET MY **KNIVES HAND-SHARPENED**?

Ho Ching Kee Lee
G/F, 66–68 Tong Mei Rd, Mong Kok
2543-7352

WHERE IS A GOOD PLACE TO LOOK FOR **APPLIANCES**?

Fortress
• G/F, Yu Sung Boon Bldg, 107 Des Voeux Rd Central
  2544-4385
• 2/F, Shun Tak Centre
  200 Connaught Rd Central, Sheung Wan
  3152-3111
www.fortress.com.hk
Many locations.

Broadway
7/F–9/F, Times Square, Causeway Bay
2506-1330 / 2506-0228 / 3426-4098
www.ibroadway.com.hk

Best Hong Kong
2/F, Plaza Hollywood, 3 Lung Poon St, Diamond Hill
2326-9563

Gilman Home Appliances
- G/F, 52 Gilman St, Central
  2524-3554
- UG/F, Leighton Centre
  77 Leighton Rd, Causeway Bay
  2881-0055
- 3/F, Ocean Centre, Harbour City
  Canton Rd, Tsim Sha Tsui
  2730-6747
- 2/F, Grand Central Plaza
  138 Sha Tin Rural Committee Rd
  Sha Tin, New Territories
  2699-0345

www.gilman-group.com

Direct Consumer Distribution Centre
56/F, Hopewell Centre, 83 Queen's Rd East, Wan Chai
2866-8812

Kenmore Appliances
1/F, The Galleria, 9 Queen's Rd Central
2525-2291
www.kenmore-by-salvador.com

Siemens Ltd
G/F, Baskerville House, 13 Duddell St, Central
2511-2323
www.siemens.com.hk

Whirlpool
- UG/F, Leighton Centre
  77 Leighton Rd, Causeway Bay
  2506-1628
- 3/F, Plaza Hollywood, 3 Lung Poon St, Diamond Hill
  3115-2928

www.whirlpool.com.hk

Bosch
2565-6161
www.bosch.com

Wing On Department Store
See page 325

WHERE DO I BUY CHEAP OR SECOND-HAND APPLIANCES?

Kingsway Appliances
G/F, 28 Aberdeen Main Rd, Aberdeen
2814-8770
www.kingswayappliances.com
Good selection of used appliances ranging from washers / dryers to refrigerators. Competitive prices but no warranty.

WHERE CAN I GET THE CHEAPEST DAILY-USE ITEMS FOR THE HOME?

Japan Home Centre
See page 336
IKEA
See page 317

Man Fung ....
13/F, Coda Plaza, 51 Garden Rd, Mid-Levels
2571-4027
*Similar to Japan Home Centre, and also carries a toy
selection.*

JUSCO $10 Plaza ....
- 1/F, Pacific Plaza
  410 Des Voeux Rd West, Sai Wan
  2291-6236
- Mezzanine, Wing Tak Mansion
  15 Canal Rd, Wan Chai
  2892-1812
- Basement, Metropole Bldg
  416–426 King's Rd, North Point
  2561-2198
- 3/F, Chong Hing Square
  601 Nathan Rd, Mong Kok
  2388-3171
- 2/F, Kowloon City Plaza
  128 Carpenter Rd, Kowloon City
  2382-6616
- 1/F, Tseung Kwan O Plaza
  1 Tong Tak St, Tseung Kwan O
  2207-4172

*Tupperware, gift boxes, loot bag items for kids' parties,
kitchen utensils, stationery and everything under the sun.*

WHERE CAN I BUY A **HOME SAFE**, SIMILAR TO THE
ONES THEY USE IN HOTEL ROOMS?

YS Safe Co. ....
3/F, 13–17 Wah Shing St, Kwai Hing
2833-6354
*Manufacture their own "Victory" computer-operated
safes using technology from Germany. Prices start from
$2,000. They also manufacture their own filing cabinets;
great for the home office.*

Safeguard Ltd
2/F, Hang Wai Comm. Bldg
231–233 Queen's Rd East, Wan Chai
2572-9290 / 8573-8491
www.safeguardchubbsafes.com.hk
*Authorised distributor of all types of Chubb safes,
including commercial safes. Will sell you individual units.*

Bestwell Furniture Ltd
G/F, 57 Wellington St, Central
2523-0608

PriceRite ....
- 1/F, Hollywood Plaza
  610 Nathan Rd, Mong Kok
  2782-0129
- 9/F, Dragon Centre
  37K Yen Chow St, Sham Shui Po
  2725-3018
- Podium, Mei Foo Sun Chuen, Phase 3, Mei Foo
  2371-3707
- G/F, Site 2, Wonderful Worlds of Whampoa
  Hung Hom
  2926-5200
www.pricerite.com.hk
See website for other outlets.

EVERYTHING HOUSE & HOME

POSH

- G/F, Hong Kong Trade Centre
  161 – 167 Des Voeux Rd Central
  2851-0899
- G/F, 251 Hennessy Rd, Wan Chai
  2789-9777
- G/F, Perfect Comm. Bldg
  20 Austin Ave, Tsim Sha Tsui
  2722-7016
- G/F, 486 Nathan Rd, Yau Ma Tei
  2385-8585

www.posh.com.hk

WHO OFFERS **SAME-DAY DRY-CLEANING SERVICE**?

Kleaners

L1, IFC Mall, 8 Finance St, Central
2295-0088
20% surcharge for same-day service.

Martinizing Dry Cleaning

- 1/F, World-Wide Plaza, 19 Des Voeux Rd Central
  2526-9643
- G/F, 7 Glenealy, Central
  2525-3089
- G/F, Caravan Court, 141 – 145 Caine Rd, Mid-Levels
  2803-7138
- G/F, Great Eagle Centre
  23 Harbour Rd, Wan Chai
  2827-7060
- G/F, 69D Sing Woo Rd, Happy Valley
  2833-5368
- G/F, 114G Boundary St, Prince Edward
  2337-0139

www.martinizing.com
Trusted American chain dry-cleaners with many locations worldwide.

Clean Living

- MTR Central Station (Exit F, H), Central
  2523-0549
- 2/F, Entertainment Bldg, 30 Queen's Rd Central
  2868-3669
- Queensway Plaza, 93 Queensway, Admiralty
  2528-2603
- G/F, Great Eagle Centre
  23 Harbour Rd, Wan Chai
  2877-3133
- G/F, Sino Plaza
  255 – 257 Gloucester Rd, Causeway Bay
  2834-1112
- G/F, Progress Comm. Bldg
  9 Irving St, Causeway Bay
  2972-2728
- G/F, Tsimshatsui Mansion
  36 – 50 Lock Rd, Tsim Sha Tsui
  2723-7873
- 5/F, Flat A, Eldex Ind. Bldg
  21 Ma Tau Wai Rd, Hung Hom
  2333-0141

www.cleanliving.com.hk
See website for other locations; only same-day service outlets are listed here.

EVERYTHING HOUSE & HOME

Jeeves of Belgravia
- 1/F, The Galleria, 9 Queen's Rd Central
  2973-0101
- LG/F, Jardine House, 1 Connaught Place, Central
  3119-7200
- G/F, 10 Yik Yam St, Happy Valley
  2574-9393
- 3/F, 33 Hysan Ave, Causeway Bay
  2973-0077

Collection and delivery: 2552-7557
Customer service: 2973-0071
www.jeeves.com.hk
Many locations. Also offers leather and suede restoration, shoe/handbag repair, atmospheric barrier protection packaging, stain guard, and more. Free pick-up and delivery service with minimum $300.

WHERE CAN I TAKE MY EXPENSIVE CLOTHES FOR EXPERT **STAIN REMOVAL AND DRY CLEANING**?

Goodwins of London
Great Food Hall, LG, Pacific Place
88 Queensway, Admiralty
2918-1400
Pick-up/Delivery: 2812-2400
www.goodwinsoflondon.com
Excellent full-service dry-cleaner. Expect to pay for the quality.

Jeeves of Belgravia
See above

Park Avenue Clothes Care Specialist
- 1/F, The Forum, Exchange Square
  8 Connaught Place, Central
- G/F, 33 Robinson Rd, Mid-Levels
  2536-9533
- G/F, Yee Fat Mansion, 2 Min Fat St, Happy Valley
  2155-9393
- Block 9, City Garden, City Garden Rd, North Point
  2807-1133
- G/F, MTR Kowloon Station, Kowloon
  2302-4020

www.parkavenuehk.com

Martinizing Dry Cleaning
See page 340

WHO IS A MORE **REASONABLY PRICED DRY CLEANER** FOR EVERYDAY CLOTHES?

Clean Living
See page 340
Reasonably priced, professional and reliable. One day service at 10% extra charge, same-day service 20% extra.

Scargos
2813-1231 / 9202-1555 / 2552-9911
www.scargos.com
Reliable, reasonably priced dry-cleaner near Stanley. Pick-up and delivery.

Kenlea Dry Cleaner
2569-8696 / 9688-2211
Alex will come to your home to pick up and deliver dry-cleaning. Reliable for everyday clothes (no suits or formal wear).

Vogue Laundry
- MTR Hong Kong Station, Central
  2147-5233
- G/F, 35 Caine Rd, Mid-Levels
  2122-9323
- Basement, Three Pacific Place
  1 Queen's Rd East, Wan Chai
  3555-4009
- G/F, Empire Court, 2–4 Hysan Rd, Causeway Bay
  2504-2318
- G/F, Park Comm. Centre
  180 Tung Lo Wan Rd, Causeway Bay
  2807-2683
- G/F, 5–13 Fortress Hill Rd, Fortress Hill
  2887-1332
- G/F, Cityplaza, 18 Taikoo Shing Rd, Tai Koo
  2907-0138
- G/F, Devon House, Taikoo Place, 979 King's Rd, Tai Koo
  2561-2898
- 3/F, The Westwood, 8 Belcher's St, Kennedy Town
  2542-7022
- 1/F, Service Annex, 100 Cyberport Rd, Cyberport
  2989-6388
www.voguelaundry.com

Tai Pan Valet Shop
G/F, 109 The Repulse Bay Arcade, Repulse Bay
2812-6488

British Dry Cleaners
G/F, 2 Star St, Wan Chai
2866-8355
Hotline: 2564-7581
www.britishdrycleaners.com

Mei Yen Laundry
G/F, Yick Fat Bldg, 32 Yau Man St, Quarry Bay
2565-0848

Well Supreme Laundry
2/F, Discovery Bay Plaza, Discovery Bay, Lantau Island
2987-5151

WHERE CAN I BUY A PROFESSIONAL CLOTHING STEAMER?

Trade Style Ltd
7/F, Siu Wai Ind. Centre
29–33 Wing Hong St, Lai Chi Kok
2559-5533
www.tras-group.com
A Jiffy steamer from the US will make ironing look professional. These are the same steamers that the shops use and are especially effective on knits and thinner fabrics that are difficult to press using an iron.

WHERE CAN I FIND A GOOD CARPET CLEANER WHO SPECIALISES IN STAIN REMOVAL?

Easy Carpet Care Systems
4/F, Loyong Court Comm. Bldg
212–220 Lockhart Rd, Wan Chai
2519-9828
www.easycare.com.hk

Viking Carpet Care
26/F, Universal Trade Centre
3–5 Arbuthnot Rd, Central
2556-9553
www.scanasia.com/viking.html

Fortune Cleaning & Pest Control Service Co. Ltd
9/F, Goldfield Ind. Centre
1 Sui Wo Rd, Fo Tan, New Territories
2394-2976

WHO CAN I BRING IN FOR **PEST CONTROL**?

Biocycle ....
11/F, Lock Kui Ind. Bldg
6–8 Hung To Rd, Kwun Tong
3575-2575
www.biocycle.com.hk

Asia Pest Control
8–10 Prince's Terrace, Mid-Levels
2523-8855

ISS Thomas Cowan Co. Ltd
12/F, North Somerset House, Taikoo Place
979 King's Rd, Quarry Bay
2861-0303
www.yp.com.hk/issthomascowan
Specialises in termite infestations.

Pesticide Services
14/F, Block A, Sea View Estate 2
2 Watson Rd, North Point
2570-7028
www.pesticide.com.hk

Truly Care
15/F, Nan Fung Centre
264–298 Castle Peak Rd
Tsuen Wan, New Territories
2458-8378
www.trulycare.com.hk

Goatee Toni
www.goateetoni.com
If you've got a snake problem, call Goatee Toni who will catch and release the snake in an unpopulated area as opposed to calling the police who will likely just "get rid" of it.

I HAVE UNWANTED **FURNITURE AND HOUSEHOLD ITEMS**. WHO I CAN **GIVE** THEM TO WHO CAN ALSO PICK THEM UP FROM MY HOME?

Crossroads International
Crossroads Village
2 Castle Peak Rd, Tuen Mun, New Territories
2984-9309
www.crossroads.org.hk
This registered non-profit organisation takes quality goods and redistributes them to people in need both locally and internationally. They accept household, office and classroom furniture, bedding and fabric, medical provisions, electrical items, computers, household goods, clothing, stationery, books and educational toys.

EVERYTHING HOUSE & HOME

WHERE CAN I GO TO **DISPOSE OF OVERSIZED RUBBISH,** INCLUDING HOUSEHOLD ITEMS?

Central/Western District:
- Lan Kwai Fong Refuse Collection Point:
  Beside the Lan Kwai Fong sitting-out area, Central
- Man Kat St Refuse Collection Point:
  Junction of Man Kat St and Connaught Rd Central
- Gage St Refuse Collection Point:
  38–42 Gage St, Central
- Robinson Rd Refuse Collection Point:
  Junction of Robinson Rd and Castle Rd, Mid-Levels
- Arbuthnot Rd Refuse Collection Point:
  Junction of Arbuthnot Rd and Caine Rd, Mid-Levels
- Kennedy Rd Refuse Collection Point:
  Underneath the junction of Kennedy Rd and the
  Cotton Tree Drive flyover, Mid-Levels
- Queensway Plaza Refuse Collection Point:
  Queensway Plaza, 99 Queensway, Admiralty
- Peak Galleria Refuse Collection Point:
  Peak Galleria Bus Terminus, The Peak
- Lok Ku Rd Refuse Collection Point:
  G/F, 21–23 Lok Ku Rd, Sheung Wan
- Shek Tong Tsui Refuse Collection Point:
  Shek Tong Tsui Municipal Services Bldg
  470 Queen's Rd West, Sai Wan
- Smithfield Municipal Services Bldg Refuse Collection Point:
  Basement, Smithfield Municipal Services Bldg
  12K Smithfield Rd, Kennedy Town

Wan Chai District:
- Paterson St Refuse Collection Point:
  Junction of Paterson St and Gloucester Rd, Wan Chai
- Gloucester Rd Refuse Collection Point:
  Opposite 250 Gloucester Rd, Wan Chai
- Lockhart Rd Refuse Collection Point:
  224 Lockhart Rd, Wan Chai
- Luard Rd Refuse Collection Point:
  Junction of Luard Rd and Johnston Rd, Wan Chai
- Star St Refuse Collection Point:
  Junction of Star St and Sun St, Wan Chai
- Shiu Fai Terrace Refuse Collection Point:
  Opposite 7 Shiu Fai Terrace, Wan Chai
- Cross Lane Refuse Collection Point:
  Junction of Cross Lane and Bullock Lane, Wan Chai
- Sing Woo Rd Refuse Collection Point:
  Junction of Sing Woo Rd and Yik Yam St, Happy Valley

Eastern District
- Wing Hing St Refuse Collection Point:
  15 Wing Hing St, Tin Hau
- Oil St Refuse Collection Point:
  3 Oil St, Fortress Hill
- Java Rd Refuse Collection Point:
  99 Java Rd (Java Rd Market), North Point
- Tanner Rd Refuse Collection Point:
  63 Tanner Rd, North Point
- Marble Rd Refuse Collection Point:
  Marble Rd opposite King's Rd Playground, North Point
- Mansion St Refuse Collection Point:
  41 Mansion St, Quarry Bay

EVERYTHING HOUSE & HOME

- Quarry Bay Market Refuse Collection Point:
  Quarry Bay St, Quarry Bay
- Hing Man St Refuse Collection Point:
  Junction of Hing Man St and Oi Yee St, Sai Wan Ho
- Sai Wan Ho St Refuse Collection Point:
  2A Sai Wan Ho St, Sai Wan Ho
- Tung Hei Rd Refuse Collection Point:
  At side of 28 Tung Hei Rd, Shau Kei Wan

Southern District:
- Tsung Man St Refuse Collection Point:
  19 Tsung Man St, Aberdeen
- Tin Wan Close Refuse Collection Point:
  Next to 9 Tin Wan Close, Tin Wan
- Repulse Bay Refuse Collection Point:
  Next to 33 Beach Rd, Repulse Bay
- Stanley Beach Rd Refuse Collection Point:
  Next to car park opposite 20 Stanley Beach Rd,
  Stanley
- Shek O Refuse Collection Point:
  Next to Shek O Main Beach Car Park, Shek O
- Ap Lei Chau Municipal Services Building
  Refuse Collection Point:
  8 Hung Shing St, Ap Lei Chau
- Stanley Temporary Market Refuse Collection Point:
  Next to Stanley Temporary Market
  Stanley Main St, Stanley

HOW ABOUT SOMEWHERE I CAN **DROP OFF USEFUL CLOTHING**, ETC. TO PASS ON TO PEOPLE IN NEED?

Salvation Army
www.salvation.org.hk
Collection Centres:
- 11, Wing Sing Lane, Yau Ma Tei
  2332-4433
- G/F, 31 Wood Rd, Wan Chai
  2572-2879

Family Stores:
- G/F, 29 Wing Hing St, Causeway Bay
  2887-5577
- G/F, Man Kwong Court
  12F–12G Smithfield Rd, Kennedy Town
  2974-0882
- G/F Tung Hong Bldg
  139 Shau Kei Wan Main St East, Shau Kei Wan
  2535-8113
- Yue On House, Yue Wan Estate, Chai Wan
  2558-8655
- 8 Tung Sing Rd, Aberdeen
  2873-4666
- G/F, 98 Stanley Main St, Stanley
  3197-0070
- G/F, 1A Cliff Rd, Yau Ma Tei
  2332-4448
- Xing Hua Centre, 433 Shanghai St, Mong Kok
  3422-3205
*See website for other Family Stores in Kowloon and
New Territories. They can also arrange a pick-up service
upon request for heavy items or large quantities of
donations.*

EVERYTHING HOUSE & HOME

WHERE CAN I HIRE A RELIABLE **PART-TIME NANNY OR BABY-SITTER**?

Rent-a-Mum
4/F, 33 Robinson Rd, Mid-Levels
2523-4868
www.rent-a-mum.com
Reliable, experienced Western nannies who can be hired for short-term baby-sitting.
The Nanny Experts Ltd
2335-1127
www.thenannyexperts.com

WHERE DO I FIND A GOOD AGENCY TO HIRE A **LOCAL LIVE-IN HELPER**?

ACJ International Recruitment
8/F, Skyline Comm. Centre
77 Wing Lok St, Sheung Wan
2591-5127
More expensive than most, but highly recommended by expats looking for helpers with great references.
Josie James Personnel
1/F, Lap Fai Bldg
6–8 Pottinger St, Central
2377-2568
www.josiejamespersonnel.com
Also good for expats and a cheaper agency fee.
Emry's Employment Agency
• 11/F, Wah Ying Cheong Bldg
  158–164 Queen's Rd Central
  2815-6060
• 11/F, On Hong Comm. Bldg
  145 Hennessy Rd, Wan Chai
  2545-0032 / 3110-1491
www.emrysemploymentagency.com

WHERE CAN I LOOK FOR A **FILIPINO HELPER ONLINE**?

Amah Net
2/F, United Centre, 95 Queensway, Admiralty
2869-9330
www.amahnet.com
AsiaXpat
www.asiaxpat.com

WHERE CAN I FIND AN **EMPLOYMENT AGENCY** THAT BRINGS IN DOMESTIC HELPERS FROM THE PHILIPPINES?

Homeasy Services Ltd
11/F, Yue Shing Comm. Bldg
15–16 Queen Victoria St, Central
2776-2900
www.homeasy.com.hk

Jem Employment & Trading
11/F, Kai Tak Comm. Bldg
66–72 Stanley St, Central
2850-5970
www.jememployment.com

Overseas Employment Centre Ltd
2/F, Commercial House
35 Queen's Road Central
2524-6195
www.overseas.com.hk
Comprehensive website with downloadable forms and documentation.

I AM LOOKING FOR A **PART-TIME HELPER**. HOW CAN I HIRE ONE?

Prestige Home Services
8/F, Cameron Comm. Centre
458–468 Hennessy Rd, Causeway Bay
2893-7387
www.phshk.com
Specialising in part-time helpers. Rates start at $70/ hour, which includes travel cost and insurance.

Merry Maids
20/F, Sun Ying Ind. Centre
9 Tin Wan Close, Aberdeen
2857-4038
www.merrymaids.com.hk
Hourly, long-term or one-off cleaning.

Swan Hygiene Services
7/F, Cityplaza, 18 Taikoo Shing Rd, Tai Koo
2741-3731
www.swanservices.com.hk

WHERE CAN I HIRE A **CANTONESE OR MANDARIN-SPEAKING HELPER**?

W F Employment Service (Lao Ban)
11/F, Cameron Comm. Centre
458 Hennessy Rd, Causeway Bay
2877-3511

Good Help Services Co.
3/F, World-Wide Plaza
19 Des Voeux Rd Central
2530-1743
Angie can help you find a part-time or full-time Chinese helper. She can also find you a temporary helper while your helper is away.

Smart Living
2317-4567
www.erb.org/smartliving/en
A government training centre that can assist you to find part-time Mandarin- and/or Cantonese-speaking help.

EVERYTHING HOUSE & HOME

I AM DECORATING FOR A PARTY. WHERE CAN I
PICK UP GORGEOUS **FLOWER ARRANGEMENTS**?

See florists, pages 350–351.

WHERE IS A GOOD PLACE TO BUY INEXPENSIVE
SIMPLE GLASS VASES, LARGE AND SMALL?

Brighton Flori-Art Plaza
G/F, 1 Flower Market Rd, Mong Kok
2787-2203

Nice Garden
G/F, 3 Yuen Po St, Mong Kok
2787-3933
*There are a few other stores with no English name within
a few stores of Nice Garden that also carry a good
selection of glass vases.*

Flowerland Horticulture
G/F, 68 Flower Market Rd, Mong Kok
2142-7827
*This shop has a good selection of inexpensive vases, big
and small.*

Sun Kee Trading Co.
G/F, 5–7 Yuen Po St, Mong Kok
2380-8331

Wai Bun
G/F, 186B Prince Edward Rd West, Mong Kok
2395-3778 / 2395-1660

WHERE IS A GOOD PLACE TO BUY **LARGE POTTED
PLANTS** FOR A GOOD PRICE?

Brighton Pot Plant Centre
G/F, 28 Flower Market Rd, Mong Kok
2380-5113
A garden centre with great choices for plants.

Kwan Kwan Garden Co.
G/F, 204 Prince Edward Rd West, Mong Kok
2393-4123

Art Mount Ltd
G/F, 202 Prince Edward Rd West, Mong Kok
2787-3218
Tastefully potted plants and bonsai.

Mountain City Plant Co.
G/F, 221 Sai Yee St, Mong Kok
2395-0618

P&F Garden
50 Shui Choi Tin Village, Victoria Rd, Pok Fu Lam
2812-0948
www.pnfgarden.iyp.hk

Chun Hing Gardening & Landscaping
1 Wong Nai Chung Rd, Happy Valley
2572-6430 / 2573-5408
www.chunhinggarden.com

Cheung Kee Garden Ltd
Tai Chung Hau, Sai Kung, New Territories
2526-2138

Greenhouse Nursery
42 Tai Chung Hau, Fung On Village
Sai Kung, New Territories
2573-3627

EVERYTHING HOUSE & HOME

WHERE CAN I BUY **BONSAI PLANTS**?

Kwan Kwan Garden Co. ....
G/F, 204 Prince Edward Rd West, Mong Kok
2393-4123

Long To Flower Shop ....
G/F, 220A Prince Edward Rd West, Mong Kok
2399-0992

Prince Florist ....
G/F, 2 Yuen Ngai St, Prince Edward
2380-1982

WHERE CAN I BUY **GARDENING TOOLS AND FLORIST SUPPLIES**?

Brighton Garden Centre
G/F, 8 Flower Market Rd, Mong Kok
2380-9807

Brighton Cut Flower Centre
G/F, 18 Flower Market Rd, Mong Kok
2380-9136

WHERE CAN I BUY A **REAL CHRISTMAS TREE AND DECORATIONS**?

Chun Hing Gardening & Landscaping
1 Wong Nai Chung Rd, Happy Valley
2572-6430 / 2573-5408
www.chunhinggarden.com
Fresh-cut Fraser, Noble and Douglas fir trees from the US. Also wreaths, garlands, poinsettias and accessories. You can bring your kids to choose their own tree, which can be delivered to your home. From 2 to 20 ft., their trees are always nice. You can pre-order with a 30% deposit before late November for slightly better prices.

P&F Garden
50 Shui Choi Tin Village, Victoria Rd, Pok Fu Lam
2812-0948
www.pnfgarden.iyp.hk
A reliable place to order your Noble or Douglas fir Christmas tree for home delivery. They also carry wreaths, garlands, poinsettias and more. You can also go to choose your own tree.

Wah Kwong Stationery Printing Co. ....
G/F, Waga Comm. Centre
99 Wellington St, Central
2523-0356
A plentiful source of cheap, seasonal decorations.

Abies Danica Ltd
2/F, Hankow Centre
5–15 Hankow Rd, Tsim Sha Tsui
2574-9877
www.royalfir.com

Anglo Chinese Florist
• 1 Lyndhurst Terrace, Central
  2921-2986
• G/F, 28 Peel St, Central
  2845-4212
• G/F, 22 Stanley St, Central
  2526-3511
www.anglochinese.com

Hong Kong Island Landscape Co. Ltd
Lin Tong Mei Tsuen, Fan Kam Rd
Sheung Shui, New Territories
2369-8367
www.hkil.com.hk

Cheung Kee Garden Ltd
Tai Chung Hau, Sai Kung, New Territories
2526-2138

Sophie's Xmas Trees
42E Ma On Shan Village (Ha Pun Shan)
Ma On Shan, New Territories
2649-6280
www.sophieshk.com

Lily Flowers
Pok Fu Lam Rd, Wah Fu
2551-3307

Greenhouse Nursery
42 Tai Chung Hau, Fung On Village
Sai Kung, New Territories
2573-3627

WHERE CAN I FIND THE MOST **CREATIVE AND INNOVATIVE FLORISTS?**

Ovo Garden
G/F, 22 Queen's Rd East, Wan Chai
2529-2599
www.ovogarden.com.hk

agnès b. Fleuriste
- L3, IFC Mall, 8 Finance St, Central
  2805-0631
- L1, Pacific Place, 88 Queensway, Admiralty
  2918-1680
- 1/F, 111 Leighton Rd, Causeway Bay
  2895-1300
- LG1, Festival Walk, 80 Tat Chee Ave, Kowloon Tong
  2265-8388
www.agnesb-fleuriste.com

Boris & Matthew
G/F, 25 Jervois St, Sheung Wan
2854-2934
www.bnm.hk

Gary Kwok Flowers
3/F, Hopewell Centre, 183 Queen's Rd East, Wan Chai
8200-9226
www.garykwok.com

Armani Fiori
1/F, Chater House, 11 Connaught Rd Central
2532-7766

HOW ABOUT A **RELIABLE FLORIST** WHO WILL GET THE JOB DONE ON TIME AND WELL?

Anglo Chinese Florist
See page 349

Juju Flowers
G/F, 4–6 On Wo Lane, Central
2521-9911
www.juju.com.hk

EVERYTHING HOUSE & HOME

Greenfingers Florist Co. Ltd
- G/F, Tung Tze Terrace
  6 Aberdeen St, Central
  2827-8280 / 2827-8923
- G/F, 37 Austin Rd, Tsim Sha Tsui
  2730-5376 / 2735-4878
- 7/F, Mai Tak Ind. Bldg
  221 Wai Yip St, Kwun Tong
  2343-6362
www.greenfingers.com.hk

I'M LOOKING TO GET MY **GARDEN LANDSCAPED**. WHO DO YOU RECOMMEND?

Chun Hing Gardening & Landscaping
1 Wong Nai Chung Rd, Happy Valley
2572-6430 / 2573-5408
www.chunhinggarden.com
Ito Futon
G/F, 46 Morrison Hill Rd, Wan Chai
2845-1138
www.itofuton.com.hk
Artland Nursery
G/F, 7D O'Brien Rd, Wan Chai
2519-9939
www.yp.com.hk/artland
Kalok Horticulture
1K Mang Kung Wor Rd, Sai Kung, New Territories
2719-3039
www.kalokhort.com.hk

WHERE CAN I BUY A **BARBECUE**?

Barbecues Galore
12/F, Horizon Plaza
2 Lee Wing St, Ap Lei Chau
2792-7268
Barbecues, bug repellers, gazebos and accessories from Australia, with prices starting from $2,200. They also sell outdoor heat lamps.
Wing On Department Store
See page 325
See also outdoor furniture stores, page 352.

WHERE CAN I ORDER **GAS** FOR MY **BARBECUE**?

Kwok Fu Gas Co. Ltd
G/F, 1 Eastern St, Sai Ying Pun
2817-8828
Kong Lee Gas Co.
G/F, 217 Hollywood Rd, Sheung Wan
2543-2895
Tai Fat Hong Petroleum Co.
G/F, 320A Des Voeux Rd West, Sai Wan
2540-5249
Kong Fu Gas Co.
G/F, 216 Des Voeux Rd West, Sai Wan
2817-8828

EVERYTHING HOUSE & HOME

WHAT IS A GOOD SOURCE FOR **OUTDOOR FURNITURE**?

Indigo Living
See page 313

Everything Under the Sun (Resource Asia Hong Kong Ltd)
9/F, Horizon Plaza, 2 Lee Wing St, Ap Lei Chau
2554-9088
www.resourceasia.com.hk
*Established in 1996, with offices in Portugal, Hawaii,
Thailand and Australia, Resource Asia carries an
extensive collection of high-quality outdoor furniture and
accessories, including its flagship brand Gloster.*

House & Garden
16/F, Horizon Plaza, 2 Lee Wing St, Ap Lei Chau
2555-8433
*Outdoor furniture, accessories, kitchen and houseware
and more.*

Garden Gallery
• 7/F, Horizon Plaza, 2 Lee Wing St, Ap Lei Chau
  2553-3251
• Office:
  4/F, Leader Ind. Centre, 57–59 Au Pui Wan St
  Fo Tan, New Territories
  2602-8622
www.gardengallery.com.hk
*Imported products from the US, Australia and Europe.
Garden Gallery specialises in outdoor furniture, lighting,
patio heaters, insect killers, barbecues, etc.*

Alberobello Outdoor Accessories
G/F, 5 Gordon Rd, North Point
2979-4444
www.alberobello.com.hk

Aloha Outdoor Furniture
8/F, Horizon Plaza, 2 Lee Wing St, Ap Lei Chau
2552-0036

Movee Boyee Creative Products
• 17/F, Block 1, Golden Dragon Ind. Bldg
  152–160 Tai In Pa Rd, Kwai Chung, New Territories
  2457-5412
• G/F, 23 Po Tung Rd, Sai Kung, New Territories
  2792-7679
• G/F, 741 Tai Kei Leng Chuen
  Yuen Long, New Territories
  2475-2193
www.moveeboyee.com
*Reasonably priced source for outdoor furniture, benches,
sunshades, made in China.*

Warric
4/F, 2–10 Lyndhurst Terrace, Central
2527-7369
www.warric.com
High-end, stylish imported outdoor furniture.

I'D LIKE TO INSTALL **BUG SCREENS** ON
MY WINDOWS. WHERE CAN I DO THIS
INEXPENSIVELY?

Chun Fat Window Engineering
Room I, Wing Kin Ind. Bldg
4–6 Wing Kin Rd, Kwai Hing, Kwai Chung
2423-3601

EVERYTHING HOUSE & HOME

Man Chong Aluminum Decoration
G/F, 604 Shanghai St, Mong Kok
2566-3022

I HAVE A SMALL **TERRACE** THAT WOULD BENEFIT FROM SOME **OUTDOOR WOODEN DECKING**. WHO DO YOU SUGGEST I CONTACT?

Hop Sze Timber Co. Ltd
G/F, 220 Gloucester Rd, Wan Chai
2833-6069
www.hopsze.com
Full range of indoor and outdoor wooden flooring.
Wonderfloor International Ltd
G/F, 271 Lockhart Rd, Wan Chai
2728-9373 / 2360-5175

WHERE DO I FIND A REPUTABLE PLACE TO **BUY A PET**?

Mega Pet
• G/F, 17 Cannon St, Causeway Bay
  2626-0915
• G/F, 149 Tung Choi St, Mong Kok
  2626-0875
www.megapet.com.hk
The pets that they sell apparently come from Australia. The shop also offers pet grooming, immigration, insurance and funeral services. You have to be very careful buying a pet in Hong Kong. In general, we recommend adopting your pet instead (see below).

WHERE CAN I GO TO **ADOPT A PET**?

SPCA
5 Wan Shing St, Wan Chai
2802-0501
www.spca.org.hk
Hong Kong Alleycat Watch
9310-0744 / 6076-1652
www.hkalleycats.com
Hong Kong Dog Rescue
698 Victoria Rd, Pok Fu Lam
2875-2132
www.hongkongdogrescue.com
Adoption Sundays are held at Whiskers and Paws, 2–5pm (see below).
Whiskers N Paws
10/F, Horizon Plaza, 2 Lee Wing St, Ap Lei Chau
2522-6200
www.wnp.com.hk

WHERE CAN I FIND A GOOD STORE FOR **PET SUPPLIES**?

Whiskers N Paws
See above
Dog One Life
• G/F–3/F, 459 Lockhart Rd, Causeway Bay
  3105-5550
• 4/F, EMAX, 1 Trademart Drive, Kowloon Bay
  3105-5904
www.dogonelife.com.hk

EVERYTHING HOUSE & HOME

MOVE IT . BUILD IT . FIX IT . LEASE IT . DESIGN IT . PARTY IT . CLEAN IT . PICTURE IT . DISCOUNT IT . HOUSE IT . FURNISH IT . FRIEND IT . BEST

Best Pedigree Cattery Ltd
G/F, 30 Cannon St, Causeway Bay
2834-1957
Specialising in cat needs. They offer free delivery service with a minimum purhase.

My Dear Pet Shop
G/F, 20 Cannon St, Causeway Bay
2838-0803

Noble Pet Shop
G/F, 1 Yuen Yuen St, Happy Valley
2552-0728
www.noblepetshop.com

Mega Pet
See page 353

Red Carrot
G/F, 189–191 Tung Choi St, Mong Kok
2393-3869
www.redcarrot.com.hk

Classic Pet Shop
8 Cannon St, Causeway Bay
2838-6617

Chinchilla and Pets Shop
Basement, President Shopping Centre
527 Jaffe Rd, Causeway Bay
2895-5502
Good source for hamsters, chinchillas, rabbits and supplies.

Puppy Doggy
G/F, Kennedy Town Bldg
27 Kennedy Town Praya, Kennedy Town
3427-3500
www.puppydoggy.com.hk

Pawette
G/F, 3 Shing Hing St, Central
2537-9999
www.pawette.com.hk
Deluxe pet boutique salon and spa for your VIP—Very Important Pet.

WHERE CAN I ORDER **PET FOOD** BY PHONE OR ONLINE AND HAVE IT DELIVERED?

Whiskers N Paws
10/F, Horizon Plaza, 2 Lee Wing St, Ap Lei Chau
2522-6200
www.wnp.com.hk
Delivery with minimum purchase. Non-HK Island delivery also available. Call for frequency.

Creature Comforts
9773-0372
www.creaturecomforts.com.hk
Offers home delivery of pet food and general medication free to Hong Kong Island.

Three Dog Bakery
LG/F, Yee Fung Bldg
1A Wong Nai Chung Rd, Happy Valley
2836-6760
www.threedog.com.hk
Delivery available at a minimum of $500 purchase.

EVERYTHING HOUSE & HOME

I NEED A REPUTABLE **VETERINARIAN**.

Valley Veterinary Centre
G/F, 34 Yik Yam St, Happy Valley
2575-2389 (24 hours)
Dr Lloyd Kenda is one of the most respected vets in the industry. Services include full surgery, hospitalisation, dentistry, in-house X-ray machine, in-house lab, 24-hour emergency service, house calls, pick-up/delivery (they have their own wagon and driver), registration for all vaccinations and certification. Open every day.

The Ark Veterinary Hospital
LG/F, True Light Bldg, 100 Third St, Sai Ying Pun
2549-2330
www.thearkvets.hk.com
Open 24 hours.

Mid Levels Veterinary Centre
G/F, 28 Mosque St, Mid-Levels
2140-6581 / 7899-2179 a/c 888

The Cat Hospital
G/F, 37 Aberdeen St, Central
2975-8228
www.9lives.com.hk

Island Veterinary Services
G/F, Block B, Discovery Bay Plaza
Discovery Bay, Lantau Island
2987-9003

Australia Veterinary
G/F, 29 Man Tai St, Whampoa Estate, Hung Hom
2330-5252
www.yp.com.hk/australiavet

Animal Medical Centre
• G/F, Wai King Mansions
  22 Aberdeen Main Rd, Aberdeen
  2553-6003
• G/F, 126 Wharf Rd, North Point
  2512-1277
• G/F, 16D Victory Ave, Mong Kok
  2713-4155
The Mong Kok branch is available 24 hours.

Creature Comforts
9773-0372
www.creaturecomforts.com.hk
Dr David Gething makes house calls by appointment, servicing all areas.

I'M INTERESTED IN **HOLISTIC AND NATURAL PET CARE AND SUPPLIES**. ANY SUGGESTIONS?

New Age Shop
G/F, 7 Old Bailey St, Central
2810-8694
www.newageshop.com.hk
Paola Dindo (a.k.a. The Animal Whisperer) has long been known to many as a protector of animals and has helped solve many problems between animals and their human companions. Paola makes house calls. Reservations made through the New Age Shop.

Wise Pet
www.wisepet.com
2652-2337

Tin Hau Pet Hospital
G/F, Wilson Court, 41 King's Rd, Tin Hau
2104-2000
www.5elementsvet.com
Vet clinic and acupuncturist by appointment only.

WHERE CAN I TAKE MY DOG FOR **CANINE EDUCATION/TRAINING**?

Pacific Dog and Training Service Ltd
122 Kam Sheung Rd, Yuen Long, New Territories
The Petzone Training and Practice Centre
G/F, 41 Tai Tsun St, Tai Kok Tsui
2381-8500
Beginner's course in dog grooming teaches pet care and nutrition, bathing and grooming techniques, as well as basic pet training and communication skills.
Whiskers N Paws
10/F, Horizon Plaza, 2 Lee Wing St, Ap Lei Chau
2522-6200
www.wnp.com.hk

IS THERE A **DOG TRAINER** WHO WILL COME TO MY **HOME**?

Jack Suen
2576-2745
Jack will come to your home to train your pet.

WHERE IS A CONVENIENT PLACE ON HONG KONG ISLAND THAT I CAN TAKE MY **DOG FOR A WALK** AND POSSIBLY LET HIM RUN FREE?

Victoria Peak Garden
Located at the very top of Mt. Austin Rd where there is a small car park. From here, walk down through several tiered gardens. This is a popular place for dog enthusiasts and you can usually find somewhere to let your dog run free.
Bowen Rd, Mid-Levels East
Between Magazine Gap Rd and Stubbs Rd, this 4km-long path with gorgeous city views is an ideal place to walk your dog. Keeping your dog on a leash is probably the best as the trail can be quite busy and there have been previous incidents of dog poisoning.
Lugard Rd, The Peak
Another path offering spectacular views from the top of Hong Kong Island. Again this 3km loop can be quite busy and a leash is recommended.
The Promenade, Deep Water Bay to Repulse Bay
Between the north end of Repulse Bay and past Deep Water Bay to just below the country club is a 2km-plus waterside path offering an ideal setting for a walk with your pooch.
Aberdeen Country Park
Pok Fu Lam Country Park
Tai Tam Country Park
With many access points on Hong Kong Island, these three parks link together and offer endless trails and paths. Many of the trails are ideal for letting your dog run free.

EVERYTHING HOUSE & HOME

IS THERE A RELIABLE **PET GROOMING** SERVICE?

Academy of Modern Pet
1/F, Tak Wah Mansion
290–296 Hennessy Rd, Wan Chai
2891-6190
www.agroomer.com

Hong Kong Doggie House
G/F, 5 Peace Ave, Mong Kok
2712-9986
www.hongkongdoggiehouse.com
One of the best and most well-known pet grooming shops in Hong Kong.

Miss Pet II
G/F, 9 Yuk Sau St, Happy Valley
2838-3799

Deedi's Doggies
G/F, Fung Woo Bldg, 65A Sing Woo Rd, Happy Valley
2575-5781

D.O.G.S.
G/F, 16C Shan Kwong Rd, Happy Valley
2838-4811

Dogfather's Mobile Groomer
1/F, Fairview Mansion, 84 Robinson Rd, Mid-Levels
9460-0389
www.dogfathers.com.hk
Jin Hay is certified in Canada, England and Hong Kong. He is an excellent groomer who comes to your house.

Grooming with Tracey Cajilig
2311-3730 / 9709-0193
Home visits only.

Stanley Pet Station
G/F, 10 Wong Ma Kok Rd, Stanley
2813-7979

Whiskers N Paws
10/F, Horizon Plaza, 2 Lee Wing St, Ap Lei Chau
2522-6200
www.wnp.com.hk

Pawette
G/F, 3 Shing Hing St, Central
2537-9999
www.pawette.com.hk

Dogotel
G/F, 124E Argyle St, Mong Kok
2711-0019
www.dogotel.com

WE ARE LEAVING HONG KONG AND WANT TO BRING OUR PET WITH US. WHO CAN HELP US WITH **PET RELOCATION**?

Aeropet
16/F, Fullagar Ind. Bldg, 234 Abereen Main Rd, Aberdeen
2744-3330
www.aero-pet.com
Excellent service. Call Angela Yeung.

Export-A-Pet
G/F, Marina Cove Shopping Centre
380 Hiram's Highway, Sai Kung, New Territories
2358-1774
www.export-a-pet.com
Hong Kong's leading specialist in pet relocation, both coming into and leaving Hong Kong.

WHERE CAN I FIND INFORMATION & REGULATIONS ON **IMPORTING A PET** INTO HONG KONG?

Agriculture and Fisheries Department
Animal Management Centre
5/F, Cheung Sha Wan Government Offices
303 Cheung Sha Wan Rd, Cheung Sha Wan
2708-8885
www.afcd.gov.hk

WHERE CAN I FIND A **GOOD KENNEL**?

Ferndale Kennels
SX-2031 Pak Tam Chung, Sai Kung, New Territories
2792-4642
www.ferndalekennels.com

Kennel Van Dego
1–3 Shek Hang Village, Yan Yee Rd
Sai Kung, New Territories
2792-6889
www.kennelvandego.com

Dogotel
G/F, 124E Argyle St, Mong Kok
2711-0019
www.dogotel.com

WHERE CAN I BUY AN **AQUARIUM** AND SUPPLIES?

Aquatech
G/F, 9 Haven St, Causeway Bay
2119-0229
www.aquatech.com.hk
Ask for Kenny.

King's Aquarium
G/F, 150 Tung Choi St, Mong Kok
2393-3566

Max Aquarium
190 Tung Choi St, Mong Kok
2787-6128
www.maxaqua.com

Ocean World Aquarium
G/F, 207 Tung Choi St, Mong Kok
2381-8382

Rivulet Aquarium Centre
G/F, 205 Tung Choi St, Mong Kok
2787-0398

Tony's Aquarium Co. Ltd
G/F, 26–28 Gordon Rd, Causeway Bay
2571-3700
www.tonyaqua.com

WHERE CAN I FIND SOMEONE TO **SERVICE MY FISH TANK REGULARLY**?

Hoi Tsuen Aquarium Maintenance Co.
7238-9009 (pager)
Mr Tso speaks English and can also build, stock and maintain your custom fish tank regularly in your home.

Aquatech
G/F, 9 Haven St, Causeway Bay
2119-0229
www.aquatech.com.hk

Reef Link Aquatic Engineering
6333-4323
Contact Phyllis Lin.
Tony's Aquarium Co. Ltd
G/F, 26–28 Gordon Rd, Causeway Bay
2571-3700
www.tonyaqua.com

WHERE DO I FIND A GOOD **RESIDENTIAL ARCHITECT**?

Alexander Stuart Designs Ltd
5/F, 15B Wellington St, Central
2526-6155
Alec Stuart has lived and worked in Hong Kong since 1991. He specialises in interior architecture and teaches a course on Hong Kong architecture at the Academy for Performing Arts.
Original Vision
22/F, 88 Gloucester Rd, Wan Chai
2810-9797
www.original-vision.com
Contact Adrian McCarroll.
Stephan James (Plan 3 Asia Ltd)
8/F, Carfield Community Bldg
77 Wyndham St, Central
2525-3037 / 2521-2757
Team HC
10/F, China Merchants Bldg
152–155 Connaught Rd Central
2581-2011
www.teamhc.com
The fabulous husband and wife duo offer architecture and interior design at its best. For residential and commercial. Not for the budget conscious!
MAP
21/F, Asian House, 1 Hennessy Rd, Admiralty
2877-9282
www.maphk.com
Specialising in large commercial projects, MAP also does high-end residential overhaul.
Johnny Li (Li & Co. Design Ltd)
4/F, Yuet Lai Bldg
43–55 Wyndham St, Central
2526-8326 / 9400-1729
Specialty in residential and retail/hospitality architecture and interiors.

WHERE CAN I FIND A GOOD **INTERIOR DESIGNER**?

Team HC
10/F, China Merchants Bldg
152–155 Connaught Rd Central
2581-2011
www.teamhc.com
Kenneth Ko Designs Ltd
15/F, On Wah Bldg
41–43 Au Pui Wan St
Fo Tan, New Territories
2604-9494
www.kennethko.com

Deborah Oppenheimer Interior Design
2592-7415 / 9459-0704
www.doid.com.hk
With an established reputation for high-end residential interior design, Deborah favours clean lines and combining different influences for an elegant, unpredictable look. She covers both structural and decorative elements.

Nicole Cromwell Interior Design Ltd
2521-9299
www.nicolecromwell.com

candace.collective
1/F, 171–177 Hollywood Rd, Central
6706-7921
www.candacecollective.com
Specialises in funky loft designs on a budget, bringing a New York vibe to Hong Kong.

Alex Cary & Associates Interior Design
19/F, Rice Merchant Bldg
77–78 Connaught Rd West, Sheung Wan
3422-8126
www.alexcaryinteriors.com

Leigh Chiu Designs
13/F, Ying Point Bldg
69–71 Peel St, Central
2559-1250 / 9506-3222
www.leighchiudesigns.com

Emma Hann Interior Design
2812-0400 / 6686-7779
emhannid@gmail.com
Residential and commercial interior designer who has lots of experience. Very practical, edgy, creative and easy to work with.

Toland Sherriff (Domain)
27/F, Yan's Tower
27 Wong Chuk Hang, Aberdeen
9880-8641
toland@netvigator.com
Specialises in residential interior decorating. Clean contemporary meets modern glamour.

Jason Caroline Design
14/F, 39 Wellington St, Central
2517-7510
www.jasoncarolinedesign.com
Specialises in high-end residential architecture and interior design.

Victoria Ho (Lagoon Design Ltd)
9491-3133
Specialises in residential and commercial interior design.

Obelisk Design Co. Ltd
15/F, Keybond Comm. Bldg
38 Ferry St, Jordan
3188-9818
www.obelisk.com.hk
Specialises in residential and commercial interior design. Versatile and able to accommodate different styles.

EVERYTHING HOUSE & HOME

WHO CAN HELP ME **DESIGN AND PLAN MY KITCHEN**?

Kitench Leader Ltd
G/F, 13 Leighton Rd, Causeway Bay
2836-0280
www.kitench.com
Ask for Harris or Eva.

Koda Kitchen
22/F, Lucky Bldg, 39–41 Wellington St, Central
2899-2878
www.kodakitchen.com

Via
See page 314

Sigmann
G/F, Siu On Centre, 188 Lockhart Rd, Wan Chai
2828-3438

East Asia Giotto
G/F, Yue Xiu Bldg, 160–174 Lockhart Rd, Wan Chai
2151-0806
www.eagiotto.com

Great Treasure Ltd
2/F, Amber Comm. Bldg
70–74 Morrison Hill Rd, Causeway Bay
3118-7449 / 3118-2449
www.cristal.com.hk

Royal Kitchen Design Co. Ltd
G/F, 169 Wong Nai Chung Rd, Happy Valley
2805-6128
www.haecker-kuechen.com.hk

Kitchen Design
2/F, Lucky Plaza, 315–321 Lockhart Rd, Wan Chai
2572-5727

HOW ABOUT FOR **REDESIGNING MY BATHROOM**?

The Professional Depot
G/F, 371 Lockhart Rd, Wan Chai
3106-6008

Pacific Bath Collection
G/F, 189 Lockhart Rd, Wan Chai
2528-2230
www.pacificbuilding.com.hk

Colour Living
G/F, 333 Lockhart Rd, Wan Chai
2510-2666
www.colourliving.com

WHO CAN PUT A **FIREPLACE** IN MY HOME?

Design & Distribution Link Ltd
G/F, Ruttonjee Centre, 11 Duddell St, Central
3113-8728 / 2868-0991

I'M MOVING INTO A NEW HOUSE. WHERE CAN I FIND A **FENG SHUI MASTER / CONSULTANT**?

Kenneth Luk
130 Austin Rd, Tsim Sha Tsui
8101-8078
Kenneth Luk is a Feng Shui Master who has been practising for over 20 years. He offers consultations in both Cantonese and English.

Raymond Lo
12/F, Star House, 3 Salisbury Rd, Tsim Sha Tsui
2736-9568 / 9024-9438
www.raymond-lo.com
Popularly know as "Feng Shui Lo", Raymond Lo is a professional feng shui consultant, author and lecturer. He has appeared on numerous TV shows worldwide, written newspaper columns and lectured at universities and elsewhere. He also teaches feng shui courses.

Master Pak Wai
4/F, Hang Shun Bldg
33 Boundary St, Jordan
6056-4618 / 9056-4618
www.pakwai.com

Peter So Man-Fung
12/F, Rightful Centre, 11–12 Tak Hing St, Jordan
2780-3675

Chow Hong-Ming Fortune Telling ....
8/F, Prosperous Comm. Bldg
54–58 Jardine's Bazaar, Causeway Bay
2895-1887

Lee Sing Tong
27/F, Richmond Comm. Bldg
107–111 Argyle St, Mong Kok
3188-9091

WHERE CAN I FIND A GOOD **ALL-PURPOSE HANDYMAN**?

Eddy Wong (Wong Kwong Kee Decoration)
2571-2385 / 9080-7769

Jackson
9096-3337

Herman
9486-4914
Herman speaks English and is good for all basic maintenance jobs, from hanging heavy mirrors to fixing leaks to painting. He can also source extra labour for larger jobs.

Tom Hardcastle
2865-7060
Since 1993, Tom has specialised in electrical work, plumbing, carpentry and general maintenance.

Tony
9518-8311
Tony speaks English and is a reasonably priced and reliable handyman and contractor.

Anthony Alexandrou
6900-7501
Aussie offering good rates for handyman and property maintenance service.

Ezyfix Home Improvement Experts
G/F, 18 Clarence Terrace, Sai Wan
2522-6226
www.ezyfix.com.hk

CD&I
5/F, Lan Kwai House, 6 Lan Kwai Fong, Central
2815-7929
www.cdihk.com
Ask for Mark.

EVERYTHING HOUSE & HOME

MOVE IT . BUILD IT . FIX IT . LEASE IT . DESIGN IT . PARTY IT . CLEAN IT . PICTURE IT . DISCOUNT IT . HOUSE IT . HANDY IT . FURNISH IT

WHERE CAN I FIND A RELIABLE **CONTRACTOR** TO CARRY OUT MY HOME RENOVATIONS?

CAD Contracting
6/F, Federal Bldg, 369 Lockhart Rd, Wan Chai
2891-7733 / 9099-8988
Very good quality contractor, speak with Kane Chan.

CAT Contractors
9236-8864
Reasonably priced, speak with James Moon.

Light & Colour Ltd
10/F, Workingberg Comm. Bldg
41–47 Marble Rd, North Point
2811-0328 / 9101-3340
Owen Ngau speaks English and has a graphic design background. He has a good sense of design and is very good at getting things done efficiently.

Wellform Decoration Engineering
9/F, Kwai On Factory Estate
103–113 Tai Lin Pai Rd, Kwai Chung, New Territories
2663-2751
Reliable, good value, tidy, creative and good design and engineering. Ask for Ah Kwong. You must speak Cantonese or have someone reliable who does to deal with this contractor, but they are very good.

Kin's Building Materials & Contracting Ltd
19/F, Shinyam Comm. Bldg
163 Johnston Rd, Wan Chai
2575-4457
Contact Felix Chow.

Kuen Lee Contracting Co. Ltd
9/F, Block A, Wing Hin Factory Bldg
31–33 Ng Fong St, San Po Kong
2396-0985
Contact Matthew Leung.

Opus Design
18/F, Lee West Comm. Bldg
408–412 Hennessy Rd, Wan Chai
2121-1497 / 9733-7328
www.opusdesign.com.hk

Susana Lau
9277-4745
Susana is a very reasonably priced contractor who speaks English and can do anything. She is also very busy!

WHERE CAN I FIND A GOOD **PAINTER**?

Golding Decoration
9074-5231
Colin Golding has 12 years of painting experience in Hong Kong.

Ryan Rufus
6735-9076
ryanrufus@gmail.com
Fabulous reliable Australian painter and odd-job man. Competitive rates. Mainly covers Clear Water Bay and Sai Kung area.

Tung Tai Interior Design and Decoration
2/F, Johnston Court, 30 Johnston Rd, Wan Chai
2380-9615
www.repaintjob.com

EVERYTHING HOUSE & HOME

Unitek HK
9/F, Empire Land Comm. Centre
81–85 Lockhart Rd, Wan Chai
2984-9381
www.unitekhk.com

Mr Hammer
G/F, 11 North St, Kennedy Town
2816-6383

WHO DO I CALL TO GET AIR-CONDITIONERS INSTALLED OR FIXED?

Ming Service Centre
Canny Ind. Bldg, 33 Tai Yau St, San Po Kong
9077-5053
Reliable, honest specialist in air-conditioning, electrical and water works. Speak to Ming.

Alan Engineering
G/F, 14 Merlin St, North Point
2887-6638
In addition to air-conditioners, also a good source for an electrician or plumber.

Whirlpool
14/F, Wilson Logistics Centre
24–28 Kung Yip St, Kwai Chung, New Territories
2406-9138
www.whirlpool.com.hk

Wah Shun Electric
G/F, King's Centre Shopping Arcade
193 King's Rd, North Point
2566–2166

Hang Lee Air Conditioning & Electrical Engineering Co.
G/F, 38 Sheung Sha Wan Rd, Sham Shui Po
2725-7565 / 9097-5292
www.hang-lee.com.hk

Johnny Electrical & Decoration Co.
2729-1516 / 9097-5292

WHERE CAN I FIND A 24-HOUR ELECTRICIAN/PLUMBER?

Tsang Sui Kee
G/F, 66A Tung Lo Wan Rd, Causeway Bay
2824-2723 / 9078-3836
www.locksmith-hk.com
Locksmith, plumber, electrician and welder.

General Electric Shop
2522-6266

WHERE CAN I FIND A LOCKSMITH?

Chat Kee Locksmith
G/F, 138 Pei Ho Rd, Sham Shui Po
2562-3078
24-hour service.

Leung Pui Kee
G/F, 116 Wellington St, Central
2544-3272
Contact Ms Wong.

Kong Yung Kee Locksmith
18 Queen's Rd Central
2522-9800

Wai Kee Locksmithing Works
G/F, 370 Des Voeux Rd West, Sai Wan
9031-5691 / 2549-1178
Contact Mr Wong.
Mr Locksmith
G/F, 14 Merlin St, North Point
2887-6638
A to Go Chi Shun Locksmiths
G/F, 522 Lockhart Rd, Causeway Bay
2832-4125
www.atogochishun.biz.com.hk
24-hour locksmith.

WHERE CAN I FIND A GOOD **HARDWARE STORE**?

Yuen Tung Co.
G/F, 36 Lyndhurst Terrace, Central
2851-6811
*Conveniently located shop with a bit of everything, from
hardware items to a 24-hour electrical repair service.*
Chow Shing Metal Co.
G/F, 112 Thomson Rd, Wan Chai
2573-1378
Modern Home Decoration Supplies Co.
G/F, 254 Lockhart Rd, Wan Chai
2511-5228

WHERE DO I FIND A **GOOD PAINT STORE**?

Dai Cheung Paints & Hardware
98 Wharf Rd, North Point
2887-2339
Cheong Fat Ho ....
G/F, Tung Wai Comm. Bldg
22 Fleming Rd, Wan Chai
2507-2420
www.cheongfatho.iyp.hk
Yuen Fat Ho
G/F, 77 Hollywood Rd, Central
2546-8020
Tung Shing Metal ....
G/F, 132–134 Jervois St, Sheung Wan
2544-5239
Berger Paints ....
6/F, 239–241 Wing Lok St, Sheung Wan
2544-3768
www.bergerpaints.com

WHERE DO I BUY ENVIRONMENTALLY FRIENDLY NATURAL PAINT?

Ecotec Natural Paint Ltd ....
• G/F, 385 Lockhart Rd, Wan Chai
  2847-3378/ 2847-3379
• 5/F, Premier Home Forum, HITEC
  1 Trademart Drive, Kowloon Bay
  2847-3379
www.ecozmo.com
*Manufactured in Germany using only safe, non-toxic
raw materials with no paint odour. A good selection
of colours for indoor as well as outdoor paints, glaze,
wood stain and wax.*

Natural Living ....

G/F, Yue On Comm. Bldg
385 Lockhart Rd, Wan Chai
2847-3378
www.naturalliving.hk
In addition to paint, they also carry a large range of natural and organic products for body and home.

Berger Paints ....

6/F, 239–241 Wing Lok St, Sheung Wan
2544-3768
www.bergerpaints.com

I'M LOOKING FOR **PROPERTY AGENTS** WHO WILL UNDERSTAND EXPATRIATE NEEDS AND EXPECTATIONS. WHERE SHOULD I START?

Habitat
19/F, Time Centre, 53–55 Hollywood Rd, Central
2869-9069 / 9779-0233
www.habitat-property.com

Landscope
31/F, Hopewell Centre, 183 Queen's Rd East, Wan Chai
2866-0022
www.landscope.com

Savills
• 23/F, Two Exchange Square
  8 Connaught Place, Central
  2842-4400
• 21/F, Tower 6, The Gateway
  9 Canton Rd, Tsim Sha Tsui
  2378-8688
• 13/F, Tower 2, Grand Century Place
  193 Prince Edward Rd West, Kowloon
  2622-9222
• 6/F, Block A, Discovery Bay Plaza
  Discovery Bay, Lantau Island
  9287-1919
www.savills.com.hk

Jones Lang LaSalle
28/F, One Pacific Place, 88 Queensway, Admiralty
2846-5000
www.joneslanglasalle.com.hk

Colliers
57/F, Central Plaza, 18 Harbour Rd, Wan Chai
2828-9888
www.colliers.com/markets/hongkong

Asia Pacific Properties
14/F, Wilson House, 19–27 Wyndham St, Central
2281-7800
www.asiapacificproperties.com

Stately Home
G/F, 49A Bonham Rd, Mid-Levels
www.statelyhome.com.hk

Sallmanns Residential
29/F, Universal Trade Centre, 3–5 Arbuthnot Rd, Central
2537-5338
www.sallmannsres.com

Knight Frank
4/F, Shui On Centre, 6–8 Harbour Rd, Wan Chai
2877-5511
www.knightfrank.com

Landmark Asia Realty
14/F, Times Square, Tower 1
1 Matheson St, Causeway Bay
3571-9122 / 2506-1008
www.landmarkasia.com.hk

Manks Quarters Ltd
2 Kennedy Terrace, Mid-Levels
2522-5114
www.manksquarters.com

Property Man
2869-5128
www.hongkongpropertyman.com

Home Life Property
8/F, Silverstrand Mart
2 Silver Cape Rd, Clear Water Bay
2719-0606
www.homelife.com.hk
Specialists in Sai Kung and Clear Water Bay.

Island Property
7/F, Arion Comm. Centre
2–12 Queen's Rd West, Sheung Wan
2155-3138
www.islandproperty.com.hk

Lifestyle Homes
5/F, Discovery Bay Plaza, Discovery Bay, Lantau Island
2914-0888
*Discovery Bay property agent offering the largest
portfolio of sales and rentals of live-aboard house boats.*

WHERE CAN I FIND AN ESTABLISHED **REAL
ESTATE** COMPANY THAT CAN SHOW ME A LOT OF
PROPERTIES IN DIFFERENT PRICE RANGES?

Centaline Property Agency Ltd
Head office:
5/F, New World Tower, Tower 1, 18 Queen's Rd Central
2521-8402
web.centanet.com

Midland Realty
• G/F, 23 Queen's Rd East, Admiralty
  2921-8228
• G/F, 87 Wan Chai Rd, Wan Chai
  2923-5851
• G/F, 6 Cambridge Rd, Kowloon Tong
  2926-7938
www.midland.com.hk/eng
See website for more locations.

LJ Hooker
G/F, Cameo Court, 63–69 Caine Rd, Mid-Levels
2869-8822
www.ljhooker.com.hk

Century 21
G/F, 18 Arbuthnot Rd, Central
2850-6363
www.homesearch.com.hk

Ricacorp
Head office:
13/F, Centre Point, 181–185 Gloucester Rd, Wan Chai
2506-0008 / 2574-5732
www.ricacorp.com

House Hunters
7/F, Wyndham Place, 40–44 Wyndham St, Central
2869-1001
www.househunters.com.hk

Full Harvest Property
15/F, Nam Fung Tower, 173 Des Voeux Rd Central
2873-0055
www.fhproperties.com.hk

Hong Kong Property
- Island South / The Peak:
  16E Shouson Hill Rd, Shouson Hill
  2923-7355 / 2813-1318
- Admiralty, Mid-Levels:
  Moonstar Court, 2A–2G Star St, Wan Chai
  2922-3188 / 2524-3950
- Happy Valley:
  G/F, 165 Wong Nai Chung Rd, Happy Valley
  2923-7323 / 2573-0768 / 2923-5633
- Mid-Levels West:
  G/F, 46–48 Robinson Rd, Mid-Levels
  2803-0688 / 2921-2668
www.hkp.com.hk

WHERE CAN I FIND AN ESTABLISHED
INTERNATIONAL RELOCATION COMPANY THAT ALSO
DOES **LOCAL MOVES**?

Crown Relocations
Crown Worldwide Bldg, 9–11 Yuen On St
Siu Lek Yuen, Sha Tin, New Territories
2636-8388
www.crownrelo.com/hongkong

Santa Fe Transport International
18/F, C.C. Wu Bldg
302–308 Hennessy Rd, Wan Chai
2574-6204
www.santaferelo.com

Asian Tigers
17/F, 3 Lockhart Rd, Wan Chai
2528-1384
www.asiantigers-hongkong.com

Relocasia
13/F, Gee Tung Cheong Ind. Bldg
4 Fung Yip St, Chai Wan
2976-9969
www.relocasia.com

Four Winds International Removers
5/F, Len Shing Ind. Bldg
4A Kung Ngam Village Rd, Shau Kei Wan
2885-9666
www.agsfourwinds.com

Links Moving
11/F, Champion Bldg
287–291 Des Voeux Rd Central
2366-6700
www.linksmoving.asia

Prudential International Moving
9/F, Block B, New Trade Plaza
6 On Ping St, Sha Tin, New Territories
2618-6888
www.prudentialmovers.com

EVERYTHING HOUSE & HOME

WHERE CAN I FIND A **MAN WITH A TRUCK** TO MOVE A FEW PIECES OF FURNITURE AND OTHER SMALL ITEMS?

Dhillon's Logistics & Removal
9853-3476
dhillon3@netvigator.com
Mr Kwai
9779-7659
Murphy Luk .... 🏷️
9436-1883
Easygoing and reasonably priced, Murphy will also help you to physically move the item. Sundays only.

I AM LOOKING FOR A REASONABLE **LOCAL MOVING COMPANY**. ANY IDEAS?

Yiu Ming Removal Co. Ltd .... 🏷️
8/F, Chai Wan Ind. City, Phase 2
70 Wing Tai Rd, Chai Wan
2887-8605 / 2976-9841
Inexpensive, trustworthy, reliable local mover.
Tai Kow Lo Transportation Co. Ltd
G/F, 43 Fuk Chak St, Tai Kok Tsui
2392-7108
www.yp.com.hk/taikowlo/
Ask for Miss Leung.
Jumbo Transportation Ltd
1/F, Block B, Vincent Mansion
18–20 Mercury St, North Point
2578-9669
www.yp.com.hk/jumbomovers
A good local mover, but they do require supervision, especially with fragile items. Contact Michael Chang.

I'M LOOKING FOR **MINI STORAGE** THAT I CAN HAVE REGULAR ACCESS TO.

The Store House Ltd
2548-4049
www.thestorehouse.com.hk
Ask for Joel Wai–he is very busy, but very helpful.
Store Friendly
24-hour hotline: 8202-0811 / 3579-8886
www.store-friendly.com
Hong Kong Storage
2817-6486
www.hongkongstorage.com
SC Storage
8177-7778 / 8204-4916
www.scstorage.com
RoomPlus (Self Storage) Ltd
ROOM+ Kwun Tong Bldg
338 Kwun Tong Td, Kwun Tong
2331-7331
www.roomplus.com.hk
Selfstorasia
13/F, Gee Tung Cheong Ind. Bldg
4 Fung Yip St, Chai Wan
2976-9969
www.selfstorasia.com

EVERYTHING HOUSE & HOME

I'M LOOKING FOR A **SERVICED APARTMENT**/SHORT-TERM LET. WHERE SHOULD I START LOOKING?

Kush
Office:
• G/F, 111 High St, Sai Wan
Locations:
• 255 Des Voeux Rd West, Sai Ying Pun
• 222 Hollywood Rd, SoHo
• 111 High St, Sai Wan
2850-5866
www.kushliving.com

Shama
• 2/F, 26 Peel St, Central
   2103-1713
• G/F, 52 Hollywood Rd, Central
   2103-1713
• G/F, 8 Hospital Rd, Mid-Levels
   3607-9000
• G/F, 1–3 Sik On St, Wan Chai
   2865-9889
• 7/F, 8 Russell St, Causeway Bay
   2202-5555
• 151 King's Rd, North Point
   3788-2888
• 74–78 Nathan Rd, Tsim Sha Tsui
   3513-0088
www.shama.com
An established serviced apartment chain, offering well-appointed units, good service and amenities that are consistent through each location.

Atria ....🌿
Office:
• 11/F, Carfield Comm. Bldg
   75–77 Wyndham St, Central
Boutique Studios:
• Aberdeen St, Central
• Glenealy, Central
• Staunton St, Central
• Lan Kwai Fong, Central
• Wellington St, Central
Green Residences:
• Green Span – 19 Lyndhurst Terrace, Central
• Shelley Vert – 11 Shelley St, Central
• Culture Vulture – 13 Old Bailey St, Central
• Robin's Nest – 19 Gage St, Central
• Boho Chic – 29–31 Aberdeen St, SoHo
3119-8250
www.atriastudios.hk
www.atriaresidencies.hk
Atria offers boutique studios and green residences for eco-friendly customers.

Ovolo
2 Arbuthnot Rd, Central
3105-2600
www.home2home.hk/ovolo/ovolo_overview.html

Four Seasons Place
8 Finance St, Central
3196-8228
www.fsphk.com

Pacific Place Apartments
Pacific Place, 88 Queensway, Admiralty
2844-8361
www.pacificplace.com.hk

Hong Kong Parkview
88 Tai Tam Reservoir Rd, Tai Tam
2812-3456
www.hongkongparkview.com

The Repulse Bay – De Ricou Serviced Apartments
109 Repulse Bay Rd, Repulse Bay
2292-2888
www.therepulsebay.com

The Stanley Oriental Hotel
2/F, 90B Stanley Main St, Stanley
2899-1688
www.stanleyorientalhotel.com.hk
Stylish interiors with gorgeous views, away from the hustle and bustle, for short term let, or to put up out-of-town guests.

Ice House
38 Ice House St, Central
2836-7333
www.icehouse.com.hk

The HarbourView Place
Elements Mall, 1 Austin Rd West, Kowloon
3718-8000
www.harbourviewplace.com

New World Apartments
24 Salisbury Rd, Tsim Sha Tsui
2734-8989
www.newworldapartments.com.hk

Eaton House Furnished Apartments
• 3–5 Wan Chai Gap Rd, Wan Chai
• 100 Blue Pool Rd, Happy Valley
• 4H Village Rd, Happy Valley
3182-7000 / 8109-9683
www.eatonhousehk.com

The Gateway
23/F, Prudential Tower, Harbour City
25 Canton Rd, Tsim Sha Tsui
2119-3000
www.gatewayapartments.com.hk

The V
• 1 Castle Rd, Mid-Levels
  3602-2388
• 180 Jaffe Rd, Wan Chai
  3602-2388
• 9 Yee Wo St, Causeway Bay
  3602-2388
• 25 Tung Lo Wan Rd, Causeway Bay
  3140-8408
• 68 Sing Woo Rd, Happy Valley
  3602-2388
• 535 Canton Rd, West Kowloon
  2332-5560
www.thev.hk

The Putman
202 Queen's Rd Central
2233-2288 / 2233-2233
www.theputman.com
Ultra-modern "long-term hotel" apartment suites for the discerning guest.

I'VE GOT SOME HIP FRIENDS COMING INTO TOWN. CAN YOU RECOMMEND ANY **BOUTIQUE HOTELS**?

JIA
1–5 Irving St, Causeway Bay
3196-9000
www.jiahongkong.com

Hotel LKF
33 Wyndham St, Central
3518-9688
www.hotel-lkf.com.hk

The Upper House
Pacific Place, 88 Queensway, Admiralty
3698-1000 / 2918-1838
www.upperhouse.com

The Mira Hong Kong
118 Nathan Road, Tsim Sha Tsui
2368-1111
www.themirahotel.com
New modern contemporary décor with plenty of restaurants to offer in the middle of a shopping locality. They allow you to choose your room style and colour scheme from the four they have to offer.

W Hotel
1 Austin Road West, Kowloon
3717-2222
www.starwoodhotels.com

I'VE FRIENDS COMING IN FROM OUT OF TOWN. WHERE CAN THEY FIND GOOD VALUE, **BUDGET ACCOMMODATION**?

Helena May
35 Garden Rd, Central
2522-6766
www.helenamay.com
Very reasonably priced accommodation for women only, with shared bathroom and includes Continental breakfast. Co-ed studio suites available in a separate wing. Non-members welcome with a small additional fee. For more information, contact Phoebe Wong.

Mingle Place
• At The Eden
  148 Wellington St, Central
  2850-6289
• On The Wing
  105 Wing Lok St, Sheung Wan
  2581-2329
• By The Park
  143 Wan Chai Rd, Wan Chai
  2838-1109
• With The Star
  139 Wan Chai Rd, Wan Chai
  2838-1109
www.mingleplace.com

Ice House
38 Ice House St, Central
2836-7333
www.icehouse.com.hk

The Garden View – YWCA .... 🏷
1 Macdonnell Rd, Mid-Levels
2877-3737
hotel.ywca.org.hk

Bishop Lei International House .... 🏷
4 Robinson Rd, Mid-Levels
2868-0828
www.bishopleihtl.com.hk

Sohotel .... 🏷
139 Bonham Strand, Sheung Wan
2851-8818
www.sohotelhongkong.com

Butterfly .... 🏷
• Butterfly on Prat
  21 Prat Ave, Tsim Sha Tsui
  3962-8889
• Butterfly on Morrison
  39 Morrison Hill Rd, Wan Chai
  3962-8333
www.butterflyhk.com

WHERE IS A GOOD PLACE TO BUY **BARGAIN
ELECTRONICS AND MOBILE PHONES**?

Apliu St, Sham Shui Po
Between Nam Cheong St and Yen Chow St
Beware of pickpockets, con-artists, and faux items!
See also EVERYTHING SHAM SHUI PO, page 189 – 191.

WHERE CAN I FIND A REPUTABLE SHOP FOR
CAMERAS AND VIDEO EQUIPMENT?

A&A Audio and Video Centre Ltd
L1, Pacific Place, 88 Queensway, Admiralty
2845-3670

Johnny's Photo and Video Supply Ltd
1/F, Admiralty Centre, Tower 2
18 Harcourt Rd, Admiralty
2877-2227
www.johnnysphoto.com.hk

Universal Audio & Video Centre
• L1, IFC Mall, 8 Finance St, Central
  2801-6411
• L1, Pacific Place, 88 Queensway, Admiralty
  2801-6422
www.universal-av.com

Broadway
7/F – 9/F, Times Square, Causeway Bay
2506-1330 / 2506-0228 / 3426-4098
www.ibroadway.com.hk
Many locations.

Fortress
• G/F, Yu Sung Boon Bldg, 107 Des Voeux Rd Central
  2544-4385
• 2/F, Shun Tak Centre
  200 Connaught Rd Central, Sheung Wan
  3152-3111
www.fortress.com.hk
Many locations.

EVERYTHING HOUSE & HOME

Best Hong Kong
2/F, Plaza Hollywood, 3 Lung Poon St, Diamond Hill
2326-9563
Megastore carrying appliances, electronics, homeware, and much more.

WHERE IS A **GOOD PLACE TO START FOR A HOME ENTERTAINMENT SYSTEM**?

Fortress
See page 373
Broadway
7/F–9/F, Times Square, Causeway Bay
2506-1330 / 2506-0228 / 3426-4098
www.ibroadway.com.hk
Best Hong Kong
2/F, Plaza Hollywood, 3 Lung Poon St, Diamond Hill
2326-9563
Chung Yuen
7/F, Times Square, 1 Matheson St, Causeway Bay
2506-3515
www.chungyuen.com.hk

WHERE CAN I GET A SERIOUS **HOME AUDIO SYSTEM**?

Bang & Olufsen
- L2, Pacific Place, 88 Queensway, Admiralty
  2918-0007
- 3/F, One Hysan Ave, Causeway Bay
  2882-1782
- 3/F, Ocean Terminal, Harbour City
  Canton Rd, Tsim Sha Tsui
  2730-6844
- LG1, Festival Walk, 80 Tat Chee Ave, Kowloon Tong
  2265-7860
www.bang-olufsen.com
Bose
- G/F, Tak Shing Bldg, 20 Des Voeux Rd Central
  3100-0080
- 8/F, Times Square, 1 Matheson St, Causeway Bay
  2836-3181
- 2/F, Elements Mall, 1 Austin Rd West, Kowloon
  2196-8195
- 3/F, Ocean Centre, Harbour City
  Canton Rd, Tsim Sha Tsui
  2688-6887
- 6/F, New Town Plaza, Phase 1
  Sha Tin Centre St, Sha Tin, New Territories
  3422-8298
www.bose.hk
Audio Evidence
The Sound Chamber
4/F, Chekiang First Bank Centre, 1 Duddell St, Central
2418-0088
www.audioevidence.com
King's Audio
25/F, Capital Trade Centre, 62 Tsun Yip St, Kwun Tong
2345-2323
www.kingsaudio.com.hk

EVERYTHING HOUSE & HOME

New Lee Tung Audio Visual Engineering Service Co.
17/F, Radiant Centre, 7 Cannon St, Causeway Bay
2147-0696
www.newleetungav.com
Call before you go as hours are sometimes sporadic.

WHICH ARE SOME OF THE MAIN **COMPUTER COMPANIES** IN HONG KONG?

Acer
• Acer Care Service Centre
  18/F, Prosperity Place, 6 Seng Yip St, Kwun Tong
  2520-2000
• 2/F, Mong Kok Computer Centre
  8 Nelson St, Mong Kok
  2771-3326
www.acer.com.hk

Apple
Communications & Services Experts Ltd
• 6/F, Stanhope Plaza, 734 King's Rd, Quarry Bay
• 11/F, Wai Fung Plaza, 664 Nathan Road, Mong Kok
2915-7883
www.appleclub.com.hk

Ultimate PC & Mac Gallery
• G/F, World Trust Tower, 50 Stanley St, Central
  2899-2239
• G/F, 99 Des Voeux Rd Central
  2110-9009
• 11/F, Windsor House, 311 Gloucester Rd, Causeway Bay
  2881-1069 / 2881-6320
• G/F, Devon House, Taikoo Place
  979 King's Rd, Quarry Bay
  3107-0804
• G/F, 29A Cameron Rd, Tsim Sha Tsui
  3422-3788
• 2/F, Mongkok Computer Centre
  8 Nelson St, Mong Kok
  3591-8901
www.upcmac.com.hk

Dell
2969-3113
www.dell.com.hk

Hewlett-Packard
Customer Care Service Centre
25/F, Cityplaza 1, 18 Taikoo Shing Rd, Tai Koo
2599-7000
www.hp.com.hk
Includes Compaq.

IBM
14/F, Chinachem Exchange Square
1 Hoi Wan St, Quarry Bay
2825-6580 / 2516-3939
www.ibm.com/hk

Sony
2/F, Man Yee Bldg, 60–68 Des Voeux Rd Central
2882-0101
www.sony.com.hk

Fuji Xerox
2513-2513
www.fujixerox.com.hk

EVERYTHING HOUSE & HOME

DO YOU HAVE ANY RECOMMENDATIONS FOR
GOOD **COMPUTER MALLS**?

Wan Chai Computer Centre
130 Hennessy Rd, Wan Chai
Golden Shopping Centre
94A Yen Chow St, Sham Shui Po
The In Square
10/F – 12/F, Windsor House
311 Gloucester Rd, Causeway Bay
www.windsorhouse.hk
298 Computer Zone
298 Hennessy Rd, Wan Chai
Star Computer City
2/F, Star House
3 Salisbury Rd, Tsim Sha Tsui
2730-4382
Mong Kok Computer Centre
8 Nelson St, Mong Kok
*Three floors of independent computer shops carrying
hardware, software, and accessories. Very reasonable
prices and fairly reliable.*

WHAT ARE SOME OF THE **BETTER SHOPS** AT **WINDSOR
HOUSE'S IN SQUARE COMPUTER MALL**?

Vertex Technology Co. Ltd
11/F, Windsor House
311 Gloucester Rd, Causeway Bay
2576-4869
www.vertexhk.com
Ultimate PC & MAC Gallery Ltd
11/F, Windsor House
311 Gloucester Rd, Causeway Bay
2881-1069 / 2881-6320
www.upcmac.com.hk
DG Lifestyle Store
11/F, Windsor House
311 Gloucester Rd, Causeway Bay
2504-4122
www.dg-lifestyle.com
Sunlite Computronics Ltd
11/F, Windsor House
311 Gloucester Rd, Causeway Bay
2576-2067
www.sunlite.hk
CD Express
11/F, Windsor House
311 Gloucester Rd, Causeway Bay
2881-0171
www.cdxpress.com.hk
Specialising in computer games.
2C Co. Ltd
10/F, Windsor House
311 Gloucester Rd, Causeway Bay
2504-2128
www.2c.hk
Computer accessories and software.

EVERYTHING HOUSE & HOME

WHERE IS A GOOD PLACE TO BUY SOFTWARE?

Advance Software Ltd
2/F, Wan Chai Computer Centre
130 Hennessy Rd, Wan Chai
2591-5201
www.advance-software.net
A great shop used by pros and students alike.
See computer malls, previous page.

WHERE CAN I BUY APPLE COMPUTERS AND GADGETS?

New Vision Technology Ltd
UG/F, Winway Bldg, 50 Wellington St, Central
3157-0979
www.newvision.com.hk
Ultimate PC & Mac Gallery Ltd
See page 375
DG Lifestyle Store
• L2, IFC Mall, 8 Finance St, Central
  2295-4488
• 2/F, Wan Chai Computer Centre
  130 Hennessy Rd, Wan Chai
  3107-0588
• 9/F, Times Square, 1 Matheson St, Causeway Bay
  2506-1338
• 11/F, Windsor House
  311 Gloucester Rd, Causeway Bay
  2504-4122
• L5, MegaBox, 38 Wang Chiu Rd, Kowloon Bay
  2359-0005
• 6/F, New Town Plaza, Phase 1
  Sha Tin Centre St, Sha Tin, New Territories
  2692-2488
• G/F, Citywalk
  1 Yeung Uk Rd, Tsuen Wan, New Territories
  2941-0182
• L5, Terminal 2, Hong Kong International Airport
  2769-1288
www.dg-lifestyle.com

I WANT TO SET UP A WEBSITE. WHO DO YOU SUGGEST I CONTACT FOR WEB-DESIGN AND HOSTING?

Base Creative Consultants
16/F, Oriental Crystal Comm. Bldg
46 Lyndhurst Terrace, Central
2530-8164
www.basecreate.com
Hong Kong Hosting
www.hkhosting.com
Professional web hosting services from $100.
J-Design
6493-4662
www.j-design.com.hk
Pachosting
2575-0575
www.pachosting.com

EVERYTHING HOUSE & HOME

WHERE CAN I CREATE A **PERSONAL WEBSITE OF MY WEDDING**?

Merry-me.com
6296-7867
www.merry-me.com
Contact Christine to create a stylish website to share your beautiful memories with friends and family.
Happy Moments
3116-1508
www.happymoments.net

I WROTE MY PROMOTIONAL MATERIAL; NOW I NEED A **GRAPHIC DESIGNER**. WHO DO I CONTACT?

J-Design
6493-4662
www.j-design.com.hk
candace.collective
1/F, 171–177 Hollywood Rd, Central
6706-7921
www.candacecollective.com
A design studio specialising in web-design, marketing campaigns and photo shoots.
Salon de Pigeon
3/F, Po Yick Bldg, 17–19 Hillier St, Sheung Wan
2544-5664
www.salondepigeon.com
A creative studio providing event production, graphic design, photography, video and motion graphics.
PPC Ltd
18/F, Parkview Centre, 7 Lau Li St, Tin Hau
2504-3911
www.powerpointcreative.com
Speak with Gary Jones.
Amass Communications Ltd
18/F, Park Comm. Centre, 180 Tung Lo Wan Rd, Causeway Bay
2573-9285
www.amass.com.hk
An advertising company that has great graphic designers.
Whitespace
15/F, Bonham Centre
79–85 Bonham Strand, Sheung Wan
2869-9081
whitespace.hk

IS THERE A PROFESSIONAL IT EXPERT WHO CAN **FIX MY HOME COMPUTER**?

IT Experts Net
16/F, Amtel Bldg
144–148 Des Voeux Rd Central, Sheung Wan
9237-4870
www.itexpertsnet.com
After working with Morgan Stanley, Merrill Lynch and Lloyd's of London, Greg Spinos started this company in 2002. He specialises in website design, maintenance, project management, computer security, troubleshooting and virus elimination.

Elite Multimedia
G/F, World Trust Tower, 50 Stanley St, Central
2123-1423 / 2123-1428
IT Help
9686-6563
ithelphk@gmail.com
*Sathish can come to your office or home to deal with
hardware, software, Internet, handheld problems and more.*
Quickhand
19/F, Vulcan House
21 –23 Leighton Rd, Causeway Bay
2838-6189
www.quickhand.com.hk
Computer Troubleshooters
23/F, World-Wide House
19 Des Voeux Rd Central
2270-1305
www.comptroub.com
Computer Services Hong Kong
2572-2867 / 9147-0230
chrisk@netvigator.com
*Christopher Krishnan is highly professional and will
come to your home to fix any computer glitches.*

WHERE CAN I TAKE **COMPUTER COURSES** TO GO
OVER BASICS OR TO LEARN NEW SOFTWARE?

See page 245.

WHERE CAN I GO TO GET MY **CAR WASHED/DETAILED**?

Challenger
www.challenger.com.hk
*Deep cleaning and detailing done while you shop.
Several locations within major shopping mall parking lots.*
NTI Express Auto Care
G/F, 368 Kwun Tong Rd, Kwun Tong
2345-2193
www.nti.hk
*As similar as it gets in Hong Kong to a North American
style drive-through car wash.*

WHERE CAN I FIND A GOOD **CAR MECHANIC** WHO
SPEAKS ENGLISH?

Autosuite
G/F, 37A Lyttlelton Rd, Mid-Levels
2559-7648
*Raymond Yeung and David Cheung offer friendly,
reasonably priced car repairs. Helpful in sourcing
economical ways to fix your car by using used parts,
such as windshields.*
Southern Garage Ltd
• G/F, 11 Village Rd, Happy Valley
  2572-0893
• G/F, Block A, 33 Yip Kan St, Wong Chuk Heng
  2555-7997
*They specialise in fine European cars. Good service,
honest and dependable. Mr Zheung, the boss, speaks
English well.*

British Repair & Auto Service
G/F, 41 First St, Sai Ying Pun
2559-6007

Fookie Motors Co. Ltd
G/F, Paramount Bldg, 12 Kai Yip St, Chai Wan
2565-6166
Pick-up and delivery service.

AutoWRX
DD215, Hong Tsuen Rd, Sai Kung, New Territories
6505-8605
www.autowrx.com.hk

Cheung Wah Kee Motor Services
G/F, 1–9 Lin Fa Kung West St, Tai Hang, Causeway Bay
2807-3208
www.cwkmotor.com

Hong Kong Automobile Association
391 Nathan Rd, Yau Ma Tei
2739-5273
www.hkaa.com.hk
Call 2304-4911 for 24-hour emergency rescue service.

HP Cars
• Unit A, Gee Tung Chang Ind. Bldg
  4 Fung Yip St, Siu Sai Wan, Chai Wan
  2558-0222
• 215 Hong Tsuen Rd, Tui Min Hoi
  Sai Kung, New Territories
  2791-4145
www.hpcars.hk.com

Diligence Motor Service Co.
G/F, Tung Fat Bldg, 55D Kam Ping St, North Point
2516-7202

Ngai Shing Motor Co. Ltd ....
52 Ngan Fung St
Fung Wong New Village, Wong Tai Sin
2328-6391
Pick-up and delivery service.

WHERE CAN I HIRE A CAR TO GO TO THE AIRPORT?

Winson Wu
8100-0612
24-hour taxi service to the airport at fixed price.

Hawk Rent A Car
10/F, Corporation Park
11 On Lai St, Sha Tin, New Territories
2516-9822
www.hawkrentacar.com.hk
A range of 8 cars available.

WHERE CAN I RENT A CAR?

Avis
www.avis.com.hk

Hawk
www.hawkrentacar.com.hk

Rhino Car Hire Hong Kong
www.rhinocarhire.com

Any Car Hire
www.anycarhire.com

Hong Kong Limousine Service
www.hongkonglimousineservice.com

RENT IT . BUILD IT . FIX IT . LEASE IT . DESIGN IT . PARTY IT . CLEAN IT . PICTURE IT . DISCOUNT IT . HOUSE IT . RENOVATE IT . FURNISH IT

EVERYTHING HOUSE & HOME

WHERE CAN I **RENT FURNITURE**?

Indigo Living
See page 313
Rental department: 2552-3550
Home Essentials
G/F, Lok Moon Mansion
29–31 Queen's Rd East, Wan Chai
2870-1400
www.homeessentials.net
Tree
See page 313
Tequila Kola
• 2/F, Prince's Bldg, 10 Chater Rd, Central
  2520-1611
• 1/F, Horizon Plaza, 2 Lee Wing St, Ap Lei Chau
  2877-3295
www.tequilakola.com

WHERE CAN I RENT A **BICYCLE**?

Friendly Bicycle Shop
Mui Wo, Lantau Island
2984-2278
*Jacky Chan rents mountain and leisure bikes. Lantau is a
great place to ride both on the road and on trails.*
Tai Po Market
Tai Po, New Territories
Tai Mei Tuk, New Territories ....
*Several rental places in both locations. Many also rent
children's bikes.*

WHERE CAN I RENT **BABY EQUIPMENT** INSTEAD OF
BUYING IT?

YWCA Baby Equipment Rental ....
3/F, 1 Macdonnell Rd, Mid-Levels
3476-1346
www.esmdywca.org.hk
*Rental equipment is donated by members and is in good
condition. Most items rent for $50/week.*

WHERE CAN I RENT A **SEWING MACHINE** FOR A
COSTUME-MAKING PROJECT?

YWCA
3/F, 1 Macdonnell Rd, Mid-Levels
3476-1346
www.esmdywca.org.hk
Bernina and Singer sewing machines rent for $100/week.

WHERE CAN I FIND A DEPENDABLE **LOCAL COURIER
OR MESSENGER**?

City Courier Service Ltd
9/F, Yip Fat Ind. Bldg, 75 Hoi Yuen Rd, Kwun Tong
2389-0161
www.citycourier.com.hk
*A full-service local courier for deliveries, pick-up and
more.*

EVERYTHING HOUSE & HOME

Morning Express Courier
3/F, Kin Yip Plaza
9 Cheung Yee St, Cheung Sha Wan
2370-8222
www.mechk.com
A full-service courier for local, China and international deliveries. They can pick up from your home at an additional charge. They also offer personal messenger service for paying bills, collecting mail, applying for licences and visas, etc. It occasionally takes a while before they put an English-speaker on the phone, though.

WHO CAN HELP ME **COURIER** SOMETHING TO CHINA?

China Courier
• 10/F, Eastern Harbour
  28 Hoi Chak St, Quarry Bay
• G/F, Po Lung Centre
  11 Wang Chiu Rd, Kowloon Bay
2516-6213
www.china-courier.com.hk

EMS Worldwide Express Mail Service
www.ems.com.cn/english-main.jsp
They offer domestic (China) COD service.

I NEED A LARGE, **INTERNATIONAL COURIER** SERVICE. WHO DO I CALL?

DHL
2400-3388
www.dhl.com.hk
24-hour service.

FedEx
2730-3333
www.fedex.com/hk_english

Hong Kong Post
2 Connaught Place, Central
2921-2288
www.hongkongpost.com

TNT
2331-2663 / 2331-2266
www.tnt.com
24-hour service

UPS
2735-3535
www.ups.com

Royale International Couriers
General enquiry: 2318-0370
24-hour pick-up hotline: 2218-5888
www.royaleasia.com

WHERE CAN I FIND A GOOD **PERSONAL ACCOUNTANT**?

Armando Y C Chung & Co. Certified Public Accountants
12/F, Golden Star Bldg, 20 Lockhart Rd, Wan Chai
2866-6011
Ask for Frank Ngan.

C K Lam & Co.
7/F, Fourseas Bldg, 208–212 Nathan Rd, Jordan
2866-2116
Speak with Miranda or Billie regarding Hong Kong tax and accounting issues.

Citiac Management Consultancy
4/F, Wah Kit Comm. Centre
300 Des Voeux Rd Central, Sheung Wan
2566-1126
www.citiac.com
Peter Cheung is great for small to medium businesses. In addition to accounting services, he also deals with all aspects of consulting for a small business.

LLB Accounting Services
• 7/F, 80 Gloucester Rd, Wan Chai
• 21/F, Sunshine Plaza, 353 Lockhart Rd, Wan Chai
2374-1211
www.llbaccounting.com
Contact Graham Dove.

WHICH ARE A FEW **LARGER, MORE COMPREHENSIVE ACCOUNTING FIRMS**?

Deloitte Touche Tohmatsu
35/F, One Pacific Place, 88 Queensway, Admiralty
2852-1600
www.deloitte.com

Ernst & Young
62/F, One Island East, 18 Westland Rd, Quarry Bay
2846-9888

Grant Thornton
• Head office:
  6/F, Nexxus Bldg, 41 Connaught Rd Central
• Branch office:
  6/F, Sunning Plaza, 10 Hysan Ave, Causeway Bay
2218-3000
www.gthk.com.hk

Horwath Hong Kong
38/F, Central Plaza, 18 Harbour Rd, Wan Chai
2526-2191
www.horwath.com.hk

KPMG
8/F, Prince's Bldg, 10 Chater Rd, Central
2522-6022
www.kpmg.com.hk

PricewaterhouseCoopers
22/F, Prince's Bldg, 10 Chater Rd, Central
2289-8888
www.pwchk.com

WHERE CAN I FIND A **TAX ADVISER** WHO SPECIALISES IN CERTAIN COUNTRIES?

USAsia Tax
63/F, The Centre, 99 Queen's Rd Central
2851-8049
www.usasiatax.com
Call Fergus Tong or Agnes Chang for US tax services, tax planning and tax return preparation.

Mint Tax Consulting Ltd
18/F, Wheelock House, 20 Pedder St, Central
2987-9821
www.mint-tax.com
Specialising in US and Hong Kong taxes, Caroline Tsui and Gary Ho have over 10 years' experience each with Big Four accounting firms.

Azure Tax Consulting
10/F, Lippo Centre, Tower 2, 89 Queensway, Admiralty
2123-9370
www.azuretax.com
Azure deals with US, UK, Australian, PRC and Hong Kong taxes and tax issues.

Lipsher Accountancy
7/F, The Garley Bldg, 53 Graham St, Central
9469-6105 / 2526-6744
web.mac.com/prctaxman/prctaxman.com

Lehman Brown
17/F, Jubilee Centre, 18 Fenwick St, Wan Chai
2426-6426
www.lehmanbrown.com
Specialising in Chinese taxation.

I NEED ADVICE ON MY **WORK VISA** AS WELL AS **STARTING UP A BUSINESS**. WHO CAN HELP?

Suzanne Liu Duddek
16/F, Kinwick Centre, 32 Hollywood Rd, Central
2868-1287
www.hongkongcpa.com
The accounting expert for expats, offering accounting, audit, tax, company secretarial and company formation.

Bridges Executive Centre
20/F, Central Tower, 28 Queen's Rd Central
2159-4888
www.bridgescentre.com
Business start-up and working visa experts.

Dearson Winyard International
9/F, Printing House, 6 Duddell St, Central
2116-8283
www.dwiglobal.com
Global work visa and immigration specialists.

Asian Corporate Services Ltd
8/F, Pacific House, 20 Queen's Rd Central
2877-2290
www.acshk.com

WHERE CAN I FIND AN **IMMIGRATION CONSULTANT**?

Emigra
21/F, Sunshine Plaza, 353 Lockhart Rd, Wan Chai
2783-7183
www.hongkongvisas.com
Immigration and visa services for Hong Kong and over 80 other countries. Ask for Lath Olavath.

VISION Relocation
2/F, Shui On Centre, 6–8 Harbour Rd, Wan Chai
2824-8135
www.visionrelocation.com
Specialises in visa and immigration issues.

Lloyden Consultancy Ltd
19/F, 128 Lockhart Rd, Wan Chai
2151-8082
www.lloyden.com

Paul Mak
9350-8213
Specialises in local immigration issues such as Hong Kong permanent residency.

EVERYTHING HOUSE & HOME

I NEED **INSURANCE ADVICE**. WHO CAN I TALK TO?

RS Insurance Brokers
5/F, Winsome House, 73 Wyndham St, Central
3106-2938
www.rsib.com.hk
Professional advice for all types of insurance including life, medical and household. Ask for Ira Storfer.

Trans-Pacific Insurance Brokers
15/F, Chinachem Plaza, 29 Leighton Rd, Wan Chai
2838-5262
www.transpacific.hk
Ask for Julie Ho.

Navigator Insurance Brokers Ltd
2/F, Midland Centre, 328 Queen's Rd Central
2530-2530 / 9833-7335
www.navigator-insurance.com
Ask for Clive Wolstencroft.

WHERE CAN I FIND AN EXPERT WHO CAN HELP ME **WRITE MY WILL**?

Professional Wills Ltd
5/F, Block C & D, 657–659 King's Rd, Quarry Bay
2561-9031
www.profwills.com

Susan Liang and Co. Solicitors
18/F, 1 Duddell St, Central
2526-2607
www.speedysue.com

EVERYTHING
BY PHONE

Telephone PCCW Directory Assistance
1081 *English*
1088 *Mandarin*

Emergency Call
999
Police, ambulance or fire service.

Consumer Council
2929-2222
Protects the interests of consumers.

Leisure and Cultural Services Department
2414-5555
Oversees all government-run leisure and cultural services, such as sport centres, museums and libraries.

Hong Kong International Airport
2181-8888

Immigration Department
2824-6111

Hong Kong Observatory
1878-200

Time and Weather
18501 *English*
18508 *Mandarin*

Hong Kong Taxi Centre
2574-7311

The Taxi Operators Association Limited
2362-2337

Wing Tai Radio Taxi
2865-7398
2861-1011

Yau Luen Radio Taxi
2527-6324

Ho Wah Radio Taxi
2571-2929

EVERYTHING
ONLINE

DIRECTORIES / MAPS

**www.pccw.com/eng/CustomerSupport/Directories/
1081DirectoryInquiries.html**
1081 PCCW Directory Assistance online service.

www.yp.com.hk
Hong Kong Yellow Pages—Business and Consumer.

www.ypmap.com
Hong Kong Yellow Pages—map service.

www.centamap.com
Centaline Property—map service.

maps.google.com.hk
Google Map Service for Hong Kong.

WEATHER

www.hko.gov.hk
Hong Kong Observatory—current local weather report
and 7-day forecast.

www.weather.org.hk
Weather Underground—Hong Kong weather website,
including weather alerts, air pollution index and more.

www.hko.gov.hk/informtc/informtc.htm
Tropical cyclone warning bulletin, cyclone track,
warning for shipping and severe weather information
centre.

www.windguru.cz
Windsurfing forecast Hong Kong.

GOVERNMENT SERVICES INFORMATION

**www.discoverhongkong.com/eng/jsp/consulates/search-
index.jsp**
List of all consulates in Hong Kong, visa application
forms and more.

www.gov.hk/en/residents
Hong Kong local government website for residents.
"Electronic Service Deliver" is also available: pay
your parking tickets, file your tax return, apply for a
passports and other useful services to avoid queues.

www.immd.gov.hk/ehtml/home.htm
Hong Kong Immigration Department.

www.gov.hk/en/about/abouthk/holiday
Hong Kong General Holidays.

EVERYTHING ONLINE

DOMESTIC HELPERS

www.immd.gov.hk/ehtml/hkvisas_5.5.htm
Guidebook for employment of domestic helpers from abroad.

FOREIGN EXCHANGE & OTHER CONVERSIONS

www.xe.com
Up-to-date exchange calculations for all currencies.

www.timezoneconverter.com
Worldwide Time Zone conversion.

www.onlineconversion.com
Converts just about anything.

NEED-TO-KNOW WEBSITES

www.discoverhongkong.com
Hong Kong Tourism Board and all it has to offer.

www.consumer.org.hk
Hong Kong Consumer Council website for lodging complaints against companies or shops.

www.ho-sum.org
A non-profit website dedicated to promoting charities in Hong Kong, including a comprehensive list and ways to help.

www.hotel.hk
Hotel bookings in Hong Kong. Rated as one of the top frequented Hong Kong websites.

www.parkinghk.com
Helps you search for car park locations, lists parking spaces for lease or for sale throughout Hong Kong.

www.autotoll.com.hk
Get auto toll for your car.

CLASSIFIED LISTINGS

www.ownad.com
Post your own classified ads for Hong Kong on this website.

www.asiaxpat.com
Classifieds reaching the expatriate community of Hong Kong.

www.jobsdb.com.hk
Hong Kong-based recruitment site reaching the Asia Pacific area.

www.monster.com.hk
International recruitment site for Hong Kong.

EVERYTHING ONLINE

HONG KONG RADIO/NEWS

www.rthk.org.hk
Radio Television Hong Kong's website with live web-casts, archived broadcasts, podcasts and more.

www.scmp.com
The South China Morning Post's daily website showing headlines; subscription required for full access.

FOOD, ENTERTAINMENT & SHOPPING SITES

www.eatdrinkhongkong.com
Extensive guide of restaurants and bars in Hong Kong.

www.womguide.com
A word-of-mouth guide and review database to eating and drinking in Hong Kong.

www.happycow.net
Vegetarian restaurants guide and directory of natural health food stores by Happy Cow.

www.hk-weekend.com
Entertainment and events in Hong Kong, updated weekly.

www.lcsd.gov.hk
Hong Kong Leisure and Cultural Services Department website with a calendar of upcoming events, and links to local stage and concert venue websites.

www.bcmagazine.net
BC (Be Scene) magazine's Hong Kong entertainment website, updated biweekly.

www.ilovesoho.com.hk
Everything SoHo.

www.hkclubbing.com
Clubbing and nightlife guide.

www.mcb.com.hk
Hong Kong and International music news and reviews.

www.undergroundhk.com
Local music acts playing in Hong Kong.

www.lovehkfilm.com
Hong Kong film reviews, people, features and more.

www.hiphongkong.com
This website has a hip list of places to visit, shop, dine and party. Browse photos, blogs and videos.

www.dimsumandthensome.com.hk
Subscribe to this site to stay up-to-date and receive comprehensive lists of the dimsum girls' favourite places, products and services as well as what's new, what's next, and what's best in this city.

EVERYTHING ONLINE

www.lifestyleasia.com
Stay up-to-date with trends, events and lifestyle around Hong Kong and Asia.

www.hkac.org.hk
Hong Kong Arts Centre's upcoming events.

www.hkcec.com
Hong Kong Convention and Exhibition Centre's upcoming events.

www.shops.hk
Latest fashion and shopping news.

www.butterboom.com
News and upcoming fashion and various blogs. Mainly Asia-focused but they have quite a bit on Hong Kong.

PARENTING

www.geobaby.com
Find like-minded parents for recommendations and helpful tips via this online forum. This is also a great directory for other baby and toddler necessities.

www.hongkongbabies.com
Similar to the website above, this is Hong Kong's newest online parenting forum. You'll find all you need to know for raising babies and pre-schoolers in this city.

TICKET BOOKING

hkticketing.hk
Online booking for tickets to concerts, theatre, dance, musicals, circus, cinema and more, including performance information and seat selection.

www.cityline.com.hk
Online ticketing service for music, sports, dance, film, theatre and more through Urbtix and booking service for UA Cinemas.

www.cinema.com.hk
Online booking service for Broadway Circuit cinemas with reviews of current and upcoming movies.

www.thegrandcinema.com.hk
Online ticketing for The Grand Cinema in Elements Mall. Apart from the conventional movie-watching experience, you can also book the Standard Chartered Starsuite for a private movie gathering.

www.uacinemas.com.hk
Another site for booking tickets of UA Cinemas.

www.amccinemas.com.hk
Online booking services for AMC Cinemas in Festival Walk and Pacific Place.

EVERYTHING ONLINE

www.mclcinema.com
Online ticketing services for MCL Cinemas.

OUTDOORS, RECREATION & LEISURE

www.hkoutdoors.com
Dedicated to outdoor activities, places, news and more in Hong Kong.

www.exploresaikung.com
Sai Kung natural and cultural highlights, business products and services.

www.lamma.com.hk
Lamma Island local events, information and more.

www.discoverybay.com.hk
Information for visitors, residents or people relocating to Discovery Bay.

www.thepeak.com.hk
How to get there and what to do at The Peak.

www.happyvalley.hk
Shop directories and classified ads for Happy Valley.

www.hk-stanley-market.com
Suggestions for where to go and what to do in Stanley.

www.holistic.asia.com
A guide to holistic events and activities in Hong Kong.

www.hkrugby.com
Hong Kong Rugby: where to play it, coach it, watch it and more.

EVERYTHING
CANTONESE

Hello!	[Nay ho!]
Goodbye!	[Joy geen!]
Good morning!	[Jo sun!]
Have you eaten? (A common greeting)	[Nay sik jaw faan may?]
Sorry!	[Doy mm ju!]
Excuse me.	[Mm ho yee see.]
What's your name?	[Nay gyu meh meng?]
My name is…	[Ngaw gyu…]
Where are you from?	[Nay hi bin doe lay gah?]
Please.	[Mm goi.]
Thank you!	[Daw jeh!]
You're welcome.	[Mm sai haak hay.]

IN CONVERSATION

I don't understand Cantonese.	[Ngaw mm sik gwong dong wah.]
I don't understand.	[Ngaw mm ming baak.]
What is this?	[Li gaw meh lay ga?]
Where are we going?	[Ngaw day hoi bin doe?]
Why?	[Deem guy?]
Hurry up!	[Fy dee!]

PERSONAL PREFERENCES

I like…	[Ngaw jong yee…]
I don't like…	[Ngaw mm jong yee…]

GETTING AROUND

Where is…?	[… hi bin?]
Where can I find…?	[Bin doe yau…?]

EVERYTHING CANTONESE

Toilet	[Chee saw]
What time is it now?	[Yee gah gay daw deem?]
Up	[Seung]
Down	[Haa]
Left	[Jaw]
Right	[Yau]
Centre	[Jong gaan]
Front	[Cheen]
Back	[Hau]
Stop here	[Lay dou]
Go straight	[Jik hoy]

SHOPPING

How much is it?	[Gay cheen?]
This	[Lay gaw]
That	[Gaw gaw]
Can you wrap it for me?	[Mm goy bong ngaw baau.]
Do you have a new one?	[Yau moe sun gah?]
Can I have S size please?	[Yau moe sigh mah?]
Can I have M size please?	[Yau moe jong mah?]
Can I have L size please?	[Yau moe dye mah?]
Can I have XL size please?	[Yau moe gah dye mah?]

COLOURS

Red	[Hong sik]
Orange	[Chaang sik]
Yellow	[Wong sik]
Green	[Lok sik]
Purple	[Jee sik]
Pink	[Fun hong sik]
Brown	[Feh sik]
Black	[Haak sik]
Grey	[Fuy sik]

| White | [Baak sik] |

Cheaper!	[Peng dee lah!]
I am from far away.	[Ngaw ho yoon lay gah!]
My friend recommended me to come.	[Ngaw pang yau guy siu ngaw la gaa!]
I'm buying in bulk.	[Ngaw my hoe daw.]

Noodle	[Meen]
Bread	[Meen baau]
Beef	[Ngau yok]
Pork	[Ju yok]
Chicken	[Guy]
Fish	[Yu]
Milk	[Laai]
Iced/cold	[Dong]
Hot	[Yeet]
Coffee	[Gaa feh]
Tea	[Ling cha]
Coffee-and-tea mix (local specialty)	[Yin yeung]
Chocolate	[Ju goo lik]
Orange juice	[Chaang jup]
Apple juice	[Ping gwoh jup]
Soy milk	[Dau jeung]
Beer	[Beh jau]

I am a vegetarian.	[Ngaw sik jai.]
Organic food	[Yau gey sik bun]
Do you have a kids' menu?	[Yau moe yee tong chaan?]
Less...	[Siu dee...]
More...	[Daw dee...]

EVERYTHING CANTONESE

No...	[Mm yiu]
Salt	[Yeem]
Sugar	[Tong]
Pepper	[Woo jiu fun]
Spicy	[Laat]
Oil/Fat	[Yau]
MSG	[May jing]
Leaner cut (of meat)	[Sau dee]
Excuse me, can I have...	[Mm goy ngaw seung yiu...]
Ice	[Bing]
Ketchup	[Keh jap]
Chilli	[Laat jiu]
Mustard	[Guy laat]
Soy sauce	[See yau]
Fork	[Cha]
Knife	[Doe]
Plate	[Deep]
Bowl	[Woon]
Cup	[Bui]
Spoon	[Chee gung]
Chopsticks	[Fy jee]
Check please.	[Mm goy mye daan.]
Can we pay separately?	[Haw mm haw yee fun hoi bay?]
Do you take credit cards?	[Sau mm sau seun yung kaat?]

COUNTING NUMBERS

1	[Yut]
2	[Yee]
3	[Saam]
4	[Say]
5	[Mm]

6	[Lok]
7	[Chut]
8	[Baat]
9	[Gau]
10	[Sup]

FESTIVALS

New Year	[Sun neen]
Chinese New Year	[Long lik sun neen]
Wishing you prosperity! (Chinese New Year greetings)	[Gong hay faat choi]
Dragon Boat Festival	[Duen ng jeet]
Mid-Autumn Festival	[Jung chau jeet]

EVERYTHING
INDEX

aboriginal art, 307
accommodations
    boutique hotels, 372
    budget, 372–373
    serviced apartments, 370–371
accountants, 382–383
    See also tax advisers
accounting firms, 383
acupuncture, 284–285
    pets', 356
adventure
    programmes, 199
    races, 198, 200
advice
    parenting, 254, 390
    pre-natal, 282–283
aerobics, 194–195
afternoon tea, 29, 32–33
Aikido, 203
air-conditioner servicing, 364
airport
    car hire, 380
    concierge services, 223
    information, 386
al fresco dining, 18–20, 21–23, 31, 37, 67–68
alchohol rehabilitation, 281–282, 284
allergies, 277
alterations, 136–137
alternative
    dance classes, 248
    medicine, 284–286
    music, 253
animal communicators, 355
antique
    artwork, 304–305
    costumes/textiles, 304–305
    furniture, 310–312
    furniture servicing, 318
    jewellery, 150–151
    maps, 304
    photos, 304
Apple computers, 375, 377
appliances, 325, 337–338
aquariums, 358–359
architects, 359, 360
aromatherapy
    products, 300–301
    treatments, 201, 285, 289–292
art appreciation courses, 250
Art Deco furniture, 312, 315
art galleries, 304–308
arts and crafts
    See also beads
    classes (adults'), 248–250
    classes (kids'), 258–259
    supplies, 157–158, 184, 189–191, 250–251
artwork
    framing, 309
    made-to-order, 308
    restoration, 309
    shipping, transportation, hanging, 310
Asian
    art, 304–307
    spices and provisions, 88–89
asthma treatment, 277
astrology profiling, 286
athletic
    associations, 196, 199–200, 211
    training, 197–199

EVERYTHING INDEX

auction houses, 310
audio systems, 373, 374–375
babies'
    clothes, 107–108, 168–173, 187–189
    equipment rental, 381
    gifts, 153–155, 164–166, 333–334
    playgroups, 254–256
    supplies, 160–162
baby-sitters, 346
badminton, 209
bag tags, 168
bags and purses, 106–107, 117, 118, 121–122, 137–142
bakeries, 92–93
baking utensils, 81, 95, 335–337
ball and puck sports, 209–210
ballet
    classes, 262–263
    supplies, 174
ballroom dance classes, 247
bands
    hire, 227–228
    performances, 53–54, 224–225, 389–390
    recording studios, 253
barbecues, 325, 351–352
    See also BBQ meat; BBQ seafood
bars, 17–18, 49–56
    See also lounges
    great views, 17–18
    in restaurants, 52–53
    live music, 53–54
    neighbourhood, 49–50
    sports, 50–51
bartenders, 99–100, 231
bathroom
    accessories, 330–332
    designers, 361
    furnishing, 313–314
BBQ
    meat, 44, 63
    seafood, 21–23
beaches, 217–219
beaded jewellery, 153
beads, 157–158, 189–191, 251
bean bag chairs, 315
beauty treatments, 289–296
beauty treatments (men's), 296
bed linens, 315, 317, 326–327
bedding, 322, 326–327
beers, 55–56
belly dance classes, 247
bicycle
    rental, 381
    shops, 174
big-group dining, 65–66
bilingual schools, 268–269
billiards, 216
Biokinetik Exercise Technique, 200
birthday
    cakes, 94, 230, 234–235
    parties (adults'), 228–230
    parties (kids'), 231–235
boarding school consultancy, 272
boat charter/licence, 225–227
Bollywood dance classes, 247
bonsai plants, 349
bookbinding classes, 250
books, 176–181, 216–217, 285
    antique, 180, 304, 311
    art, 181
    business, 181
    children's, 176–178
    Chinese, 179
    computer, 180
    design, 181
    French, 180
    gay and lesbian, 181
    hiking, 216–217
    law, 181

EVERYTHING INDEX

medicine, 181
New Age, 285
rare, 180
second-hand, 179–180
boot camps, 198
Botox, 297–298
bouncy castle, 234
boutique hotels, 372
boutiques, 110–111, 114–120
    See also clothing
boxer shorts, 128
boxing, 204
box-making classes, 249
Brazilian
    barbecue, 44
    Jiu Jitsu, 204
    waxing, 295
breakfast, 29, 37–38
bridal salons,131
brunch, 29–30
buffets, 29–31
bug screens, 352–353
bunk beds, 324
burgers, 47–48
business cards, 185
business start-up, 384
butchers, 85–86
buttons, 189–191
Caesar cocktails, 56
cafés, 17, 80–81
cake, 94–95, 230, 234–235
    making classes, 244–245
    moulds, decorations and tools, 95
calligraphers, 184
cameras, 373–374
camps (kids'), 262
candles, 329
canine training, 356
Cantonese
    courses, 246–247
    domestic helpers, 347
    phrases, 392–396
    schools, 268–269
caps, 143
car mechanics, 379–380
cards, 183, 185–186
carpets, 328
carpet cleaners, 342–343
cars
    rental, 380
    wash/detailing, 379
cashmere, 124–125, 165, 188
casual wear
    men's, 126–127
    women's, 105–114
caterers, 99–100, 227
caviar, 40
ceiling fans, 322
ceramics
    antique, 310–312
    reproduction, 329
chairs, 315
    rental, 231, 381
champagnes, 96–99
chandeliers, 322
char siu (Chinese BBQ), 63
chartering boats/junks/yachts, 225–227
cheeky toys, 229–230
cheese, 81, 86–88
cheongsams, 132, 187–189
ch'i kung See Qigong
children's
    books, 176–178
    clothes and shoes, 168–176, 187–189
    courses, 254–263
    furniture, 323–324
    medical treatments, 274–278
    sports, 206–207, 263–266

EVERYTHING INDEX

China (maps of), 222
China (porcelain), 333–334
Chinese
    antiques/ceramics, 310–312
    desserts, 74–75
    medicinal drinks, 62
    medicine, 284–285
    restaurants, 16, 23–24, 25, 26–27, 38–39, 56–69
    tea, 84
chiropractors, 279
chocolates, 77–80
choirs (children's), 259
Christmas
    cards, 183–185
    trees/decorations, 349–350
churrascaria, 44
cigars, 99
cinemas, 223, 390–391
classified listings, 388
climbing, 196
clinical psychologists, 280–281, 285
clothes donation centres, 345
clothes steamers, 135, 342
clothing
    basic items, 113–114
    cashmere, 124–125
    cocktail dresses, 114–115
    cold weather, 147–149, 173, 187–189
    costumes, 173, 187–189
    custom-made, 129–135
    discount outlets, 111–113
    evening wear, 115
    fur, 125
    kids' See kids' clothing
    leather, 191
    linen, 188–189
    maternity, 162–163
    men's See men's clothing
    school, 175
    second-hand, 116–117
    ski wear, 147–149, 173, 215
    sports, 173–175, 187–189, 212–216
    streetwear, 117–120
    surfing, 147, 215
    yoga, 144–146, 213
clowns, 234
clubs
    golf, 215–216
    memberships, 271–272
    private, 223, 233
clutches, 137–138
coaches
    athletic, 197–198
    football, 206, 209
    hockey, 209–210, 265–266
    life, 242
    swimming, 207
    tennis, 197, 209
    triathlon, 198
cocktail dresses, 114–115
coffee
    ground, 84
    shops, 17, 80–81
    tables, 312–314
colonic irrigation treatments, 286
colour blindness tests, 276
comedy clubs, 53, 224
comfort food, 45–49, 63
communication disorders, 277
complementary health, 284–286
computer
    courses, 245
    repair, 378–379
    shops, 375–377
    software, 377
concert listings, 224–225, 389
conflict resolution, 254
congee, 61

EVERYTHING INDEX

consulates, 387
Consumer Council, 386
contact sports classes, 203–204, 263–264
contemporary
    art, 305–308
    furniture, 312–315
contractors (home renovation), 363
cooking classes, 243–245, 257–258
corrective eye surgery, 280
costume jewellery, 152–153
costumes, 187–189
    antiques, 304–305
    rental, 173
counselling, 280–281
country clubs, 233
countryside adventure, 221
couriers, 381–382
courses
    for domestic helpers, 243–244
    interest (adults'), 242–250, 252–254
    interest (kids'), 252–253, 254–263
    sports (adults'), 196–198, 199, 200–206, 211
    sports (kids'), 205–206, 207, 209–211, 263–266
craniosacral therapy, 284
creative writing classes, 261
cricket, 209
crystal, 158, 333–334
cupcakes, 230
curtains and blinds, 319–320
custard tarts , 74–75
custom-made
    art, 308
    cards, 183, 185–186
    clothing, 129–135
    furniture, 316–317, 323
    shoes, 135–136
cycling, 210, 213–214, 381
D.I.Y. craft supplies, 184, 189–191, 250–251
dai pai dong, 65
daily-use items, 338–339
dance classes
    adults', 247–248
    kids', 262–263
date spots, 20–21
day camps, 262
decorative items (home), 333–335
deejay See DJ
deep tissue massages, 294
delicatessens, 86–87
denims, 117–120, 187–190
dental whitening, 296–297
dentists, 274–275, 296–297
dermatologists, 297–298
designer clothes, 110–113, 114–117
    second-hand, 116–117
designers
    fashion, 114–115, 129–130
    graphic, 378
    interior, 359–361
    jewellery, 149–150, 157
    web, 377–378
desks, 315
desserts, 74–80
diamonds, 157
diaper bags, 164
dieticians, 278
dim sum, 56–58
dirt biking, 234
disco balls, 230
discount outlets, 111–113
dishes, 333–334, 335–337
disposal
    clothing, 345
    furniture and household items, 343–345
    oversized rubbish, 344–345
diving, 208, 210, 220
DJ, 227–228

dogs
    See also pets
    training, 356
    walking places, 356
domestic helpers
    classes, 243–244
    hire, 346–347
donations, 343, 345
dragon boat races, 208, 210–211
drama
    classes, 259–260
    listings, 223, 389–390
drawing classes, 248–249
    See also arts and crafts classes
dressmakers, 129–131
dry cleaners, 340–341
dumplings, 58–60
duvets, 326–327
dyes, 328
dyslexia, 278
early childhood specialists, 254
educational resources, 166, 261
egg tarts, 74
electricians, 364
electronics, 189–191, 373–374
embroidering (linens), 327–328
employment agencies (domestic helpers), 346–347
English classes (kids'), 260–261
engraving, 335
entertainers, 234
entertainment event listings, 223, 389–390
entertainment systems (home), 374–375
equestrian, 204–205
European
    antique furniture, 312
    restaurants, 42–43
evening wear, 115
event planners, 227, 231
exercise equipment, 213
extreme sports, 205
eye examinations, 279–280
eyebrow treatments, 295
eyelash extensions, 295
eyewear, 116, 143–144, 276, 280
fabrics
    tailoring, 134, 189
    upholstery, 320, 190–191
    vintage/retro, 320
face and body care products, 300
facial and body treatments, 289–296
farms, 257
fashion *See* clothing
fasteners, 190–191, 318
feng shui
    courses, 242
    masters, 361–362
fertility specialists, 282
Filipino helpers, 346–347
fireplaces, 361
fireworks, 230
first aid courses, 243
fish tanks, 358–359
fitness clubs, 194–195
Flamenco dance classes, 247
florist supplies, 349
florists, 348–351
flower arrangements, 350–351
foot
    doctors, 279
    massages, 292
football (soccer)
    clubs, 209, 233
    training (kids'), 206
formal wear, 114–115, 129–130, 133–134
    kids', 170–171, 176
fragrances, 329
framing shops, 309

EVERYTHING INDEX

French
    books, 180
    classes, 246
    restaurants, 14–15, 25, 27–28, 42, 65
frozen
    meat, 85–86
    yoghurt, 77
furniture
    antique/vintage, 310–312
    contemporary, 312–315
    custom-made, 316–317, 323
    give-away, 343–344
    kids', 323–324
    rental, 231, 313, 381
    repair, 318
furs
    accessories, 328
    clothing, 125
    custom-made, 131
garbage disposal, 344–345
garden landscaping, 351
gardening tools, 349
gelato, 76
general practitioners, 273–274
gift boxes, 157, 182–183, 339
gift registries, 242, 333–334
gifts, 332
    for babies, 153–155, 164, 333–334
    for high-flyers, 223
girls' groups pampering session, 291–292
glass
    art, 308
    art classes, 249
glasses (spectacles), 143–144, 276, 280
glasses (utensils), 335–337
goldsmiths, 156–157
golf
    associations, 210
    driving ranges, 215
    equipment and accessories, 215–216
    simulators, 215
    training, 197
gourmet food stores, 87–88
GPs See general practitioners
graphic designers, 378
greeting cards, 182–185
grocery stores
    Asian, 88–89
    bulk provisions, 84
    online, 83
    Western, 81–83
grooming and treatments, 296–297
group
    exercise classes, 194–195
    outdoor training, 198
gym equipment, 213
gyms, 194–195
    hotel, 195
    trainers, 195, 197
    women-only, 195
gynaecologists, 282
gyrotonic exercise methods, 200
Hai Nan chicken rice, 64
hair
    removal, 296–299
    styling and treatments, 286–289
    transplants, 298
halal
    provisions, 89
    restaurants, 39
handbags, 137–141
    photo-print, 138–139
    second-hand, 139
    skins/hide, 138
handymen, 362
hardware stores, 365–366
harpists, 228
hats, 116–117, 143

EVERYTHING INDEX

health and performance supplements, 92, 299–300
healthy takeouts, 36–37
hearing tests, 276
helpers, 346–347
hen nights, 229–230
henna tattoos, 295
herbal teas, 62
herbalists, 284–285
hiking
    expeditions, 217
    outfits and supplies, 144–149, 174, 212, 216
    trails, 216–217
hip-hop classes (kids'), 263
hockey
    equipment, 214
    grounds, 205
    training (kids'), 205, 265–266
holiday cards, 183, 185
holistic healthcare, 284
    pets', 355–356
home accessories, 330–335
home audio systems, 374–375
home chefs, 100
homeopaths, 277, 284
homeware gift registries, 333–334
Hong Kong Immigration Department, 387–388
Hong Kong Observatory, 386–387
Hong Kong Tourism Board, 388
horse riding, 204–205
hospitals, 272–273
hot chocolate, 80
hot dogs, 48
hot pots, 61–62
hotels
    boutique, 372
    budget, 372–373
    online booking, 388
hypnotherapists, 285
ice cream, 76
ice hockey, 265–266
ice suppliers, 230
ice-skating, 105, 206, 265
image consultants, 296
immigration consultants, 384
    See also Hong Kong Immigration Department
Indian
    art, 306–307
    fashion, 106, 133
Indian
    provisions, 88
    restaurants, 30, 38–39, 67, 70–71
Indonesian restaurants, 71
indoor
    playgrounds, 256–257
    sports centres, 196
infant bedding, 322
inflatable games, 234
ingrown nails, 293
injury rehabilitation, 197, 202, 278
inline hockey/skating, 205, 211, 214, 266
insurance advice, 385
interior designers, 359–361
invitation cards, 185–186
Italian delicatessens, 86–87
IVF, 282
jade, 149, 151–152, 157, 191
Japanese
    provisions, 89
    restaurants, 16, 24, 30–31, 71–73
jazz
    dance classes (kids'), 263
    live music, 53–54, 224–225, 389–390
    musicians, 228
jeans, 106, 108–119, 117–120, 187–189
jewellery, 149–160
    See also diamonds; goldsmiths, jade; pearls; silver
    antique, 150–151
    boxes, 158

EVERYTHING INDEX

custom-made, 149–50, 157
    repair/reset, 156
    second-hand, 159–160
jewellery making
    classes, 250
    supplies, 157–158, 189–191, 251
Jiu Jitsu, 204
Judo, 203, 263–264
junk charter, 226–227
Kadoorie Farm, 257
Karate-Do, 203, 263–264
kayaking, 208, 217, 221
Kendo, 203
kennels, 358
kids' bedding, 322–323
kids' clothing
    formal wear, 170–171, 176
    school basics, 167–168, 175
    sportswear, 173–176, 187–191, 212
    streetwear, 170
kids' furniture, 323–324
kids' meals, 46–47
kids' sports, 263–266
kilts, 134
kindergartens, 266–269
kitchen designers, 361
kitchenware, 95, 335–337
knife sharpening, 337
Korean
    art, 306
    provisions, 89
    restaurants, 70
Kosher
    provisions, 83
    restaurants, 39
Kung Fu, 203–204, 263–264
labels (kids'), 68
lacrosse, 210
ladies' lunches, 31–32
lampshades, 320–321
landscaping, 351
language classes, 245–247, 260–261
Lasertag, 234
Lasik surgery, 280
Latin dance classes, 247
Latin-style food, 44–45
launderettes, 340–342
lawyers, 385
learning disorders, 278
learn-through-play, 254–256
leather
    clothing, 125
    desks and chairs, 315
    jewellery boxes, 158
leather and skin supplies, 191
life coach, 242
lifestyle accessories, 330–335
light and healthy meals, 35–37
lighting shops, 320–321
linen clothing, 188
lingerie, 122–124
liquor wholesale, 98–99
live music
    bars, 53–54, 224–225, 389–390
    hire, 227–228
locksmiths, 364–365
loot bag items, 189–191, 235, 339
lounges, 54–55, 56
luggages, 222
luxury boat charter, 226–227
lymphatic drainage, 284–285
MacLehose Trail, 199
magazines, 178–179, 182
makeup artists, 240–241
male strippers, 230
malls
    clothing, 104–105, 168
    computers, 376

Mandarin
    classes, 246–247
    classes (kids'), 260, 268–269
    playgroups, 256, 260
    schools, 268–269
manicures, 292–294
manual therapy, 278, 283
maps, 10–11, 216, 222, 387
marathons, 199–200
marriage counselling, 281
martial arts training, 203–204
    kids', 263–264
Martinis, 56
massages, 279, 289–292
maternity
    nurses, 283
    supplies, 160–165
    wear, 107–110, 113–114, 144, 160–163, 188–189
Maths classes, 261
mattresses, 324–326
mechanics, 379–380
medical
    services, 272–286
    supplies, 299
meditation courses, 242
Mediterranean restaurants, 18, 22, 43, 65
mediums, 286
men's bags, 141–142
men's clothing
    casual wear, 126–128
    custom-made suits, 133–134
    shoes, 127–128, 136
    socks, 107, 108, 123–124, 126, 128
    underwear, 128
messengers, 381–382
Mexican tapas bars, 44–45
Middle Eastern restaurants, 43
midwives, 282–283
milk delivery, 89
mini storage, 369
mirrors (Venetian), 333
mobile phones, 189, 373
monogramming (linens), 327–328
mountain biking, 210, 217
mountaineering, 211
movers, 368–369
movie ticketing, 223, 390–391
murals, 317
murses, 141–142
music
    event listings, 224–225, 389–390
    live, 53–54, 224–225, 389–390
music and movement, 256
music classes
    adults', 252–253
    kids', 253, 259–260
    toddlers', 256
musical instrument stores, 253
nail treatments, 292–294
nannies, 283, 346
napkins, 334
natural paints, 364
nature appreciation, 257
naturopaths, 277
needlework supplies, 251
neighbourhood haunts, 49–50
Nepalese restaurants, 70–71
netball, 209
New Age resources, 286
new mothers, 282–283, 390
newspaper delivery, 182
noodles, 60–61
nostalgic memorabilia, 304
nursing supplies, 160, 161, 163–164
nutritionists, 278
NY-style delis, 47
obstetricians, 282

EVERYTHING INDEX

off-the-beaten track eateries
    Asian, 21–23, 187–189
      Western, 67–68, 187–189
open water races, 200
opticians, 276, 280
optometrists, 280
organic
    face and body products, 300
      food stores, 89–92
      meals (vegetarian/vegan), 37–38
orienteering, 198–200, 211
orthodontists, 275
osteopaths, 279, 284
outdoor
    furniture, 313, 352
      wooden decking, 353
outlets, 111–113
Outward Bound, 198–199
oyster bars, 40
paediatricians, 274
painters (home), 363–364
painting
    classes, 248–249
      classes (kids'), 258–259
      murals, 317
      restoration, 309
paints, 365
Pakistani restaurants, 70–71
paper, 183–184, 186
parachuting, 211
paradiving, 208
paragliding, 211
Paralympic sports, 211
parenting
    advice, 254
      websites, 390
party
    catering, 99–101
      grams, 230
      invitations, 185–186
      paraphernalia, 235
      planners, 227, 231
      supplies, 235
      venues, 18–20, 225–229, 231–234
patio dining , 8–20
pearls, 157–158, 189
pedicures, 292–293
Peking duck, 64
performing arts
    classes, 259–260
      shows, 223, 387–388
Persian rugs, 328
personal styling, 296
personal trainers, 194–95, 197
pest control, 343
pet
    adoption, 353
      grooming, 357
      medical care, 355–356
      relocation/immigration, 357–358
      training, 356
      shops, 353
      supplies, 353–354
photo albums, 182–183, 238
photocopies, 184
photographers
    baby and family photos, 236
      parties, 237
      portraits, 237
      special events, 236
      wedding, 239–240
photographic canvas, 309–310
photography
    albums and accessories, 182–183, 238, 251
      classes, 248
      equipment, 373–374
      professional developing, 237–238
photos (vintage), 304

EVERYTHING INDEX

physiotherapists, 278–279, 283
piano lessons, 252
pilates, 200–201
pillows, 324–327
pizzas, 19, 21, 22, 45–47, 102
plants, 348–351
plastic surgeons, 298
    kids', 276
plates, 333–334, 335–337
playgroups 254–256
plumbers, 364
podiatrists, 279
pole dance classes, 248
pool cues and accessories, 216
post-natal conditioning, 197
posture correction, 197
pots and pans, 335–336
potted plants, 348–349
pottery classes, 249–250
Power Plate, 197
pre-natal
    advice, 282–283
    yoga, 197, 200, 264
pre-schools, 266–269
preserved fruit (Chinese), 75
primary schools, 268–271
printed gift boxes, 182–183
printers, 185–186
printing finishes, 183
prints, 308
private clubs, 223
private kitchens, 26–28
property agents, 366–367
psychics, 286
psychologists, 280–281
public holidays, 367
pyjamas, 172
Qigong, 285
Qipao tailoring, 132, 187–189
racquet sports, 209
Raleigh Challenge, 199
rattan furniture, 313, 324
real estate agents, 367–368
recording studios, 253
reflexology massage, 285, 292
rehabilitation supplies, 194, 299
Reiki, 285
relocation companies, 368–369
    See also pet relocation
remedial massages, 279
rental
    baby equipment, 381
    bicycles, 381
    bouncy castle, 234
    cars, 380
    costumes, 173
    furniture, 231, 313, 381
    sewing machines, 381
    table, chairs and tableware, 231
restaurants
    al fresco, 18–20, 21–23, 31, 37, 67–68
    casual, 49–50, 60, 64–65
    Chinese, 16, 23–24, 25, 26–27, 38–39, 56–67
    date spots, 21
    delivery service, 101–102
    distinct/historic décor, 23–24
    for kids, 46–47
    French, 14–15, 25, 27–28, 42, 65
    good value, 33–34, 62–66
    great views, 14–18
    halal, 39
    in Sham Shui Po, 190
    in Stanley, 18–19, 21–22, 24, 44–45, 188
    Indian, 30, 38–39, 67, 70–71
    Indonesian, 71
    Japanese, 16, 24, 30–31, 71–73
    Korean, 70
    kosher, 39

light meals, 35
Mediterranean/Middle Eastern, 18, 21–23, 43, 65
neighbourhood, 28, 29, 37, 49–50
Nepalese, 70–71
off the beaten track, 21–23, 67–68, 187–190
Pakistani, 70–71
party venues, 18, 46, 229
private kitchens, 26–28
special occasions, 20–21, 25–26, 40, 66–67
spicy, 27, 69–71
Thai, 19, 22, 34, 65, 68, 69–70, 100
vegetarian/vegan/organic, 30–39, 71
Vietnamese, 64–65, 73–74
with bar scene, 52–53
ribbons, 189–191
riding schools, 205
road running, 198–200
roller sports, 205, 210
rollerblading
     classes, 205
     gear, 214
romantic dining, 20–21, 25–26
rowing, 211
rubbish collection, 344–345
rugby, 209, 265, 391
rugs, 305, 311, 315, 328
running races, 199–200
safes (home), 339–340
sailing, 210–211
salad bars, 35–36
salons (hair), 286–289
sandwiches, 36–37, 92
sari, 106, 133
sauces (Chinese), 88–89
saunas, 194
scene-and-be-seen bars, 54
school
     bags, 167–168
     clothing, 175
     debentures, 271–272
schools, 266–272
Science classes, 258
scrapbooking classes, 250
seafood
     restaurants, 15, 22–23, 28, 39–40, 61–62, 67–69, 229
     shops, 86
secondary schools, 268–271
second-hand
     bags, 139
     books, 179–180
     designer clothing, 116–117
self-improvement courses, 242–253, 254
sequins, 158, 189–191
serviced apartments, 370–371
serving pieces, 335
set lunches, 15, 16, 28, 33–35, 72–73
sewing machines (rental), 381
sexual health, 282
Sham Shui Po, 189–191
shipping (artwork), 310
shoes
     kids', 168, 174–176
     men's, 127–128, 136
     women's, 104–105, 110, 115–116, 132, 135–136, 140
shooting, 211
sight tests, 276, 279–280
sign language (for babies), 254
silk wear, 188–189
silver
     engraving, 334
     home accessories, 334
     jewellery, 153–155
singing classes 253
     kids', 252, 259
skateboarding
     parks, 205
     gear, 214
skating rinks, 206, 265

ski wear, 105, 128, 147–149, 205, 211, 214–215, 266
    kids', 173
skin treatments, 298–299
sleepwear, 172, 187, 331
slimming treatments, 294
snake removal, 343
snooker cues and accessories, 216
snowboarding clothes, 215
soccer *See* football
socks, 128
sofa upholstery, 190–191, 316–317, 319
softball, 210
solicitors, 385
Southeast Asian art, 306–307, 311
spas, 289–292
specialists (medical), 273–282
speciality food stores, 87–88
speech tests, 277
spicy food, 27, 69–71
splashing pools, 207
sports
    bars, 50–51
    centres, 196
    clothing, 120–122, 144–149, 173–176, 187–189, 212–216
    equipment, 174–175, 212–216
    grounds, 198
sports injury specialists, 197, 202, 278–279
squash, 209
stain removal
    carpets, 342–343
    clothes, 341
Stanley, 187–189
stationery, 178, 183–185, 251, 339
steakhouses, 40–42
steamers (clothes), 135, 342
steams/saunas, 194
stem cell storage, 283
storage, 369
street markets, 105
streetwear, 117–120, 190
    kids', 170
string quartets, 228
strollers, 160–162
suits, 133–134
sunglasses, 143–144
    kids', 276
surf wear, 128, 147, 175, 187, 215
survival games, 211
Swedish massages, 285, 295
sweets, 77–80
swimming
    associations, 210
    lessons, 207
    open water races, 200
    pools, 195, 207, 233
swimwear, 105, 124, 144–146, 212
    kids', 174
tablecloths, 231, 327, 334
tables, 312–317
    rental, 231, 381
tableware, 335–337
    gifts, 333–335
    rental, 231
Taekwondo, 203, 263–264
Tai Chi classes, 203
tailors
    cheongsam, 132
    dresses, 129–134
    redesign, 131
    suits, 133–134
takeout options, 36–37, 100–101
tanning salons, 295
tapas, 44–45
tattoo
    artists, 295, 298–299
    removal, 299
tax advisers, 383–384
    See also accountants

EVERYTHING INDEX

TCM *See* traditional Chinese medicine
team building programmes, 199
tennis
    associations, 209
    coaches, 197, 205, 209
    courts, 208–209
    racquets, 174, 212
terrace wood decking, 353
textiles, 134, 189–191
    antiques, 304–305
Thai
    antique furniture, 311
    art, 306
    massage, 291
    provisions, 88
    restaurants, 19, 22, 34, 65, 68, 69–70, 100
towels, 175, 327, 331
toys
    educational, 166
    libraries, 257
    limited edition, 166
    model and collectable, 167
track fields, 198
traditional Chinese medicine, 284–285
traditional Indian clothing, 133
trail races, 199
travel
    Hong Kong countryside, 221
    vaccinations, 221
travel agents
    online services, 221
    personal travels, 219–220
    special holidays, 220
    sports and adventure, 220–221
triathlons, 198, 200, 211
tricycles, 174
trimmings, 191
T-shirt printing, 134–135
tutorial classes, 261
ultimate frisbee, 211
underwear
    kids', 172, 187
    men's, 128
    women's, 122–124
upholstery, 190–191, 317–320
useful websites, 387–391
vaccinations, 221
vegetarian food, 30, 35–39, 71, 389, 394
veterinarians, 355
video equipment, 373–374
videographers, 240
Vietnamese
    art, 305–307
    restaurants, 64–65, 68, 73–74
Ving Tsun, 203
vintage
    fabrics, 320
    fashion and accessories, 116, 131, 137, 143, 151, 160
    furniture, 312–313
    photos, 304
vitamins and supplements, 91–92, 299–300
voice disorders, 277
voice lessons, 252–253, 259–260
waiters, 231
wakeboarding, 208
wall panels/stickers, 317–318
warehouses, 369
watches, 150, 159–160, 332
water delivery, 83
water sports, 208, 210
watering holes, 51–52
waterskiing, 208
waxing, 290, 294–295, 300
web design and hosting, 377–378
wedding
    cakes, 95
    gowns, 131
    favours, 241

    invitations, 185–186
    makeup, 240–241
    men's tailors, 133–134
    musicians, 227–228
    photographers, 239–240
    planners, 238–239
    websites, 378, 240
    wine registry, 95
    wines, 95–97, 241
will writing, 385
windsurfing, 208, 210, 387
wine
    cellars, 97
    fridges, 98
    merchants, 95–97
    online purchase, 97–98
    with personalised labels, 97, 241
    wholesale, 97
women-only gyms, 195
woodwind quartets, 228
work visas   384
    See also Hong Kong Immigration Department
wraps (food), 37
yachts charter/licences, 225–227
yarn supplies, 251
yoga
    See also pilates
    classes (adults'), 201–202
    classes (kids'), 264
    clothes and accessories, 144–146, 213
    learn to teach, 264
    private instructors, 202
yoghurt, 77